Prince Eugene of Savoy

MEN IN OFFICE

General Editor:
Professor Ragnhild Hatton

DEREK McKAY

Prince Eugene
of Savoy

with 43 illustrations

THAMES AND HUDSON

For Louise and Katie

*Printed in Great Britain by
Latimer Trend & Company Ltd, Plymouth*

Contents

Preface

It is now more than a decade since Max Braubach completed his five-volume life of prince Eugene. This was the culmination of Braubach's own long research on the prince and of a century of German and Austrian scholarship. Surprisingly, little of this work has been made available to the English reader. The biography by Nicholas Henderson, while good on Eugene's artistic interests and military career, is incomplete on him as a statesman. I have tried myself to look at the many sides of the prince's life and also to say something about his adopted country, Austria.

I am grateful to a number of people for their help during the writing of this book. The officials of the Austrian State Archives, the Austrian National Library and the Lower-Saxon Archives were remarkably tolerant of my German and never failed to produce the material I wanted. Dr Georg Schnath kindly arranged for me to see the family papers in the possession of Count Andreas von Bernstorff at Gartow. I owe a particular debt to the London Library and the British Library of Political and Economic Science. Ragnhild Hatton was characteristically generous with her time and advice, working her way through a very scrappy early draft. I profited from talks with Peter Barber. Above all I have been especially fortunate in the interest and help of Hamish Scott, who read the whole text and made numerous suggestions for improvement. Margaret Bradgate and Nett Capsey cheerfully and efficiently typed the manuscript. Finally I should like to thank my family – my wife Frances not only for reading and criticizing interminable drafts but also for her advice, patience and support throughout, and our two daughters for their continual interest despite their disappointment that Eugene was no fairy-tale prince and that there was no princess.

I

A Prince of Savoy

In August 1683 the emperor Leopold with his family and court were waiting for a miracle in the town of Passau on the Danube. Behind them, lower down the river, the city of Vienna, capital of the Habsburg monarchy and centre of the Holy Roman Empire, was cut off from the Christian world by the Turkish grand vizier, Kara Mustafa, and a besieging army of possibly 90,000 men. Between Passau and Vienna, all along the south bank of the Danube, bands of terrifying Tartar horsemen were creating panic and destruction on a scale which was to impoverish the whole area of Lower Austria for decades to come as well as robbing the Turkish army itself of food during the siege.

The Imperial court and the majority of the city's wealthy residents had made a headlong flight for safety with whatever they could carry a month before. Leopold's field army under Charles of Lorraine had failed to contain the vast numbers of the Turkish army as it advanced through Hungary towards Vienna, and there now seemed no likelihood that the emperor could relieve the city with its small garrison and remaining citizens through his own resources. Only help from outside could save his capital.

Vienna held out during the hot summer months as a relief army was desperately brought together from Poland, the Habsburg hereditary lands and the German states. Fortunately for the Imperialists Kara Mustafa's siege artillery proved weak, and he put off serious attempts to storm the city in the hope that it would surrender voluntarily and its wealth fall into his hands intact. Little was done to prevent the Polish king, John* Sobieski, and the elector of Bavaria, Maximilian Emmanuel, from joining their forces with the troops under Lorraine at the beginning of September. This combined Christian army crossed to the south bank of the Danube unopposed and took up an excellent position on the Kahlenberg overlooking Vienna.

* First names have been anglicized wherever possible.

On 12 September 1683 the Christian forces moved down to attack the Muslim camp. The Turks were outgunned and outmanoeuvred: having taken no precautions against an attack, Kara Mustafa made the basic mistake of not abandoning the siege in time and trying to beat off the enemy with his cavalry alone. A full day's fighting ended with the total defeat of the Turks and their flight towards Hungary. There was no pursuit, but Kara Mustafa's army had only one aim, to return home, which for many meant the outer limits of the Ottoman empire in Africa and Asia. The grand vizier himself was to go no further than Belgrade. Here the silken cord, dispatched by the sultan at the first news of the defeat, reached him and he was ceremonially strangled.

The plight of Vienna had aroused the conscience of both Catholic and Protestant Europe. Cash and volunteers came from all quarters. Only Louis XIV of France stood aside. Nevertheless, several members of the French nobility fought of their own accord in the battle to save Vienna. Among them was prince Eugene of Savoy.

Eugene had been born in Paris on 18 October 1663. Although he was a subject of the French king, both his parents came from Italian families. His mother, Olympia Mancini, was one of the three nieces cardinal Mazarin had introduced to Paris, all of whom were to captivate the adolescent Louis XIV. As a young woman and society hostess Olympia soon outdid all her rivals in the number of her love affairs and intrigues at court. Louis seems to have retained some affection for her until 1680, when he discovered she was dabbling in magic and love potions. She was forced to flee Paris and France for Brussels, where she fretted away the rest of her life till her death in 1708.

Olympia's husband, Eugene Maurice, prince of Savoy-Carignan and duke of Soissons, belonged to a collateral line of the ruling dukes of Savoy. A soldier in the French army, he was completely overshadowed by his wife but loyally supported her in her intrigues right up to his early death in the summer of 1673. His influence over his children had been slight but he did bring them connections with Italian and German princely houses.

The couple had five sons and two daughters: Eugene Francis (Eugène François) was the youngest boy. Neither parent spent much time with the children and stability in the family home, the Hôtel de Soissons, was provided by their father's French mother, Marie de Bourbon, princess of Carignan. It was to Marie's firm hand that the upbringing of the sixteen year old Eugene and his two sisters was entrusted when their mother fled from France with what money was left to the family. Another dependable member of the household was Marie's daughter, the margravine of

Baden, mother of Eugene's cousin and later friend and mentor in the Imperial army, prince Louis of Baden.

A younger son from a princely family, Eugene was destined for a clerical or military career. His grandmother favoured the former, and in his teens Eugene wore the tonsure and was known as the abbé de Savoie. We know little of his life in Paris before 1683 and have to depend on the hostile remarks made about him by the duchess of Orleans once he had become an inveterate enemy of her brother-in-law Louis XIV. She accused him of homosexual antics with lackeys and pages, called him 'a little slut'[1] and declared that 'he often played the woman with young people'.[2] This may well have been true given his mother's lax household and her own failure to show any affection towards him. Yet once Eugene had left France we hear no further accusations of homosexuality.

The scandals within his own family during his early life left Eugene a reserved and cautious individual who put great stress on his own honour and integrity. His training for the church seems to have given him a lasting delight in books and literary men, but it did not make him a scholar or a linguist. Throughout his life French was to remain his main language although he was fluent in Italian. His Latin was not good, and despite his half-century in the service of the house of Habsburg he never mastered German well enough to use it in writing, although he could read and speak it. As a child his favourite study had been mathematics, which was to stand him in good stead in his military career.

In February 1683, to his family's surprise, Eugene announced that he did not wish to enter the church; he intended to follow his father's example and join the French army. Since his grandmother would have none of it and refused to support him, he applied to Louis XIV to be put in command of a company. The king rejected him out of hand, probably because he looked on him as lacking in military promise. Eugene had a slight puny build, a swarthy complexion with sunken cheeks, snub nose and ever open mouth. Just as damning, however, may have been the influence of Louis's secretary of state for war, Louvois, who detested Eugene's mother because she had rejected a proposed match between one of her daughters and his son. Denied a military career in France, Eugene had to look elsewhere.

That Eugene should turn to the emperor Leopold was natural enough. The Turkish advance on Austria was encouraging other would-be crusaders to offer their services early in 1683, but more important was the fact that one of Eugene's elder brothers, Louis Julius, was already serving in the Imperial army. When the news of Louis Julius's death in a skirmish with the Tartars reached Paris on 23 July, Eugene immediately decided to go to Austria, probably hoping to take over his brother's regiment. He could expect some support from his cousin, prince Louis, margrave of Baden-Baden and a leading Imperial general, as well as from a more distant cousin, Maximilian Emmanuel, elector of Bavaria.

On 26 July Eugene and his close friend the prince of Conti fled from Paris without Louis's permission. Because Conti was a French prince of the blood efforts were made by the king's agents to stop the pair as they crossed Germany. They were caught at Frankfurt. Conti was persuaded to return, but Eugene refused and went on.

He reached Passau in mid-August and was immediately welcomed by friends of Louis of Baden, who at the time was with the army in the field. The margrave's uncle, Herman of Baden, a younger son of the ruling family of Baden, was president of the Imperial war council (*Reichshofratspräsident*) and a leader of the anti-French group at Leopold's court. This group included the Spanish ambassador Borgomanero, who was said to be consulted by the emperor 'oftener in business of importance than his own ministers'.[3] Borgomanero and the Badens were Eugene's constant protectors in the next few years, and it was in fact the Spaniard who introduced the young fugitive to Leopold on 14 August.

Although Louis Julius's regiment had already been disposed of, the emperor readily accepted the young prince as a volunteer. What probably counted with Leopold was not only Eugene's desertion of the hated Louis XIV but also his Italian background, since Italian generals were common in the Imperial army. It was, however, under the immediate command of his German cousin, Louis of Baden, that Eugene fought during the relief of Vienna.

Despite his complete lack of experience, Eugene fought bravely enough to be promised the next available dragoon regiment. He received this two months later in December 1683 and became a regular colonel in the Imperial army. The rewards of such commands were good. Regiments were thought of as their colonels' own property and were reckoned to be worth 10,000–12,000 gulden a year. A colonel sold commissions, deducted a percentage from his men's pay, charged officers fees when they were promoted and above all took a large share of any booty seized in battle and of contributions levied on enemy territory.

Although Eugene was to be promoted rapidly during the annual campaigns against the Turks in the 1680s, his income as an officer was never sufficient for a man of his position. He had arrived in Passau with little more than a ring and a small amount of money given him by Conti, but as a prince he wanted and was expected to move in the highest circles. Consequently he soon found himself in serious financial difficulties.

Although he lived in Borgomanero's house while he was in Vienna, he was forced to appeal to his relatives for money. Max Emmanuel of Bavaria is said to have advanced him 1,000 gulden at the start of his career[4] but most help came from the head of his father's house, Victor Amadeus, duke of Savoy, who in 1684 gave him 15,000 lire and then a further 20,000 after a personal visit by Eugene to Turin early the following year. Real financial security only came in 1688, when Victor Amadeus granted him the revenues from two abbeys in Piedmont, amounting to 20,000 lire a year. Before then financial embarrassment had forced him, in 1685 and 1686, to consider entering Spanish service, especially as Leopold himself did nothing to supplement his income. Such moves from one European army to another were common enough at this time, but in the event Eugene was to stay in the service of the same ruling family for the rest of his life. He never had any thought of returning to France, nor any encouragement from Louis to do so. In fact his bitterness at the king's rejection was eventually to lead to a fierce determination to humble France. As contact with his earlier life and associates was quickly lost, Eugene came to stress his origins as a prince of the house of Savoy far more than his French background.

II

Leopold I and his Empire

Eugene's new master, Leopold I, had like the prince been destined for the church and but for the death of an elder brother would never have become emperor. His clerical training had a lasting influence; throughout his life he was conscious of his religious obligations and regarded his throne as a sacred trust. He resorted continually to a religious fatalism which drove even the papal nuncio to protest that he wished 'the Emperor's faith in God were a bit less'.[1] Leopold was painfully aware of his odd physical appearance, having inherited the Habsburg family defects of a deformed mouth and unsteady legs. He tried to make up for this by a serious manner, curling moustaches, black Spanish court dress and red stockings, but he was always at a loss as to what to do with his hands and his broad feathered hat. Yet he worked harder than any Habsburg before Maria Theresa in the following century. He was morally upright, finding an outlet in music, for which he had real talent, and in that obsession with hunting which was so characteristic of his family.

Leopold lacked what Louis XIV certainly possessed: a natural capacity for ruling. Although he had a certain majesty and tried to keep overall control of government in his own hands, he proved incapable of directing the ministers in charge of the great departments of state. The English diplomat Stepney wrote home in 1693 that the emperor was 'of an irresolute wavering temper, on which the last impressions ever make the deepest marks, this occasions that he is frequently torn several ways by the different inclinations of his Ministers, who in a manner governed him by turns as if each had commanded *de jour*'.[2]

Leopold had been elected Holy Roman Emperor in 1658 but at the beginning of his reign his power as emperor was limited: in fact, Louis XIV had greater influence with the German princes. Leopold's real power came from the Habsburg hereditary lands, to which he had succeeded at the age of seventeen on the death of his father, Ferdinand III, in 1657. These lands formed a natural geographic unit around the Danube. The territories which had formed the core of the Habsburg possessions since the thirteenth century corresponded roughly to the Austria of today – Upper and Lower Austria, Carinthia, Styria, Carniola, and the mountainous Tyrol. More prosperous were the lands ruled by the Habsburgs as kings of Bohemia since 1526, which included Silesia and Moravia; these possessions became hereditary in the family only in 1627 after the suppression of the Bohemian rebellion which had led to the outbreak of the Thirty Years War (1618–48). But in another of his possessions, Hungary, Leopold still had to be elected king. All that had been salvaged from the Turkish invasions of the sixteenth century and the destruction of the old kingdom of Greater Hungary was a narrow strip of territory stretching through the Carpathians and their southern slopes, squeezing its way between Styria and Lake Balaton, and then broadening out into the Hungarian crown land of Croatia before reaching the Adriatic.

Every ruler in the seventeenth century was faced by the basic problem of how to increase his own power at the expense of local institutions and traditions. Whether kings wanted to or not, they were forced to adopt absolutist policies in response to the challenge of nobles and estates and the financial and manpower demands of international warfare. The revolt of the predominantly Protestant Bohemian estates in 1618, and similar movements in Austria, Moravia and Silesia, were crushed in a way which allowed the crown to impose a form of Catholic absolutism on all its territories outside Hungary in the thirty or so years before Leopold's accession. In comparison with France, however, Habsburg absolutism and centralization had hardly begun by the time of Leopold's reign. Although we use words like 'Austria' and the 'Austrian state', these were only beginning to have real meaning: Leopold's territories were still largely a collection of separate provinces which happened to have the same ruler. Central institutions for the provinces of the monarchy as a whole were only emerging slowly.

Habsburg absolutism rested on two planks: first, the co-operation of the church and nobility, and second, the gradual formation of a standing army and of a central and provincial bureaucracy. In the seventeenth century the former was the more important. The monarchy and its officials identified themselves closely with the Catholic Church and especially with the Jesuit order. Everywhere the church was a major landowner: the large number of her monasteries led to Austria being called a *Klösterreich*. The crown also continued to regard itself as a crusader on behalf of Catholicism.

The imposition of Catholic uniformity at home went hand in hand with an increase in monarchical absolutism at the expense of the independent political role of the nobility. Instead the nobles were drawn into partnership with the crown. This was particularly true of Bohemia where the rebel Protestant nobility was rooted out and replaced by a loyal Catholic and often non-Bohemian aristocracy, which acquiesced in the crown's destruction of the legislative powers of the estates, the former centre of aristocratic power and independence, and accepted in return an increasing number of the chief administrative and ministerial posts. A similar but less drastic policy was carried out in the Austrian lands. However, there were limits to the monarch's powers. Although Austria and Bohemia were ruled directly through central institutions in Vienna, at a local level the ruler shared power with the nobility. Even in the Bohemian lands the right to vote contributions for the upkeep of the army was left in the hands of the noble-dominated estates. Everywhere the latter also performed an essential role in local administration and were an effective bar to direct government intervention. Permanent committees and officials of the estates acted with the ruler's own representatives in collecting taxes and recruiting and quartering troops.

Although the nobility was determined to grant as little as possible in taxation, it was willing enough to serve the dynasty, and throughout the Habsburg possessions the nobles constituted the mainstay of the emperor's rule. In Hungary the monarchy was also supported by the Catholic magnates. Aristocrats monopolized every office at Vienna, in the provinces and in the army; the capital also attracted nobles from all over Europe, especially from the Holy Roman Empire and Italy, most of whom were rapidly assimilated. The only exception to this aristocratic monopoly was a steady stream of recruits to the administration by lawyers, often from west Germany, who rose to power through the legal institutions of the Holy Roman Empire.

Throughout the seventeenth century in the Habsburg lands departments of state with distinct functions were being created while separate institutions for the various provinces were disappearing. Yet even in the eighteenth century there was much overlapping and competition between the various departments which the emperors themselves did little to resolve. A major problem of duality was also produced by Leopold's position as Holy Roman Emperor which entailed the existence of Imperial institutions in Vienna.

The old Imperial court chancery (*Reichshofkanzlei*), which had acted both as a foreign office and domestic chancery for the Holy Roman Empire as well as for the Habsburg hereditary lands, was gradually being superseded for the latter by the court chancery (*Hofkanzlei*). This development coincided with the emergence of the Habsburg monarchy, or

Austria, as an entity separate from the Empire and a great power in its own right. The court chancellor (*Hofkanzler*) eventually became the most important minister of the crown, if only because of the range of his responsibilities; but Leopold and his immediate successors leaned indiscriminately on ministers from all departments for advice, including the head of the Imperial chancery, the Imperial vice-chancellor (*Reichsvizekanzler*). The *Hofkanzlei*'s powers were in any case limited by the existence in Vienna of separate chanceries for Bohemia and Hungary.

The chamber (*Hofkammer*) also suffered similar interference in the financial sphere from the war council (*Hofkriegsrat*) and the court chancery at Vienna and from the estates at a provincial level. What revenues were received were both inadequate and badly managed. On occasions only a third of the income existing on paper was actually collected, and during wartime the situation deteriorated rapidly. In the wars between 1689 and 1714 Austria undoubtedly suffered the largest gap between expenditure and income of all the belligerents. The financial weakness of the monarchy seriously hampered its role as a great power and, in fact, to wage war the emperor had to depend on outside subsidies. Even with foreign help the monarchy still needed to resort to heavy borrowing, either from abroad, as from the Dutch in the 1690s, or from the Imperial court Jew, Samuel Oppenheimer, and later from the Vienna City Bank.

Many of the problems created by Leopold's weak leadership and his divided and overlapping ministries could have been solved if there had been an effective supreme body where the emperor and the heads of departments could discuss general problems and formulate policy. A small secret conference (*Geheime Konferenz*) was set up by Leopold for this purpose in 1659 but it soon became too large and ineffectual. It was not till the start of his son's reign in 1709 that a new effective conference of the major ministers was instituted, but even this was largely confined to discussing foreign policy.

Although seventeenth-century governments, especially those in western Europe, were becoming increasingly aware of the role they could play in developing their countries' wealth and their own revenues, it was only in the reign of Charles VI (1711–40) that the Habsburgs seriously undertook state encouragement of industry and trade. Economic advance in Leopold's reign was disappointing: what success there was took place on the estates of the nobility. The real answer to the crown's financial problems would have been realistic taxation of these estates, but the nobility evaded taxes and, like the ecclesiastical landowners, prospered. During the second half of the seventeenth century, especially in Bohemia, the landowners, clerical and lay, developed into industrialists as well as extensive farmers producing for a large domestic and international market. This development was bought at the expense of the towns and the peasantry. The decline of the towns as centres of trade and industry was hastened by the peasants being forced to buy directly from their lords' shops, mills and inns, and by the lords' preference for exporting and buying directly from outside the Habsburg lands. The large-scale urban building carried out after 1683 was mainly the work of the aristocracy and the church, using men and materials from their own estates. Although urban decline was less apparent in Vienna with the vast needs of the court, the capital itself was changing from a city dominated by burghers to one of aristocratic palaces and monasteries.

The position of the peasantry was far worse in the Habsburg lands than in most of Germany. In the former the peasants were being reduced to the level of serfdom. In the rich agricultural areas of Bohemia, Moravia, Habsburg Hungary, and increasingly in Lower Austria as well, the landowners, like those in other parts of Europe east of the river Elbe, were no longer content to live off rents and occasional labour services but wanted the peasants to work on the demesne land and in manorial industries to produce for a cash market. Peasant holdings were reduced in size, peasant labour services drastically increased and the freedom of the peasants to leave their estates was curtailed. Between 1683 and 1702 prince Ferdinand Schwarzenberg managed to treble his income, not by improved agriculture but merely by increasing his peasants' burdens. It was the peasant who also paid the bulk of indirect and direct taxation as well as the dues to the church. The baroque splendour of central Europe was built on the backs of these men and women.

The crown did not interfere in this subjection of the peasantry: it could not, unless it wanted to overturn society. Habsburg absolutism was linked too intimately with the loyalty of the church and nobility. Both the peasantry and the towns were victims of a monarchical-aristocratic-clerical system, which was hardly modified until the late eighteenth century.

Leopold's absolutist position was weakest in the lands he ruled as elective king of Hungary. Here the Magyar nobles were supreme. At each royal election the diet at Pressburg (Bratislava) imposed conditions on the new ruler and had the permanent right to rebel if he broke Hungarian law, a law made by the diet. The French minister Grémonville was astonished to note in 1667 that Leopold was forced to bow before 'an insolent populace and the power of an assembled diet which believes itself equal, if not superior, to its master'.[3] Free from taxation and all-powerful in local administration, the nobles benefited from the same increasing subjection of the peasantry that we have seen taking place in Bohemia. Although the majority of these magnates and gentry in the flat central part of Hungary was now Catholic, the Germans in the towns and the Magyar nobles of mountainous Slovakia remained Protestant. Their religion had been guaranteed by an edict of toleration issued by Leopold's father Ferdinand III in 1645, a concession which Leopold was to try continually to end.

The crown's weak position in Hungary was made worse by the situation across the eastern border. Here a large area of the old kingdom of Hungary was ruled by the Turks through military governors. This territory provided toleration for Protestants and a refuge for rebels from Habsburg Hungary. The border was undefined and the whole area was the scene of interminable fighting. It was accepted 'that in times of peace, it is allowable for both sides . . . to make incursions upon each other, to rob and drive away cattle, and to fight in the field with strong parties both of horse and foot'.[4]

From his accession Leopold and successive ministers had been determined to end the unsatisfactory position of the crown in Habsburg Hungary. A means to do so lay in the nobles' own unwillingness to defend the country from Turkish incursions. A defence force of German garrison troops had to be provided by the emperor and paid for largely by the Bohemian and Austrian estates. These became more firmly entrenched in Hungary after the Austro-Turkish war of 1663–64, when a Turkish move towards Vienna was defeated by the Imperial army under Montecuccoli at St Gotthard on the river Rába (Raab). In the following two decades the Austrian government tried to curb the Magyar nobility, using the same means that it had employed against the Bohemians after the Thirty Years War. The country was put under military rule and Protestantism suppressed, but this led to widespread rebellion and guerrilla war. Eventually in 1681 the monarchy had to admit defeat. The overall result of the struggle was to weaken Habsburg Hungary and to invite further Turkish invasion.

A compelling reason for Leopold to compromise in Hungary was his wish to concentrate on western Europe. During the 1660s and early 1670s Austrian policy had aimed at conciliating Louis XIV of France and working with him for a peaceful partition of Spain and her empire in Europe and overseas in the event of the death of the Spanish king, Charles II. A chronic invalid from youth, Charles was not expected to live long nor to have any children. While Louis could only claim the succession for his children through his marriage to Charles's half-sister Maria Theresa, Leopold had claims based on his own marriage to the young king's sister Margaret Theresa, a string of previous marriages between his family and their Spanish cousins, and promises in the will of the last king Philip IV and in a family compact of 1617.

Leopold's conciliatory attitude towards Louis changed with the extension of French territorial ambitions during the war against the Dutch (1672–78). The emperor was forced to assume the role of champion of the independence of the Holy Roman Empire from France and to join an alliance with the Dutch and Spain, a grouping which was to form the basis of Austrian alliances for the rest of the century.

Despite the signature of peace with Louis XIV in 1679, the war left a permanent anti-French party in Vienna. Leopold himself condemned anything French, refusing to hear the language spoken at court, encouraging the use of Italian instead, and resisting the German tendency to ape everything French. For the next three decades Austrian Habsburg policy was directed towards keeping the Spanish succession in the Austrian branch of the family and winning back those parts of Alsace and the three bishoprics of Metz, Toul and Verdun in Lorraine which had been ceded to France at the peace of Westphalia in 1648. From the 1680s onwards Leopold also had to assume the religious-cultural mission of defending central Europe from the Turks, as well as being faced by recurring rebellion in Hungary. As it proved impossible to isolate these problems in western and eastern Europe from each other, the Austrian monarchy was burdened with enormous military and financial demands throughout Leopold's and his son Joseph's reign – Austria's political ambitions were far outstripping her material resources. But a positive result of this struggle in the short term was that Vienna's influence within the Holy Roman Empire increased under the double impact of Louis XIV's aggression and Leopold's eventual victories against the Turks, and this led to substantial support being given by the Empire.

The momentous struggle, which culminated in the emergence of Austria as a power many times her original size, began in the 1680s when Louis XIV tried to perfect an impenetrable eastern frontier for France. His means, while bullying, violent and terrorizing, were not those of open warfare but consisted rather in a steady erosion of neighbouring territory through a policy of laying claims to dependencies of lands already ceded to France. At the same time he was building a massive defensive fortress system around France. Nothing stood in his way. The major German princes felt too scared to oppose him. Austria was drained financially from her last war against France and in 1679 she was struck by a devastating attack of plague which forced the Imperial court into pathetic, fearful journeys from Vienna and then from Prague. By late 1681 Louis had occupied the Imperial free city of Strasbourg which completed his control of Alsace and seemed the key to the Rhineland. This was followed two years later by the French seizure of most of Spanish Luxembourg.

The majority of Leopold's ministers, including the president of the war council, Herman of Baden, and Borgomanero, wanted to resist Louis, but the papal envoy and clerical elements in Vienna urged the emperor to lead a European crusade against the Turks. In the event he was forced to look eastwards because of action by the Turks themselves, but almost to the very last he chose to ignore the dangerous situation which was building up in the Balkans in 1681–82. In Constantinople a new grand vizier, Kara Mustafa, hoped to secure his position through an attack on Vienna. This project of the 'Golden Apple' offered him vast wealth and military prestige, and the leading Magyar rebel, Thököly, in asking for his help, provided a sufficient excuse to intervene in Hungary.

These Turkish ambitions were encouraged by Louis XIV: they would allow him to squeeze the German princes and Spain harder. But his own actions in the Rhineland in the early 1680s were leading to a revulsion of feeling against him, and new rulers in Saxony, Hanover and Bavaria were moving towards agreement with Vienna. In January 1683 the young and impetuous Maximilian Emmanuel of Bavaria signed a defensive pact with Leopold, offering his help in the east and the west. It was this alliance, together with one concluded with John Sobieski of Poland in March, which saved Leopold during the summer of 1683 when the Turks finally surrounded his capital.

III

The Conquest of Hungary

As he entered the Imperial capital for the first time on the night of the victory over Kara Mustafa, five years of campaigning against the Turks lay ahead of prince Eugene. These years were to mark him out as one of the most promising of the emperor's younger commanders, but he might instead have been faced with the immediate and difficult decision of whether to fight not the Turks but his late ruler, the king of France. There was strong pressure from the anti-French group in the Imperial court to disengage in the east and to send the Imperial forces westwards to face the great 'Christian Turk', Louis XIV. French troops had in fact begun to bombard cities in the Spanish Netherlands a few days before the relief of Vienna, following a rash declaration of war by Spain. But the whole weight of the clerical party and especially that of the fiery court preacher and confidant of Leopold, Marco d'Aviano, favoured a crusade against the Ottomans. The military leaders, Max Emmanuel and duke Charles of Lorraine, also supported this idea, and it was Charles's stand which was probably decisive. Besides being the emperor's brother-in-law, the duke was known to be fervently anti-French and would have been the one with most to gain by a war in the west: his duchy of Lorraine was still occupied by the French as he had refused to accept it back on terms offered by Louis at the peace of 1679. In any case a war of some kind in Hungary had to be fought because the sultan, Mehmed IV, saw no reason to make peace: his control of Hungary was as firm as ever.

In March 1684 Leopold concluded the Holy League with Poland and Venice against the Turks. The alliance was enthusiastically supported by pope Innocent XI, who contributed large sums to the war and ordered the clergy throughout southern Europe to do the same. Now for the first time in Leopold's reign, and for that matter since the first siege of Vienna in 1529, Austrian policy seriously envisaged destroying Turkish rule in Hungary. But a necessary corollary was Leopold's agreement to

the great French diplomatic triumph of the truce of Ratisbon (Regensburg), signed in August 1684, by which Leopold and Spain recognized
Louis's recent gains, including Strasbourg and Luxembourg, for twenty
years.

We know comparatively little about Eugene's life during these first
campaigns against the Turks. Indeed it would be surprising if we did,
since as a young officer he is only mentioned briefly by contemporary
observers as having been at such a battle or siege. In Eugene's own surviving correspondence, largely to his Savoyard cousin Victor Amadeus,
he is as reticent about his own feelings and experiences as he was always
to be. Although he took part in all the Turkish campaigns up till 1688
and distinguished himself by his bravery, it would be absurd to claim
that he had any significant impact on them. His main achievement in
these years was to establish himself as a professional soldier under the
protection of leading men in the Imperial army and to take full advantage
of what family connections he possessed. He had to prove his military
ability, as much for his own personal respect as for the promotion it
would bring, and he set about this with a determination unusual for a
man of his class, studying hard and forcing himself to endure physical
discomfort. He seems to have had little inclination for anything else and
to have relished the work involved in running his own regiment. He was
very much the young dedicated professional officer to be found in any
army then and now. On the whole these do not appear to have been
particularly lonely or unhappy years. The companionship of the camp
sufficed. Moreover, after 1685 he was to have the company of other
young French aristocrats in the Imperial army, in particular that of
Charles Francis, prince of Commercy. A son by the natural daughter of
the previous duke of Lorraine, Commercy had also been refused a regiment by Louis XIV before coming to Vienna in the autumn of 1684. He
was two years older than Eugene and may have known him in France.
The two men soon became inseparable friends and almost from the beginning Commercy acted as Eugene's right-hand man on campaigns.

His commander-in-chief, Charles, duke of Lorraine, was a straight-
forward modest soldier with simple tastes, who had come under the
spell of Marco d'Aviano, sharing the Capuchin priest's belief in a
Christian crusade. Although he was a competent general in battle, he
had a slipshod approach to strategy and to supplying his troops. Largely
because of this his attempt to take Buda, the centre of Turkish power in
Hungary, failed miserably in the summer and autumn of 1684 as his army
collapsed from hunger and disease in rain-sodden trenches. But the
following year he brought the whole left bank of the Danube as far east

as Buda under his control and then defeated the Turkish field army at Esztergom (Gran) in August.

Large-scale financial support from the church was now reaching the Imperialists and there was no shortage of men. In 1685 Lorraine's army was nearly 100,000 strong; of these troops 60,000 were Austrian and 38,000 were from the Holy Roman Empire. The German princes, like the emperor himself, had built standing armies during and after the Thirty Years War, and they were quite willing to hire them out. The conquest of Hungary was to be as much a German as an Austrian achievement.

While the Imperial armies had a supply system of sorts and did not have to depend on ransacking their campaigning areas like the Turks, the poor desolate plains and swamps along the Danube and its tributaries posed massive provisioning problems for the Imperialists, although in time a partial solution was found by making effective use of these waterways. As early as the winter of 1685–86 it was proving impossible to quarter troops in Hungary: the whole countryside between Buda and Vienna was rapidly becoming a wasteland with its peasants fleeing to the mountains in the north. When the fifteen year old illegitimate son of James II of England, the later duke of Berwick, reached Buda in July 1686, he did so '. . . with a good appetite, having lived since my depart of Vienna upon bread and wine, for we could not find upon the road the least thing to eat. Hungary is the miserablest country in the world, for it is plundered every day or else by the Christians or the Turks or sometimes by both.'[1]

As a commander of a regiment Eugene had his share of difficulties in Hungary. At the siege of Buda in 1684 his troops had suffered as badly as any and after the siege was raised only a remnant could be put into winter quarters in Bohemia and Moravia. Eugene never stayed with his troops during the winters but copied the other military commanders' practice of a summer campaign, then a return home to Vienna or their palaces in Germany. As he had no home of his own to go back to – he was still a lodger with the Spanish ambassador – he used the opportunity to travel south to Turin early in 1685 to ask for money from Victor Amadeus of Savoy. He needed to rebuild his ruined regiment – at this stage in his career he was putting more financially into the army than he was getting out of it. In the following winter of 1686 he went further afield, visiting his mother in Brussels; it was their first meeting since she had fled from Paris six years earlier. The visit was a long one and they found time to sail to Spain, where Olympia seems to have tried to obtain a marriage or military post for her son, although we cannot be sure of this. In any case Eugene returned to Vienna in time for the 1686 campaign with neither. The attempt to re-establish some kind of bond with his mother must also be judged a failure; he did not bother to see her again until just before she died more than twenty years later.

Eugene's closest ties were now not with his own family but with other young aristocrats who had left their country for service in Hungary in much the same way as he had. By 1686 there were countless non-German princes and nobles in the Imperial army. The war was increasingly taking on the appearance of a crusade. Despite Louis XIV's disapproval many French aristocrats went as well; and when James II's natural son arrived he found an 'abundance of English'.[2] The capture of Buda in the summer of 1686 was hailed as a victory for Europe as a whole: Leopold was beginning to be thought of as the champion of all Christendom rather than as the intolerant Catholic that he in many ways was.

The prize of Buda was nearly lost because of quarrelling among the Imperial generals. It was inevitable that disputes should break out as so many of the leaders were ruling princes. The elector of Bavaria, Max Emmanuel, had married Leopold's only child by his first wife in 1685. He and his close friend and supporter, Louis of Baden, were both obstinate and quick-tempered young men, who were particularly impatient with the more cautious Charles of Lorraine. They believed Max Emmanuel's electoral rank and family relationship to Leopold should have given him precedence over the duke or at the least an independent command. But Lorraine was determined to keep control of the whole field army and he got his way because of the support of Leopold. Lorraine had other powerful allies in the papal nuncio Buonvisi and in the tireless Marco d'Aviano, who accompanied the army, preaching in Italian to uncomprehending but enthusiastic troops. In June 1686, therefore, Lorraine was able to surround Buda with his whole army, though the commanders continued to quarrel throughout the summer months as the siege ran true to form and led to far greater losses than would have been suffered in an actual battle. During one of the many costly assaults Eugene, who was attached to the wing under Max Emmanuel, received his first slight wound. On 2 September the city fell and, despite attempts by the commanders to prevent it, Buda was sacked and burned, the Imperial troops killing all the Turks they could find. This may have been Eugene's fault. According to a contemporary account he and his dragoons had been posted outside the city to guard against any Turkish relief attempt, but he 'forsook his post, and let loose his soldiers, crying out to give no quarter to the Janisaries'.[3] But considering their losses during the siege and their 'scarce and rotten' food,[4] some plundering and slaughter was inevitable, and was seen by the troops as their right.

The capture of Buda was the first major gain from the Turks in central Europe since the conquests of Suleiman the Magnificent in the early sixteenth century. It was followed by a collapse of Turkish resistance throughout Hungary as far as Transylvania and Serbia, with Pécs (Fünfkirchen), Szeged (Szegedin) and even Arad falling to the Imperialists before the end of 1686. Eugene himself accompanied Louis of Baden in a deep strike down the Danube into southern Hungary as far as Osijek (Esseg) before returning to Vienna in mid-November.

Buoyed up by their success several of the Imperial generals, including Eugene, made their way with Max Emmanuel to Venice for the carnival in January 1687. Both the city and its carnival were firm favourites with the European aristocracy, especially with those taking part in the Grand Tour. But while his comrades passed their time with receptions, balls and love affairs, Eugene seems to have found more enjoyment in visiting the famous arsenal and shipyards. The journey also gave him another chance to see Victor Amadeus whom he visited in February. He had made it clear to his cousin both by direct letters and through the Savoyard minister in Vienna, Tarino, that he could not afford to stay in Imperial service without further financial help. Once again Victor Amadeus gave him money, and the next year the gift of revenues from the two Piedmontese abbeys finally provided him with the permanent security he needed. The duke's generosity undoubtedly came from a desire to help a member of his own family, but the two men also seem to have got on well with each other personally, and much of the information we have about Eugene in these early years comes from his fairly regular correspondence with Victor Amadeus.

In the spring of 1687 the pressure from Max Emmanuel for an independent command became too strong for Leopold to resist, and he reluctantly allowed him to take part of the army along the river Tisza to besiege Peterwardein (Petrovaradin). Louis of Baden and Eugene accompanied him, but the operation was short-lived. Max found neither food nor forage on the Tisza and had to rejoin Lorraine. The joint Imperial army of 60,000 men eventually came up against a larger Turkish force under the grand vizier, Suleiman Pasha, which was protected by the guns of the fortress of Osijek. The Imperial army was forced to retreat, the troops short of food and even drinking water and harassed by Tartar raids. It was decided to make a stand near Mohács, where king Louis of Hungary had been killed and had lost his kingdom to the Ottomans in 1526. In the ensuing battle of Berg Harsan (Nagyharsány) on 12 August 1687 the Turks were decisively beaten. It was the kind of full-scale battle Lorraine had wanted and knew could only be won by employing the whole army rather than by allowing his subordinates to fritter parts of it away on numerous sieges. In the battle Eugene had stood out for his bravery in leading cavalry charges and he was granted the special honour of riding to Vienna to report the victory in person to the emperor. Leopold responded with a gift of a portrait of himself set in diamonds.

Berg Harsan opened the way into Serbia for the Imperialists and destroyed the power of the Turks in the Hungarian plain for good. The most immediate effect, however, was that the demoralized retreating Ottoman army mutinied, a revolt which soon spread to Constantinople, where the grand vizier was killed and sultan Mehmed IV deposed. For a year Turkey was paralysed.

The latent quarrels between Lorraine and his two subordinates, Max Emmanuel and Louis of Baden, erupted again after Berg Harsan and the two princes left the Imperial camp for Vienna. Eugene was careful, despite their patronage, not to identify himself with his German cousins in their quarrels. He therefore stayed behind with the duke who wanted to round off the year's campaign by attacking Transylvania, a vassal principality of the sultan's which so far had been largely untouched by the war.

The Imperialists marched north along the Tisza, a route which Eugene was to follow more than once in the future. It proved a harrowing experience. Heavy September rain turned the countryside into knee-deep mud, and there was no wood available for heat or cooking. The troops lived on 'dry bisket softened with bad water, such as was found in the ditches'. Many became ill and their horses died 'for want of forage'.[5] When they eventually crossed the Tisza into Transylvania, the Imperialists followed what had become a general practice of seizing Turkish civilians and demanding ransoms for their release.[6] During the siege of Buda a hundred Turkish women had been captured and sold as slaves, although the prettier of the women taken were often kept by the soldiers themselves.

The ruler of Transylvania, prince Apafi, did not resist the Imperial troops but quickly paid a large tribute and agreed to provide winter quarters. Lorraine and his officers, including Eugene, were therefore back in Vienna before the end of the year, but the army left behind was one of occupation; the way was being prepared for annexation and this followed gradually over the next ten years. The victories of 1685 and 1686 also had a direct effect on Leopold's position in Habsburg and former Turkish Hungary. The lands taken from the Turks were disposed of directly by the crown, while in September 1687 the diet was assembled at Pressburg and forced to make the throne hereditary in the Habsburg family and to abolish the right of legal rebellion.

The prospects for the campaign in 1688 were better than ever because of the confusion in the Ottoman empire, but Lorraine was unable to take advantage of them himself. His health had been poor for some time and the march into Transylvania undermined it further. Max Emmanuel was now given sole charge. Despite the romantic figure which this slight, sensual, almost effeminate-looking prince presented, he had much in common with his predecessor. Both he and Lorraine showed their best during a battle – Marco d'Aviano described Max as 'all fire and flame'[7] – but neither could be bothered with the details of campaigning. The elector's aim for his first campaign as commander-in-chief was one which seemed fitting to his ambition, to seize the capital of Serbia, Belgrade, the only major city in the northern Balkans still in Turkish hands.

The city proved easier to take than Buda, for on the approach of the Imperialists, the Turkish troops and civilians in the suburbs fled, burning their houses as they left and packing what they could onto boats which took them down the Danube. Only the Serbs and Jews remained and a Turkish garrison shut itself up in the citadel. Eugene was the first commander on the scene but there was no repetition of the atrocities at Buda; the troops were allowed to pillage what little had been left behind and the inhabitants were spared.

Eugene was not to see the surrender of the citadel at Belgrade. During the siege he was badly wounded in the knee by a musket ball and had to be carried home to Vienna. The flesh took from September till December to close. In addition he was beginning to suffer from bronchitis and sinusitis which had first affected him some months before after the march into Transylvania. He was to be troubled by this during most winters for the rest of his life, a condition which his incessant snuff-taking aggravated.

The 1688 campaign was to be Eugene's last against the Turks for a number of years; instead he was to be called on to fight in the war which broke out in the west with France. His five years in Hungary had brought him the rank of lieutenant-general (*Feldmarshall-Leutnant*), to which he had been promoted in November 1687. He was also making an impression as a military leader, Lorraine informing the Spanish ambassador at his promotion that he possessed far greater talents than one would expect from a man of his age: he was then twenty-four. A year later the French soldier Villars, who had served with Eugene under Max Emmanuel, reckoned him nineteenth in the ranks of the emperor's

generals and added: 'The Prince of Savoy is thought a brave man, having
as much good sense as spirit, enjoying studying and being set on becoming the good officer he is certainly capable of becoming; he is full of
ambition, zealous about anything which has to do with glory but even
more to be commended by his sincere and true devotion to duty.'[8]

The fall of Belgrade in 1688 marked the limit of Imperialist gains
against the Turks. Over the next few years the war with France, the con-
sequent reduction of German forces in Hungary and the partial recovery of the Turks saw an erosion of the Imperial position and the loss
of Belgrade in 1690. Yet there was no serious threat to Habsburg control
of Hungary, the wars having shown that the Turks were no match for
considerably smaller German armies in the field.

The Imperial army owed its superiority in the Balkans to the work of
an Italian, Raymond Montecuccoli, who as commander-in-chief and
president of the war council (1668–80) applied the lessons he had learned
as a young commander during the Thirty Years War. His great achievement was to refashion the Austrian infantry on the pattern of the
Swedish army of Gustavus Adolphus. He made it more mobile by
abandoning the large unwieldy *tercios*, solid blocks of men over 2,000
strong, for battalions half this size which could adopt several formations
besides the conventional squares. At the same time he reduced the number of men armed with the long 14–18 foot pike, a cumbersome defensive weapon, and increased the number of musketeers. After his death
mobility was improved further by replacing the heavy and unreliable
matchlock guns with lighter and more rapid-firing flintlocks. This
change began in the 1680s but was not completed in the Austrian army
before the first decade of the eighteenth century. A further innovation of
these Turkish wars was the gradual replacement of the pike, first with a
shorter boar spear and then with plug, ring and socket bayonets fixed to
the musket barrels. All infantrymen could now be armed with the same
weapon and every man could act as a defensive and offensive unit. The
French army which was far more advanced than the Austrian army in so
many fields, especially in its organization, was much slower in adopting
the bayonet.

Montecuccoli also copied from the Swedes their use of light field
artillery and equipped the Austrian army with one or two guns, varying
from 3- to 24-pounders, for every 1,000 men. Although he was primarily an infantry general, he also made important changes in the
cavalry to bring it into line with other western armies. Making up about
a third of an army, cavalry was very expensive because of the cost of the
mounts and the need to provide fodder. It was also the élite of an army,

appealing naturally enough more than the infantry to young noble recruits. Under Montecuccoli it became an increasingly versatile instrument which could be used either for charging the enemy with the sword or discharging shot at them. The heavily-armoured soldier on horseback was now a thing of the past. By the 1680s the heavy cuirassiers, used primarily for their shock-power, were equipped with armour only to protect their head, chest and back, and arms. Under white cloaks they wore brown leather tunics, white jackets and red pantaloons; for weapons they carried a sabre, carbine and a brace of pistols. The lighter dragoons, who were Eugene's favourite troops, provided rapid fire-power on different parts of the field. Like the cuirassiers they wore white cloaks and black three-cornered felt hats but boasted more brightly coloured uniforms of blue, red or green. They could fight on foot or on horseback – they acted rather like a mounted infantry – and usually carried an arc-handled sword and a carbine, although later they adopted the bayonet flintlock. While cuirassiers and dragoons were common to all western armies, the Austrians during the 1680s also came to depend on Croat horsemen, hussars, who stood out with their fur-edged dolmans. They were used for raiding opposing armies or local communities, for foraging and intelligence work. Croat infantry, similarly clad in furs and armed with carbines and sabres, were also used as irregulars.

It was their increased fire-power and mobility which gave the troops of the emperor and the German princes a decided advantage against the Turks. Neither the bayonet nor the flintlock had been introduced into the sultan's armies and his infantry, the janissaries, relied on matchlocks and their skill as swordsmen. Light artillery was unknown and the intricate manoeuvres and squares of western armies were totally alien to the Turks, who had huge numbers of undisciplined irregular troops in their armies and depended on large half-moon formations to envelop and swamp the enemy. Wave upon wave of janissaries and spahis (Turkish cavalry) would advance in mass rushes which could not be regrouped. The German troops only needed to keep their nerve and hold their formations for their superior fire-power to mow down the Turks. The more fiercely the Turks charged the more men they lost. Victory was won through superior defence, but Eugene was to show in later years that the Turks could also be beaten when attacked. One advantage the Turks continued to enjoy for a long time, however, was their bands of Crimean Tartar horsemen, who, armed with little more than bows and arrows, were unleashed in swift devastating raids against supply bases and local communities. Eventually an answer was found to this menace by sending hussars after them.

IV

War in Savoy

Just as Belgrade was falling to Max Emmanuel in September 1688 French troops were crossing the Rhine into the Holy Roman Empire at several points. Louis XIV and his war minister Louvois hoped that a limited show of force would not only encourage the Turks to continue the war in the Balkans but also that it would make the emperor and German princes confirm France's earlier gains at the truce of Ratisbon.

Louis had to take this action because he was all too aware that his paramount position of 1684 had collapsed. Then his unrivalled military strength and a number of judicious bribes to German states had given him more influence in the Empire than Leopold, while around France's northern and eastern borders a chain of defensive works was being constructed by the great fortifications expert, Vauban. Although this 'iron barrier' was nearly complete in 1688, by then Louis was isolated in Europe and confronted by powers determined to humble him.

The most determined of Louis's enemies was the Dutch stadtholder, William of Orange. He had been urging the other European powers to combine against France, since before the truce of Ratisbon, hoping to create a balance to her power if not to destroy her. But he had received little response. However, the situation changed dramatically after 1685 when Louis made the mistake of expelling French Protestants by the revocation of the edict of Nantes. Infuriated German Protestant princes, particularly the elector of Brandenburg, turned against him, at the very time when Leopold's successes in Hungary were increasing his prestige and creating the image of a ruler fighting on behalf of all Christendom.

Worried by the hostility of the German states in 1686–87, Louis decided to frighten them back into obedience, and in 1688 he pressed for the election of a pro-French candidate as archbishop-elector of Cologne as well as upholding the claims of his sister-in-law, Elizabeth Charlotte, duchess of Orleans, in the Palatinate. Although it was William of Orange who did most to rally German resistance to these threats, he was now finding increasing support in Vienna for a determined stand. The emperor's closest advisers, Borgomanero and the court chancellor Stratmann, managed to persuade Leopold to give tacit support to a military venture of William's own: an invasion of England to force his Catholic father-in-law, James II, onto the anti-French side. Leopold was to insist, however, that the Protestant William give assurances about the safety of the British Catholics as well as a promise of support for Austrian claims to the Spanish succession.

This hostile coalition existed in embryo when Louis's troops crossed into the Empire in September 1688 and began to lay waste the Palatinate. Instead of intimidating the German princes, the French action had the opposite effect and the English minister at Ratisbon reported that 'The French have so enraged the Germans with the many outrages they have committed . . . that the several states were never so united and animated to revenge them.'[1] Compromise was now impossible and the full-scale war which Louis had hoped to avoid became certain; it was to last for nine years until 1697. The attack on the Palatinate also gave William the opportunity to invade England, where he and his wife Mary were made joint sovereigns after the rapid flight of James II to France. They were supported by a parliament determined to defend this Protestant succession against their old king and his French protector.

There were never any doubts that Austria would join in the struggle against France; all the military and political leaders as well as Leopold were in favour of doing so. The only question was whether the emperor should end the Turkish war. Leopold's clerical advisers urged him to continue the crusade in the Balkans, and by taking this advice he committed himself to a contest completely beyond the resources of his monarchy.

In May 1689 Leopold signed the Grand Alliance with the Dutch, which aimed at forcing France back to her 1659 frontiers. The alliance was soon joined not only by England and Spain but also by the majority of German princes, including Max Emmanuel of Bavaria; it was the princes who would provide the bulk of the manpower for the coming war against France. Leopold now appeared to be, and in many ways was, the champion of the interests of the whole Holy Roman Empire rather than of his own dynasty or hereditary lands. His ultimate objective in this Nine Years War was to undo the territorial settlements of the last forty years and to compel France to restore all of Alsace as well as the three bishoprics of Metz, Toul and Verdun. Leopold's own influence in the Empire had recovered dramatically from the disastrously low ebb of the first years of his reign; his new-found authority was based on the willing co-operation of the majority of the princes, who had come to see that their private interests had to take second place before the over-riding menace of Louis XIV. The most tangible sign of this change was the election of Leopold's eldest son Joseph as King of the Romans in January 1690: he could now succeed his father as emperor immediately on his death without a further election.

The Nine Years War (1688–97) was to settle down rapidly into a contest of indecisive manoeuvres and sieges as the allies tried and failed to destroy the French fortification network in Flanders and the Rhine-land. It became a matter of which side collapsed first through financial exhaustion. While Louis was quite prepared for a war of this kind, the allies, particularly William, looked desperately for a way out: the answer seemed to lie in Italy and it was here that Eugene was to make his first impact as a commander in his own right.

The war began predictably enough for Eugene, who was now twenty-five: he followed his protector Max Emmanuel to the Rhine and had charge of three cavalry regiments at the siege of Mainz during the summer of 1689 where he received a slight head wound. He might well have stayed on the Rhine for the rest of the war in a comparatively minor position since there were plenty of German ruling princes jostling for high commands. But in 1690 new prospects opened up when his cousin Victor Amadeus joined the Grand Alliance.

For more than ten years Victor Amadeus had suffered virtual French control of his duchy through two fortresses garrisoned by the French at Casale and Pinerolo. While he was determined to be free of these, he had no intention of exchanging a French master for a Spanish one in neigh-bouring Milan or an Austrian one from the north. Throughout his long reign he was to shift continually from one alliance to another so as to maintain his independence and to grab what he could for Savoy. By necessity he learned to play things close to his chest and as early as 1687 the French minister in Turin remarked that 'his heart is covered with mountains like his country'.[2] Much the same policy was pursued by Max Emmanuel of Bavaria in the coming years, and it was one which prince Eugene, despite his debt to both men, found difficult to understand or to forgive. For him loyalty was one of the chief attributes of military and public life.

In June 1690 Austria and Spain finally concluded long drawn-out negotiations with Victor Amadeus and promised to send troops from the Empire and Milan to help him expel the French from his territories. The Maritime Powers* were willing to back this alliance with continual financial aid, partly because this new theatre of war would divert

* This was the name usually given by contemporaries to the English and Dutch.

French resources from elsewhere but also because they originally hoped it might prove the weak link in France's defence system. As William III's minister in Vienna, Paget, put it: 'a doore is now opened into France, bigg enough I think for us to get in at, and enter ye strong man's house'.[3]

Soon after the alliance was signed Eugene, now promoted to general of cavalry, arrived in Turin with his close friend Commercy to take command of five regiments of Imperial troops being transferred to Italy. Eugene's close family relationship with Victor Amadeus made him a natural choice to lead the small Imperial force but his persuasive friends in Vienna, Borgomanero, chancellor Stratmann and the Savoyard ambassador Tarino, had also pressed his case. Unfortunately these men could not ensure that Eugene's troops arrived quickly enough to save him from feeling humiliated, for as he wrote to Tarino, 'I am useless here without troops and we will be accused of only coming here to go into winter quarters.'[4]

The Imperial troops were needed badly because Louis XIV was determined to punish Victor Amadeus and had ordered his general, Catinat, to use his substantial force to burn large tracts of the mountainous parts of Savoy and of the plain of Piedmont. Intimidation of this sort was widely used by the French throughout the war and it was all too easy for them to destroy the rice, corn and maize fields in the Po valley and to burn villages and isolated cottages. The few attempts by the peasants to retaliate by ambushing French troops were met by hanging anyone found carrying arms. In a desperate attempt to stop this destruction Victor Amadeus rejected Eugene's advice and insisted on 18 August 1690 on engaging the French at Staffarda with his own and Spanish troops. Only Eugene's command of the Savoyard cavalry and his conduct of the retreat, which Catinat considered 'carried out well and with firmness',[5] saved his militarily inept cousin from disaster.

When Eugene's troops eventually arrived little could be done because the Spanish generals raised countless objections: in Eugene's words, 'they want to do absolutely nothing'.[6] He had to be satisfied with small raids against the enemy. In one of these in September he was unable to prevent his men, used to the brutality of the Turkish wars, acting in a way almost unknown in the west: they castrated and then killed two hundred French prisoners. The usual western practice was to exchange prisoners with the enemy, although some French troops taken on the Rhine by the Imperialists were sent to serve in garrisons in Hungary.[7]

When winter came the troops had to be found quarters. Following the policy that it was best to have someone else pay for these, Vienna ordered Eugene to quarter his men in the Montferrat, which belonged to the pro-French duke of Mantua. The duke tried to prevent this by encouraging the peasantry in bands a thousand strong to ambush Eugene's troops. Short of food and with their pay in arrears, the Imperialists sacked villages and hanged anyone found armed. Eugene had little heart for this kind of warfare, blaming it on his own government's deficient financial and supply services. Whereas Catinat could always depend on vigorous support and firm direction from home, Eugene could not and every winter during the campaigns in Italy he was forced to leave his troops and cross the Alps to plead personally at the Imperial court for their arrears to be paid and satisfactory provision made for the coming year.

Over the next five years he saw at first hand the defects in the Imperial government. Although both the court chancellor Stratmann and the Imperial vice-chancellor Königsegg were determined enemies of France and grasped the urgency of the situation, they were the exception and were both dead by 1694. A particular source of disappointment was Rüdiger Starhemberg, who had been made president of the war council in 1688. While he inspired confidence because of his earlier bravery in defending Vienna from the Turks, he had little administrative ability and to outside observers he appeared a prematurely-aged fop with little political influence.[8]

Eugene soon realized the worthlessness of most of the ministers but he was equally aware that the main blame lay with the emperor. At the beginning of 1693 he wrote bitterly to his cousin Louis of Baden: 'No one thinks of anything but eating, drinking and gambling; they trouble themselves about nothing else. . . . The tragic circumstances in the Empire [France appeared on the point of invading south Germany] certainly disturbed the Emperor for the space of an hour. But luckily on that same day there was a procession, and he forgot anything else.'[9]

Although the inertia at home continually irritated Eugene, on a more personal level he had the frustration of being rapidly reduced to a subordinate military position. While he had been senior enough to command the small body of Imperial troops in Savoy in 1690, in the following years the size of the Imperial force was considerably increased by the addition of mercenary troops paid for by the Maritime Powers. Consequently the allied army became too large for a junior officer and minor prince like Eugene to command and he had to be satisfied with a secondary role under men who proved incapable of outmanoeuvring Catinat and forcing him to a decisive battle.

In 1691 Max Emmanuel arrived to take command, bringing with him the Neapolitan Caraffa, who had won an infamous reputation for his cruelty to Protestant rebels in Hungary. Despite the Bavarian elector's renown as a brave and dashing leader, he did little more than bombard Catinat's armed camp during the summer and autumn. When Catinat retaliated, Max showed that whatever he lacked as a strategist, he could make up for in bravado: on being asked by the French where his quarters were so that their gunners would not fire on that part of the camp, he replied 'everywhere'![10]

Although Eugene won a minor success himself on 28 June 1691 in relieving the town of Cuneo, a success well publicized in Vienna and Germany, he was fretting at this indecisive warfare. However, he carefully avoided criticizing the elector and that winter went with him to Venice, even joining him in the gaming rooms. At this stage in his career Max Emmanuel might still have held the key to his future and in any case Eugene bore no personal ill-feeling towards him. He did, however, criticize Caraffa. Knowing that his comments would be passed on, he wrote to Tarino in Vienna that 'no one could be less of a soldier' than Caraffa and that his army was in a state of 'confusion and disorder which could never be matched'.[11] Eugene himself was beginning to impose the strict discipline on his own regiments which he always demanded later.

When Max Emmanuel gave up his Italian command to become governor of the Spanish Netherlands in 1692, the allied statesmen in Vienna were convinced that the only man capable of leading and revitalizing the campaign in Savoy was Eugene. In January 1692 the English minister Paget pressed for the prince to be given command under Victor Amadeus's nominal leadership, as he believed Eugene was '. . . a very worthy person, and greatly esteemed for a prudent goodly commander . . . all yt was well don last year in those parts was performed by his courage and conduct; he knows the country perfectly well, is well beloved, and obeyed by ye soldiers'. Unfortunately the court was not prepared to take this step.[12] Leopold preferred men he knew well and therefore sent another Italian and notorious looter, Caprara, to act as immediate subordinate to Victor Amadeus, who was put in overall command for 1692.

Caprara had an excellent chance for a decisive campaign because while the number of his troops was stepped up, Louis withdrew many of his own to concentrate them in Flanders. But instead of trying to reduce the French fortresses of Casale or Pinerolo, Caprara embarked on a punitive raid into southern France, burning and seizing all he could find as far as Grenoble. Louis had calculated quite correctly that the allies would do no more than 'burn some villages in my country' and he was willing enough to allow this.[13] Eugene, who took part in this raid with Caprara, is said to have remarked to Commercy, 'Didn't I say I would only return to France sword in hand? Louis exiled my mother, the Countess of Soissons, and I have just exiled thousands of his subjects by making them flee from their houses and country.'[14] Although the story is unconfirmed Eugene was certainly a hard and unforgiving enough man to have said this; more than thirty years later a French observer found that he still felt very bitter at Louis's treatment of him and his family.

After a further inconclusive campaign in Piedmont in 1693, culminating in a minor French victory at Marsaglia in October, Caprara was sent to Hungary the following year. Eugene's hour had now come as there was no one of equivalent standing who could command in Italy. He was therefore detailed to act under Victor Amadeus for 1694, but was given specific instructions to proceed cautiously. Caprara had warned that Eugene was inclined to be over-hasty.

A cautious policy was inevitable in any case, not only because of the failure of the Imperial government to provide Eugene with either the men or the means for effective action but also because of the attitude of Victor Amadeus, who throughout 1694 continually prevaricated and vetoed an active policy. In fact the duke was negotiating secretly with the French, having been finally convinced by Marsaglia that the only way to prevent further devastation of his countryside and to obtain the French fortresses was by selling his support to Louis. The French king responded, although the talks proceeded very slowly. When Eugene at last persuaded the allied army to besiege Casale in July 1695 he was amazed that the fortress immediately surrendered. But Louis had agreed to this in the spring through a secret agreement made with Victor Amadeus by the French governor of Pinerolo, Tessé. What Louis ultimately wanted was a separate peace with Victor Amadeus to neutralize the Italian theatre of war. Victor Amadeus, however, was a slippery customer and would only agree after further French concessions. Following a meeting with him Tessé remarked that he had just made 'a journey to the most difficult, most suspicious, most indecisive prince that could ever be'.[15] The duke held out till May 1696 when Louis promised that Pinerolo would be handed over to him. Consequently the following month he declared an armistice, invited the other allies to agree to the neutrality of Italy for the rest of the war and threatened to join his troops to those of France if they proved unamenable.

Although Eugene's suspicions of Victor Amadeus increased considerably after the surrender of Casale, he remained largely in the dark about his activities. The armistice finally revealed all and Eugene was never to trust his cousin again; their relations were strained for the rest of their lives, although Eugene continued to pay due deference to the duke as head of his own family and to write to him fairly intimately for a further ten years.

During the summer of 1696 while they waited for replies from Madrid and Vienna to Victor Amadeus's armistice proposals, Eugene and the commander of the Spanish troops, Legañez, moved eastwards to cover Milan. In September Victor Amadeus joined his troops to those under Catinat and there now seemed a real danger that together they would attack Milan. Eugene appealed to Leopold to decide quickly whether to fight on or to abandon Italy.

Leopold vacillated for a long time. The Maritime Powers urged him to hold out, as they feared that Louis would be able to transfer his troops from Italy elsewhere and force the allies to make a general peace on his terms. But Leopold had no forces of his own left to send into Italy and the Spaniards were scared of losing Milan to Louis. On 7 October 1696 Austria, Spain, Savoy and France signed the treaty of Vigevano which neutralized Italy. Catinat's troops were transferred northwards and William III never forgave Leopold for taking this 'villainous step'[16] which quickly led to the disintegration of the Grand Alliance and to a general peace with France.

The war in Italy had never represented a very high priority for the Austrians. It had largely been the Maritime Powers who had encouraged it in the hope of diverting French energies from Flanders and the Rhine;[17] the idea of trying to invade France herself from the south-east was never a serious possibility. The Austrians had preferred to concentrate on the Rhine, feeling there was no territory for them to gain in the peninsula. Yet their interests were to shift dramatically towards Italy almost immediately after the war when the prospect arose of acquiring Spain's provinces there. At the time the ruler to gain most was Victor Amadeus who achieved independence from France and had Pinerolo and Casale restored to him. However, the agrarian communities in Piedmont and Savoy paid heavily for these gains: they were forced to work as sappers or waggoners, their crops and houses were burnt and their animals seized for food and transport.[18]

The military honours undoubtedly went to Catinat who had been able to take full advantage of the incompetent or shackled allied commanders. He was a master of the inconclusive and defensive strategy so dear to Louis himself. Eugene did well to survive the disappointing and very frustrating campaigns with an enhanced reputation. He emerged as the one general determined on action and a decisive result. He was now

considered fit to command an army in his own right and had been
created a field-marshal in 1693 (this was less of a distinction for a man of
thirty than might be thought, as there were no less than twenty-two
field-marshals in the Imperial army in 1705). The war also marked his
definite commitment to serve under the house of Habsburg. Still unmarried and with hardly any contact now with his own family, his only
home apart from the army was Vienna, and during the war he had begun
buying property there.

The indecisive and sluggish campaigns in Italy were repeated on a
larger scale elsewhere during the Nine Years War. This must have been
particularly galling to the young generals who had fought in Hungary in
the 1680s. The Turkish army had been much inferior in all but size to
the German one, whereas in the west the armies on both sides were
roughly matched. At the same time the whole development and approach to fighting of western armies in the late seventeenth century was
to encourage indecisive warfare.

The growth of the centralized state in western and central Europe
went hand in hand with the development of large standing armies. This
was a continuing process from the previous century, but in the late
seventeenth century, especially in France but also elsewhere, there was a
more determined effort by governments to control and regulate their
armies. Recruiting, financing and supplying were administered more
directly by the state, and uniforms, arms and drill were regularized. Perhaps the easiest task was finding the men: the money usually ran out
before the supply of manpower. Troops were recruited in winter when
fieldworkers in an almost totally agrarian society were unemployed.
Those who joined voluntarily were usually men without farms of their
own, more often than not younger sons. Famine conditions would
automatically swell the number of recruits. But at times the demands on
manpower became too pressing and there was resort to compulsory
conscription, particularly of vagrants. A man's religion was of little
account when he was recruited: Protestants were tolerated in Leopold's
army. While cavalrymen were comparatively well off, the ordinary infantryman, who had not yet become the automaton of Frederick the
Great's army, had lost the position of respect which he enjoyed in the
sixteenth century. He was an expendable article, easier to replace than
cavalry horses. He was paid no more than a day labourer, that is when he
was paid at all. Cut off from contact with his family and former community, poorly fed and clothed, despised and hated by the local populations where he served, the infantryman was inevitably brutalized, taking
what opportunity he could to desert or to revenge himself on the civilian

world around him by outbursts of looting and physical violence.

The chief problem for governments in the seventeenth century with large armies (up to a quarter of a million strong in wartime) was to finance and adequately supply them. The latter was particularly difficult because there had been no developments in agriculture or transport in continental Europe to cope with the increasing demands of warfare. During the Thirty Years War armies had largely depended on seizing what they could on the march and eating their way through a countryside. It was impossible to support the larger armies in this way; in areas like Hungary they would have starved and even in fertile Lombardy and the Netherlands there would have been huge problems of collection and distribution. Governments, therefore, amassed food as well as arms before a campaign and stored them in magazines sited in strategic places. They then drew on these to supply their armies during the campaigning season.

The wide-scale undisciplined looting of food and goods carried out in the Thirty Years War was abandoned. When areas were devastated, as in the Palatinate or in Savoy-Piedmont, it was done largely as a form of intimidation or to rob the enemy of supplies or future tax revenues. In place of indiscriminate looting the practice was growing of imposing contributions or financial exactions on enemy or neutral territory under the threat of burning crops or villages. This gave the local population some protection if they paid up, provided armies with a regular source of income for buying provisions and gave commanding officers plenty of opportunity for growing rich, opportunities which Caraffa and Caprara in particular had used to the full.[19] Similarly, cities were only plundered after sieges if they refused to surrender.

The actual mobility of armies was restricted by their dependence on maintaining contact with their magazines, an effective range being about 140–160 kilometres. No army could carry all its supplies: it has been calculated that merely to carry sufficient fodder for horses and draught animals as well as the grain, handmills, bricks and firewood to bake bread for an army of 60,000 men for a month would have needed a transport train of 11,000 carts, a monster 198 kilometres long.

The supply system in the Imperial army was probably the worst in western Europe. It was well known that the Imperial troops would tolerate worse food than other armies and were used to starving. It was felt sufficient to supply them with bread, biscuit, salt and some kind of drink, but even in the better-off French armies it was never possible to provide a daily meat ration. Soldiers in the late seventeenth century probably received a third of the calories and protein thought necessary in the First World War for garrison troops. They consequently could hardly march 20 kilometres a day, suffered continually from scurvy and were an easy prey to epidemics, especially of dysentery and typhoid in late summer and early autumn, when they ate vast quantities of unwashed and unripe fruit.

During Eugene's lifetime most of the supplying of food, clothing and ammunition in the Imperial armies was carried out by Jewish contractors. The most famous of the 'court Jews' was Samuel Oppenheimer, who had extensive international contacts and credit. He charged heavily for his services but he always ran the risk of not being paid.

Fodder was not usually supplied to the armies from magazines. Hay and corn were simply mown down with no regard for the peasants, four or five days' supply being taken at a time. Inevitably the supply of fodder, which was dependent on weather and terrain, affected mobility. In winter everything came to a stop because it was impossible to forage for animals on the move. At most there were only a hundred days a year available for campaigning and a great deal of this time was spent manoeuvring to cut and defend supply lines.

The difficulties of providing adequate supplies, the lack of mobility, the fact that even a beaten enemy could use the winter to recuperate without fear of attack, and the deliberate French emphasis on fortified frontiers meant that warfare in this period was a long drawn-out affair of several years' campaigning, which financial exhaustion as much as military defeat brought to a close.

V

Zenta

As the Imperial army, now little more than a ragged rabble, retreated towards Milan in September 1696 and it seemed all too clear that the Italian war was over, Eugene wrote to Leopold asking to be considered for the campaign against the Turks in Hungary the following year. With his request went a similar one from prince Commercy, who had been his closest friend and subordinate throughout the past decade of fighting.

In Hungary by the mid-1690s a stalemate had developed as the Imperialists concentrated their energies on the Rhine. Their leading generals also moved west, Lorraine and Max Emmanuel in 1689 and then Louis of Baden in 1692. On the other hand, despite the forceful leadership of sultan Mustafa II who led his troops in person, the Turks had not recovered sufficiently to win back the vast areas lost to the Christian armies in the 1680s, with the exception of Belgrade. There were, however, few signs that Mustafa was prepared to agree to peace and recognize the loss of Hungary: only total military defeat would bring him to this. But the Imperialists seemed incapable of delivering the final blow, particularly under the leaders who succeeded Baden like Caprara and then from 1696 Frederick Augustus, elector of Saxony.

The elector, still in his mid-twenties, was a man of great physical strength, soon to be known as 'Augustus the Strong'. His sexual appetite was vast; the number of his children was said eventually to equal the days in a year. To those who knew him, like the English diplomat Stepney, his appointment came as a surprise. He did not actually take 'a billiard-table and tennis court with him to the camp' as Stepney had predicted,[1] but he was nevertheless a disastrous commander. He had been appointed mainly because he brought 8,000 Saxons with him and it was difficult for Leopold to be rid of him. He ignored the advice of the experienced Imperial generals who soon despised him. One of them a French émigré, Rabutin, was particularly outspoken, pointing out to the war council that 'the honour or advantage of being an elector do not in themselves produce the intelligence or talents of a captain'. He despaired at the thought of another campaign under Frederick Augustus: 'our soldiers have lost their courage . . . ; they have no Lorraine or Prince Louis to lead them. Surely we can find generals like them?' Starved of resources because of the war with France, as well as being inadequately led, the army was collapsing as a fighting force and was having to live almost completely off the local population in Hungary. Even a hardened campaigner like Rabutin, while recognizing 'that the people must be sacrificed rather than the troops', was 'filled with pity for the misery . . . of these poor people'.[2] Conditions were even worse than those described four years earlier by an English agent journeying south from Vienna:

> . . . the heats, natts and scarcity of food were very severe upon us, and after wee past Buda our faces were so marked that any man would have imagined it had been the small pox. . . . [At Osijek] the garrison look generally like dead men, I pray God send me well out of it for I never was in so dreadfull a place that I can remember.[3]

One way out of the predicament was for the Imperial court to appoint an able subordinate who could stand up to Frederick Augustus. Eugene was the obvious choice especially as he wanted to go to Hungary. Both Louis of Baden, who was now in command on the Rhine and corresponded frequently with Eugene, and the president of the war council, Rüdiger Starhemberg, urged this course on Leopold. But the emperor was reluctant to abandon his preference for men he knew well like Caprara and refused to come to a decision during the winter of 1696–97. He finally gave way in April 1697, a month after receiving this remarkable tribute to the thirty-three year old Eugene from Starhemberg: ' . . . [he knew] no one with more understanding, experience, application and zeal for Your Imperial Majesty's service, or with a more generous and disinterested temper, and possessing the esteem of his soldiers to a greater extent than the Prince.'[4]

If one hurdle had been overcome, there was still the problem of Frederick Augustus himself. It was to be solved by the Saxon elector's entry into the contested election for the Polish throne, vacant since the death of John Sobieski the previous year. Just before the summer campaign began, he left for Krakow and was eventually elected king, taking the title Augustus II. Although the evidence is not conclusive it seems that both Eugene and Rüdiger Starhemberg had a hand in encouraging him to enter the contest and in winning him Imperial support in Poland. They clearly did so in order to get rid of him. As it was too late to appoint a new commander-in-chief, Eugene replaced him and at the beginning of July he went south to join the army for his first really independent command.

On 27 July the Imperial forces were drawn up in front of the strong fortress of Peterwardein on the north bank of the Danube to welcome their new commander. There was a striking difference between him and their previous leader. The prince was physically unprepossessing and clearly indifferent about his own appearance. Although he wore a full-bottomed wig, he had long since abandoned the usual officer's tunic of pearl-grey cloth with sky-blue flecks, edged with gold braid. He preferred a plain brown tunic and was soon known by the troops as their 'little Capuchin'.

The 30,000 Austrian, Saxon and Brandenburg soldiers greeted him with a ceremonial salute. The regimental colours, with the Imperial eagle on one side and the Virgin or motley saints on the other, made a brave enough sight, but the prince was unimpressed. He reported to Leopold that he found the army in a state of 'indescribable misery'. Discipline had collapsed and there was not 'a kreuzer piece'[5] in the war chest to pay the troops. He had to borrow 1,000 gulden immediately from one of his generals. Nevertheless, Eugene had able subordinates – Commercy, who was already indispensable as his second in command and as a cavalry leader, Guido Starhemberg and Heister, fine infantry generals with long experience of warfare against the Turks. He was also his own master.

Whatever hopes prince Eugene may have entertained for the campaign, little was expected generally. When Rüdiger Starhemberg had held a war council in May with Frederick Augustus and Eugene, it had been concluded that the only possible course of action was to stand on the defensive around Peterwardein and to repel any Turkish incursion into southern Hungary or Transylvania. And when the new commander left Vienna, he did so with a warning from Leopold 'to act cautiously and avoid getting involved in any action without a good chance of success'.[6] Caution seemed all the more necessary because of the outbreak in June of a revolt in Upper Hungary around Tokaj of peasants and poor nobles protesting against the quartering of marauding troops. The uprising caused widespread panic as far west as Vienna,[7] and although the young Lorrainer, prince Vaudémont,* was to suppress it quickly Eugene opened his own campaign with an uneasy eye to the north.

Taking his defensive role seriously, Eugene began by strengthening his

---

* Charles Thomas Vaudémont was yet another Lorrainer, the grandson of duke Charles IV by a morganatic marriage. He entered Imperial service at the age of fourteen in 1684 and like his cousin Commercy soon became a close friend of Eugene's.

position along the line of the Danube and the Tisza from Peterwardein
to Szeged and setting up magazines at various points. All supplies had to
be brought down the Danube, as the area of operations was completely
bare. At this time, before the drainage schemes of the following two
centuries, the countryside north of the Danube and west of the Tisza was
largely composed of vast swamps often covered by stagnant water. There
were few trees and vegetation often consisted of no more than low
bushes and reeds. During the very hot summers this fenland dried up
rapidly, leaving armies short of water and grass. River transport was
therefore essential to both Austrians and Turks who depended on large
galleys and small flat-bottomed boats (*caïques*), in the Austrian case
manned largely by Croats and Serbs. These fleets often engaged in fierce
river fights independently of their respective armies. When contrary
winds held up the ships, as happened to those carrying grain in July,
serious difficulties could arise for the Imperialists. But just as serious was
the danger that supplies might not be sent by the contractors. Eugene
was to have little sympathy with the genuine difficulties of their chief
contractor, Oppenheimer, and at one point wrote urging Leopold 'to
make the Jew keep up the supplies properly, since it's definitely preferable
that a Jew's credit should suffer than that Your Imperial Majesty's crown
and sceptre be imperilled'.[8]

On 19 August sultan Mustafa crossed the Danube near its junction
with the Tisza. His success against Caprara and Frederick Augustus the
previous year had made him very confident: special carts followed him
loaded with chains intended for the German generals and soldiers. He
was not surprised, therefore, when Eugene retreated along the Tisza to
Zenta. The prince's object, however, was to join up with Vaudémont's
troops, now freed from suppressing the revolt in the north, and with
cavalry being brought by Rabutin from Transylvania. After doing so,
he returned to his positions in front of Peterwardein, with an army now
50,000 strong. During this gruelling march, which took a fortnight in the
fierce heat of late summer, a measure of discipline was instilled into the
Imperial army.

Mustafa was stunned to see Eugene return. The Turkish intelligence
system was poor, although the Austrians used their hussars to good
effect. Faced by this new situation, the sultan decided not to risk an attack
on the Imperialists whose rear was covered by the defences of Peterwardein. Instead he moved off along the Tisza to seize Szeged and then
cross the river into Transylvania where he hoped to levy contributions
and carry off slaves.

On hearing of the direction of the Turkish march and certain, from his hussars' reports, that Mustafa was short of cavalry and handicapped by too many raw recruits, Eugene pushed his troops after them. The sultan lost his nerve; scared of being trapped between the advancing Germans and their garrison at Szeged, he began to cross the fast-flowing Tisza at Zenta on a bridge constructed of sixty boats, hoping to be able to march into Transylvania along the other bank. But Eugene's troops were close behind. Despite the marshy ground which hindered the cavalry, the army was forced on in ten-hour marches. Eugene had abandoned all ideas of a defensive campaign for one of outright attack.

On the morning of 11 September a Turkish pasha was captured and brought in by the hussars. The prince threatened, in his own words, 'to hack him into pieces on the spot'.[9] The terrified Turk, seeing the Croat horsemen draw their sabres, divulged that though Mustafa had already crossed the river at Zenta with most of the artillery and baggage, the grand vizier and all the infantry had not. This chance was too good to miss. Riding ahead with the hussars and ordering the army to press on behind, Eugene reached the high ground above Zenta in the late afternoon. There in front of him, protected by only a wall of carts and some cannon, was the bulk of the Turkish infantry waiting its turn to cross the river. Although there were less than four hours of daylight left, he immediately decided to bring up the army for an attack. Using a half-moon formation and with the minimum of preparation, the Imperialists struck. During the ensuing battle Eugene quickly took advantage of a sandbank and shallow water near the boat bridge which allowed Guido Starhemberg and the infantry on the left wing of the Imperial forces to get behind the Turkish defences from the river side. By nightfall the battle was won. Eugene reported to the emperor with an almost poetic touch: 'This great and signal victory and this considerable battle drew to a close with the day itself; it was as though the sun decided not to set until it could see and cast its rays on the triumph of Your Majesty's arms.' In fact the slaughter of the janissaries went on till ten o'clock at night. Very few prisoners were taken for, as Eugene explained, 'The soldiers got worked up to such a pitch that they spared no one and butchered all who fell into their hands despite the large sums of money which the Pashas and Turkish leaders offered them to spare their lives.'[10] Possibly 20,000 were killed and a further 10,000 drowned in the river. The grand vizier had also been cut down by his own men as they struggled to get over the bridge. On Eugene's side only about 300 were killed.

The next day as the Imperial army crossed the river, its waters still full of floating Turkish dead, the enormity of the victory became clear. The Turkish infantry had been totally destroyed, while the sultan and his cavalry had fled towards Temesvár (Timişoara) abandoning their heavy guns and their camp. There was a huge amount of booty, including a war chest of 3 million piastres, 9,000 baggage carts, among them the ones bearing the chains intended for the Imperialists, 6,000 camels and 15,000 oxen. Battle trophies included the grand vizier's seal of office and seven horse-tail standards.

The victory had been won by Eugene's quick decision on the day and his determination almost from the beginning to use his not inconsiderable army offensively. Given Mustafa's mistakes and the poor quality of the Turkish troops, the prince had acted boldly but not rashly. He recognized his army's limitations and made no attempt to follow up the victory by an attack on Temesvár or Belgrade so late in the season. The onset of heavy rain made it vital to put the troops into winter quarters before the army fell apart. Already on 27 September over a thousand of his men had fallen sick. This he felt was only to be expected after 'six weeks in these wastes, where wood in particular cannot be found, where there is no forage and almost all the water has to be taken from stagnant pools'.[11] He himself, however, decided to take Commercy and Starhemberg with 6,000 cavalry and some light guns on a rapid month-long terror raid across 'rude and unbeaten'[12] mountain and forest tracks into Bosnia. Widespread burning of the countryside by this force culminated in the sack of the important but undefended trading centre of Sarajevo with its hundreds of white minaretted mosques. Eugene noted in his campaign diary 'a terrible confusion amongst the Turks'.[13] The Imperial raiders then made their way back across the Sava into Hungary with 'a great quantity of Turkish cloth, with many Turkish women, . . . a great quantity of small and great cattle',[14] at the same time 'burning everything to our right and left belonging to the Turks as we marched'.[15]

In November Eugene returned to Vienna and had his first taste of a triumphant reception – public celebrations, the presentation of an expensive sword from Leopold, and the striking of a special medal with an idealized portrait of the prince on one side and five half-dressed maidens cavorting with Turkish weapons and standards on the other. The victory turned Eugene into a European hero – twenty Italian and German pamphlets were written about the battle of Zenta – and he was to continue to capture general interest for the next quarter of a century. As a *miles christianus** he was splendid propaganda material for religious pamphleteers, who praised his practical Christianity.[16]

With Zenta the Austrians had something more tangible to celebrate than the disappointing peace signed with France at Ryswick at the same

* Christian soldier.

time. The victory was also conclusive enough to bring the Turkish war to an end: both the emperor and the sultan wanted peace. However, they had to wait for the Maritime Powers, who had offered to act as mediators, to arrange one. Such negotiations always took a long time, especially those with the Turks, so that a further campaign in the summer of 1698 was unavoidable. As the Turkish field army kept out of harm's way across the Danube at Belgrade, Eugene spent the summer marching and countermarching around Peterwardein. In August three of his dragoon regiments came near to mutiny because of lack of pay. This had to be crushed by hanging twenty men, shooting a further twelve and making the other culprits run the gauntlet – the ceremonial thrashing by long double lines of troops which was the most common form of punishment in Imperial armies of the time.

By the end of the year the peace negotiations opened between the Turks and all their Christian enemies, who since 1695 had included the Russians as well as the Imperialists, Venetians and Poles. Eugene together with other Imperial generals was consulted on the strategic aspects of the settlement but the negotiations were left entirely to the diplomats, and on 26 January 1699 the treaty of Karlowitz (Karlovci) was signed. All Hungary and Transylvania, except for the Banat of Temesvár, were handed over to the emperor, Azov to the Russians, Podolia to the Poles, and parts of the Dalmatian coast as well as the Morea to Venice. Less than twenty years before Vienna itself had been threatened by Turkish strongholds no more than 100 kilometres away; now the nearest fortresses were at Temesvár and Belgrade, both of which were more threatened than threatening. From being a border province, Austria became the centre of a huge central European empire. The peace was also to foster in Leopold a new determination to face Louis XIV, strengthened as he now was by great territorial gains and possessing capable generals.

The actual expulsion of the Turks was of more value to the monarchy than the lands gained from them. The conquered areas, except for Transylvania, were largely a desert. What population was left felt loyalty to no one; conditions in Hungary were to become even worse between 1703 and 1711 when the Magyars rose in revolt under Francis II Rákóczi. Yet almost from the beginning large numbers of peasants from south-west Germany and Lorraine began to sail down the Danube to settle in what they called 'Greece'. At the same time Slovaks from the Carpathians and Serbs, Jews, Greeks and Rumanians from the Turkish empire itself also moved into the area, and the work of resettlement began.

VI

Two Years of Peace

The collapse of the Turkish empire in central Europe contributed to striking changes in the appearance of Vienna. The 1690s saw the beginnings of the transformation of the city from a fortified frontier town, hemmed in by its own walls and the Danube, into the expanding centre of the Habsburg empire and even of Germany. As the Turkish menace receded the inner city which had been battered by Kara Mustafa's bombardment was rebuilt, and outside the walls new buildings appeared in the suburbs which had been burnt by the besieging Turkish army. The inner area was turned into a 'city of palaces', the winter homes of the nobility; at the same time summer garden palaces sprang up in the suburbs. In this way Vienna was being divided into two distinct parts, a division preserved today by the wide Ringstrasse which encircles the city along the lines of the old fortifications.

Within the old part of the city the Hofburg palace had been a separate, somewhat cramped, Imperial enclave. It was to remain so and hardly changed after the siege. Though Leopold completely rebuilt his suburban palaces, the Favorita and Laxenburg, which had been gutted by the Turks, his building efforts were on a much less grand scale than those of his subjects: he lacked the money with which to compete.

The aristocracy, lay and clerical, spent vast sums on their palaces in the last years of Leopold's reign and those of his sons. They were victims of a disease, of a 'building bug' (*Bauwurm*), as it was called. We find the elector of Mainz writing sympathetically to his nephew Frederick Schönborn, the Imperial vice-chancellor and an avid builder, in the 1710s: 'Building is a devilish thing. Once you begin there's no stopping.'[1] The biggest spenders of all were the Liechtenstein family. Prince Adam Liechtenstein, 'Adam the Rich', who was believed by one observer in 1701 to be 'the richest subject in Europe having near $\frac{m}{400}$ Dollars yearly income', had no qualms about his extravagance but considered it a social duty: 'As God Almighty has bestowed such wealth on me, I want to give away 30,000 gulden a year in alms, not to idle beggars . . . but to needy artisans and labourers.'[2]

The reconstruction of Vienna was less impressive than it might have been. Large unfashionable areas remained untouched, and these became more crowded as houses were torn down elsewhere to construct the palaces. It was these parts which suffered badly from the plague in 1713. Yet even the aristocratic quarter around the Hofburg often proved somewhat of a disappointment to visitors. When a Hanoverian described the city in 1730 he found its palaces 'in splendor and magnificence . . . greatly surpass the hotels of Paris', but the streets where they were situated were 'very narrow and winding'.[3] Some fifteen years earlier Lady Mary Wortley Montagu had complained it was difficult to

> . . . observe the fine fronts of the palaces, though many of them well deserve observation, being truly magnificent, all built of fine white stone [it was actually stucco painted white], and excessive high, the town being so much too little for the number of people . . . the builders seem to have projected to repair that misfortune by clapping one town on the top of another, most of the houses being of five, and some of them of six storeys . . . [4]

The narrow streets and tall buildings made the inner city a dark place at the best of times. Street lighting was poor: the Viennese joked that 'the lights are there so that you can see the dark better'. Ordinary citizens carried lanterns around with them. The nobility did not venture out on foot but went everywhere in their coaches and sedan chairs.

Leopold made up for his modesty as a builder by the sums he poured into his music and pageants. Grand colourful ritualistic displays seemed to fulfil a need felt by the upper classes in the baroque era. These could take the shape of religious processions or of the great ballet to celebrate Leopold's marriage in 1667 performed by a cast of a thousand, the music provided by two hundred players on board a full-size galley floating on an artificial pond in the middle of the Burgplatz. These court displays were for the entertainment of the whole Viennese aristocracy, and the pageantry and cultural life of the city was largely that of the court. On the other hand the sombre Spanish dress and etiquette imposed in the Hofburg was in marked contrast to that of the world of the aristocrats in their palaces outside. Town life for the nobility was a very sociable one of exchanging receptions, dinners and games of cards. Card playing, despite occasional Imperial prohibitions against high stakes, struck foreign visitors as being almost as much an obsession as the 'Belly cheer . . . which the Austrians generally think of most'.[5] These visitors, especially aristocratic ones from the Holy Roman Empire and increasingly from other European countries on their way to Italy as part of the Grand Tour, were readily accepted into Viennese society. Many of them, used as they were to a world of aristocratic privilege, found the pride and ostentation of the Viennese insufferable. In 1715, for example, the English envoy and ex-soldier Lord Cobham was so upset by it all, that he asked to be re-called.[6] A year later Lady Mary Wortley Montagu described them as 'never lively but upon points of ceremony', and told a correspondent the remarkable tale of two ladies whose coaches had met in a narrow street, sitting in them till two o'clock in the morning because neither would give way.

> Eventually the Imperial guards came to separate them and even then they refus'd to stir till the expedient was found out of takeing them both out in chairs at exactly the same moment, after which it was with some difficulty the *pas* was decided between the 2 coachmen, no lesse tenacious of their rank than the ladys.[7]

The quarrels among servants over precedence led, as elsewhere, to numerous brawls, counterparts of their masters' duels. A particularly fierce fight between lackeys outside Louis of Baden's house in 1682 had to be broken up by prince Louis leaning out of his window and hurling hand grenades into the street so that the ball he was giving inside could proceed in peace.

Late seventeenth-century Vienna was already a remarkably racially-mixed city with a population growing steadily from 80,000 in 1690 to 135,000 in 1721. While the aristocracy absorbed Spaniards, Italians, Magyars and Frenchmen, at a lower level there were large numbers of Slav immigrants as well as Jews. The expanding population was increasingly one whose sole function was to service the court and the aristocracy, lay and clerical.

For nearly three years after his return from the last campaign against the Turks Eugene could play a full part in this aristocratic society. His foreign ancestry was no handicap, especially as Italian and French were spoken as frequently as German in such circles. Above all Eugene had the time and the money. He had no governmental responsibilities, and during peacetime his only concern was his dragoon regiment. He was by now a rich man, although there is some doubt about the size of his income. His personal accounts were destroyed after his death. We do know, however, that in 1699 he told Villars that he only received 50,000 livres (about 37,500 gulden) a year from his position as field-marshal in the Imperial army. He had, of course, his income from the abbeys in Savoy, and in 1698 and 1702 Leopold gave him land confiscated in southern Hungary at Siklós and Vörösmarton. These estates included much marshland and, considering the condition of Hungary and its agriculture at this time, they are likely to have yielded little in the way of rents. Presumably he took a sizeable share of the booty at Zenta, but it seems that the bulk of his income derived from his Savoy revenues until he became president of the war council in 1703.

What money he had was used carefully and channelled largely into buying property. He kept out of debt and settled those he had run up in Paris before his flight. Having no interest in acquiring land for the rents it produced, he did not buy a country estate,[8] where he might live as 'quite a gentleman farmer' like his friend Guido Starhemberg.[9] Instead he concentrated on establishing himself in Vienna close to the centre of political power. At some point early in the 1690s he bought a house in the Himmelpfortgasse near St Stephen's Cathedral and gradually acquired the houses on either side. By the time he returned from his victorious campaign against the Turks, a fine town palace had been built for him here and it was to be continually extended and adapted over the years. He also bought a piece of sloping land in the south-eastern suburbs with fine views of the city and the Kahlenberg. By 1700 gardens were being laid out and it was clearly his intention to build the palace which was to become the future Belvedere when he could afford it. In 1698 he had also purchased the island of Czepel in the Danube below Buda, paying 15,000 gulden in advance and another 70,000 over the next two years. By 1701 plans were already in hand for a palace on this site.

These purchases and his military position made the prince an accepted member of the Imperial aristocracy. While other foreigners, like Montecuccoli, Caraffa and Caprara, had been similarly assimilated, they had sealed this with their own or their children's marriage into the native families of the Habsburg lands. But in 1698 Eugene was still unmarried at thirty-five. Given his military career, there was nothing extraordinary in this, although now was the time for him to marry and establish a family of his own. In a period of arranged matches there would have been no problem in finding a bride, and we have already seen his mother's attempt to promote a marriage in Spain. In 1690 Louis of Baden suggested that Eugene should marry his sister-in-law, Frances of Sachsen-Lauenburg. The two actually met briefly. Eugene had been described to the princess as 'a brave and gallant gentleman, who also knows German well'.[10] But neither seems to have taken to the other, and we hear no more about it, nor of further attempts to arrange a marriage for him. One sound reason for Eugene's staying unmarried was that the revenues from the Savoyard abbeys would be lost once he ceased to be celibate.

What were the prince's relations with women? The short answer is that no one knows. German and Austrian historians have been remarkably reticent in discussing them,[11] and this can be contrasted with the intense curiosity of Swedish historians about Eugene's contemporary, Charles XII, another military genius who did not marry. It is difficult to do more than speculate in Eugene's case because of the lack of firm evidence. He was extremely guarded in writing and conversation about his own feelings.[12] If he ever did confide them to anyone, we have no record of it. We have to depend largely on the reports of foreign envoys and of the generals who served with him. It is clear that he did not shy away from women in society, but there is no reliable indication of a mistress of any sort until his late forties and fifties. On the other hand, it is unlikely that casual liaisons would have been reported. There were also no suggestions of homosexual relations after he left Paris – French agents and ministers and other hostile observers would have been quick to note this, but they did not. On the whole the evidence points to an indifference towards physical or close emotional relations, which was part of a make-up which stressed self-control both in actions and speech.

Contact with his own family was very slight after the months spent with his mother in 1686. He never saw his sisters who died, still unmarried, in middle age. Of his brothers, Louis Julius was dead by 1683, another, Philip, died in 1693. The eldest, Louis Thomas, who served in the French army till he fell out with Louis XIV, tried unsuccessfully to make a military career elsewhere and then arrived on Eugene's doorstep in Vienna in 1699. The prince managed to get a regiment for him in 1702, but he was killed the same year on the Rhine. He was the only one of Olympia's children to marry and to have legitimate offspring, and Eugene looked on the latter as his own heirs.

Of more importance to prince Eugene than his family in these early years were his friends in the army, especially the two French-speaking Lorrainers, Commercy and Vaudémont. Another friend was St Saphorin, a French-speaking Swiss, who admitted to having only 'bad German' when he was vice-admiral of the Imperial Danube fleet during the Zenta campaign. It is interesting that St Saphorin at this time was collecting books and reading them, and it may well be that Eugene was already doing the same.[13]

Eugene did not limit his circle of friends in Vienna to other French-speaking exiles. He had close contact with some of Leopold's ministers – with Stratmann and Königsegg from the early 1690s, and with the Bohemian chancellor Kinsky till his death in 1699. He was also beginning to associate with a group of younger men who came from leading Austrian families but were as yet only on the fringes of political power: Kinsky's nephew John Wenzel Wratislaw, Philip Louis Sinzendorff, son of a corrupt former president of the chamber, and Gundaker Starhemberg, a much younger half-brother of Rüdiger Starhemberg and a cousin of the infantry general Guido Starhemberg. Although these men as yet had no direct influence on Leopold, they were reaching the ear of the Imperial vice-chancellor Kaunitz and above all of the heir apparent, king Joseph. All of them had easy access to court circles, where Eugene was also respected enough by Leopold at this time to be invited to take part in some court functions. In 1698, for example, the Russian tsar Peter visited Vienna in an unsuccessful bid to persuade Leopold to continue the war with the Turks. Leopold held a masked ball (or *Wirtschaft*) for the tsar in the conservatory of the Favorita. The guests were asked to ignore the grand furniture and mirrors, and the hundreds of wax candles in gold and silver candelabras, and to imagine themselves in a country inn. The emperor and empress played the innkeeper and his wife, while others came dressed as brigands, gypsies and peasants. Eugene was given the special honour of being head waiter to the innkeeper, while Peter enjoyed himself hugely as a Frisian peasant lad with an eye for the girls.

By the turn of the century Leopold appeared to outsiders to be at the height of his power. He had imposed the humiliating peace of Karlowitz on the Turks and the future of his dynasty seemed secure with two healthy sons, Joseph born in 1678 and Charles in 1685: Joseph had been elected his successor in both Hungary and the Holy Roman Empire. Yet Leopold's government had probably reached an all-time low both in terms of its effectiveness and of the quality of its ministers. The emperor had no forceful adviser to compensate for his own lack of drive. As he grew older he came to depend on what was familiar, on what had proved its worth by mere survival, and in this his ministers were no exception. All tended to be obstinate indecisive men like the emperor himself. The court chancellor count Buccelini was a Fleming with no grasp or interest in his assigned field of foreign policy. The *Obristhofmeister* and the head of the conference – itself a large ineffective body – was the lethargic count Harrach. The burden of foreign affairs was in practice carried by the Imperial vice-chancellor Dominic Kaunitz. A seasoned diplomat, he saw that the governmental machine could not run itself, but he was very much an isolated case among the ministers and the administration continued in its old incompetent way. The chamber under Salaburg as president remained chaotic, and the army was reduced and neglected. As Leopold himself spent more and more time in religious observances, real hopes for change lay with a change of monarch.

Completely blind to the faults of his government, Leopold was as keen to preserve and extend his dynastic rights and international prestige as Louis XIV. After Karlowitz he drifted towards a new war with France over the question of the succession to the Spanish throne. But as his régime had neither the diplomatic nor political expertise to reach a satisfactory settlement, the initiative fell to others.

Although the Maritime Powers and Spain signed peace with France at Ryswick on 20 September 1697, Leopold delayed his signature for another month as the news of Zenta made the Imperial court talk of 'carrying on the war themselves'.[14] It was an empty boast and merely served to show that 'the Augustissima Casa never did anything when they should'.[15] Even though Leopold failed to win back any significant part of the gains made by France in Germany over the previous fifty years, the allies as a whole received more in the peace than they deserved: Louis recognized William III in England and restored Lorraine, Luxembourg and some of the Rhine fortresses, although he kept Alsace and Strasbourg. He was prepared to make these concessions because he wanted to end the war and to separate the Maritime Powers from Austria before Charles II of Spain should die and open up the question of the Spanish succession.

Once peace was made European diplomacy turned inevitably and almost exclusively to this problem. It was not a new one: it had existed ever since the accession of the delicate four year old Charles II in 1665. With no heirs of his own body, the sickly Spanish king's death had been constantly rumoured and predicted over the past thirty years. His obstinacy in refusing to die led one diplomat to suggest that it 'would be a shorter way to knock him on the head rather than all Europe should be kept in suspense with the uncertain state of his health'.[16]

All Europe was concerned about his successor because of the extent of Charles's empire: besides Spain and the colonies, he ruled over the Southern Netherlands and Luxembourg, and in Italy he possessed Milan, Naples and Sicily, Sardinia and enclaves on the Tuscan coast. Unfortunately Charles's nearest relatives were the rulers of the two major European powers, France and Austria. Both Louis and Leopold were sons of Spanish princesses and had married ones. In Leopold's case the issue was more complicated as his Spanish wife only produced one child before her death, the archduchess Maria Antonia, who married Max Emmanuel of Bavaria. At her marriage she was forced to renounce her claims to Spain in favour of her father. Leopold intended to keep these claims within his own direct line, that is for himself and the sons by his third marriage to the German Eleonora of Pfalz-Neuburg. Although he always insisted that this claim was for himself as head of the Habsburg family, he never seriously intended that either he or his elder son, Joseph, should rule over Spain; instead the latter was to pass to his younger son, the archduke Charles, who significantly had been christened with the name of the Spanish king. Moreover Leopold was prepared, despite his strong dynastic feelings, to contemplate a partition of the inheritance, though he refused to discuss one while Charles II was alive.

The other European powers looked with horror at the prospect of the entire Spanish empire passing into either French or Austrian hands. The ideal solution would have been the accession in Spain of an independent ruler, and this is what the Spaniards wanted. The obvious candidate was the child of Maria Antonia and Max Emmanuel of Bavaria. Unfortunately this 'Bavarian baby' died in 1699, leaving the prospect of a direct Austro-French confrontation. While Austrian and French ministers struggled in Madrid to influence the king and the factions around him to make a will in their favour, attempts were made to achieve a diplomatic settlement.

After Ryswick both Louis XIV and William III were prepared to try seriously to settle their own and European problems by diplomatic means: there was a mutual recognition that they were too exhausted to contemplate further war. Both preferred to work with each other, reach agreement and then present it to Leopold as a *fait accompli*: this was because of the notorious difficulties in negotiating with Vienna. After an earlier agreed solution was ruined by the death of the Bavarian baby, William and Louis settled on a second partition treaty in June 1699. By this treaty Spain, the Indies and the Southern Netherlands were to pass to the archduke Charles, while Louis's own immediate heir, the dauphin Louis, was to inherit the Italian lands. At this stage Louis intended, with William's blessing, to exchange these territories for those of the dukes of Lorraine and Savoy and thus strengthen France directly by the addition of their duchies.

While this was fine on paper, it ignored the feelings of the native Spaniards who did not wish to see their empire split up. It also stood little chance of acceptance by Leopold, since the areas assigned to his family were not those which he wanted. The problem was that William III, conscious of the strategic importance of the Southern Netherlands to England and the United Provinces, and of the economic interests and ambitions of both the latter states in the Iberian peninsula and Spanish colonies, could not allow French control in these areas. It would be safer to allow French expansion into Italy or Savoy and Lorraine.

From 1697 the Imperialists were determined that if they gained nothing else they must be granted control of Milan because it was an Imperial fief and 'because of its fertility & vicinity to the Emperour's hereditary countries, & its being therefore very tenable & an inlet into Italy, & the only means by which they cd prevent that whole country falling into the hands of the French'.[17] The Imperial vice-chancellor Kaunitz even went so far as to say in the conference in August 1699, without contradiction, that Leopold 'should demand Milan, Naples and Sicily; the rest can be taken by whoever wants it'.[18] The Imperialists were therefore totally opposed to the partition treaty which would lead to their being 'shut out of Italy'.[19]

From the start Leopold and his ministers showed a determination to fight and even to occupy Milan as soon as possible. What they failed to do, however, was to make direct proposals of their own to the other powers for a settlement until it was too late, nor did Leopold make it clear that he would accept a partition or even that he intended his younger son rather than himself to inherit the Austrian share. This was understandable because he felt that the claim was his own God-given right and that it was up to him, not to international treaties, to transfer his rights to his son. His recent gains by the peace of Karlowitz put him in a strong enough international position at this time to be uncompromising; of most importance, however, was that he believed that Charles II was still far from death in 1700 and that the Austrian party in Madrid would eventually persuade him to leave the whole inheritance to his Austrian cousins.

Unfortunately Charles II died in November 1700 and in his will left the whole empire to Louis XIV's younger grandson, Philip of Anjou. It was hoped in Madrid that Philip, who was asked in the will to renounce his claims to France, would keep the Spanish empire separate and intact, being able to count on the superior strength of France to maintain the Spanish possessions. Louis XIV quickly accepted the will for his grandson, and Leopold just as quickly rejected it: it was clearly far worse than the partition treaty. Nevertheless the emperor did recognize that he would have to accept some kind of partition, although he was determined, as he said in the conference, 'to keep Italy above all'.[20] He showed unusual energy in pushing forward the desultory preparations which had been in hand since the beginning of 1700 to seize Milan and to install the archduke Charles there. On 18 November 1700, the night he heard from Paris of Charles II's death, he ordered Rüdiger Starhemberg to discuss the venture with Caprara, Eugene and Commercy, and only three days later Eugene was appointed to command a force of 30,000 men which was to enter Italy the following year.

These moves had been carried out entirely on Vienna's own initiative and little had been done to ensure outside support. Although an alliance was made with Brandenburg in November 1700 – the price was Leopold's agreement to the elector Frederick's calling himself king in Prussia – and both Hanover and the Palatinate were on even closer terms with Vienna, nothing could be hoped for from the Italian states, and it was also still unclear how the Maritime Powers would act. Because of difficulties in both England and the Republic, William could not oppose Philip's accession and had to acknowledge him as Philip V. Louis had also won over Max Emmanuel of Bavaria and his brother the elector of Cologne by letting Max continue as governor of the Southern Netherlands and hinting at more permanent control. French troops had entered the Southern Netherlands and were allowed into Milan – being shipped through Finale – at the beginning of 1701 when the Spanish administration and the governor, Charles Henry Vaudémont (the father of Eugene's close friend), declared for Philip. French garrisons were also accepted by neighbouring Modena and Mantua, and in the south Naples also acknowledged Philip. To complete French control of Italy, in April 1701 Victor Amadeus of Savoy married his daughter to Philip of Anjou, renewed his alliance with France and agreed to help in the event of war.

By the beginning of 1701 Leopold had been outmanoeuvred diplomatically by Louis and had merely his own military resources to fall back on. Only a small force had been assembled for dispatch to Italy and nothing had been done to overhaul the financial system, facts which Louis knew full well through his minister in Vienna, Villars. But what the Austrian ministers calculated on, and in this they were proved right, was that an initiative on their part would force the Maritime Powers to act against France; if Eugene's army won in Italy it would encourage them to join, and if it lost it would frighten them into resisting an unacceptable increase in French power.

VII

The Outbreak of the War of Spanish Succession

Leopold and his ageing ministers' determination to fight for the succession faltered during the first months of 1701 as it became clear that the Maritime Powers were not rushing to help, but both his son Joseph and Dominic Kaunitz encouraged the emperor to stand firm. That the Italian campaign went ahead at all was largely due to Eugene's own efforts. He had to bear most of the burden of preparing the expedition because of the paralysis of the war council: the vice-president Caprara died in February 1701, and Rüdiger Starhemberg, already fatally ill, died in June. What ambitions Eugene might have had for either office were disappointed and Leopold made the predictable and disastrous decision to appoint as president a time-serving courtier, count Henry Mansfeld, prince of Fondi. He proved inept and complacent, completely out of touch with the needs of the men in the field.

At the end of May Eugene joined his troops at Rovereto in the Tyrol. Nearly 30,000 strong, they were in good shape: with only one war on Leopold's hands it had been possible to send 'the choice of all the Emprs forces'.[1] Eugene had sole command and insisted on picking his own subordinates, all close friends, Commercy, Guido Starhemberg and Vaudémont, even though the latter's father, as Spanish governor of Milan, had declared for Philip V. Although prince Eugene's eventual target was the conquest of Milan and Naples, his immediate problem was equally formidable: how to enter Italy. All the north of the country from Savoy to the borders of Venice was occupied by France and her Savoyard and Spanish allies. Catinat, once more in command, had blocked up all the passes leading from the Tyrol into Lombardy and the French were 'boasting that the Imperial army would have to grow wings to get into Italy'.[2]

There was no alternative but to find a new route and Eugene decided to take his army over the mountains further east, even though they were thought to be impassable and a march by this route would infringe Venetian neutrality. Hundreds of Tyrolean peasants were conscripted to shovel away snow and cut paths through the wild Terragnolo and Fredda valleys before the troops could drag their animals and artillery through. Early in June the bulk of the army had crossed the mountains 'without mishap',[3] emerging between Verona and Vicenza into what was Venetian territory. It was a remarkable feat and contemporaries quickly compared the crossing with that of Hannibal; engravings of it were published almost at once. Eugene, who was little given to boasting, wrote to Leopold that 'it was amazing that an army and its artillery had crossed such dangerous and precipitous mountains where there had been no roads at all before and where no one could recall even a small cart having been through'.[4]

Catinat was completely taken by surprise and he never regained the initiative. Nothing seemed to go right for him and he became increasingly depressed. Unsure whether Eugene intended to march south towards Naples or to move towards Milan – he did in fact make for the latter – he spread out his troops which made it easier for Eugene to cross the large number of canals and rivers in this part of north-east Italy. French intelligence reports were poor, whereas Eugene had much better information, accompanying scouting parties in person and closely questioning any prisoners brought in.[5] Although he had capable subordinates, the main burden of the campaign fell on his shoulders, and it is astonishing that he found time to send long reports to the emperor as well as keeping an official campaign diary: his reports were far more detailed than those sent by most commanders, including Marlborough.

Prince Eugene had never had any other aim than that of forcing his way into Milan, but he kept his intentions, even his day-to-day plans, to himself and his closest aides. By an amazing series of feints and surprise moves, which tied the French in knots, he managed to cross both the Adige and Mincio before the end of August and thus opened up safe supply routes to his magazines in the southern Tyrol. The larger French force merely withdrew before him. Catinat realized too late that he should never have let the Austrians take the initiative, and he himself admitted to Louis XIV that 'Up to now, sire, our war has not been a successful one.'[6] Louis recognized this all too well and had been particularly incensed at the news of a sharp defeat suffered by part of the French force at Carpi on 9 July. To Catinat's excuses that he was worried about keeping contact with his magazines, the king retorted:

The Imperialists are marching through a country unknown to them; they have neither magazines nor safe places, yet nothing stops them. You have towns and rivers close by you and all the country is on your side. I have warned you that you are dealing with an enterprising young prince: he does not tie himself down to the rules of war, whereas you want to follow them and let him do anything he wants.[7]

Catinat had to go, but unfortunately Louis made the mistake of replacing him with the ageing duke of Villeroy, who was a much better courtier than soldier but was a favourite of Louis's wife, Madame de Maintenon, and a childhood friend of his own. He had also been a frequent visitor to Eugene's home during the prince's childhood. When Villeroy arrived in late August he was confident of success even though by then the French army had retreated even further, crossing the Oglio into Lombardy and abandoning the duchy of Mantua.

Instead of being intimidated when Villeroy and his larger army moved over to the offensive, Eugene welcomed the prospect of a decisive battle. He waited on the eastern side of the Oglio to be attacked, choosing his ground carefully and drawing up his troops and guns in front of the small fortress of Chiari. Streams protected his lines on three sides and, as there was not enough room for a cavalry engagement, he could count on a frontal attack by the French infantry. He knew the enemy well enough now to predict that they would stake everything on a ferocious preliminary attack, and he was proved right. On 1 September Villeroy brushed aside Catinat's warnings about the strength of the Imperialists' position, remarking acidly that Louis 'had not sent so many brave men just to look at the enemy through their spy glasses'.[8] With '3 shouts of Vive le Roy' the French infantry advanced, to be mown down by Eugene's troops, who were lying flat and fired at point-blank range.[9] Two thousand French were killed with only trifling Imperialist losses. Chiari was a foretaste of the bloody infantry engagements which were to follow in most battles in this War of Spanish Succession.

Villeroy went to pieces during the battle and Catinat, despite being wounded, had to organize a retreat. The French dug themselves in only a mile or so away from the Austrians on the same side of the Oglio, and here the two armies stayed put for the next two months. Villeroy was too shaken to risk another battle, while Eugene realized that the French force was in too good a defensive position to be attacked.

Both sides were waiting for the other to strike camp first, hoping to attack them then. As autumn advanced conditions deteriorated in both camps. Fodder was so short that Eugene's horses sometimes had to eat fallen leaves. But the French suffered most because their camp was on marshy ground, and they moved out first in mid-November, managing to cross the Oglio with only small losses and going into winter quarters in Milan. Here they proved an increasingly unpopular burden: contributions of over 5 million livres in cash for the soldiers' pay and lodgings and of over 2 million in fodder had already been imposed.[10] Most of this had to be taken by force. While the French and the local peasants had engaged in sporadic fighting all along, Eugene's relations with the local communities had been good. He kept tight control of his men, insisting that only forage be taken and that the peasants be allowed to gather their harvest in peace. He executed four dozen troops for minor acts of looting, and told Leopold that he had 'imposed more severe discipline than has possibly ever been seen in an army'.[11]

For his winter quarters Eugene occupied the pro-French duchy of Mantua, levying contributions and seizing quarters for his men. He had to do this to survive, for during the year he had received far less help from home than he expected. What cash had been sent was largely the result of Leopold's own efforts rather than those of the war president Mansfeld, who was busy consolidating his position among the other ministers and trying to oust Kaunitz.[12]

Despite his financial difficulties, there is no doubt that the campaign was a success for Eugene. Although the French were still in Milan, their position was weak. At the end of the year Villeroy doubted whether he could hold on to the province because of the hostility of the local population. He warned Louis that 'he must abandon the war in Italy or make an effort in the coming year to put the affairs of this country on a sound footing'.[13] Eugene, on the other hand, seemed firmly established in Italy and, as he had hoped at the start, the success of his campaign persuaded the Maritime Powers to come to the aid of the emperor. The prince had kept William III informed of his progress in Italy[14] and since the beginning of the year his friend Wratislaw had been in London as Imperial minister, pressing for assistance. On 7 September 1701 the Maritime Powers and Leopold signed the Grand Alliance of The Hague and prepared to join in the war the following spring. They reached agreement on a new division of the Spanish empire. While Philip was to be left with Spain and its colonies, Leopold agreed to be satisfied with the Italian lands and – on Anglo-Dutch insistence – the Southern Netherlands. For their part, the Maritime Powers were to be allowed to seize what Spanish colonies and trading concessions they could.[15] Both sides worked on the assumption that Leopold's share would go to the archduke Charles.[16] William III was to die before the English and Dutch could enter the war and his death also brought to an end the personal connection between England and the United Provinces. But the two countries remained determined to achieve a partition of the Spanish empire, the lead being taken in the Republic by the grand pensionary Heinsius and in England by the chief ministers of the new ruler, queen Anne, Godolphin at the treasury and Marlborough as commander-in-chief of the English army.

In 1702 Louis was not only faced by a conflict in Italy but also by one in the Netherlands and along the Rhine, where Leopold now had enough support from the German princes to mount a further campaign* which aimed at reversing France's gains of the previous half-century. But for the Austrians the main area of interest was now Italy where they could make direct territorial gains, and this was reflected in their intention to spend twice as much there as in Germany. All Leopold's ministers were indifferent to Spain itself, looking on it 'as a mere carcass, scarce worth the having unless accompanyed with the Dominions in Italy, which are supposed to be the flesh and vitals'.[17] However they could only make feeble efforts to win these provinces in 1702, and the Maritime Powers, as yet, had little interest in seeing Austrian control there.

During the first months of 1702 the Imperial army rotted away before Eugene's eyes in its quarters in Mantua. Up to fifty men had to be billeted in every derelict house, while others had to sleep on the bare ground, often living on bread and water. The troops received pay for only one out of the five winter months because what cash Eugene received had to be spent on buying food from Venice and Ferrara. To make up for his small numbers and inadequate supplies, Eugene was driven reluctantly to use unconventional tactics against the French. During the winter, when custom normally decreed that all military activity cease, he decided to seize the town of Cremona in Lombardy where Villeroy had his headquarters, hoping to do so before the French army billeted in the surrounding countryside could prevent him. His widespread intelligence system, which included intercepting letters and employing agents as far away as Genoa, provided the opportunity. One of Commercy's contacts in Cremona, a priest, reported that a dried-up sewer led under the walls of the town into his own cellar. Consequently in pouring rain on the night of 31 January/1 February 1702 a few grenadiers squeezed through the sewer, killed the guards at the nearest gate and opened it for Eugene's cavalry and infantry. The French were completely surprised and large numbers of their officers, including Villeroy himself, were captured half asleep as they struggled to rouse their men.

* Under prince Louis of Baden

But pockets of the French held out, especially the Irish soldiers, whom Eugene considered 'the best of the enemy troops'.[18] By five in the afternoon the prince decided against further costly hand-to-hand street fighting and beat a rapid retreat before a French relief force arrived. What had begun as a master stroke had turned sour and Eugene remarked to one of his French prisoners as they left, 'I am always unlucky and nothing goes right for me.'[19] Nevertheless the French had been humiliated by the loss of their commander-in-chief and they were so unnerved that they evacuated the whole area between the Adda and Oglio.

Although the capture of Villeroy was a European sensation and a sore embarrassment to Louis XIV, it proved a blessing in disguise for the French. While Villeroy was taken to a pleasant enough temporary imprisonment in Graz, Louis replaced him with a very different commander, the duke of Vendôme. A career soldier since the age of twelve, he was a grandson of Henry IV and first cousin to Eugene. He was notorious for sleeping till late in the afternoon, for his slovenly dress and familiarity with his soldiers, but he was a vigorous commander in the field and capable of countering Eugene's manoeuvres. He was soon to head a combined Franco-Spanish-Savoyard force of 80,000 men, whereas Eugene had at most 33,000 troops. Moreover Vendôme was able to count on firm support from Versailles, while Eugene was left largely to fend for himself.

Before the 1702 campaign opened the prince realized there was no point in appealing to either Leopold or Mansfeld. Therefore in March and April he resorted to writing to the Jesuit Father Bischoff, whom he did not know personally but who was believed to have some influence with both Leopold and Joseph. In asking for his support, he claimed that he was being unfairly criticized in Vienna by men 'who like to puff themselves up with brave words, but who have not the smallest understanding or experience of war. . . . My manner of conducting war is ridiculed as being Croatian . . . I am provided with neither money nor supplies.'[20] In late May Eugene was reduced to threatening Leopold that, as he had received no money for two months, '. . . at the end of the campaign I shall resign my command. I can no longer bear the fearful burden which torments me night and day of losing the Emperor not only the glory of his army but also his crown, sceptre, army, land and people.'[21] When one of his cavalry generals, the Hungarian Pálffy, was sent to appeal in person to Leopold, he merely received tender enquiries about the prince's health, the emperor asking if it was 'true that Your Highness had turned quite grey and had begun to look so ill? To which I [Pálffy] countered by asking how he could expect anything else when your letters received no reply, let alone money or deliveries.'[22]

As long as the army of Italy was starved of men and resources the most Eugene could do was to tie down as many French troops as possible. The pattern of the Nine Years War was therefore being repeated. Throughout the spring of 1702 Eugene managed to hold the lines of the rivers Mincio and Po, positioning himself strongly in the duchy of Mantua; but he knew it was only a matter of time before his army collapsed from within. Cash was so short that even the officers were having to do without their weekly stipends; desertions were heavy and the food situation would soon become critical. Once the spring and early summer grass was finished there would be no money to buy fodder. Supplies from the Tyrol, always spasmodic, were drying up, while 'the country of Mantua being destroyed to that degree, that the peasants are run away, and left their lands uncultivated'.[23] Relations with the local population had deteriorated badly, and it was now the turn of the Imperialists to be ambushed and to retaliate by hanging those found with arms and by destroying houses and farms where attacks took place.

By July the army, forced to operate in the swampy countryside of Mantua, and physically weak, was hit badly by fever. Despite appeals to Vienna there were no physicians attending the troops; when Commercy became ill he had to be treated by one of the ordinary camp surgeons. At the best of times medical provision for Imperial, or any, armies was poor. In 1701 two waggons sufficed to carry the medical supplies for the whole of Eugene's army; in 1697 Guido Starhemberg had complained that his soldiers in Hungary had only been given useless purgatives and sweating powders. The war commissariat department (*Generalkriegskommissariat*) insisted that careful attention and patience were far more effective in curing common soldiers and N.C.O.s than expensive medicine, and the department always tried to limit its total annual expenditure on medical services to 40,000–70,000 gulden. Physicians rarely accompanied the armies: officers usually had to send for local men, while for the ordinary soldiers there were only the ill-trained company surgeons.

By August 1702 Eugene had reached the point of desperation. He had to take drastic action, staking all on a 'lucky hitt', so that his army could find safe quarters for the winter months; otherwise he would have 'to return by the way of Tyroll, leaving the French entirely masters of Italy'.[24] Therefore on 15 August he tried to surprise a third of the French army which was encamped at Luzzara under Vendôme. But he failed to drive the French from their camp before nightfall brought to an end a bloody infantry battle, where the fire had been so fierce that Eugene described it as 'so great on both sides that none of the oldest generals, officers or soldiers remembered having seen anything like it in the past wars'.[25] The French lost 4,000 men and the Imperialists half this number. One of the victims was prince Commercy, killed by a ball in the throat. At the sight of his body, Eugene burst into tears: he had clearly suffered a great personal blow in the death of his closest friend of the past twenty years.

Although Eugene proudly described the bravery of his army in his account of the battle to the emperor, the engagement had settled nothing except to deter Vendôme from precipitate action during the coming months. In fact the two armies stayed put in fortified camps close to each other for the rest of the campaigning season. Eugene's force appeared near to total collapse: the unpaid troops tried to desert, the horses died and the prince was horrified to see his officers forfeiting their dignity and respect by going on foot like their men.[26] At last on 5 November Vendôme moved into winter quarters and Eugene could look for quarters for his own army, moving further down the Po to Carbonara, although he knew there would be no fodder or straw, as both armies had already effectively scoured the whole area. He described the condition of his men to Leopold at this time: 'We are at the end of November and the troops have not yet received their pay for the previous winter, let alone the summer. Meanwhile the men are having to go naked.'[27]

Eugene had no doubts that the main fault lay at Mansfeld's door. The president of the war council was certainly incompetent and, according to the English diplomat Stepney, was guided more 'by personall than publick interests'[28] as well as being 'full of odd notions, whereas his business requires practice and not speculations'.[29] He probably never bothered to read Eugene's long complaining letters and it was often two months at a stretch before he replied. When he did, it was merely to counsel patience and to suggest standing on the defensive until help could be sent, promising that enough troops would be sent to Italy in 1703 to conquer Naples as well as Milan.[30] At the same time he was assuring Leopold that Eugene already had a large enough army and that he was exaggerating the cost of supporting it. He was also quick to blame the prince in front of Stepney for ruining his own army 'by operations in the winter, whereby they have been rendered incapable to act as they might have done in the spring'.[31]

While Mansfeld only made a bad situation worse, the strain on the monarchy's finances and resources of having to support a war in both Italy and Germany was unbearable. In a meeting with Stepney in December 1702 Harrach, Mansfeld and Kaunitz stressed that they intended to spend 5 million pounds on the war the following year, which was more than the total British war effort.[32] On the other hand, although the Imperialists had committed themselves on paper to field 130,650 men at the beginning of 1702, in fact during this year they deployed no more than 40,000 in Italy and 20,000 on the Rhine.

By late December 1702 the force in Italy had been reduced to 20,000 men. These Eugene left in winter quarters in Mirandola and Modena under Guido Starhemberg's command; he himself had finally decided to go to Vienna to press his case in person after further threats to resign throughout the autumn had produced no effect. He reached the Imperial capital on 8 January 1703, much to Mansfeld's dismay, as the latter had been trying 'to keep him at a distance, and out of the way of telling his story with its disagreeable circumstances'. The president had already been criticized fiercely by Louis of Baden, and this criticism had been strongly supported by Leopold's heir, Joseph, who had been in Germany during the summer and had been furious at the inadequate help sent to Baden.[33]

Although Eugene arrived in Vienna full of despair and frustration over the 1702 campaign, he brought a great European reputation with him. The attack on Cremona and even the battle of Luzzara had been celebrated throughout the allied capitals: at least these engagements seemed more worthy of celebration than the stalemate which had soon developed on the Rhine and in the Netherlands. Yet the campaign had hardly been a success: Eugene had had to give up any hope of forcing his way into Milan, while after Luzzara his army had rotted away uselessly. Not unnaturally Vendôme felt somewhat peeved at the reputation Eugene continued to enjoy, even in France, and at the lack of credit he himself received. On 1 December he wrote to the French war minister Chamillart, explaining that the nature of the terrain with its many rivers and canals made it difficult to drive out a tenacious enemy, and adding: 'but if you would care to look at the map and see where we were when the campaign began and where we are now, you must agree that if he [Eugene] is a clever man, he has at least been an unlucky one'.[34]

VIII

President of the Imperial War Council

When Eugene returned to Vienna in January 1703 all the hopes of conquest and expansion, which had led the monarchy into war nearly two years before, seemed to have collapsed utterly. Austria herself was now faced by the direct threat of invasion from across the border in Bavaria, where Max Emmanuel had declared openly for the Bourbon powers in August 1702.

Now approaching forty, prince Eugene struck most people by his dress and conduct as a 'modest, plain man'.[1] He was a serious taciturn character, completely out of step with the elegant and self-satisfied men around Leopold. Although he was now highly respected and 'favourably rec'd by everybody', he was to become increasingly depressed during the first months of the year as he tried and failed to cajole and threaten the emperor and his chief ministers into taking their situation seriously and doing something about it. His health suffered visibly under the strain and the English minister Stepney, who saw a close resemblance between the prince and William of Orange, felt his constitution did 'not promise a long thread'.[2]

The key figure in the Austrian war machine was clearly Mansfeld, president of the war council. Eugene tried to be pleasant with him, even taking his first meal with him on his return to Vienna, but his patience quickly wore thin as he listened to the urbane president's empty eloquence. He bombarded him with weekly memorials, demanding action, and he became increasingly contemptuous. In his private correspondence he labelled Mansfeld and Salaburg, the president of the *Hofkammer*, 'these two asses'.[3] To Guido Starhemberg in Italy he wrote that 'talking to the ministers is like talking to a wall'.[4] When he saw Mansfeld's plans for the summer campaigns, he was speechless: 'I have never seen anything so ridiculous in all my life.'[5] Whenever Eugene managed to see Leopold, the emperor would listen sympathetically but answer in a way which showed he hoped to 'get shutt of' the prince, and then do nothing:[6] 'It is impossible to speak more forcefully than I have by word of mouth and letter. The master knows it and promises to remedy it, but the execution is lacking. He writes *un billet piquant* and believes he has done a lot.'[7] Neither pleas nor further threats of resignation had any effect.

By mid-May prince Eugene was still in Vienna and had no intention of returning to Italy precipitately, largely because he had good reasons to believe that there would soon be a change of ministry, which would benefit himself and the army.[8] He had come to recognize that his own problems in Italy were part of a greater whole: Mansfeld and Salaburg had to be replaced by men with drive and enthusiasm if the war was to be won and the monarchy saved. His assurances to Guido Starhemberg that he did not want to become president of the war council himself – 'I have declared that far from seeking it, I would not accept it'[9] – should not be taken too seriously.

From the beginning of the year there had been an increasingly power-ful group at work in Vienna determined on making Leopold dismiss Harrach, Mansfeld and Salaburg. Eugene had firmly supported this op-position, but he had not taken the lead himself and had in fact been less vocal in his criticism of the old ministers than had Louis of Baden. The opposition was led from within the Imperial family by Leopold's son Joseph, who wrote to Louis of Baden in April: 'My great task now is to persuade the Emperor to change them . . . if it doesn't happen soon, it will be too late.'[10] Behind him stood his uncle the elector palatine, the empress Eleonora's brother, who wanted a vigorous war against France. He sent a minister to Vienna in 1703 to press Leopold to sack Mansfeld, writing that 'he wishes him hang'd and offers to pay for the rope'.[11] The Imperial vice-chancellor Kaunitz, who had largely been excluded from meetings of the conference by Harrach, was working towards the same end, and brought with him the support of his two young protégés, Sinzendorff and Wratislaw. But the most important figure in holding the opposition together was the still largely unknown prince Salm, Joseph's former tutor, who had become a member of the conference and was a determined advocate of defending Germany from France.

The emperor stuck obstinately to his old ministers, ignoring both the pressure from within the court and even such pointed warnings as that given him in March by count Traun, landmarshal of the Lower Austrian estates, that 'if more vigour were not used both their country and family would be utterly ruined . . . for that the States of Austria would allways find a master, whereas ye House of Austria was not as sure of enjoying what they now possess'.[12] Harrach was such an old friend that only death would separate him from Leopold, but the emperor was almost as attached to Mansfeld and Salaburg. Both were certainly loyal and un-corrupt, while Mansfeld was also cultured and persuasive.[13] Salaburg had tried to run the chamber as best he could within the existing system. His misfortune was to run foul of most of the native Viennese bankers, who would not lend to him, so that he had to advance large sums of his own money[14] and depend heavily on loans from Oppenheimer to finance the war. The accounting machinery of the *Hofkammer* was inadequate and its officials unable to cope with the extraordinary demands of wartime. It had estimated that 23.5 million gulden were needed for the 1702 cam-paign, but the contributions extracted from the various estates with in-creasing difficulty, loans floated on the security of mining and other revenues, and various expedients, had produced only half this amount.

Both Mansfeld and Salaburg were as much the victims of the ills of the monarchy as their cause. Most responsibility lay with the ageing and fatalistic Leopold who clung to the servants he knew, closed his eyes to the realities of an expanding war and trusted that further 'miracles' would save the day. Stepney put the blame for the situation on the 'grievances and abuses of a long and indolent reign' and felt that any future ministers, especially those managing the finances, 'will certainly be out of breath likewise in a year or two; and then cast away'.[15] What was needed was a radical change of emperor, ministers and the whole governmental system.

Almost to the last Leopold showed no signs that he would dismiss his old ministers. But in June Bavarian troops had established themselves in the Tyrol, where Max Emmanuel found many Habsburg subjects willing to change allegiance, while in Hungary a small-scale revolt which had broken out in May was gaining frightening momentum. Far worse, however, were the results of the death on 1 May of the 'court Jew' Samuel Oppenheimer. In reporting his death Stepney commented that 'the man was very useful',[16] but this was hardly the half of it. Under Salaburg, besides being responsible for the contracting of all military sup-plies, he had also begun to handle most of the government's credit. Al-though Leopold objected to his dependence on Oppenheimer, he came to accept it as a necessary evil, like co-operating with Protestant allies. Oppenheimer's financial empire collapsed at his death. His son desper-ately tried to stave off the demands of creditors, but the crown, which was said to owe the Oppenheimer firm 18 million gulden,[17] had no cash to save it from bankruptcy. The government's credit collapsed as well and it was unable to raise a penny, Salaburg himself admitting that Austria had suffered 'a blow more fatal than anything France could devise'.[18]

By the end of June even Leopold's nerve snapped: he sacked Salaburg and promoted Mansfeld to *Obristkämmerer*, a post with few duties but which kept him in daily contact with the emperor. Gundaker Starhemberg and Eugene replaced these ministers at the head of the chamber and the war council. Everyone, including the prince himself, recognized that he was the only possible successor to Mansfeld. Both Leopold and Joseph were surprised that he imposed no conditions when accepting the post except that he should have their support.

Essential to the success of the new order was to be Eugene's co-operation with the new president of the *Hofkammer*, Gundaker Starhemberg, 'his intimate friend'.[19] The chamber and the war council now worked closely together and a real effort was made by Starhemberg to meet military priorities. Recognized as a financial expert and enjoying close contacts with Viennese banking circles, Starhemberg had been vice-president of the *Hofkammer* and had strongly opposed Salaburg's policy of massive loans and dependence on Oppenheimer. Wealthy enough himself not to be corrupt, he intended a thorough reorganization of his department. Financial reforms were worked out in several long conferences of the chief ministers under the chairmanship of Joseph. A preliminary attempt was made to solve the government's credit problems by setting up a state (*Giro*) bank in August 1703, but it was less successful than had been hoped and was replaced in 1706 by government dependence on the more successful Vienna City Bank which Starhemberg himself directed. For the first time realistic estimates were made of revenues and expenditure, and a serious effort was made to finance the difference by extending indirect taxation. However, it was to prove impossible to persuade the estates to relax their control over their own contributions. Although Starhemberg's measures could not produce an immediate change, from 1704 the situation gradually improved despite the continual high war expenditure – about 25 million gulden a year. The Maritime Powers provided help in the form of loans – the Dutch lent 5.9 million gulden and the English 3.5 million during the war – and by paying directly for mercenary regiments attached to the Imperial armies. Once the allies began to make gains of their own, the Imperialists were able to meet some of the cost of the war through impositions raised from occupied Italy and Bavaria.

As *Hofkriegsratspräsident* Eugene had become head not only of the war council but also one of the emperor's inner circle of ministers who could be expected to be consulted on all important matters. He was the first president since Montecuccoli to remain an active commander. Of his fellow generals only Baden could approach him in experience and success. Although he had to remain at the centre of government for the time being, he continued to assure both Guido Starhemberg in Italy and the allied ministers in Vienna – and he probably believed it himself – that he would return south before the end of the year. He had two main tasks: to reorganize the Imperial armies into an effective fighting force and to work out a strategy which would drive the Bourbons out of Italy and the Empire and also destroy French power. He realized that the latter called for closer co-operation with the Maritime Powers.

He knew the army would not change overnight: in November 1703 he was to write that it would 'take time to bring an army into being again as so many years have been spent ruining it'.[20] But he took immediate steps to improve morale, keeping in weekly contact with his commanders and sending words of encouragement and whatever cash was available. More couriers were dispatched in his first two months of office than in the whole of the previous year. By persuading Leopold on 5 September to forbid colonels to sell commissions in their regiments, he tried to improve the quality of officers. All appointments now had to go through the war council, and Eugene also tried to use the council to enforce discipline in the armies. Soon after becoming president he ordered one of his generals in the Tyrol to clamp down on looting and to hang soldiers who tried to desert. A similar tough line was taken over the courtmartialling and execution of the governor of Breisach for surrendering the fortress to the French.[21]

Refashioning the army would be a long undertaking, but vital decisions on how to make the best use of the existing forces had to be taken immediately. Bavaria's entry into the war had allowed Louis XIV in 1703 to stay on the defensive in the Netherlands while making an all-out assault on the Empire and Austria. Despite his personal debt to Max Emmanuel, Eugene had no doubts about the need to retaliate. He had told Stepney as early as 9 January 1703 that 'we ought with all imaginable dispatch to gett into the Elector's country, and (upon his refusall to comply) lay it all to waste'.[22] Mansfeld had suggested that the Italian army should be employed for this purpose, but Eugene argued strongly and successfully against such a move, pointing out that it would be 'absolutely impossible to get it back there as long as the French had one in Italy'.[23] He saw the importance for the emperor of maintaining at least a defensive army in Italy to sustain the political ambitions of the monarchy: Italy was the only part of the Spanish empire that Austria could conquer by herself without having to depend on the goodwill of the Maritime Powers.

By June 1703 the elector had been strengthened by French troops brought by Villars and was free to take the initiative. Although Villars wanted an immediate assault on Vienna, believing it to be defenceless, Max Emmanuel, who had defeated one Austrian army sent against him in March, insisted on an expedition to the Tyrol which he hoped to conquer for himself. This proved a fiasco. The peasants who had at first welcomed Max Emmanuel turned against him once his army began to behave badly, and bitter guerrilla war was waged against the elector's troops. On becoming president Eugene quickly dispatched a force of 3,000 men to strengthen this peasant resistance. By September the Bavarians were expelled from the Tyrol, and the prince's insistence on keeping Imperial troops in Italy also meant that Vendôme, who had been ordered by Louis to co-operate with Max Emmanuel's expedition in the Tyrol, arrived there too late and with too few men. Vendôme's intervention ended almost as disastrously as the elector's and he was forced to withdraw into Italy.

The failure of the Franco-Bavarian attack on Austria in 1703 was due as much to good luck and local peasant initiative as to Eugene's actions and encouragement. The potential threat to the Austrian monarchy from this quarter remained, however. By the end of the year, although the Tyrol and other Austrian provinces were free, the whole Danube valley in south Germany as well as the Rhine forts of Breisach and Landau were in enemy hands.

The continuing crisis here, and increasingly that in Hungary as well, meant that Eugene could not rejoin his troops in Italy in the autumn of 1703. Guido Starhemberg, left facing Vendôme's superior army throughout the year, had quite naturally felt deserted and resentful. His letters to Eugene became colder, and from this time a fierce animosity developed between the two men. After his first months in office Eugene was receiving letters from his commanders, and particularly from Guido Starhemberg, very similar to those he himself used to send to Mansfeld. Although some recruits had been dispatched to Italy and more financial help had been allocated there than elsewhere, Starhemberg complained in September 1703 that of his 50,000 men only 18,000 were fit for service and that he wanted to resign.[24]

Eugene felt no happier about his own position. After only a month as president of the war council he also began to talk of resigning. The main obstacle to effective action was Leopold, and Stepney had rightly predicted that there would be no proper reformation while 'the present master' lived.[25] Although he had visibly deteriorated by the autumn of 1703, suffering from painful swollen legs, and in the opinion of his physician was unlikely to survive the winter, the emperor did not die and remained very much his old self.[26] He paid little heed to Eugene's pleas for firm direction on his own part, even though the prince himself declared that he had spoken to him 'more fiercely than any minister to date'.[27] Above all he did nothing to stop the opposition which still continued within the court and government to the changes wanted by Eugene and Gundaker Starhemberg. Mansfeld, as well as Harrach, criticized the younger men and encouraged Leopold's natural inclination 'to pass the rest of his life with the least inconvenience'.[28] It was difficult to get the rest of the ministers to take the situation seriously or even to assemble for meetings of the conference. Just as dangerous was a feeling among officials that nothing could be done to save the situation. By November Eugene wrote in exasperation to Guido Starhemberg, 'I would rather be a galley-slave than serve as president for war or a general in this way.'[29]

After six months with Eugene in office the military position of the monarchy had become even worse than when he took over. The chief immediate danger at the end of 1703 came not from the still undefeated Bavarians but from the alarming spread of the Hungarian revolt. Peasant despair after the devastations of the Turkish wars and subsequent crushing taxation, coupled with feudal burdens, had led to the revolt. Some of the magnates and gentry, led by the great landowner Francis II Rákóczi and encouraged by Louis XIV, managed to turn the peasants' anger into a war for the restoration of the old Hungarian constitution and even for the defence of Protestantism. By late 1703 the rebels controlled most of Hungary and bands of their horsemen were raiding as far as Moravia and Lower Austria. Vienna itself was gripped by a panic as people streamed into the walled area of the city from the suburbs and provinces.[30]

In mid-December Eugene went in person to Pressburg (Bratislava). He was appalled at the situation he found, reporting to the war council on 22 December that 'in short there is nothing anywhere, and I can't make something out of nothing'.[31] Although he allowed such loyal Magyars as Esterházy to negotiate with the rebels, this was largely to gain time. He distrusted Rákóczi, who had been a neighbour of his in Vienna, and he wanted the rebellion suppressed by force. Meanwhile Joseph worked hard in Vienna organizing help: horses were sent from the Imperial riding stables and the University; large sums of money were advanced by rich nobles like Liechtenstein and Czernin; the nobles, merchants and officials contributed towards levies and 'of the meaner inhabitants every house is to provide a foot soldier'.[32] But these measures, together with troops rushed eastwards from the Tyrol, were only sufficient to allow Eugene to strengthen the Danube crossings in an attempt to isolate the rebellion. There was no possibility of an offensive against the rebels.

In mid-January 1704 the prince left Pressburg on the news that the Bavarians had taken Passau. Vienna was terrified as the capital seemed trapped between the Hungarians and Max Emmanuel. The Dutch minister Bruynincx was convinced that Austria was finished. He wrote home on 16 January:

> Everything here is quite desperate; the monarchy is on its last legs and will go down in a general military collapse unless there is some miraculous intervention of the Almighty . . . It looks as though the enemy will soon be at the gates of Vienna – advancing from both sides. There is absolutely nothing to stop them. There is no money. There are no troops. Nothing for the defence of the town. And we will soon be without bread. I fear that a general uprising is likely, because you cannot imagine with what unrestrained venom people speak of the Emperor, of the Government, and of the clergy.[33]

If the court had wanted to flee, there was nowhere for it to run.

In the days immediately before his return to Vienna, Eugene's appraisal of the situation had been almost as gloomy. He had no faith in divine intervention and reminded Joseph that 'The proverb says that God helps him who helps himself.'[34] Yet the crisis passed: Austria's enemies could not believe they had merely to march on Vienna. The Bavarians halted at Passau, while the Magyar rebels stayed in Hungary except for periodic short raiding parties.

Leopold had remained impassive during the critical days but the danger proved useful since it enabled Joseph to gain greater control. It was he who urged Eugene to return from Pressburg, and he now presided regularly over the conference, which met four times a week.[35] He insisted on emergency taxes on the nobility and clergy, and his confessor, Father Bischoff, convinced Leopold of the morality of these measures.[36] During the first half of 1704 support for a more dynamic policy also came from the elector palatine, who came to Vienna in person to repeat his advice that Leopold should rid himself completely of his old ministers. He left in August, however, without achieving his aims and Bruynincx commented, 'if an angel had come down to this court from heaven, he would have fared no better'.[37]

Yet the situation in Austria had changed since the previous year. Harrach, Mansfeld and Buccelini might still hold office, but they were ignored by foreign diplomats, and it was clear to all that Joseph, Kaunitz, Eugene and the elector palatine now decided the emperor's military and foreign policy.[38] Perhaps the most encouraging sign for the future was the beginning of genuine diplomatic and military co-operation among the allies. The man chiefly responsible for closer Austrian ties with the latter was Eugene's friend Wratislaw, the Austrian minister in London, who had formed an excellent working relationship with the English commander-in-chief in the Netherlands, Marlborough. Before the end of 1702 Wratislaw had impressed on London the importance of an Imperialist presence in Italy, and in January 1703 the secretary of state, Nottingham, had offered an Anglo-Dutch subsidy of 100,000 pounds as well as help from the English fleet in the Mediterranean if the Imperialists raised a large force for Italy. This offer came to nothing because the Dutch refused to contribute their share, but the negotiations are interesting in showing the confidence which the English now had in Eugene; they intended to pay the money only if it went directly to him in Italy, bypassing the normal channels in Vienna.[39]

A tangible result of joint allied diplomacy in 1703 was that Victor Amadeus, who had become increasingly dissatisfied with his satellite position, was persuaded to desert Louis XIV. Although Eugene had been careful not to initiate discussions with his cousin while he had been in Italy, as he was afraid of being accused of treason, once he returned to Vienna he was 'all along privy to the negotiation' with Savoy and took part in talks with an agent of Victor Amadeus.[40] It is doubtful whether the duke would actually have broken with the French in 1703, given the weakness of the Imperialists in Italy, if the English minister in Turin, Richard Hill, had not inadvertently divulged the negotiations to the French in September. Vendôme's immediate seizure of Savoyard troops pushed Victor Amadeus into signing a treaty with the allies in October, by which he was promised Anglo-Dutch subsidies and military help from 15,000 Austrian troops, as well as the cession of the Montferrat and part of the duchy of Milan in any eventual peace settlement. He proceeded to encourage his subjects to engage in guerrilla warfare against the French, while Guido Starhemberg received orders from Vienna to break through the French lines and to join up with Victor Amadeus in Piedmont. Starhemberg managed this successfully in December and January 1703–04 after a brilliant series of winter manoeuvres. Victor Amadeus's defection undoubtedly weakened the French in Italy, despite their superior numbers, as they now had to concentrate on destroying him as well as defending the duchy of Milan.

Another straw in the wind was the decision of the Portuguese king Peter to sign an offensive alliance with the Maritime Powers in May 1703. This alliance envisaged a direct attack on Spain and the installation there of the archduke Charles in place of Philip V. The English hoped to gain a monopoly of Portuguese trade and through a change of dynasty in Spain to obtain commercial concessions in the Spanish overseas empire.

Leopold only joined this Portuguese alliance reluctantly: he was afraid that while it might bring his family Spain it might also lose them Italy. Neither did he wish to be separated from his favourite son Charles. His eventual agreement during the summer of 1703 reflects both his weakness and the strength of the Maritime Powers. The dispatch of the archduke to Spain greatly extended the original aims of the allies, who were now committed to a war for the transfer of the whole Spanish inheritance to the Habsburg family. But the emperor could give Charles no support of his own: he was sent to Spain 'almost as naked as he came into the world'.[41] After a tearful scene with his father – both men knew they would never see each other again – the nineteen year old archduke set out first for The Hague and then for England to join an Anglo-Dutch expedition to Portugal. Leopold and his elder son Joseph formally handed over their claims to the Spanish succession to Charles. But at the same time Charles was forced by a secret family compact, which Joseph insisted on, to agree that the duchy of Milan and Finale should go to the main branch of the family under Joseph.[42] The two brothers also agreed that both the Spanish and Austrian monarchies were to be inherited by the surviving brother or his male heirs if the other died without sons. It is not known whether Eugene was a party to these agreements, but it is probable that he was not since they were regarded as private family matters.

Although the overall aim of the Austrian government throughout the War of Spanish Succession was to prevent the hegemony of the house of Bourbon in Europe, a more specific Austrian goal was to seize and hold on to as much of Italy as possible. It was here that Austria's greatest military effort was made against France; the other areas of operations were largely forced upon her. As the war developed she came to demand Spain for the archduke almost as dogmatically as she demanded Italy, but Spain always remained secondary to the latter and became a feasible objective only because of massive allied victories elsewhere. Austria herself consistently refused to deploy more than token forces in Spain. In military terms it still seemed more important to strengthen the Rhine barrier, although the Imperial princes were expected to shoulder the main burden of the war in Germany. When Austrian forces were sent to the Southern Netherlands from 1708 onwards, they went there not so much to conquer them for the archduke Charles as to exert pressure on France to concede an acceptable general peace. What is often forgotten is that probably the major part of Austria's military resources, particularly after 1707, were tied up not in the struggle with the Bourbons but with suppressing the Hungarian rebellion. As ever Austria's ambitions were to outrun her actual means.

IX

Blenheim

In the third year of the war the military prospects of the Austrian monarchy appeared grim. As long as Max Emmanuel stood by Louis and his army remained undefeated, there was always the danger of an attack on Vienna and of total collapse. Throughout 1704, therefore, all other issues had to take second place: Victor Amadeus and Starhemberg would have to hold out as best they could in Italy, and in the east little could be done except keeping the Magyar rebels at bay. While agreeing to let the Maritime Powers try to mediate a settlement with the Magyars, none of Leopold's ministers bothered to hide the fact that this was meant to buy time and that they intended to suppress the revolt by force as soon as they could. Eugene told a shocked Dutch ambassador, who complained about Imperial troops burning two hundred villages in Transylvania, that 'he wished it had been two thousand, for as much as that whole people was rebellious'.[1]

In southern Germany at the beginning of 1704 the position of Max Emmanuel of Bavaria was strong. He and the French general, Marsin, who had replaced the arrogant and forthright Villars, occupied the whole Danube valley from Ulm to Passau with a Franco-Bavarian force of 40,000 men. On the Rhine at Strasbourg, marshal Tallard was waiting with 36,000 French troops, hoping to move them through the Black Forest to join those already in Bavaria under Marsin. Prince Louis of Baden commanded a similar number of Imperial troops manning the Lines of Stollhofen, a twenty-five mile stretch of fortifications opposite Strasbourg intended to protect central Germany from France. The largest concentrations of troops were much further north in the Netherlands, where Villeroy, at liberty again but none the wiser, was defending the Spanish provinces with 46,000 men against a much larger Anglo-Dutch army, 70,000 strong, under Marlborough.

In terms of overall allied strategy there was a clear need to correct the imbalance in south Germany if Vienna itself were not to fall. By

February 1704 Eugene, Joseph and the elector palatine were all agreed
that only military help from the Maritime Powers could save them from
Max Emmanuel. The most they probably hoped for at this time was the
transfer of a number of troops south to strengthen Baden or for Marlborough to mount an attack on France along the Moselle which would
free Louis of Baden for action against Bavaria. But the Austrian minister
in London, Eugene's friend Wratislaw, was working for Marlborough
to bring an Anglo-Dutch army in person into Germany as far south as
the Danube. This enormously fat, engaging and intelligent Bohemian
noble, still in his early thirties, was already completely trusted by the
English commander-in-chief. It seems likely that the idea of a march to
the Danube and an eventual juncture with an Imperialist force to crush
Bavaria was Wratislaw's own. Unfortunately, the need for secrecy* and
to commit as little as possible to paper means that we cannot be absolutely certain. The answer might lie in the correspondence which is
known to have passed between Wratislaw and Eugene, but this has never
been found.[2] We do know, however, that the Austrian government
seized the opportunity when it was offered and that Marlborough in 1703
had been thinking of sending troops to operate on the Moselle and
further south to save the Empire. By August 1703 he had grasped the
need for a proper war strategy, so that, as he put it, 'the whole Con-
federate army might be helping to each other'.[3]

When Marlborough and Wratislaw reached The Hague from England
at the end of April 1704, the English captain-general had fixed on the
ambitious plan of an expedition to the Danube. He was to keep this
secret from all but a close few in London and Vienna till his army was
well on its way. He felt by now that the venture was vital to the whole
outcome of the war for, as he wrote to Godolphin in London on 1 May,
'I am very sensible that I take a great deal upon me. But should I act
otherwise, the Empire would be undone and consequently the Confed-
eracy.' Success would also consolidate his own and his close ally Godolphin's position at home and silence the opposition from those Tory
politicians who wanted England to fight the French at sea rather than on
land. Therefore, when Marlborough officially communicated his plans
to Vienna through Wratislaw on 5 May, he demanded that the Imperialists should 'put all other schemes aside and . . . operate with
Marlborough against the Elector'. He also wanted them to send Eugene
for 'It is absolutely necessary that I should have a supporter of his zeal
and experience.'[4]

* Not only from the French but also from the Dutch who naturally wanted the
Anglo-Dutch army to operate as close to their borders as possible.

The question which must have tormented Marlborough most was whether Leopold and his ministers would let him down. They did not. Before his message reached Vienna, it had been decided in a conference on 12 April 1704 that Eugene should go to Germany in person to deal with the elector of Bavaria. The conference also rejected the suggestion from Louis of Baden that the Imperialists should mount an offensive on the Moselle and only act defensively against Max Emmanuel. Nothing was said in the conference about Marlborough's coming to the Moselle, let alone to the Danube. When Leopold received official notice of the expedition in mid-May, he wrote at once to Wratislaw to assure him that a force under Eugene would meet Marlborough, and on 14 May Baden was told bluntly by letter that 'I will not consent to any other operation at the opening of this campaign.'[5]

Prince Louis was likely to prove a problem. Marlborough had insisted that Eugene be sent because he had not been impressed by Baden's campaign in 1703, but the dispatch of the president of the war council might well be resented by Louis who was still commander-in-chief, or lieutenant-general, of the army of the Empire. Despite their close association in the past and their agreement over Mansfeld, the two cousins were no longer the warm friends they had been when Eugene was the junior partner. Although Baden had won brilliant successes against the Turks and was known popularly as 'Turkish Louis', now nearly fifty he was an extremely touchy man, especially when suffering from gout. He had also become wedded to a static concept of warfare, built round fortresses and strategic manoeuvres, of the kind he had pursued along the Rhine during the Nine Years War. Eugene and Marlborough both realized that this strategy could not produce the decisive victory they wanted. Moreover, there was some suspicion that Baden was sympathetic towards Max Emmanuel, and this suspicion increased in May 1704 when he failed to stop Tallard bringing French reinforcements for Marsin's army through the Black Forest. Like other allied statesmen, prince Louis would have preferred to negotiate a settlement with the elector, but he differed from them in being prepared for these talks to continue almost indefinitely, and in showing extreme reluctance to attack Bavaria. While Eugene was frequently infuriated by his cousin, he never suspected treachery and his subsequent efforts to deal kindly with him came not only from tact but also from a sense of past obligation. Yet, when he left Vienna on 25 May he took with him powers from Leopold to override Baden if necessary. For the moment the emperor seemed to have full confidence in Eugene and he kept in direct secret correspondence with him throughout the year.[6] Harrach and Mansfeld were still close to the emperor, but he now listened to the advice of the duke of Moles, who had been Charles II of Spain's ambassador in Vienna and was a firm political ally of Wratislaw.[7]

When Max Emmanuel heard that Eugene had left Vienna for Germany, he wrote to Louis XIV: 'It is certain that the Prince of Savoy can only have come to the seat of war to carry out some great project.'[8] He knew only the half of it.

On 19 May what Winston Churchill called Marlborough's 'scarlet caterpillar' of red-coated troops set out from Bedburg, completely unaware that ahead of them was a two hundred and fifty-mile march from the Netherlands to the Danube. No contemporary army was better equipped or provided for: Marlborough had the money and was concerned for his men. Supplies were waiting at every stop during the march and at Heidelberg, for instance, each man received a new pair of shoes. Despite spells of hot sun and of heavy soaking rain, the army found its passage through the small Rhineland villages easy and almost enjoyable. As it marched its strength was increased from an initial 19,000 or so to 40,000, swelled by troops from the German states and others hired from Denmark. Of these troops only 9,000 were British nationals and the contingent of Dutch in the army was considerably greater than this number.

By a series of feint manoeuvres Marlborough tricked not only the Dutch leaders into letting him go but also kept the French confused and helpless while he marched. As he had hoped, Villeroy followed him with a great part of his army from the Netherlands on the French side of the Rhine, so that there was no real danger to the allied forces left guarding the Dutch frontier. The march to the Danube took five weeks and during this time important decisions were being made by the Imperial generals.

In the first week of June Eugene reached Baden's headquarters near Ulm, where he had moved the bulk of his army from the Lines of Stollhofen. On the 8th Wratislaw joined them: he had accompanied Marlborough's expedition intending to smoothe out any difficulties which might arise with Baden or Eugene, since the English general had so far met neither. By now the Imperialists had assembled large numbers of troops of their own in southern Germany to reinforce Baden, and it was hoped by both Marlborough and Eugene that some of them could co-operate with the English army against Bavaria. The rest of the Imperial troops would be needed on the Lines of Stollhofen to prevent a French move across the Rhine or further French reinforcements being pushed through the Black Forest to help Max Emmanuel and Marsin. Baden seemed the obvious choice for this command, as it would call for his undoubted strategic ability. Therefore in a council of war with Eugene and Baden, Wratislaw tried to persuade him to undertake it. But prince Louis wanted to stay at the centre of the coming action and cleverly turned the tables by saying to Wratislaw: 'Try to persuade the Prince to do so. For in the army he is the only man who could be entrusted with a command so responsible and subject to so many risks.' Eugene quickly replied: 'The Emperor has sent me into the Empire to serve under the command of his Lieutenant-General [Baden], and as I have never made difficulties about going wherever duty called me, I am quite ready to carry out the order of the Lieutenant-General.'[9]

Eugene was undoubtedly flattered by this appeal, and by accepting it he avoided a direct clash with his cousin; there was in any case a real chance that Baden would act decisively once joined with Marlborough. Eugene's ready acceptance of the Rhine command seems to show that he had never seen Marlborough's march to the Danube as an event which urgently required his personal co-operation with the English commander. The difficult strategic position at Stollhofen may have genuinely attracted him: Villeroy was known to have brought his force from the Netherlands and to have joined up with the rest of Tallard's troops at Strasbourg opposite the Lines.

On Monday 9 June Eugene rode out with Wratislaw to Marlborough's camp at Mundelsheim on the Neckar in Württemberg. The two men took to each other at once and stayed together till the Friday. It was to be one of the few lasting friendships of Eugene's life. Only three months later Stepney was surprised to see how 'our generalls live in as perfect harmony as if they were brethren'.[10] In an undated letter to the duke of Savoy written about the time of this meeting Eugene described Marlborough as 'a man of high quality, courageous, extremely well-disposed, and with a keen desire to achieve something; with all these qualities he understands thoroughly that one cannot become a general in a day, and he is diffident about himself'.[11] Although both men occasionally criticized one another during the coming campaign, they recognized that each wanted decisive military action. Both of them bore far heavier domestic political responsibilities than most generals and were completely committed to the destruction of the paramount position of Louis XIV. Yet they were so unalike: the Englishman was some ten years older and had still not commanded in a major battle, although he had served his military apprenticeship under Turenne as long ago as the 1670s. An adroit diplomat, politician and courtier, he was also strikingly handsome, even in late middle age, able to charm anyone with his smile and conversation. He was also a family man, fiercely loyal to his wife, intent on creating a dynasty and notoriously mean. Plagued by severe headaches, his letters are full of references to his health. Eugene on the contrary never mentioned whether he felt well or not. An unimpressive, even ugly man, he showed little interest in money, family, women or flattery, and subordinated everything to military success.

The one disappointment in this first meeting was Eugene's news that he intended to go to the Rhine while Baden co-operated with Marlborough. He warned him that prince Louis was a difficult man but told him in confidence that the emperor had given him full powers if necessary 'to take such measures as not to leave him [Baden] with the army'.[12]

On 13 June all three commanders met in the courtyard of the Lamb Inn at Gross Heppach to the east of Stuttgart. Their meeting passed off well enough with agreement that Baden and Marlborough were to command on alternate days, although it was tacitly assumed that the overall command was Marlborough's. The next day Eugene left for the Rhine.

Marlborough and Baden's joint army of 50,000 men was some five thousand stronger than the Franco-Bavarian force which had camped at Ulm since May. Eugene was in a much weaker position on the Rhine, with only 30,000 men to oppose Villeroy's army of 50,000. But to the prince's surprise and relief the French did not use their superiority to launch an attack, partly because the Rhine was very full but more because of confusion at the French court. Worried that Max Emmanuel would make his peace with the allies, Louis XIV ordered Tallard to lead a further 26,000 men through the Black Forest to reinforce the elector and Marsin. On receiving news of this Eugene decided to take the risk that Villeroy might move into Germany with the rest of the French force, and he left only 12,000 men to guard against this eventuality at Stollhofen while with his remaining 18,000 men he followed Tallard. The risk proved worth taking because Villeroy stayed where he was.[13]

To begin with, the French had some success. Eugene was unable to catch up with or halt Tallard's army as it struggled through the difficult mountainous country of the Black Forest during July. Tallard looked after his men and himself very well: with his army went 8,000 waggons loaded with bread, flour and biscuits, and for himself 'two mule trains laden with good things to eat – and wines too'. Even so his soldiers plundered the countryside through which they passed, with the result that 'the enraged peasantry eventually killed several thousand of our men before the army was clear of the Black Forest'.[14] This kind of conduct was typical of all the French armies in this campaign. The French colonel de la Colonie described the earlier behaviour of the troops under Marsin in Swabia in this way:

> On their arrival at each camping-ground it was their custom to go and seek for wood and straw, and under this pretext they set out in organised parties, turn and turn about, to scout and pillage the country; . . . They brought in four or five hundred sheep at a time, besides cows and oxen, from pasturages far away from the camp, where the inhabitants had believed themselves to be quite secure from robbery of this sort.[15]

Meanwhile things had not gone well for the joint force of Marlborough and Baden. To add teeth to negotiations with the elector and to open their way into Bavaria, they had stormed the strong enemy position of the Schellenberg at Donauwörth on the Danube. After a costly victory on 2 July, Marlborough and Baden's resolution seemed to fail them, and the elector and Marsin were able to shelter behind the protective fortifications at Augsburg to wait for Tallard. The allied leaders ignored Eugene's advice, received through Wratislaw, to attack again before Tallard arrived. One reason for the delay, as Marlborough explained to Godolphin, was 'making our bread follow us; for the troops I have the honour to command cannot subsist without it, and the Germans that are used to starve cannot advance without us'.[16] He decided, despite protests from Baden, 'to burn and destroy the Elector's country, to oblige him to hearken to terms'.[17] During July perhaps 500 Bavarian villages were sacked. According to the Hanoverian general Bellingk, 'The villages were prosperous and thickly populated and it distressed every officer to see 40 or 50 more villages go up in smoke in an hour.'[18] The remarkable Irishwoman, Mother Ross, who served in British armies in the 1690s and 1700s for more than ten years before her sex was discovered, described the destruction:

> We spared nothing, killing, burning, or otherwise destroying whatever we could not carry off. The bells of the churches we broke to pieces, that we might bring them away with us. I filled two bed-ticks, after having thrown out the feathers, with bell-metal, men's and women's clothes, some velvets and about a hundred Dutch caps, which I had plundered from a shop; all which I sold by the lump to a Jew, who followed the army to purchase our pillage, for four pistoles.[19]

The elector was forced to disperse his army far and wide in a desperate attempt to stop the destruction. Although he was badly shaken and his family begged him to change sides, he stood his ground.

While this had been going on and he had been shadowing Tallard, Eugene had become increasingly worried that no decisive action had taken place and feared that the English army would soon be thinking of returning home. He wrote to the duke of Savoy: ' . . . I cannot admire their performances. They have been counting on the Elector coming to terms . . . they have amused themselves with . . . burning a few villages instead of, according to my ideas, which I have put before them plainly enough, marching straight upon the enemy . . . ' He realized that Marlborough must want a decisive result since 'If he has to go home without having achieved his objective, he will certainly be ruined',[20] and that the main problem was Baden, who, he informed the emperor on 31 July, was 'very difficult to bring to any operation'.[21] Baden's chief aim seemed to be to do no more than to get into a favourable position for the next year's campaign. On 30 July Wratislaw wrote to Leopold that Baden's reply to demands for action was that 'you do not understand war, and this ends the discussion'. He therefore felt that only Eugene could save them because 'The one person he cannot say this to is the Prince.'[22] In fact but for Eugene's arrival on the scene it is unlikely that a decisive action would have taken place.

On 3 August Tallard's forces joined up with those of Marsin and the elector at Augsburg. Three days later Eugene, who had been close behind, left his troops encamped behind the Kesselbach, a small tributary of the Danube to the east of Höchstädt, and rode over with only one servant to the Baden-Marlborough camp nearby. He found to his relief that Baden had just agreed to take 15,000 men to besiege Ingolstadt, the last remaining strongpoint in Bavaria. With Baden out of the way, Eugene and Marlborough were quickly able to agree on joining their armies together for an attack on the enemy. The allied general Schulenburg observed them at close hand and had this to say of their talks in his diary:

> . . . The map was spread out before him on the table like a chess-board, and Eugene studied the moves. He was all fire and flame. At last he had found a being who understood him, who appreciated the circumspection of his plans and who thought in the same way as he did. Marlborough's handsome face glowed! But he listened with the cool ardour of the Englishman, and was amazed at all Eugene's precautionary measures. Why did the Prince consider so many possibilities when one was enough for victory?

Schulenburg added later: 'It is part of Eugene's character to see difficulties and obstacles before beginning a task. When the moment for action arrives, then he is all strength and activity.'[23]

Meanwhile the enemy were arguing heatedly: Tallard's pleas for caution were overridden by the elector and Marsin who wanted to attack Eugene's force before it joined Marlborough's. On 10 August Eugene, who was back with his army, saw the first signs of the enemy's advance troops and wrote urgently to Marlborough: 'Everything, milord, consists in speed and that you put yourself in movement to join me tomorrow without which I fear it will be too late. In short, the enemy is there . . . '[24] Marlborough rushed his troops over to join the prince, but the French stayed put, continued to argue and were even unaware that the allies had come together.

On 12 August Eugene and Marlborough made a preliminary reconnaissance, protected by a screen of 2,000 horsemen. Next they observed the enemy positions through a spyglass from the church tower at Tapfheim. The French army, probably a little stronger than the allies, some 56,000 against the allies' 52,000, was camped in a four-mile line, stretching from some woods and the village of Lutzingen in the north down to another village, Blindheim (the name was anglicized to Blenheim and gave its name to the ensuing battle), on the Danube itself. Tallard's force lay between Blindheim and another village, Oberglau, in the centre, while that of the elector and Marsin was positioned between Oberglau and Lutzingen. The two parts of the French army were kept a little apart to prevent a disease among Tallard's horses spreading. In front of the whole French army was a stream, the Nebel. Although most of their subordinates thought the French position too strong, Marlborough and Eugene had no hesitation in deciding on a battle for the following day.

That night, while the French and Bavarian generals were oblivious of what was in store, neither allied commander slept. When Marlborough went over to see the prince at two o'clock on the morning of the 13th, he found him busy writing letters. An hour later bugles and drums signalled for the troops to move out. Through the dark and the early morning mist they advanced in nine columns, five under Marlborough nearest to the Danube and the other four under Eugene to the north. It was only at six o'clock that the French spotted allied troops massing on the marshy land on the opposite side of the Nebel, and even then Tallard took an hour before he was convinced a battle was in the offing. By this time Marlborough's troops were ready for action, but it was midday before Eugene had made his way across the more difficult ground to reach his agreed position further up the stream where it ran deeper and faster. Meanwhile Marlborough's troops built crude pontoons over the Nebel and lay down in their ranks to avoid the worst of the accurate artillery fire from the French.

The allied plan was for Eugene to use 16,000 men in a containing

action against Marsin and the elector's 23,000, while the bulk of the
allied army, some 36,000 strong, was deployed by Marlborough to
destroy Tallard's 33,000. Marlborough concentrated his infantry on his
left, opposite most of the French foot concentrated in and around the
village of Blindheim. On his right he mixed foot and horse opposite
Tallard's left which consisted almost entirely of cavalry. Tallard did little
to change his dispositions from where his men were camped. He was
badly handicapped by poor eyesight, but seems to have intended to
allow Marlborough's force over the stream and then to drive it back.

When the battle began in the early afternoon Marlborough made his
main effort in the centre against Tallard's left wing. His troops crossed
the Nebel largely unimpeded and to Tallard's dismay soon established
themselves strongly: the interspersing of infantry and cavalry meant that
the horse could be shielded after every charge by the infantry firing
effective volleys by platoons. The wide field of yellow stubble in front
of the stream was ideal for the ferocious sabre-wielding cavalry charges
Marlborough excelled in. Tallard's cavalry was outnumbered and received no protection from the French infantry uselessly bottled up round
Blindheim. The battle was won in the late afternoon when Tallard's
cavalry broke and fled, many being swept into the Danube. His infantry was then surrounded and forced to surrender. Eleven thousand
prisoners were taken, including the unfortunate Tallard.

Further north Eugene had managed to hold on. Although no real
attempt was made by the two French armies to coordinate, there had
been a dangerous moment when some of Marsin's infantry, the Irish
'Wild Geese',* attacked Marlborough's flank. The situation was saved
by the hard-pressed Eugene answering Marlborough's request for the
loan of some cavalry. The prince's position was very difficult because of
his smaller numbers and the undoubted ability of the elector. He consequently demanded far more from his men than they could give, although he did not spare himself and, according to the Prussian general
Grumbkow, it was 'almost a miracle that he escaped the danger'.[25] After
leading his left wing of Imperial cavalry in three unsuccessful charges, he
shot two of his troopers to prevent a general flight. Then declaring in
disgust, 'I wish to fight among brave men and not among cowards',[26]
he joined the right wing of Prussian and Danish mercenary infantry. A
murderous stalemate was resolved when the news of Tallard's disaster
caused the elector and Marsin to retreat. They escaped largely intact
through the gathering darkness: Eugene's troops were too exhausted to
follow.

* Irish Catholic troops in French service.

The battle had been won and lost on Marlborough's part of the field, where he had kept tight control over operations by his own presence unlike the half-blind Tallard who was never in the right place at the right time. Marlborough had been prepared to accept heavy losses to achieve victory – as many allies, 12,000, were killed and wounded as the enemy. According to the English general Richard Kane, 'those under Prince Eugene suffered most'.[27] Eugene's holding operation had been as crucial to the whole battle as had his pressure for action in the days leading up to it.

Both men were full of praise for each other. There was no criticism or denigration of Eugene in Marlborough's account of the battle to his wife (though some has been read into it):

... the army of M de Tallard, which was what I fought with, is quite ruined; that of the Elector of Bavaria, and the Marshal de Marsin, which Eugene fought against, I am afraid has not had much loss, for I can't find that he had many prisoners ... had the success of Prince Eugene been equal to his merit, we should in that day's action have made an end of the war.[28]

He was, however, as critical of the Imperial cavalry's performance as Eugene had been: their losses, unlike the other troops under the prince, were a mere 200 dead and wounded.[29] Because of this Marlborough felt he could only send a compliment, rather than a proper letter to the emperor, 'since I could not say anything of their troups, Prince Eugene with the Imperial troups having been repulsed twice, so that if wee had not succeeded thay must have been cut to peeces'.[30] Had Eugene wanted to, he could have complained that he had been given the more difficult task in the winning of 'the most complete victory for more than a hundred years'.[31]

The allies captured a good deal of booty: 5,400 waggons of food and ammunition, 34 coaches containing the women of the French officers, 334 mules loaded with plate, the war chest and 40 large cannon. This was divided among the allied contingents, the ordinary soldiers being given their share at once and also being allowed to strip their own and the enemy dead. Although Marlborough had taken almost all the prisoners he shared them equally with Eugene, partly out of politeness and so that the Imperialists might exchange them for men lost in the campaign the previous year, but also because it was more convenient. The captured Bavarian troops were sent to serve in Hungary and Italy, but vague talk of trying the officers as traitors to the Empire came to nothing.[32] The beaten Tallard, who was wounded and had lost his own son in the battle, was treated very kindly by Marlborough before being sent to England.

It was observed, however, that Eugene went out of his way to be cold towards the French prisoners.

There was a marked difference in the rewards granted to the victors by their respective rulers. While Marlborough was given a dukedom and the promise of a palace (Blenheim) to be built at the expense of the nation, Leopold merely paid 6,000 gulden to the city of Vienna for Eugene to have the right to be exempt from impositions or billeting in his palace in the Himmelpfortgasse.

The battle of Blenheim was probably the most decisive of the war. It freed Vienna from the Franco-Bavarian threat and delivered south Germany into allied hands. At the same time it firmly cemented the Grand Alliance and established the ascendancy of the Godolphin-Marlborough ministry in England. Much more significant, however, and this was something grasped by contemporaries at once, was that in one afternoon the forty-year supremacy of Louis XIV and the French army had been shattered: France herself now had to face the real danger of invasion.

Although Marsin and the elector managed to get their army away from Blenheim almost intact, it disintegrated as the men fled demoralized through the mountains of the Black Forest back to France. As they pillaged their way home, angry peasants picked off many of the troops, and most of their baggage was burnt or abandoned on the march. The Flemish general Mérode-Westerloo made his personal sacrifice during the flight by serving up forty bottles of wine at a dinner party. Max Emmanuel accompanied the French, having decided to reject peace offers from the allies, to abandon his electorate till better times and to resume his position as Philip V's governor in the Spanish Netherlands.

At the close of November the Imperialists had regained Landau on the Rhine and Marlborough had taken Trier on his way back to the Netherlands. No further trouble need be feared within Germany. Local resistance from Bavarian troops in the electorate was over by mid-November when Max Emmanuel's wife agreed to hand over the whole of Bavaria to the emperor to stop further devastation by the Imperial army. Eugene arrived in Munich at the end of November, and stayed there for a month. During this time he organized the quartering of the bulk of the Imperial army in Bavaria for the winter, as well as setting up a military administration primarily intended to channel Bavarian revenues into the Austrian treasury. While the basic institutions of government and system of office-holding were left intact, Bavaria was treated as a conquered province which paid for its ruler's treason to the emperor by being forced to contribute heavily to the Imperial war effort till the peace of 1714.

X

The Accession of Joseph I

After Blenheim the military initiative clearly lay with the allies who decided that Marlborough in 1705 should try to break into France along the Moselle, while the Imperialists held the Rhine and concentrated on northern Italy. The conquest of the Spanish territories in Italy was what Vienna desired most, and if the Maritime Powers had little sympathy with these ambitions, they nevertheless saw that Savoy had to be relieved and a further front maintained against France. During 1704 Victor Amadeus and Guido Starhemberg had clung to the area around Turin while a small Imperial force was all but pushed back into the Trentino. Although Eugene had ignored the appeals for help from this quarter, he was determined to raise and lead a sizeable army there in 1705. However, he had no intention of doing so as he told Starhemberg in a somewhat tactless letter, considering what Guido had suffered, 'until I see a proper army raised rather than another make-shift job . . . , so that I do not jeopardize my honour and reputation'.[1] In the event what should have been a year of consolidation in Italy turned into one of near disaster, as Eugene strove to prevent the collapse of firm control of the war by Vienna and to hold together yet another pitifully-equipped army under his command in the peninsula.

When Eugene returned to Vienna from Bavaria at the end of 1704, he found that far from being treated like a conquering hero, his influence had actually decreased. While he had been away, and especially when Joseph joined the army on the Rhine for some months after Blenheim, the emperor had begun to listen once again to his old friends, Harrach, Mansfeld and Buccelini. Mansfeld interfered in the war council and both he and Buccelini tried to obstruct Gundaker Starhemberg's work at the *Hofkammer*. Eugene therefore threw his whole weight behind Wratislaw, who was emerging as the foremost opponent of the old ministers. Viennese wits remarked with an obvious dig at the two men's physical size that 'formerly great St Xopher carried little Jesus, but now the picture is reversed'.[2] But their co-operation had little practical effect: Leopold rejected the proposal that Wratislaw be appointed governor of Bavaria, and in March 1705 Stepney was sure that Wratislaw would have no influence while the emperor lived.[3]

Nor was Eugene getting his way in the military sphere. Throughout 1704 he had pressed Leopold without success to dismiss Heister, the commander in Hungary, whom he felt was both incompetent and aim-lessly terroristic. The prince wanted the rebels crushed quickly 'with fire and sword'[4] to end a continual drain of men and money. But it was above all over Italy, where he was concerned personally, that Eugene felt most angry. He found that next to nothing had been done to prepare for the coming campaign before he returned, and even then he was left to deal with everything almost single-handed. By March 1705 he decided to bring things to a head by threatening to resign if Heister was not dis-missed, and if the revenues from Bavaria were not wholly devoted to the war effort and enough money found for the Italian campaign. He then made a point of staying away from court.[5]

Eugene's conduct may well have been the result of personal resentment as well as professional frustration. There was probably more than a grain of truth in Stepney's observation that the prince was

> sour'd upon the applause and rewards which the D. of Marlborough found in England, and his eye was evil because nothing of that kind was shewd him here; he could not forbear giving broad hints of this even in his discourse with me, whereby he discover'd where the shoe pinched; under the disguise of an affected modesty and indifference, he has as great a stock of ambition as any man ... [6]

But he must also have been aware of what lay ahead of him in Italy: another humiliating campaign similar to that of 1703. What was so galling to him as a military commander was not so much the praise Marlborough received but the latter's ability to raise an army which could do justice to his military gifts.

After two weeks' delay Leopold resolved the impasse by seeing Eugene for a quarter of an hour and satisfying him on the main point of providing sufficient money for Italy. In doing so he had rejected the advice of his friends to call Eugene's bluff by sacking him and appointing Heister president of the war council and Guido Starhemberg com-mander in Italy.[7] But it was not in Leopold's nature to dismiss anyone and, moreover, he knew the bad effect such a step would have on the allies.

In accepting Leopold's worthless assurances and leaving for Italy on

18 April, Eugene went 'more like an apostle than a general, for he has no money'.[8] The Dutch minister Bruynincx predicted gloomily that 'the coming campaign will not be a happy one'.[9] The prince himself was no more optimistic and he must have been particularly disturbed at his relations with Leopold. However, the emperor was already a dying man. He died on 5 May after weeks of discomfort from wind, constipation, swollen limbs and worry over his 'Dear Charles' in Spain. His death caused genuine grief among the court and people of Vienna in marked contrast to his earlier unpopularity.[10] After serving the same man for more than twenty years, Eugene also had some affection for him, but with Joseph as emperor he knew things would be easier.

Prince Salm, who became *Obristhofmeister* immediately on Joseph's accession, assured Stepney a fortnight later that the new emperor 'was resolved to supply all that Prince Eugene shall stand in need of'.[11] Considerable sums were sent,[12] but before the end of the campaign Eugene complained that he had received nothing like the amount promised him. However, his army's performance was to be largely limited by the inadequacy of the measures taken during Leopold's last months as emperor. The situation would have been even worse if Marlborough had not gone to Berlin at the end of 1704 to hire 8,000 Prussians, to be paid for by the Maritime Powers, for Eugene's use in Italy during the 1705 campaign.

Eugene faced a virtually impossible task. The army waiting for him at Rovereto in April had become, in Guido Starhemberg's words, a 'riotous parliament',[13] with desertions running at fifty a day and its officers unpaid for fifteen months. The new recruits were little better, some arriving with matchlocks or with no guns at all; Joseph later confiscated and sent all the guns that could be found in Bavaria. Few magazines had been set up, and there was a serious shortage of carts and materials for bridging rivers, which meant Eugene's mobility would be severely limited.

The French army opposing him was large and still led by the capable Vendôme, who never underestimated his adversary, since, as he admitted in March 1705, 'just one false move during the whole campaign could ruin everything'.[14] He had the difficult task of mopping up Savoyard resistance and of preventing the Austrians breaking into Lombardy from the Trentino. Turin was not to fall to the French that year even though no outside help was to reach Victor Amadeus and the latter was to quarrel continually with Guido Starhemberg, who was a competent but very tetchy general.[15] Starhemberg had some excuse for this because he suffered continual pain from a spear head lodged in his shoulder since the siege of Buda some twenty years before. Instead of concentrating on taking Turin, Vendôme moved most of his men into Lombardy to keep the Imperialists out. This was evidently what Eugene wanted him to do. Faced by increasing difficulties and with a force no more than 30,000 strong, the prince never seriously tried to break into Lombardy or through to Victor Amadeus in Savoy but worked to create a diversion large enough to make Vendôme ease the pressure on Turin.[16]

Eugene managed to establish himself east of the Oglio by June, but all further attempts by him to move westwards were thwarted by Vendôme's skilful covering of the remaining rivers and Eugene's difficulties in crossing them. Continuous heavy rain swamped the roads and caused the rivers to burst their banks, drowning thousands of people.[17] In a situation where he found 'every little ditch is like a river'[18] but had no boats or the proper materials to construct bridges, Eugene was helpless. As the summer wore on he gradually lost control of events. His supply system had almost totally broken down and he was reduced to a primitive day-to-day improvisation. Sickness and desertion were rife and he was unable to push the troops hired from the German princes as hard as he would have liked. However, he remained self-assured and kept his force together as best he could. We have a description of his daily routine at this time, drawn up by a French spy who had infiltrated his camp:

> He seems a very energetic man, frequently on horseback, and maintaining strict discipline . . . he always eats two meat dishes by themselves at midday, drinks a good deal of local wine from a silver tankard and then has some cheese and whatever fruit is in season. He does not eat supper but retires and rises very early.[19]

In the circumstances Eugene would have preferred to sit it out until winter and concentrate on establishing himself where he was, but desperate appeals from Victor Amadeus and criticism from home of his growing 'of a suddain so wonderfully circumspect'[20] goaded him into action. On 16 August he made a bloody and unsuccessful attempt to seize a crossing on the river Adda at Cassano.

When Eugene eventually called off the campaign in November, he had spent a further three months of frustrating and unproductive manoeuvring. It had proved a humiliating experience, especially towards the end of the campaign when he had been forced to condone plundering and watch his men laughing at their officers' orders. As he told Marlborough, his army was 'ruined, the horses worn out with past fatigues, no sure footing in the country'.[21] But he had kept what was left of his army in a position to renew the struggle the following year and had reduced the pressure on Victor Amadeus sufficiently for the latter to survive in Turin. He justified himself by emphasizing that the war had not been 'one of conquest . . . but a war of diversion' which tied down 80,000 enemy troops.[22]

Elsewhere the allies' main hope for 1705, Marlborough's campaign along the Moselle, had also ended in failure. In Hungary there was still no end in sight to the rebellion, which was absorbing 20,000 Imperial troops. In November 1705 Bavaria rose in revolt against the Imperial occupation. Already in February of that year the roads had been full of dangerous swarms of beggars, left homeless by the ravages of the 1704 campaigns,[23] and the peasants were increasingly driven to open rebellion by the heavy taxes, billeting and the extensive recruiting which Eugene had urged very strongly. He now pressed for punitive measures and by the end of the year military force, executions and deportations to Hungary had brought Bavaria to heel.

The alliance could not afford another year like 1705, when all the gains made at Blenheim seemed to have evaporated. It was clear that the main problem in Italy was cash, and it was equally clear that this could only come from the Maritime Powers. Marlborough had been in correspondence with Eugene throughout 1705 and was well aware of the prince's problems, both Eugene and Wratislaw having threatened that without outside financial help the emperor would be forced to withdraw completely from the peninsula. It is doubtful whether this threat was intended seriously, as it would have meant the abandonment of Austria's main war aim. But Marlborough needed little convincing and on 5 October 1705 wrote to Wratislaw: 'It seems to me high time to think seriously about this war in Italy, a war which employs so great a number of enemy troops, who would fall upon our backs elsewhere if we were driven out of it.'[24] During the autumn after the campaigning season was over, Marlborough undertook a marathon journey throughout Germany to hire more mercenary troops to be paid for by the Maritime Powers to join the Prussians already in Italy. In November he came to Vienna and promised a loan of 250,000 pounds (about 2 million gulden), but he insisted that it should be paid directly to the prince and used exclusively in Italy. Although Eugene did not return to Vienna in time to see Marlborough, when he did arrive there he was able to plan with far more confidence for the following year's campaign. With the promise of English cash and the firm support of the new emperor, he was determined to break through to Victor Amadeus in Savoy during 1706.

Joseph was a very different man from his father, for, as Stepney put it, 'the blood of the Palatin family has gott the better of the Austrian'.[25]

Short and stocky, with blue eyes and blond hair, he had escaped the
Habsburg jaw. Not yet thirty, Joseph was energetic and active, a vora-
cious hunter who took full advantage of the great variety of animals still
to be found close to Vienna.* Unlike his father, Joseph had his mistresses.
Although he was careful not to cross his wife Amelia openly, as he grew
older and it became clear that she would not have any more children,
particularly a son – they had two daughters – he spent more time with his
women and in hunting. His favourite, count Lamberg, was described by
a French agent in 1707 as 'a man whose only merit is that he is a good
huntsman and an excellent pimp for his master'.[27]

Having grown up at a time when the Habsburgs had greatly increased
their power in the Balkans and in the Empire, he was inevitably a far
more confident ruler than his father. He did not share in the latter's
religious fatalism, and had been brought up by his tutor Salm to resent
clerical, particularly Jesuit, influence. Violently anti-French, he had a
keen sense of dynasty and pride in being German. He emphasized the
Imperial dignity by the magnificence of his clothes and jewels and by his
more high-handed attitude towards the Imperial princes, and he probably had more influence in the Empire than any other emperor in the
seventeenth or eighteenth centuries. He sat in on the conferences of his
ministers and could make sound judgments. He ensured that he was
obeyed, but at the same time he lacked the persistence to pursue a
radical transformation of the administration or even to insist that there
should be unity among his ministers. He was also inclined to spend
lavishly in both time and money on his own pleasures.[28] There was no
sense of wartime austerity at court: the *Fasching* carnivals were still held
every January, and in July 1708 Joseph's birthday was celebrated 'with an
opera at night, presented in the garden of the . . . Favourite, where all
the actors appeared on horseback, and in triumphal chariots, after the
manner of the antient Romans'.[29] On the other hand he kept his mistresses, confessors and personal favourites well in the background and
listened to the abler men around him. He recognized and usually supported Eugene's supremacy in military affairs; for example in a conference of 8 October 1705 he insisted that everything possible should be
done to support him in Italy. He was the most effective emperor the
prince served and the one he was happiest under. The successes of his
short reign (1705–11) cannot be attributed solely to his servants: Joseph
also played his part.

---

* An Englishman commented in 1707 that 'The Court has been at thirty miles
distance from hence three days hunting of bears, an animal I would rather goe
something out of my way to avoid than travel thirty miles to pursue.'[26]

Immediately on his accession Joseph dismissed Harrach, Mansfeld, Buccelini and Heister, and appointed prince Salm *Obristhofmeister* and president of a smaller *Conferenz* of up to five ministers. The court chancery was divided into two and a first and second *Hofkanzler* appointed, Seilern and Sinzendorff, both protégés of Joseph's uncle, the elector palatine; Seilern was a conscientious lawyer from the Empire and an artisan's son. But the direction of foreign policy now really lay outside the *Hofkanzlei* and fell to Wratislaw, who dominated it from the rather unusual position of second Bohemian chancellor, where he was free from the routine of the *Hofkanzlei*. The Imperial vice-chancellor, Kaunitz, died in 1705 and was replaced by the young nephew of the elector of Mainz, Frederick Charles Schönborn, who as yet had little influence and was kept out of the conference. As Gundaker Starhemberg was confirmed as president of the chamber and as Eugene remained in his posts, power came to reside completely in the hands of men who had associated with Eugene in his struggle against the old ministers. Most of them were still in their thirties and forties and were determined to assert and expand Austrian power. Stepney, who had quarrelled violently with Wratislaw over Austria's insistence on suppressing the Hungarian rebellion by force, condemned them as 'a sett of young ministers violent and arrogant'.[30]

The weaknesses of the new régime were twofold: the inevitable divisions which soon appeared among the ministers and the permanent financial problems which made them heavily dependent on help from the Maritime Powers. Once Joseph became ruler a more determined effort could be made by Gundaker Starhemberg to rationalize the use of what funds were available. After 1705 Imperial finances were not to get into the desperate plight of the Salaburg era again and the revenues which were not dependent on the estates doubled. But the basic problem of inadequate contributions from the estates remained throughout this and the following reign.

The divisions between the ministers appeared almost at once. Even before Leopold's death, the duke of Moles, who was a close friend of Wratislaw, was trying to supplant Starhemberg as president of the chamber. Although Moles was to leave Vienna as ambassador to Charles in Spain in 1706, a great deal of hostility remained between Starhemberg and Wratislaw until the latter's death,[31] and this led to similar coolness between Starhemberg and Eugene in these years. But more important were the attempts by the rude and domineering prince Salm to make himself the real director of the whole government. The uncle of Joseph's wife Amelia and an Imperial prince in his own right, he saw Wratislaw and Eugene as standing in his way to supreme power. In fact what really stood in his way, besides his own chronic ill health, was Joseph himself, who suffered but did not like his former tutor.

Salm had fought in the Turkish wars and considered himself, not unreasonably, something of a military expert. He was highly critical of Eugene's Italian campaign of 1705, and this criticism was reinforced by Guido Starhemberg when he returned to Vienna at the end of the year before replacing Heister as commander of the Imperial forces in Hungary. Guido claimed that Eugene could have brought direct help to Victor Amadeus if he had wanted to.[32] For his part Eugene was angry because he believed Salm had failed to back up his Italian campaign and was interfering in the running of the *Hofkriegsrat*. To be fair to Salm, the war council was hardly likely to run with maximum effectiveness when the president, Eugene, could only be there in the winter. There was inevitably plenty of resentment at what seemed to be Eugene's attempt to control everything and to consider no other interests except those involved in winning the war, particularly winning it where he was actually in command. In a stormy conference on 22 March 1706 Eugene was told to his face in front of Salm, but evidently not by him, 'that since the time of the Friedlander [Wallenstein] it had been a maxim of the house of Austria not to entrust the sword and the purse to the same person', and that he was 'not to have anything to do with financial matters except by express order'.[33]

While Eugene was away the main opposition to Salm came from Wratislaw. Although he had little support from the other ministers, except Moles, Wratislaw had the decided advantage of the deep trust and friendship of both Joseph and his brother Charles in Spain. He acted as the essential link between the two brothers, who had been deeply suspicious of each other before Charles left Austria. All the time the archduke (or Charles III as he was called by the allies) was in Spain, Wratislaw kept up an intimate and affectionate correspondence with him, often being addressed by Charles as 'My fat one'. He was one of the first ministers to grasp that Charles might eventually inherit the Austrian throne, if Joseph and Amelia did not have a male heir. In such a case, as he wrote to Charles at the end of 1706, it would be unrealistic for him to rule both Germany and Spain, although he could rule Germany and Italy.

Although the ministerial quarrels led to a great deal of bitterness throughout Joseph's reign, they were largely personal disputes; all the ministers were equally determined to fight France as vigorously as possible. The quarrels did little to undermine Eugene's military position, as Joseph himself paid scant attention to Salm's military advice and showed plenty of personal initiative in backing up Eugene's requests for help in Vienna.

The one area where there was a difference in policy was that Salm, usually backed by the first *Hofkanzler* Seilern, saw Joseph mainly in terms of his position as head of the Empire, whose chief interest should be to defend German territorial integrity against France and to regain the lands lost to her. Wratislaw was more concerned about the development of Austria herself as a great power with territorial ambitions in Italy and, to some extent, in Bavaria. He was ready not only to renounce Habsburg claims in Alsace but also in Spain and the Spanish Netherlands, if only the Spanish lands in Italy could be kept. Despite his friendship with the archduke Charles, he was always to be deaf to his appeals for Austrian military help in Spain. While Eugene shared these ideas of Wratislaw in the main, he nevertheless saw the need for at least a strong *Reich* barrier against France.

XI

Turin and Toulon

If there was an *annus mirabilis* of the War of Spanish Succession, it was surely 1706, when the allies conquered northern Italy and most of the Southern Netherlands and forced the French king into an increasingly desperate struggle for survival. Although it was a year in which both the English and Austrian commanders-in-chief won stunning victories separately, the success of the Austrian campaign in Italy depended heavily on the Maritime Powers. Not only did the English loan pay for five months' campaigning but large numbers of troops in Eugene's army were German auxiliaries hired by the Maritime Powers – these increased in strength during 1706 from 18,000 to 28,000.

The Italian campaign began on a note of disaster. As Eugene came to join his troops in mid-April, he found them being driven back into the mountains around Lake Garda after being sharply beaten by Vendôme at Calcinato on 19 April. He managed to organize an orderly retreat and took the loss of 3,000 dead calmly enough, refusing to courtmartial Reventlau, who had been left in charge, as it would only 'show that not everyone can command an army'.[1] He spent the next two months training and distilling tough discipline into the men he had and waiting for the arrival of the auxiliary troops from Germany. Able to pay his men regularly, he could now insist that they behave in an orderly fashion, and it was his boast during the year that both peasants' and nobles' homes were safe and that crops were brought in undisturbed.

Eugene stayed in the mountains throughout May and most of June 1706; this lulled the French into a sense of false security. Vendôme constructed defensive lines along the river Adige, which he felt sure Eugene would never breach; in the west La Feuillade appeared certain to take Turin during the summer. But Turin held on, skilfully defended by the Imperial general, Daun, and La Feuillade's troops wasted their energies in fruitless chases after Victor Amadeus and his cavalry in the mountains which surrounded the city.[2]

When Eugene felt ready to move at the end of June, he marched south along the Adige, finding a weak spot in the French defences at Rovigo and crossing there on 6 July. He then continued southwards, upsetting Vendôme's calculations that he would have to keep close to the Tyrol and his magazines. By mid-July Eugene's army crossed the Po and began to move westwards along the Po valley. Outflanked, his strategy of defending the Adige in ruins, Vendôme was still cheerfully optimistic, writing to the French war minister Chamillart, on 10 July: 'As to the siege of Turin you can count on it definitely that Prince Eugene cannot upset it; there are plenty of places where we can stop him if he is thinking of trying to come to its rescue.'[3]

It was fortunate for Vendôme's reputation that he left Italy at this point, being recalled urgently to take command in the Netherlands. Here Villeroy's army had been smashed by Marlborough at Ramillies on 23 May and was retreating in disorder, leaving the whole of the Spanish Netherlands, and possibly France itself, open to the Anglo-Dutch army. Eugene cannot have been sorry to see the back of the man who had effectively parried all his moves in Italy since 1702.

Louis XIV replaced Vendôme by his young nephew the duke of Orleans, who was to be heavily dependent on the advice of his generals, particularly of Marsin, who accompanied him to Italy. Unfortunately Marsin was a singularly unlucky commander, having shared in the defeats at Blenheim and Ramillies; during the coming months he suffered from acute, almost incapacitating depression. Both men made the initial serious error of concentrating on protecting Lombardy from a flank attack by Eugene instead of blocking his march to Turin: they refused to believe he was making straight for the besieged city.

During July and August Eugene's army continued westwards along the south bank of the Po, meeting hardly any French opposition. Although he had 30,000 men, Eugene could do without the magazines in the Tyrol because he had enough money to buy food on the march. The main problem, in sharp contrast to the previous year, was heat and drought: the soldiers had to march by moonlight. Nevertheless by 29 August the army reached Carmagnola where Victor Amadeus was waiting for it with his small force.

Orleans finally realized that Eugene's destination was Turin and rushed there with what men he could to strengthen La Feuillade's besieging army. The French commanders argued fiercely over what to do. La Feuillade and Marsin rejected Orleans's proposal to move out and attack the enemy and insisted that they should wait for Eugene's army in their entrenchments surrounding the city. It was out of keeping with

French military thinking, especially that of Louis XIV himself, to seek a decisive battle in the manner of Eugene and Marlborough, but Marsin also felt that any action on his part would be useless. He wrote to Chamillart on 6 September in a letter which he entrusted to his confessor:

> ... this letter is only to be delivered to you once I am dead ... Ever since I received the King's orders to go to Italy I have been unable to rid myself of the conviction that I shall be killed in this campaign; and thoughts of death ... force themselves on me and possess me at every moment of the day and night ... P.S. At this minute the enemy are crossing the Po.[4]

Eugene and Victor Amadeus were indeed crossing the river in preparation for an attack on the French army from the west the following day. Four days earlier, on 2 September, they had observed the French from the top of the high Superga hill and had seen that they were unprepared for an attack and particularly vulnerable at one point. Eugene had remarked triumphantly to his cousin: 'They seem already half beaten to me.'[5] It was this weak point that the Imperial and Savoyard army attacked early in the morning of 7 September. The Imperial grenadiers and Prussian infantry under prince 'Bulldog' Anhalt-Dessau broke through the French defences and let the cavalry in. Eugene was prepared for heavy losses and did not spare himself. Two of his personal servants were killed in the attack and he himself was thrown from a wounded horse. Even though only a part of their army was beaten, and their casualties were a third less than those of the Imperialists, the French raised the siege and fled. Orleans was wounded twice but managed to organize the retreat. The unfortunate Marsin's fears came true: badly wounded in the thigh, he died after one of Victor Amadeus's surgeons amputated his leg. A general massacre by the Imperialists of the French wounded was only prevented by Eugene stepping in quickly to prevent it. Five thousand men and 3,000 horses, as well as most of the French baggage, were captured by the victorious army.

Eugene's march across northern Italy had kept the newspaper-reading public in the allied countries on tenterhooks during the summer; his defeat of a much larger French army and his relief of Turin led to a great outburst of public excitement, particularly in England. Marlborough was delighted, for although Eugene's victory rather overshadowed his own success at Ramillies, no one had worked harder for the relief of Turin than he had. He wrote to his wife, 'It is impossible for me to express the joy it has given me; for I do not only esteem but I really love the prince.'[6] For his part Eugene readily acknowledged that the victory had only been possible because of English cash.

The battle of Turin was immediately followed by the occupation of Lombardy by the Imperialists, the French troops there following the example of those under Orleans in Piedmont and shutting themselves up in garrisons. On 26 September Eugene and Victor Amadeus entered the city of Milan and found most of the local population ready to welcome a change of masters. Troops could now be quartered there and in neighbouring Parma at will. Parma, Tuscany and some of the Papal states were immediately forced to pay contributions, which during the next year, 1707, amounted to 2 million gulden. These were badly needed, because once the English money ran out the Imperial army was as poor as ever.[7] By March 1707 Eugene was again complaining bitterly at being starved of funds, and he wrote a heavily sarcastic letter to prince Salm, who had expressed his incredulity that Eugene's army had been kept short of reinforcements and supplies by the Imperial government and had wondered how in any case difficulties could arise in 'such a pleasant and fertile country' as Italy. He told Salm, 'All this is just as possible and natural as that such a pleasant and rich country as the Austrian monarchy can never fulfil requests for money, credit and supplies because of maladministration.'[8]

Despite these perennial financial problems, by the beginning of 1707 the Imperial army was in an impregnable position in northern Italy. The defeat at Turin following on that of Ramillies plunged Louis XIV into despair. While struggling to present a brave face, he is said to have shed tears when alone with Madame de Maintenon. Even in public the strain was beginning to show: he had been kind to his old friend Villeroy, comforting him after Ramillies with 'Monsieur le Maréchal, one is no longer lucky at our age',[9] but when La Feuillade appeared at court Louis turned his back on him. Eventually he concluded that his main priorities must be to defend the northern frontier of France and to support Philip V in Spain, where the archduke Charles and Anglo-Dutch troops had established themselves in Catalonia. Hoping to salvage the French forces still in Italy, Louis negotiated with Eugene during the winter. On 13 March 1707 Eugene signed a convention allowing all Bourbon troops to leave: he did this to avoid having to mop up the remaining garrisons, although inevitably his action angered the Maritime Powers.

Soon after the victory of Turin Eugene had been appointed viceroy of Milan. This post with a salary of 150,000 gulden a year was Eugene's reward, and the gift marked a great political coup for the prince and Wratislaw. Although Charles conferred the dignity on him from Spain, Eugene's real orders were to come from Vienna: this was an attempt to

hide from the allies the secret family compact of 1703 which had
assigned Milan to the Austrian branch of the Habsburgs.

On 16 April 1707 Eugene entered Milan in state, riding a splendid
armoured warhorse and then changing to a six-horse carriage to go to
the cathedral for a *Te Deum*. The streets were carpeted and flower-strewn,
fountains ran with the proverbial wine, and in the evening the ducal
palace was illuminated and there were bonfires and fireworks. The beginning of Austria's century and a half long rule in Lombardy was an
enthusiastic one.

One man who looked on the scenes in Milan with undisguised anger
was Eugene's cousin Victor Amadeus. He had hoped to be viceroy himself and now feared that the Austrians were trying to wriggle out of the
clause in their treaty of 1703 which promised part of Milan and the
Montferrat to him. It took a good deal of pressure from the Maritime
Powers before the emperor reluctantly began to hand over these areas
of western Lombardy in 1707 and 1708. Well in the forefront of those
who wanted to retain the territories was Eugene, who was also a firm
advocate of the decision at this time to annex Mantua outright on the
grounds that the duke was an Imperial vassal who had committed
treason. He saw the duchy as 'the key to all Italy'.[10]

The Imperialists were now in a position to put into effect what had
been a goal of Austrian policy since Leopold's reign: to assert the
emperor's feudal rights in Italy.[11] This tied in closely with Wratislaw and
Eugene's ideas of expanding there by annexing all the Spanish provinces
in the peninsula. After conquering Milan the next step for the Imperialists was to take Naples and Sicily from Philip of Anjou's supporters.
At the beginning of 1707, therefore, plans were put in train for an expedition to southern Italy. Wratislaw was the driving force behind this,
but Eugene supported what was also a project dear to both the Habsburg
brothers.

The plans for the Naples expedition went ahead in the teeth of fierce
opposition from the Maritime Powers, who felt that the Austrians could
more usefully deploy their men directly against France or Spain and
feared an unacceptable increase in Austrian power in Italy, even though
Joseph claimed to be acting on behalf of his brother. This opposition
made the Imperialists even more determined, particularly as they suspected, with some justification, that the Dutch hoped to offer Naples to
Philip of Anjou as compensation for Spain in an eventual peace settlement. Eugene worked hard to send the 10,000 troops which left for
Naples in May 1707 under Daun. During the summer and autumn the
kingdom of Naples was conquered easily enough: no help could be sent

from France or Spain because of the presence of the Anglo-Dutch fleet in the Mediterranean. The Austrians were quick 'to make the most of the kingdom' by forcing it to contribute to their war effort.[12]

While the expedition was being prepared Eugene was concerned lest the Maritime Powers show their annoyance by withdrawing the auxiliary troops from his army in northern Italy. To conciliate them he agreed to support a pet project of their own: an attack on the French port of Toulon, which Marlborough had proposed to him in a letter of 27 December 1706. The English commander-in-chief believed that an army from Italy under Eugene, supported by an Anglo-Dutch fleet, could effect what was essentially his own plan and what had become his first priority. This action would destroy the French Mediterranean fleet's base, ease the pressure in Spain and Flanders by forcing Louis to divert his forces, and allow Marlborough to bring France to a dictated peace by a simultaneous attack from the Netherlands. The early Bourbon victory in Spain at Almanza in April 1707 and then the breach of the Lines of Stollhofen in Germany by Villars the next month, following the death of Louis of Baden in January, made Marlborough even more intent on Toulon. On 5 June 1707 he wrote to Wratislaw: 'England and Holland base all their hopes on the Italian plan and are convinced that the whole future of the campaign and even of the war depends on it.'[13]

Although Eugene was personally in favour of some kind of attack on France's south-eastern border, it is clear that he never felt an expedition against Toulon was practicable but knew he would have to agree to it for the sake of Naples. In February 1707 he wrote to Joseph that 'the Provence and Toulon expedition will have to be agreed to so as not to disgust the Maritime Powers and to get the fleet [i.e. to get the fleet into the Mediterranean to cover the Naples expedition] but we should prepare secretly for Naples'.[14] Although the new English minister in Vienna, the earl of Manchester, was assured by Joseph that Eugene had positive orders to proceed against Toulon, he found all the ministers spoke 'very doubtfully of that [campaign] of France, and of the difficulties it would meet with . . .'[15]

At first Eugene raised no objections to the Toulon venture and assured the English minister to Savoy, Chetwynd, just after the Naples expeditionary force set out in May, that 'we should certainly attempt ye project agreed upon, & yt as to him he had all ready made ye necessary dispositions'.[16] But the Imperial and Savoyard force was slow to move towards France. This was partly a result of the need to see the Naples expedition safely on its way, but more important was that Victor Amadeus fell ill, the passes into France were blocked by snow for longer than usual and the Anglo-Dutch fleet did not reach Italy till mid-June. When it arrived Eugene voiced his first serious objections, and the earl of Manchester, who visited his camp at this time, came away convinced that 'they have no great mind to take Toulon . . . their whole mind is set on Italy'.[17] With the Austrian expeditionary force established in Naples, there was less need to be accommodating, and on 13 July Wratislaw wrote bluntly to Marlborough that 'we risk our army, in the sole view of pleasing England, and endeavouring to ruin the French marine'.[18]

An increasingly serious reason for Austrian reluctance and nervousness over Toulon was the position on her own northern frontier during the spring and summer. The previous September Charles XII of Sweden had taken what seemed to be the decisive step in breaking up the coalition of Denmark, Saxony-Poland and Russia which had attacked him in 1700, when he forced Augustus of Saxony-Poland to make peace at Altranstädt in Saxony and to abdicate the Polish throne in favour of Charles's protégé, Stanislas Leszczyński. During the following months from his camp in Saxony, Charles at times threatened to interfere in Silesia on behalf of Joseph's Protestant subjects, whose rights Sweden had guaranteed at the peace of Westphalia. There were also fears that he might help the largely Protestant Hungarian rebels, whom Guido Starhemberg had failed to suppress, and even that he might enter the War of Spanish Succession on the French side. To prevent a clash between Charles and Austria, Marlborough went to his camp in April 1707 only to find him preparing to move eastwards against Peter the Great of Russia and willing enough for a settlement with Austria if Joseph recognized the rights of his Silesian Protestants. Although Salm, Seilern and Schönborn pressed Joseph to stand up to Charles even at the risk of war, he sensibly listened to the advice of Wratislaw and Eugene to accept the Swedish king's terms. A war with Sweden was the last thing both men wanted at this juncture and they were dismissive of Peter the Great's offer of an alliance and help to suppress the Hungarian revolt. When Peter also proposed that Eugene should oppose the Swedish puppet, Leszczyński, as a candidate for the Polish throne, the prince hardly took this suggestion seriously. Although he left the final decision on the matter entirely to Joseph, when a Russian envoy approached him in Italy he sent him away with very general replies, for, as he confided to Marlborough, the Russian proposals were 'chimerical notions'.[19] The crisis in the north only ended in September 1707, when agreement was finally reached with Charles XII and he turned his back on Germany for his adventure against Russia and eventual defeat at Poltava.

The Toulon expedition got under way at last on 30 June when about 35,000 troops left Piedmont to move through the mountains towards the French Mediterranean coast. Although Victor Amadeus was in nominal command, real control of what were largely German auxiliary troops, paid for by the Maritime Powers, was in Eugene's hands. Within a fortnight the allies had taken Nice, meeting little French resistance, but already by 12 July Eugene was beginning to express strong doubts about continuing because of their extended lines of communication and the difficult mountainous terrain. However, in a council of war held on his flagship, the determined and obstinate English admiral Shovell supported Victor Amadeus in allaying these doubts.

The allies continued to meet minimal French opposition as they advanced. The local commander, Tessé, had at first been unsure where the enemy intended to strike but had later concentrated all available troops in Provence and Dauphiné on Toulon. Louis XIV meanwhile rushed men from the Rhine and Spain to southern France, although he was convinced that the invasion posed no real danger, declaring it was a 'rash and impracticable act . . . it will cost them dearly!'[20] But in the short run it was the local population who suffered most. Contributions were levied as a matter of course and the army, especially the Hessian auxiliaries, plundered relentlessly, neither their own officers nor Eugene having much control over them.[21] The Anglo-Dutch fleet mounted small terror raids on the coast, landing troops and burning crops. The allied devastation of Provence that summer was later calculated to have caused over 6.5 million livres damage.

As it plundered and burnt its way along the narrow coastal road, the army moved more and more slowly, suffering from heat and thirst. On 26 July it reached the outskirts of Toulon, where Tessé had had the past fortnight to organize the defences, getting 4,000 marines and peasants to level gardens and villas to construct defence works and assembling forty battalions inside the town. When he saw these defences, Eugene immediately advised a retreat in a council of war on the 28th. Although he had to accept Shovell and Victor Amadeus's demand to attack Toulon he insisted that the allies undertake a conventional siege of the town rather than immediately storming it.

During the next three weeks the allied army besieged Toulon amidst growing quarrels and difficulties. French reinforcements entered the port at will from the west and most of the Bavarian and French prisoners drafted into the Imperial army after Blenheim deserted, complaining that their bread was 'no bigger than a man's fist, and also very black'. Having to drink from contaminated streams, before long the troops were hit by the 'bloody flux' (dysentery), which was made worse because they camped in vineyards and olive groves: 'The grapes which the Germans eat every day, and the verjuice which they drink instead of wine, encreased the flux among 'em.'[22] Their officers suffered far less and maintained good relations with those of the enemy. Tessé had ice sent over every day and made Eugene a present of a topcoat.

The quarrels among the allied leaders became increasingly bitter. Victor Amadeus tried hard to keep in with the English by working closely with the young minister to his court, Chetwynd. Both accused Eugene of not pushing the siege forward energetically enough, Chetwynd writing home that 'most people here think his Highness has not had ye same mettle in this as in other things'.[23] This complaint was confirmed by the Palatine general Rehbinder, who wrote to Marlborough in despair, 'I cannot figure to myself any siege or bombardment conducted in the way I saw this business.'[24] Chetwynd also criticized the prince's organization of the army, claiming 'there is so much disorder and confusion in ye German commissariat, their artillery and everything yt belongs to them'.[25]

Eugene was quick to defend himself in his letters home. He wrote to Wratislaw that even though Victor Amadeus saw 'the great difficulties, not to say impossibilities, of this operation', he was trying to shift the whole responsibility on to him so as 'not to disgust England and Holland'. He justified his own caution: 'I readily hazard when I have the least appearance of succeeding' but 'I shall not, from complaisance for England, and for a little envoy [Chetwynd] who is here, advise a thing if I see it impossible ... It is the most difficult operation I have seen in my life.'[26] What was clear to Eugene, but not to the English, especially admiral Shovell, who did 'not understand land warfare',[27] was that even if the allies managed to take Toulon, the army could not hold on to it and would soon have to be shipped out by the fleet.

On 20 August Shovell at last agreed to a retreat because the scale of French reinforcements made the venture hopeless. The next day the allied fleet, which had been kept far from shore by contrary winds, managed to come close in and bombarded the French fleet in the harbour, although most of the French ships had already been scuttled to block the port. As these ships were never refloated, the French Toulon fleet disappeared for the rest of the war and this ensured total allied supremacy in the Mediterranean. On the 22nd the allied army moved out, marching quickly along the coast road and reaching Piedmont by the first week of September. The behaviour of the troops was as bad as ever, the route being 'marked by all sorts of violence such as fire, murder and rapes'. Chetwynd observed sarcastically that in spite of the pace, 'we have not those complaints at present of long marches, as we had before, wch I think plainly shows ye ill will with wch we went'.[28]

The idea of seizing Toulon was ill-conceived: dependent on contact with Italy along a poor coastal road, the allied forces could only have held the town by means of continuous naval support, especially as there was no thought of occupying Provence itself. A full-scale assault from the sea would have been a better idea, and in fact the destruction of the French fleet was achieved in this way. The allied venture did, however, cause Louis to divert substantial forces south at a time when he appeared on the point of a breakthrough in Spain and along the Rhine. It was unfortunate that Marlborough was unable to cash in on this in Flanders, since, as Eugene put it in a consoling letter to him, he had been 're-strained by the great circumspection of the dutch [field] deputies, who, ignorant of our profession, follow the opinion of their generals, who know nothing but defensive warfare'.[29]

The expedition finally shattered Eugene's relations with his cousin Victor Amadeus, which had not been easy for a decade. The prince was also becoming increasingly aware that the duke had ambitions for the whole of the duchy of Milan, and he warned Joseph against reducing the number of troops there. Relations between Savoy and Austria were to be bad for the rest of the war, despite their nominal alliance. Nevertheless, by the close of 1707 the Austrians had achieved a predominant position in Italy with control of Milan, Mantua and Naples. For them this had been the major objective of the war, and they could now afford to shift their military efforts elsewhere, to the Rhine and the Netherlands but also to Hungary. When Eugene left Milan for Vienna on 28 November, he left both his viceroyalty and Italy for good.

XII

The Conquest of the Southern Netherlands

By the end of 1707 the character of the War of Spanish Succession was changing. With the expulsion of the French from Italy and the increasing ability of Philip V to depend on native support in his fight with the archduke Charles and his Anglo-Dutch army in Spain, Louis began to concentrate all his efforts on the defence of France itself, falling back on the massive fortress system along his northern and eastern borders. The defeat of France would face the allies with a mammoth task.

It had become clear to Eugene during the Toulon expedition that France would never be forced to a peace acceptable to the allies by an invasion from the south-east. The allies could neither field nor effectively supply a large enough army there from Germany or even from northern Italy, and this theatre of war was in any case too far away from the centre of French power, Paris. Decisive victory could only be achieved in the north, and it was there that Eugene needed to be. Therefore, on his way back from Toulon, the prince wrote to Marlborough suggesting that the allies should stand on the defensive in Savoy and Spain during 1708 and that a new army should be built on the Moselle for him to command. This force could be used to co-operate with either the army on the Rhine or in the Netherlands, and command over it would allow Eugene to get to the northern theatre of war without offending the new commander of the Imperial army on the Rhine, George Louis, elector of Hanover, who had replaced the disastrous marquis of Bayreuth appointed after Baden's death the previous year.

Marlborough was unable to take up Eugene's offer immediately, not because it did not appeal to him but because he and his close friend and political ally, Godolphin, were in deep political trouble in England. They were gradually losing their hold on queen Anne and having to depend heavily on Whig support against Tory moves to oust them. Part of the price for this support was a firmer commitment to the war in Spain. Under Whig pressure Marlborough was forced to ask Joseph to send Eugene to Spain: it seemed that only the prince could save the situation there after a series of disasters for the allied cause during 1707. But in calling for Eugene to be sent, Marlborough felt fairly sure that the prince would refuse.

Eugene certainly did not want to go to Spain: he knew there was no chance of a sizeable army being assembled there, and on his return to Vienna at the end of 1707 he found Salm and his friends pressing for him to be sent. They calculated that once he had gone, they could persuade Joseph to make Guido Starhemberg president of the war council. The prince soon managed to turn the tables on them by getting Joseph to send Guido Starhemberg to Spain. Nevertheless the episode was annoying to Eugene and a further example of what he and Wratislaw saw as Salm's harmful influence on the war. They blamed him for Villars's success in surprising Bayreuth and crossing the Rhine during the summer and for the monarchy's persistent failure to suppress the revolt in Hungary.[1] For the first time also Eugene was beginning to express some doubts about Joseph himself, writing to archduke Charles in March 1708 that the emperor was doing nothing to end the quarrels among his ministers. In fact Joseph was now spending more time with his mistresses and hunting, even writing love letters during the conference. Salm was also firmly entrenched in power: he could depend on most of the ministers as well as on the empress Amelia. Moreover Wratislaw and Eugene dared not press for his dismissal or resignation as the alternative was worse: it looked as though Joseph would replace him as *Obristhofmeister* by cardinal Lamberg, an incompetent governor of Bavaria and the uncle of the emperor's 'chief favourite', count Lamberg.[2] Salm therefore stayed on and continued to snipe at Eugene, trying in 1708 to have him replaced as viceroy of Milan by the duke of Modena, who was related to both himself and the empress Amelia. However, Eugene managed to hold on to Milan through the support of Wratislaw and of Charles in Spain. The problem of Salm's successor was finally resolved at the end of 1708, when Eugene wrote to Wratislaw to warn Joseph that he would resign if Lamberg were appointed. This led to Joseph's assuring Wratislaw that when Salm did resign he would replace him by prince Trautsohn, who was acceptable to both him and Eugene. The emperor was also quick to write a conciliatory letter to Eugene early in 1709 when the prince stayed away from court after one of his nephews was insulted by the empress Amelia at a *Fasching* ball. And it was on Wratislaw's advice that Joseph divided the conference into two in

March 1709, creating an inner conference, which was largely intended to formulate foreign policy. But as both Salm and his ally Seilern were among its members, this step brought little immediate satisfaction to Eugene and Wratislaw.

The political uncertainty in England did not promise well for the 1708 campaign, and Marlborough for one was deeply pessimistic at the beginning of the year. However, at least Eugene would not be going to Spain but would command instead on the Moselle. On 26 March Eugene left Vienna for The Hague, hoping to meet Marlborough as soon as he reached the Netherlands from England, to work out a joint strategy for the campaign. The prince made an essential halt on the way at Hanover, where he had to break the news of the proposed Moselle army to the elector. Their meeting was not a success: both men took an instant dislike to each other and the prince reported a 'quite frosty' reception from George Louis,[3] who objected strongly to a proposal which by reducing the number of men he himself would have on the Rhine appeared to be an attempt to put him in the shade. After an unsuccessful two days Eugene went on to The Hague, where Marlborough arrived soon after.

Marlborough had left England determined that this summer should bring the decisive battle, which had escaped him the previous year and which would force the French to sue for peace. Although it was almost four years since he and Eugene had worked together, the same magic was still there and the two commanders could immediately get down to their charts to plan the campaign. Only the Dutch pensionary Heinsius was taken into their confidence.

As commander of the English forces in the Netherlands Marlborough had suffered constantly since Ramillies from the Dutch generals' and field deputies' reluctance to allow their troops to do more than cooperate with him in cautious moves to defend the Flemish cities. Eugene had no time for them and had written to the duke three years earlier in 1705: 'It is extremely cruel that opinions so weak and discordant should have obstructed the progress of your operations . . . I speak to you as a sincere friend. You will never be able to perform anything considerable with your army unless you are absolute . . . '[4] He now used his own considerable prestige and influence with the Dutch leaders to obtain a much freer hand for Marlborough. At the same time the two men agreed that Eugene's Moselle army, which was to be made up almost entirely of German troops paid for by the Maritime Powers, should assemble on the Moselle to confuse the French and then come quickly to the Netherlands to join Marlborough's forces.

The complicating factor was the elector George Louis, who had not yet agreed to the idea of a Moselle army. Therefore at the end of April Marlborough and Eugene went to Hanover for three days. Relations between the prince and the tetchy elector were no better, although George's mother, the old electress Sophia, was less hostile. She considered that Eugene was probably an acquired taste but acknowledged that he was a refined courtier with good manners and plenty of sense and spirit, despite his ugliness and addiction to his 'disgusting snuff'.[5] Marlborough, however, made a far better impression, and it was his charm and diplomatic expertise which eventually, and inevitably, extracted George's grudging consent. But the elector was not told that the Moselle army was intended to go to the Netherlands, a deception which he never forgave. After promising that his troops would be assembled within a month, Eugene left for Vienna and Marlborough returned to The Hague.

Eugene could not leave Austria till 5 June because of the demands on his time as president of the war council and the endemic problem of raising cash. The estates of the hereditary lands were becoming increasingly reluctant to disgorge more recruits and money. Taxation was steadily mounting. Even taverns used for dancing were taxed 'a florin for every fiddler who is admitted to play'.[6] The discontent at the heavy taxation was eventually to lead to fears that Bohemia would revolt.[7] In Italy the contributions raised barely supported the troops there, while in Bavaria they had to be collected by force.

Marlborough meanwhile fretted in case the French should strike first: he wrote to Godolphin on 4 June 1708, 'I would not willingly blame Prince Eugene, but his arrival at the Moselle will be ten days after his promise.'[8] Without Eugene and his troops, he would have to revert once more to a static defence of the Flemish towns seized after Ramillies two years before. In the event it was only at the end of June that two-thirds of Eugene's army assembled at Koblenz, delayed by difficulties in hiring troops from the German princes. This allowed the French to seize the initiative, as Marlborough had feared. Despite eight years of war Louis XIV was still able to field huge numbers of men: his absolutist system of government and France's large population continued to give him a fair chance of holding out longer than the allies. Max Emmanuel was given a force on the Rhine and another was sent under Berwick to guard against any attack along the Moselle from Eugene. Louis had little need to listen to Max Emmanuel's advice that with Eugene 'they had to deal with a cunning fox, who knew many tricks'.[9] Already by the end of May the king was fairly certain that Eugene's troops would move to the

Netherlands, and he therefore ordered Berwick to operate flexibly. The bulk of Louis's forces, however, were already in the Southern Netherlands, where his devout young grandson, the duke of Burgundy, had been sent to command with Vendôme under him. Louis was confident that, with Berwick's army, Burgundy would outnumber the allies and have 'the means to make a glorious campaign'.[10] Unfortunately he failed to consider how his sheltered and refined grandson would get on with the rough-and-ready 'soldiers' general', Vendôme.

For two years since Ramillies the Belgian provinces, stretching from Brussels northwards, had been controlled and administered by a joint Anglo-Dutch condominium, which was suffered sullenly by the local population. But in the first week of July the citizens of Ghent and Bruges opened their gates to Burgundy and Vendôme's army. This meant that the French now dominated the whole coastline south of Antwerp and the river and canal system of western Flanders. Heavily outnumbered by the French, Marlborough had also been outmanoeuvred. Already depressed by the prospects for the campaign and worried by the increasing crisis at home, where his wife and the queen were estranged and the Whigs pressing strongly for more ministerial posts, this proved the last straw. He suffered physical and mental collapse and seemed a broken man. He paid no attention to the demands from the Dutch field deputies for action.

On 6 July Eugene reached his camp at Assche, having rushed ahead of his army with a small escort of hussars. On embracing the duke, Eugene was shocked by his appearance and admission that 'I am sick in body and spirit'.[11] His arrival saved the situation. The confusion in the camp settled down, and Marlborough's confidence revived as Eugene took over much of the detail of staff work and shared the awful responsibility which had momentarily proved too much for Marlborough. He brought an air of firmness and confidence, telling the Prussian general Grumbkow that if the local population remained hostile, 'they must be put to the fire and sword'.[12] Another Prussian general, Natzmer, summed up the change: the army regained its 'courage . . . through God's help and with the assistance of Prince Eugene'.[13]

Within a matter of hours the two leaders had decided that the situation was too dangerous to wait for Eugene's force from the Moselle to reach them: they must act at once to prevent the French seizing control of the Scheldt and, if possible, to force them to battle. The prince agreed to stay with the duke, but in the short while that the army was preparing to march he rode into Brussels. Here his mother Olympia was dangerously, in fact mortally, ill: she died later in the year. Eugene stayed only an hour or two away, for the allied troops were already on the move. In a remarkable march from Brussels – covering fifty miles in sixty hours – the army raced along the dusty roads of western Flanders with its rich farmland and neat cottages. On 11 July they reached the river Scheldt at Oudenarde just as the French army was crossing further north. Vendôme was amazed when he heard of the enemy's presence, exclaiming 'the devil must have carried them, such marching is impossible!'[14]

The battle of Oudenarde was very different from most eighteenth-century battles which were fought between armies carefully and laboriously positioned in their lines beforehand. This engagement grew out of an initial brush between the leading columns of the two armies as Marlborough and Eugene pressed their men forward, determined to force the French to a fight before they could withdraw. Since Vendôme and Burgundy were already over the Scheldt somewhat to the north of Oudenarde, they should have had little trouble in repulsing the first allied troops as they crossed their flimsy pontoon bridges. But, as ever, there was confusion in the French command: Vendôme and Burgundy had argued throughout the campaign, and now in the battle a large body of troops directly under Burgundy stayed out of the struggle, drawn up on some high ground, causing Vendôme to write scathingly to Louis afterwards: 'I cannot comprehend how 60 battalions and 180 squadrons could be satisfied with observing us engaged for 6 hours and merely look on as though watching the opera from a third-tier box.'[15] At one point during the battle the French were surrounded and Vendôme dismounted and joined the fray with a short pike in his hand. Only desperate French resistance, contesting every hedge, ditch and cottage, staved off complete disaster and allowed most of their troops to slip away under cover of darkness and heavy rain. Even so 7,000 prisoners were taken, many through a ruse of Eugene, who ordered Huguenot drummers and officers to give the rallying calls for several French regiments.

Once again the allied commanders had co-operated remarkably and had received full support from the Dutch. While Eugene and the Dutch fieldmarshal Ouwerkerk had effectively led the allied forces on the field of battle, overall control had remained in Marlborough's hands. The two friends considered it a joint victory, the Englishman writing later in the month, 'I dare say Prince Eugene and I shall never differ about our share of laurels.'[16] There was also general praise for the enthusiasm of the young electoral prince of Hanover, the later George II, who took part in charges of the Hanoverian cavalry, a dashing figure in a red coat which he was always to treasure. Ironically the Stuart pretender James was also there but as a spectator in Burgundy's third-tier box.

We are fortunate in that one of the prisoners taken at Oudenarde was the count de Biron, who passed on to St Simon his impressions of the two allied commanders:

> He was struck by an almost royal magnificence at Prince Eugene's quarters and a shameful parsimony at those of the Duke of Marlborough, who ate the more often at the tables of others; a perfect understanding between the two in the conduct of affairs, of which the details fell much more on Eugene; a profound respect of all the generals for these two commanders but a tacit preference on the whole for Prince Eugene, without the Duke of Marlborough being at all jealous.[17]

Although all this seems to ring true from what we know of Marlborough's meanness and Eugene's detailed planning of campaigns, general Schulenburg, who was there throughout the campaign in command of Saxon auxiliary troops, believed Eugene to be less hardworking than Marlborough and certainly less of a man with a pen. He said of the prince at this time:

> Prince Eugene will often spend 3 to four hours at a time talking about the art of war; seeing that he does not write any more than he needs to, everyone comes along to where he is. Prince Eugene said on one occasion that he was certain that councils of war were only held when one didn't want to undertake anything, and besides junior officers and even the troops were given bad impressions by them; that he had never drawn up dispositions in writing except at Turin when the Duke of Savoy had wanted it, and he had not done it at other times because as soon as an army was arranged in an order of battle everyone ought to know what they had to do.[18]

The same count de Biron also passed on one of the rare comments Eugene made on his own attitude towards Louis. While they were at dinner, the two men began discussing the excellence of the Swiss troops in French service. Eugene mentioned that he thought one of the finest military posts was the colonelcy of these troops, and then added warmly:

> My father held it and on his death we hoped that my brother would acquire it. But the King preferred to make one of his natural sons colonel than to pay us this honour. He is the master and no one can gainsay him. However it is impossible not to feel rather pleased sometimes when one is in the position to make him regret his contempt.[19]

After Oudenarde Vendôme organized an orderly retreat to defensive positions around Ghent and Bruges. At the same time Berwick moved his troops from the Moselle into eastern Belgium. Even when Eugene's men joined up with Marlborough's force, the French had numerical superiority. Yet they were too shaken by their defeat to adopt anything but a defensive role for the rest of the year. Marlborough had hoped to cash in on their demoralization immediately: he made the daring proposal that the allies should end the war by marching straight on Paris, bypassing the row of massive French fortresses in front of them and depending on the navy to ship in supplies along the French coast. But Eugene was aghast at the risks involved, especially after his recent experience at Toulon of combined naval-military operations. With the support of the Dutch generals he insisted that the allied army should seize Lille first, as this fortress seemed to be the key to any attack on France. His insistence on this is interesting, as it is the first indication that he was unable to adapt his own fluid strategy of the Turkish and Italian wars to campaigning in the Low Countries and the Rhineland with their intricate fortress systems. In many ways, he, like his cousin Louis of Baden, was to become bogged down in a conservative strategy of sieges and defending supply routes.

Marlborough gave way easily enough, although he did allow himself partial criticism in writing to the Whig leader Halifax on 26 July: '... were our army all composed of English the project would certainly be feasible, but we have a great many among us who are more afraid of wanting provisions than of the enemy. However we have something of that kind in our thoughts.'[20]

The siege of Lille went ahead. Eugene undertook the convoying of a massive siege train along the roads from Brussels to the fortress under the eyes of the French armies. The cumbersome monster of 100 great siege guns, 60 mortars and 3,000 waggons, pulled by 16,000 horses and seven miles in length, made its way safely to Lille. The draught animals had been obtained by the allied armies scouring not only all the Flemish provinces but French Picardy and Artois as well. In early August these French provinces were forced to pay contributions to allied raiding parties, Louis agreeing to Artois' paying 1.5 million livres to prevent its towns being burnt. Although he had employed the same measures for years in Germany, the old king was horrified, declaring it 'contrary to laws of war'.[21]

The siege of Lille began in the second week of August 1708. Although he had never conducted a major siege before, Eugene undertook the operation, while Marlborough, with the rest of the joint allied army, covered him from attacks by Vendôme and Berwick. The siege would certainly have been a mammoth task even without the threat from the French armies; Winston Churchill called it 'the greatest siege operation since the invention of gunpowder'.[22] Lille was the showpiece of the French engineering genius, Vauban, the strongest link in the chain of fortresses across France's northern frontier. A large industrial and commercial centre, it had been one of Louis's most prized conquests of the 1660s. The allies had to construct nine miles of trenches around it, employing 12,000 peasants on the work. Inside were 15,000 troops amply supplied and commanded by a veteran of William III's siege warfare in the Netherlands, marshal Boufflers. Nevertheless both Marlborough and Eugene expected the city to fall in a matter of weeks. It was to take the rest of the year.

Although Louis insisted to his grandson, Burgundy, at the start of the siege that 'Your veritable and unique object is to conserve Lille',[23] neither Burgundy nor Berwick would risk a further pitched battle with the part of the allied army covering the siege. In desperation the French court sent their war minister Chamillart to stop the quarrels between Burgundy and Vendôme, quarrels in which Berwick had also become involved, and to persuade them to act. But he had no more success than had the letters of Louis to his grandson, which urged him to spend less time chatting to his younger brother or indulging in his hobby of astronomy. Chamillart reported finding total chaos: 'when one said white the other said black'.[24]

Lille proved the greater obstacle. The siege dragged on into late September when Eugene resorted to increasingly costly assaults. In one of these he was struck over the left eye and badly concussed, although his cocked hat took the main force of the ball. On hearing about this, Louis remarked to Madame de Maintenon and her ladies, 'I certainly don't want Prince Eugene to die but I should not be sorry if his wound stopped him taking any further part in the campaign.'[25]

The wound did mean that Eugene had to rest for a few days, and Marlborough took temporary charge. The duke had been worried about the progress of the siege and now found that the main blame lay with 'the ill conduct of our engineers', who were incompetent and fraudulent. The strain of conducting the siege in person and the worry of the previous weeks brought him close to collapse again. He had suffered continually from headaches during the summer and he now felt 'almost dead'.[26] Eugene, however, showed no signs of strain, even though, in August, there had been an attempt on his life. On opening a letter sent to him from Holland, he found it contained 'a piece of greasy blotting paper'.[27] He dropped it quickly, but he and his adjutant were both affected by fumes; when the paper was tied to a dog's collar, the animal died. Eugene shrugged off the incident, calmly remarking that he was used to this kind of thing from Italy.

It was largely through Eugene's determination that the siege was continued despite increasing problems of supply as autumn approached. Burgundy and Berwick's armies were effectively cutting the allies' communications with the coast and the north. Even Marlborough's secretary, Adam Cardonnel, feared disaster. He wrote desperately to an English under-secretary of state, George Tilson, on 24 September: 'There seems to be a great cloud hanging over our heads. . . . it were to be wisht we had quitted the siege ten days ago and the sooner we do it the better.'[28]

The army survived, however, because Marlborough managed to bring supplies on small boats across the countryside between Ostend and Lille, which the French had flooded, and by sending incessant foraging parties as far as Ypres to search for corn ' . . . in the villages, churches and castles . . . You must spare no pains nor give ear to the complaints of the peasants at this juncture for they will have hidden sufficient for their own subsistence.'[29] Although the troops were to pay for this 'bread corn' at the market price, the local farmers gave 'as little assistance as is possible'.[30]

When marshal Boufflers at last handed over the city and withdrew into the citadel on 22 October, the allies had suffered five times their losses at Oudenarde and were said to have spent nearly half a million gulden on the siege. Despite the large civilian population, mutton, beef and horse-flesh were still on sale in the city. It was not till 9 December that Boufflers surrendered the citadel, and even then Eugene and Marlborough had to agree to allow the garrison free exit to France rather than risk further costly assaults. The marshal was treated with great respect, although the pious colonel Blackader, one of Marlborough's officers who survived the war on a diet of hymns and psalms, was suitably unimpressed by 'the interview between two great men, Prince Eugene and Marshal Boufflers. I thought it all ceremony and compliment, and no reality.'[31]

The capture of the city of Lille was quickly followed by allied pushes to regain control of the Scheldt. The French armies withdrew south to winter quarters and Ghent and Bruges were reoccupied. By the end of the year, therefore, all but the most southern reaches of the Spanish Netherlands were in allied hands, as well as part of France round Lille. These gains had been achieved despite the superior French numbers and the disasters at the beginning of July. It had been a remarkable campaign, one which Eugene himself described in this way: 'He who has not seen this has seen nothing.'[32]

There is no point in trying to assess which commander deserved the greater credit: neither man thought in these terms. In many ways Eugene had become Marlborough's leading subordinate with his army almost totally paid for by the Maritime Powers, but both men considered each other equal partners and there was certainly plenty of truth in what Wratislaw wrote to the archduke Charles in Spain just after Oudenarde: 'If Eugene had not come to the Netherlands, everything there would have been spoilt, as Marlborough and the field deputies [of the Dutch] had fallen out and the army had been confounded. The battle at Oudenarde would not have taken place and only a bad peace to be looked forward to.'[33]

The war in the Netherlands had put events elsewhere in the shade. The transfer of troops northwards reduced the scale of conflict elsewhere along the Rhine and on France's south-eastern frontier. In Spain Starhemberg had barely managed to stem further Bourbon advance, although the English fleet had taken Minorca and now completely dominated the Mediterranean. All requests from the Maritime Powers for Imperial troops to be sent to Spain had been resisted because Vienna was making its main war effort in Hungary and sending as many men eastwards as possible. Eugene had supported this because he still believed that only 'the power of the sword' could end the rebellion.[34] The problem in Hungary was that almost all the agrarian population was hostile to the emperor, peasant as well as noble, and that the rebel leaders managed to organize effective guerrilla warfare which confined the Imperialists to garrison towns. During 1708, however, there were at last signs that the rebellion was being stamped out, a triumph for Heister, who had been reinstated once Starhemberg left for Spain. But Eugene gave him little personal credit for the success, criticizing his strategy as one of 'going round in circles'.[35]

XIII

The Lost Peace and Malplaquet

The fall of Lille left Louis prostrate. French money had run out and the war minister Chamillart could foresee nothing except France's defeat. The king therefore put out peace feelers to the Dutch who agreed to negotiate. As it became clear that a peace conference would take place at The Hague in the spring of 1709, the Austrian ministers had to think seriously for the first time since the beginning of the war about what terms they should demand.

Eugene returned to Vienna early in 1709 in no mood for compromise. He felt that only complete defeat would make France – this 'monster', as he called her[1] – see reason, and he was highly suspicious that the Dutch might make a separate peace. Although he usually got his way with them, he was always contemptuous of Dutch politicians, referring to Heinsius as this 'little man'. When the Dutch field deputies had spoken during a dinner the previous September about the amazing exploits of Alexander the Great, he exclaimed, 'It's because there were no Greek field deputies.'[2] Nevertheless, during discussions in February and March 1709 the conference had no doubts about putting Eugene in charge of the Imperial negotiations at The Hague. At his own and Wratislaw's request, Sinzendorff was to be sent to help him. All the ministers were agreed that they should demand the whole of the Spanish monarchy for the house of Habsburg. On Eugene's suggestion, it was also decided to use the restitution of Cologne and Bavaria as a way of forcing Louis to restore the 1648 borders of the Empire as well as all Alsace and the three bishoprics in Lorraine. In seeking to create a much stronger military barrier on the Rhine and Moselle, Eugene came closer to the position of Salm, Seilern and Schönborn than of Wratislaw, who was more interested in Austrian gains in Italy and would have been prepared to sacrifice the *Reich* barrier.[3]

Deep snow, which was said to have cut off Vienna more effectively than the Turks,[4] meant that Eugene was not back in Brussels before 27

March. On going on to The Hague he found a French agent, Rouillé, already negotiating with the Dutch. He angrily insisted that the man be sent packing unless he spoke of absolute surrender over Spain and the *Reich* frontier. When Marlborough arrived on 9 April, he supported Eugene and the Dutch fell quickly into line.

The allies could afford to be tough because of the appalling news reaching them from France. The severe winter, which had snowbound Vienna, frozen the river Thames and hastened the disastrous defeat of Charles XII's Swedish army in the Ukraine, was especially fierce in France. Here an iron frost gripped the fields from January till March, killing people, animals, trees, vines and even the seed corn in the ground. There would be no harvest that year, and even at Versailles the court had to eat oat bread during the spring. The garrisons in northern France mutinied and the country seemed defenceless.

Louis was so anxious for peace that he sent his secretary of state, Torcy, in person to The Hague in May. Torcy came not as a plenipotentiary to a formal conference but as a desperate man trying to salvage what he could through informal talks with the allied leaders in closed rooms. He found a disquieting unanimity among them. Eugene and Marlborough shared the same house and negotiated as one. The Dutch leaders, Heinsius and Buys, were determined not to separate themselves from England. Although Eugene at first suspected that Torcy had come merely to gain time, by 17 May he concluded that 'France is quite unable to prolong the war'.[5] At the end of the month Torcy was given a list of forty-two peace preliminaries to be sent to Louis; in these Eugene had gained the point on which he had insisted most – all of the Spanish monarchy, including Naples and Sicily, for the archduke Charles – but had shown himself prepared to accept a *Reich* frontier which embraced Strasbourg and part of Alsace, but which allowed France to keep the rest of the province and the three bishoprics in Lorraine. The allies had also demanded, largely on the insistence of the Dutch, who wanted an end to the conflict and to avoid a further war against Philip once peace was made with France, that the allies should occupy three French and three Spanish 'cautionary' towns on the conclusion of an armistice to ensure that Louis carried out the peace terms. If the terms were not carried out within two months, the allies would renew the war against France.[6] Louis was also specifically asked to join the allies in enforcing the peace terms on his grandson and to make him surrender Spain.

Although Eugene assured Joseph in a letter of 29 May that 'French agreement can hardly be doubted',[7] Louis was to reject the peace terms out of hand. The clauses over the 'cautionary' towns and the renewal of war after two months were resented as much as the demand that Louis act against Philip, since it was feared they would allow the allies to dismember France if they so wished. The French king preferred to risk another campaign rather than accept these conditions. He now had a new war minister, Voysin, who believed France could fight on and he had found a general, Villars, willing to do so. There were ample numbers of starving men ready to enlist and follow the bread waggons, and enough Spanish silver was now reaching the country to encourage Louis to keep buying grain abroad.

The allied leaders were dumbfounded when Torcy sent them Louis's rejection of the preliminaries. They had assumed he would have to accept them, and they had not expected the clauses over forcing Philip to surrender Spain to cause trouble, because Torcy had assured them that Louis need only command Philip for him to leave Spain. They had never believed he would have to fight his own grandson. After France's rejection of the preliminaries the Dutch were inclined to believe that Louis had never intended peace. But both Eugene and Marlborough began to remark that it had been a mistake to include demands that Louis should act against his grandson.[8] Unlike the Dutch they were prepared to accept a separate peace with France and then to undertake war against Philip to expel him from Spain. They tried to shift the blame for the failure of the talks on to the Dutch, which infuriated Heinsius because neither Marlborough nor Eugene had objected to the demands at the time. Marlborough and Eugene, moreover, had been no more accommodating in the negotiations than anyone else. Although Torcy found the prince eager to avoid petty disputes, he had been 'very firm on the essentials' and there had been stormy scenes over Alsace.[9] On the other hand, neither Marlborough nor Eugene had wanted the war with France to continue and would have preferred further talks with Louis to solve the problem of Spain, but no alternative proposals came from him. Marlborough was now approaching his sixtieth birthday and in constant poor health: peace at this stage would have been more a triumph for him than anything further war could bring. All his private letters of the time show this. Eugene was also doubtful whether the prolongation of the war would seriously change the situation and he was very aware of the vagaries of battle. He knew the Dutch would never sanction the permanent destruction of France, and he was pessimistic about the future even if Louis accepted the proposed preliminaries. He believed France would 'certainly recover in a few years and then molest her neighbours once again'.[10]

Far more intransigent had been Salm, supported by Seilern and Schönborn, who critized Eugene's surrender of Franche Comté, the Lorraine bishoprics and part of Alsace to France. Wratislaw would have been prepared to sacrifice even more but during the late spring he was often away from the conference because of ill health. This criticism infuriated Eugene, who considered it a personal attack, and he wrote to Sinzendorff, his fellow negotiator at The Hague, on 18 July: '... Salm ... is a fool who never knows what he's talking about'.[11]

Despite the French rejection of the preliminaries the allied leaders were not unduly worried, as they were confident that they would now totally defeat Louis, for as the leading Whig and Marlborough's son-in-law, Sunderland, wrote on 13 June: 'The French troops as well as the country are in such a miserable condition that either the King of France must comply with what the allies shall think necessary to demand of him, or there seems nothing can hinder our army from marching to Paris.'[12] But the allies were not to march to Paris, because Louis had found the man who could save him.

Marshal Villars had proved an impossible colleague for all who had served with him. He bragged, was ruthless and was also said to be venal. Yet no one could deny that he had been consistently successful, and Louis therefore turned to him as a last resort, giving him control of the northern armies.

As a strategist Villars shared Marlborough and Eugene's belief in movement and swift battles, but he was now to be forced to take up a largely defensive stance. The most pressing need was to feed and clothe his troops, and this he managed, after a fashion, by a mixture of bullying the court and confiscating food. Warehouses were broken into and grain seized; by mid-June he had brought some order into a hungry and ragged army which had been selling its arms and uniforms to buy food.

He did not have to face an immediate attack after the breakdown of the peace talks, because the allies had not really expected to have to fight another campaign. With their own forces larger than ever and comparatively well provided for, Marlborough and Eugene were reluctant to move prematurely through the soaking rain into the French countryside. On 9 June Marlborough informed Godolphin that 'The account we have concerning forage is so terrible that I fear that much more than the Marshal Villars's gasconading.'[13]

During the wet weather Villars dug himself in in a long stretch of fortified villages, redoubts and trenches from Douai to Béthune, which was intended to be France's last line of defence. When they saw this barrier, as Marlborough reported to his wife, 'Prince Eugene, myself, and all the generals, did not think it advisable to run so great a hazard'[14] as to attack it. Could they bypass Villars and march straight on Paris? If they did, there would be no forage ahead of them in France. Marlborough therefore reverted to his old idea of the navy supplying an invasion force through the port of Abbeville. But Eugene and the Dutch once more rejected it and he bowed to their idea of besieging Tournai. No real attempt was made to manoeuvre Villars out of his defensive positions and Louis XIV was delighted, writing that 'all the vast project of the enemy has been reduced to the single enterprise of the siege of Tournai'.[15] Why did the allies fritter away most of the campaigning season in this way, for any major siege of this sort was likely to take the whole summer? There was certainly a feeling that France was already defeated and that all that was needed was for the allies to lean on her to produce total collapse – the steady pressure of taking towns and laying waste the countryside would achieve this. Marlborough wrote in this vein to Heinsius during the siege of Tournai: 'The account of the misery and disturbances in France are such that if it continues they must be ruined . . . if it be true, the King of France will speedily be obliged to speak plainly.'[16] But at the same time the allied generals were running short of ideas and becoming understandably nervous of throwing away what they had already won. Their most brilliant victories had been those which had been forced on them by French initiative, and now this had passed to them they were proving incapable of capitalizing on their position. Throughout their joint campaigns Marlborough had always depended heavily on Eugene's advice: he appears to have trusted the prince's judgment rather than his own. Eugene's advice now was to pursue a conservative strategy: time seemed on the allies' side. But in adopting this course the allies became enmeshed in a siege strategy which, unless France collapsed at once, would take a series of campaigns to destroy her iron barrier, fortress by fortress. It was a policy which above all gave time for France's condition to change, for bad or worse, and for changes to occur within the allied states themselves. This point in the war was to be the allies' moment of supreme power: it was not to come again.

The siege of Tournai proved an awesome undertaking. The approach trenches, constructed by thousands of sappers recruited from the surrounding countryside, were soon filled with mud during the rains of July and August. Worst of all, the French had dug galleries and planted mines in the whole area in front of the town, and these had to be exploded before the fortifications could be reached. Terrified of being drowned, buried alive or blown apart, the allied troops refused to go below ground despite offers of money. Eugene and Marlborough therefore had to order them down and accompany the men themselves on occasions. Eventually Eugene produced two hundred Piedmontese miners who showed the soldiers what to do. But allied losses were very great and Tournai did not capitulate until 3 September.

Throughout the war Louis XIV had kept far tighter control of his generals' moves than the governments of the opposing states, who had left their military leaders largely free to act as they saw fit. In doing so the French king may have hamstrung them. He had certainly deterred them from bold strokes and this was especially the case now. During the summer months his orders to Villars had been to stand on the defensive and not to fight unless he enjoyed 'a great advantage'. Villars had fretted at these orders, not only because they went against his whole view of war but also because throughout August his supply situation was growing worse – his infantry were so hungry that they had to be kept away from the horses. He therefore begged Louis to let him engage the enemy, writing, 'God help us, but the more I think of the problem of food, the more I find that we must either have peace or a battle . . . ' Gradually Louis gave way and he ordered him 'to do what you believe yourself forced to do; be it to seek out or to avoid combat'.[17]

As the allies turned from Tournai to yet another siege at Mons, Villars moved out of his defensive lines to prevent this, positioning himself in the woody countryside around the village of Malplaquet and inviting the allies to attack him. On 7 and 8 September he posted the flanks of his army in two woods, leaving a gap between as a fire trap with artillery and infantry ready with crossfire. Trees were felled and chained together as defensive works, and in the woods fortifications were set up. He had plenty of time: when the allied troops approached on the 10th they might well have attacked him with their larger numbers, but they put off their assault till the following day. It seems to have been Eugene who insisted on this delay, a fatal decision which allowed the French to dig in more firmly. Villars's appearance had taken the allies somewhat by surprise and, as Eugene told Joseph in a letter of the 9th, they dared not risk an immediate attack till they had more information about the difficult terrain.[18] The time also allowed them to consult the Dutch field deputies and to wait for an extra 10,000 men from Tournai under Schulenburg, whose advice Eugene wanted over the disposition of the infantry.[19]

After the usual religious services and an issue of brandy – the second in two days – Eugene's and the other allied troops marched off at three o'clock on the morning of 11 September, making their way across the wet plain towards the enemy in the woods, 110,000 of the allies to 80,000 French. It was intended to press hard against the enemy's flanks, forcing the French to deploy troops from their centre and thus make way for a successful allied push through in this part of the field. The allies had no intention of falling into Villars's fire trap by immediately attacking the French centre. Marlborough was to hold this centre at the beginning, while Eugene and most of the German troops acted as a right wing against one wood and the Dutch under the prince of Orange did the same on the left.

The heavy French entrenchments, their use of artillery and close-range enfilading, combined with continual allied infantry assaults, made Malplaquet the bloodiest battle of the war. The impetuous young prince of Orange led his blue-coated Dutch infantry to annihilation on the left wing, while it took Eugene most of the late morning and early afternoon to force his opponents from their wood. Fighting often became hand to hand with both sides using their bayonets and musket butts. Once again Eugene was directly involved. When he was hit by a bullet behind the ear he refused to have it dressed, declaring, 'To what purpose, if we are to die here? If we live, there will be time enough in the evening.'[20]

Eventually, as the wing opposite Eugene crumbled, Villars transferred troops from his centre, allowing Marlborough to push through here. Since Villars was badly wounded in the knee, it was left to marshal Boufflers to organize an orderly retreat. The allied army was too shattered to follow.[21] Their losses had been appalling, probably reaching 25,000 dead and wounded, while the French had lost only half this. Hardened campaigners were shaken by the carnage. Corporal Bishop and his English companions on the night of the battle 'endeavoured to the utmost of our ability to get out of the noise of the wounded, but found it almost impossible, except we had gone three or four miles distance, for all the hedges and ditches were lined with disabled men'.[22] Schulenburg wrote home the next day:

> ...we are doing nothing but picking up our wounded, who greatly embarrass us as there is no town at hand where they can be sent into hospitals, so that many will be lost, and in burying our dead. The enemy dead in large numbers are still naked on the battle field and many of their wounded who have received no help so far.[23]

It took the allied troops three days to clear the woods and fields of their own casualties, while the 'Capuchins of neighbouring French towns were allowed to fetch their wounded and to bury their dead'. The Hanoverian troops eventually got their injured to Brussels by the 15th, having been held up by lack of carts, but by then most were dead. Perhaps the most telling comment on the carnage was made by the Hanoverian general, Ilten: 'In the year 1718 I saw the battlefield again while I was on a journey and the peasants assured me that for a long time they had not needed to manure their fields.'[24]

While the slaughter made Marlborough ill for the next week, it seems to have left Eugene as unmoved and impassive as ever. Although he had commented on the ferocity of the infantry fire during his first campaigns in Italy, he now seemed to accept the increasingly murderous engagements as a matter of course. Neither he nor Marlborough had any doubts about their decision to attack at Malplaquet, but we find criticism of them in the memoirs of two English officers, colonel Parker and brigadier Kane. The latter wrote: ' . . . both our generals were very much blam'd for throwing away so many brave men's lives, when there was no occasion: it was the only rash thing the Duke of Marlboro' was ever guilty of; and it was generally believ'd that he was pressed to it by Prince Eugene.'[25] There is no evidence for this accusation against Eugene or that the battle had been anything but a joint decision. In the event Marlborough was to be saddled with most of the blame for the battle. Although few of the dead were English, the battle strengthened the Tory demands for peace and produced intense criticism of Marlborough's 'butcher's bill'.

Immediately after the battle Eugene and Marlborough felt certain that Louis would be forced to submit. But they were mistaken: no peace proposals came from France. Malplaquet failed to break French resistance and Louis himself seemed determined to fight on. Villars was convinced that the allies would never risk another battle and wrote to Louis: ' . . . if God gives us the grace to lose another similar battle, your Majesty can count on his enemies being destroyed'.[26] Moreover, the news for France from elsewhere was quite cheerful. On the Rhine the elector of Hanover, whom Eugene dismissed as 'a phantom of a Prince',[27] achieved nothing; and in Spain Starhemberg made no real progress despite Louis's withdrawal of troops.

A month after Malplaquet Eugene and Marlborough's hopes of peace had evaporated. Although they went on to take Mons, the army had to be moved quickly into winter quarters in October because of heavy rain and lack of forage. During the siege of Mons the allied army's supply and transport system had broken down. Schulenburg blamed the negligence of Marlborough and Eugene for this. We also have a comment from the same man, who was a trusted infantry general, written at this time about both allied leaders. He believed Marlborough was 'the most shrewd and astute man anywhere', and that 'Prince Eugene has no other interest in life than fighting . . . [and] wishes all to bow down before the name of the Emperor'.[28] However, the impression he gained of the prince's character on campaign was very different from the rather morose and laconic figure we know from Vienna: 'Prince Eugene can bear anything without being angry, he is the happiest man in the world.'[29] Another close companion, the Prussian general Grumbkow, echoed this, describing Eugene as 'naturally and always in a very good humour at every opportunity'.[30]

When the 1709 campaign came to an end, both Eugene and Marlborough accepted that the war would have to continue. There seemed no end in sight to the bloodshed. Yet on a personal level Eugene had good grounds to be satisfied when he arrived back in Vienna on 9 December, for Salm had at last gone: he had resigned in August to trail through the German spas to death and oblivion a year later. His refusal to retire and Joseph's reluctance to insist had exasperated Eugene, causing him to write to Sinzendorff, 'these usual comedies . . . make our court ridiculous in all the foreign courts'.[31] But when Salm did resign Eugene and Wratislaw at last achieved the undisputed control they had sought for more than five years. Joseph appointed their nominee, Trautsohn, as *Obristhofmeister* and those ministers, Seilern and Gundaker Starhemberg, who had supported Salm, were quick to make their peace.[32] Wratislaw's own close relationship with the emperor was cemented by his friendship with Joseph's latest mistress, countess Pálffy, who was the daughter of one of Eugene's most valued cavalry generals.

Joseph was a generous master: all groups among the ministers seem to have benefited. Revenues from Bavaria, and estates confiscated there and in Hungary, were lavished on them. Joseph's favourite, count Lamberg, was given 250,000 gulden but Trautsohn, Gundaker Starhemberg, Sinzendorff and Wratislaw all received substantial Bavarian estates. Eugene received nothing in Bavaria, probably because he already had the post of viceroy of Milan, but on 17 December 1709 Joseph granted him a confiscated estate in Hungary worth 300,000 gulden. He never received the latter, either because no suitable estate could be found, or, more likely, because he was uninterested in adding to the land he already possessed in Hungary. Instead he was to be paid the sum in cash over a period of years.

XIV

Stalemate in the Netherlands and the Death of Joseph

During the winter of 1709–10 Eugene and Wratislaw were for the first time in full control of the Austrian government: all the major departments of state as well as the conference were in their hands or those of their friends. With the backing of the emperor they could draw on all the available resources of the monarchy for the war. Unfortunately these resources were never sufficient for the monarchy's commitments. During 1710 a further English loan – 86,950 pounds – was needed before the Imperialists could field their army in Flanders.[1] The Maritime Powers had been paying for the bread and fodder required there by the Imperialists since 1708[2] as well as for large numbers of auxiliary troops under Imperial control. The bulk of Austrian resources was being directed elsewhere. The distribution of the 133,000 troops fielded by the Imperialists in 1710 is an interesting indication of their priorities: 16,000 for the Netherlands, 10,000 for the Rhine, 12,000 for Spain, 31,000 in northern Italy, 7,500 in Naples, 5,000 in Bohemia and Silesia, and a massive 49,000 in Hungary. This concentration on Hungary was paying off, since the military position had continued to improve there under Heister during 1709.

Clearly Eugene's absences from Vienna meant that he could not exercise direct political control, and there are few signs that he wished to be regarded as principal minister like Salm. This role fell more naturally to Wratislaw and to Joseph himself. But the prince expected to be listened to over the conduct of the war and the formulation of peace aims. In September 1709 the conference approved the preliminaries he had agreed to earlier in the year at The Hague, particularly the clauses relating to the *Reich* frontier, and also agreed to his suggestion that Louis should not be forced to act against Philip. The Imperialists had been determined not to separate themselves from the Maritime Powers, but their confidence in the latter was to suffer a jolt at the end of 1709 when they discovered the terms of the Barrier treaty worked out between the English and Dutch over the Southern Netherlands. By this agreement the English Whig ministers, without consulting Vienna or the prospective ruler, the archduke Charles, and largely disregarding Marlborough's views, had promised the Dutch large commercial concessions there and an extensive fortress system in return for a guarantee of the Protestant succession and agreement to the Whig call for 'no peace without Spain'. These Whig ministers now exercised far more control over English policy than Marlborough.

When Eugene reached The Hague after an exhausting journey in April 1710, he found the Dutch already negotiating with France at Geertruidenberg. But all to no effect. Their financial exhaustion and heavy losses at Malplaquet made the Dutch try hard for peace by suggesting that Philip be allowed to keep Naples and Sicily. Although Louis welcomed this, neither the Whigs nor the Austrians would accept it. The Austrians' own proposal, put through Sinzendorff, and supported by Marlborough as well as Eugene, that the allies should not insist on Louis helping against his grandson and that they should consider a further war against Spain once peace was made with France, was rejected by both the Whigs and the Dutch, who wanted a definitive settlement. For his part Louis tried to achieve a partition of the Spanish monarchy and refused to contemplate using force against Philip, although he was prepared to provide subsidies for the allies to drive him from Spain and also to surrender all Alsace.

The negotiations failed largely because the allies, particularly the Whigs, still felt strong enough to refuse concessions, while Louis saw little reason to accept what he had refused the previous year. Although day-to-day negotiations at Geertruidenberg were largely in Sinzendorff's hands, Eugene's had been the ultimate authority for Austria's negotiations in the Netherlands. Neither he nor Marlborough can be accused personally of wrecking the negotiations, although they both were. But both men believed, as Eugene put it, that the French had 'tried in this conference to do nothing but to amuse us',[3] and neither showed the regret at the failure of the talks they had shown the previous year.

There was no alternative but to renew the war. For the allied leaders, it appeared that France had merely put off her inevitable collapse for a few more months. Before the campaign began the allies had plenty of information about great shortages on the French side, whereas by mid-April Eugene and Marlborough had a joint army of 120,000 men. This force was divided between them and the command shared as before.

Many of the auxiliary troops paid for by the Maritime Powers were attached to the part of the army under Eugene. Despite the personal popularity of the prince, some of the auxiliary generals preferred to serve with their troops under Marlborough, as Eugene seems to have exerted less control over his auxiliaries than over his own Imperial regiments, where he continually insisted on strict discipline. During the Toulon campaign the auxiliaries had behaved badly, and now the Hanoverian general Bülow was relieved when his troops were transferred to Marlborough's section, for he wrote: 'I am glad to have escaped from such a pack ... especially as Eugene's army is organized in the old Imperial way: there are wrangles over everything and also the common soldiers are so ill-disciplined that it is difficult to correct this.'[4]

The allied generals began the 1710 campaign by besieging Douai, which showed they were still wedded to a conservative siege strategy. However, Marlborough was very optimistic, feeling able to assure Godolphin that he hoped 'for a glorious campaign, in which it is likely we shall have a great deal of action ... this campaign must put an end to the war'.[5] His close subordinate, Cadogan, was even more certain that they were near 'the land of promise, and that after the taking this place there is nothing to stop our pouring into France with this great and victorious army'.[6]

Yet the campaign was to prove one of the least successful of the war. The Dutch were reluctant to face another battle, and during the year Marlborough grew increasingly depressed and inactive: his wife's bitter quarrel with the queen and the influence on Anne of the pro-peace Tories under Harley were to lead by August to the dismissal of both the Whig ministers and Godolphin. Marlborough's own position seemed threatened as well. Eugene did what he could to support him, offering to go to England on his behalf and writing to the Imperial minister there threatening to resign if Marlborough were replaced, especially by the elector of Hanover, for 'My lord duke is my especial good friend, with whom I well agree ... the good understanding between us means that much happens which would otherwise be impossible, because between us there is an equality ...'[7]

In this worrying situation during the summer of 1710 neither of the allied commanders could provide a solution to the military stalemate and no attempt was made to seek out the French army for another battle.[8] Although Louis's own position was marginally better because more men had been released from Spain, he constantly urged caution on Villars, pinning his hopes on an approach from the new Tory government in England. Villars himself was now a cripple, his shattered knee enclosed in a special iron shield. But for his threat to shoot his surgeons, they would probably have amputated his leg. Instead they had merely cut out the rotten flesh, while he lay pinned down to a table fully conscious despite having drunk vast amounts of brandy.

Although Douai fell by the end of June, the rest of the very wet season was spent in minor sieges, while Villars's forces were stretched in a new defensive line between Arras and Cambrai. After the fall of Douai, Marlborough, dejected and with his head 'perpetually hot', was coming round to the view that further decisive action was impossible and that France would eventually be worn down in two or three years by the presence of two armies living in northern France.[9]

Within the allied army itself, morale seemed to be collapsing. Schulenburg wrote home to king Augustus of Saxony-Poland that 'The confusion continues . . . in the army and I see few people who are happy; . . . piquet takes up more time than anything else and one only goes outside to have dinner with someone.'[10] Yet at the end of August Marlborough began to think again of his old idea of outflanking the French by a coastal march at least as far as Calais, depending on naval help. It was once more Eugene who refused, wanting the allies to take further French fortresses before he would agree.[11] Although, according to Schulenburg, Eugene had 'no other thought in his head' at this time 'than to fight if only the opportunity arose',[12] Villars made sure that none did. When more French fortresses had been taken by November, it was too late to contemplate Marlborough's plan, because the dreadful wet summer had been followed by even worse weather. What undoubtedly made Eugene hesitant to abandon his siege mentality was the problem of feeding troops and foraging in a famine-stricken area. Typhus, or the 'spotted fever', was spreading throughout the countryside and into the armies. Marlborough commented on ' . . . the misery of this country; at least one half of the people of the villages, since the beginning of last winter, are dead, and the rest look as if they came out of their graves. It is so mortifying, that no christian can see it, but must, with all his heart, wish for a speedy peace.'[13]

By the close of the 1710 campaign almost the whole of France's protective ring of fortresses had been cleared away. There should have been no obstacle now to prevent the allies marching on Paris, but this year was to be the last in which the allied leaders had the opportunity to work together and they let their chance slip. In Spain any hope of an allied victory disappeared when the English commander Stanhope was defeated and captured at Brihuega: it was now merely a question of time before the archduke Charles and the allied forces there were expelled.

The possibility of total victory against the Bourbons, even against France, was ebbing away fast, but the urgency of the situation was not apparent to Eugene or probably to anyone else: the Tory approaches to France for a separate peace were still a closely-guarded secret and no one knew that Joseph would soon be dead.

The Imperial government had every reason for optimism and to be satisfied with its achievements in 1710 because the Hungarian revolt was at last coming to an end. Heister had retired through ill health and had been replaced at the end of the year by a trusted Hungarian cavalry officer of Eugene's, Pálffy. Although Eugene would have preferred, as ever, for him to crush the Hungarians utterly, Pálffy negotiated with them, managing to isolate Rákóczi and pave the way for the conclusion of the peace of Szatmár (Satu Mare) in April 1711. While this settlement conciliated most of the rebels and was to be the basis for a period of relative quiet in Hungary over the next thirty years, few troops were freed immediately for Flanders or Spain. The bulk stayed where they were, partly because 'the spirit and means of rebellion were still in Hungary, the people unquiet, rambling in companies from village to village', as an English minister was told,[14] and also because the troops could live there free.

A few days before the signature of the peace of Szatmár, on 7 April 1711, Joseph suddenly fell ill: it was the smallpox. Only the previous November one of his daughters had caught it, which put everyone 'in great apprehension for his person, he never having had the distemper'.[15] At first he seemed to recover and Eugene left for the Netherlands, after another winter in Vienna, believing this. He did not see the emperor before leaving as he had not had the smallpox himself and Joseph insisted that he stay away. On 17 April the emperor was dead. His doctors may have stifled what slim chance he had of recovery – they 'not only excluded the air from his apartment, but swathed him in twenty yards of English scarlet broadcloth'.[16]

When it became known that the emperor was dying 'the consternation . . . [was] . . . inexpressible att Vienna'.[17] Wratislaw and Eugene were dismayed by his death: they had lost a friend for whom they had genuine affection, Eugene writing to Wratislaw 'I really loved this prince'.[18] They had no need to worry about their political position because the conference immediately decided to put into effect the family compact of 1703, giving the succession to Charles rather than to Joseph's daughters. Until he could return from Spain it was also decided to entrust the regency to his mother, the deeply religious empress Eleonora. There was no question of her going against Wratislaw's views, especially as he had the complete confidence of Charles, who ordered him from Spain to discuss the most important matters of state with no one else but Trautsohn.[19]

The accession of the twenty-five year old Charles was to have serious consequences for the course of the war. The Habsburg claim to the Spanish succession, which had only envisaged the direct transfer of the duchy of Milan to the main line of the family while leaving the rest to Charles, was changed by the death of Joseph to a claim to the whole inheritance for one man. Although the chances of winning Spain itself were becoming more remote, this still meant the acquisition of the Southern Netherlands and Italian lands by Austria. When Eugene reached The Hague in May, he found both the Dutch and the Tory minister, Strafford, ominously reticent about the desirability of Charles's remaining king of Spain once he became emperor.

Far more important to the Imperialists than these rumblings of future trouble was the immediate need to safeguard Charles's position in Germany and to have him elected emperor. Consequently Eugene arrived at Marlborough's headquarters unwilling to undertake any great stroke in Flanders because of the sensitivity of Germany to French moves along the Rhine. Louis XIV, for his part, was determined not to run any risks, wishing to depend on the secret peace talks which had been in train with London for some months. He told Villars explicitly on 26 April: 'I do not believe it to be àpropos for you to try to fight the enemies . . . the present conjuncture does not require that we risk any considerable action.'[20] He did, however, attempt to embarrass the Imperial election at Frankfurt by massing troops along the Rhine. It was the news of this which made Eugene on 14 June ignore pleas from both Marlborough and Heinsius and move towards the Rhine with the forces still in Austrian pay, no more than 16,000 men.

As worrying for the Imperialists as this demonstration by Louis was Charles's own reluctance to leave Spain, where he was totally convinced of his right to be king and determined not to abandon his Spanish supporters, writing to Wratislaw that this 'is not to be thought of nor to appear so'.[21] Eugene, on hearing of Joseph's death, had written asking him to return immediately, and all the other ministers had done the same. But it was July before Charles decided to leave and even then he insisted on his young wife Elizabeth staying behind in Barcelona as a pledge to his supporters in Catalonia, the last area to remain loyal to him.

During the summer Eugene stood on the defensive along the Rhine, spending most of his time in hastening the election at Frankfurt and keeping the electors loyal to the Habsburgs. Meanwhile, Marlborough had recovered his spirits enough to take yet another strongpoint,

Bouchain. But this brought a decisive turn to the war no nearer as France had still not collapsed and Marlborough's own government was more determined than ever on a peace settlement.

At last in October, just as he was landing at Genoa, the archduke Charles was elected emperor Charles VI in Frankfurt. He then moved slowly towards this Imperial city for his coronation, being joined on the road by Wratislaw and Sinzendorff. Eugene came to meet him at Innsbruck on 23 November. The new emperor was an unknown quantity: he had been an unimpressive youth, overshadowed by his elder brother, when he left for Spain eight years before. Now in his mid-twenties, he seemed much older and looked very like his father: an ugly short man with an ungainly walk. He had the Habsburg lip, large rather fierce eyes, brown hair and a ruddy complexion. Although he dressed well, the effect was somewhat spoiled by his wigs which never seemed quite right. But everyone's first impressions of him were favourable – modest, serious, aware of his responsibilities and willing to work. Neither women nor priests had any influence on him and initially the men he brought back from Spain were considered sound. He had begun his reign well by sending orders from Barcelona for all pensions to be stopped till he returned: 'the unnecessary offices are to be re-trench'd, the beginning whereof has been already made by dismissing the greatest part of the musick, the hunting equipage etc.'[22] The English minister Whitworth reported that 'King Charles seems to have more the spirit of government and good management than his predecessor.'[23]

On his return Charles immediately confirmed Wratislaw and Eugene and their supporters in power, and the only sign of future trouble was the setting up in the spring of 1712 of a Spanish council. But the latter seemed less important than Charles's past and continuing intimacy with Wratislaw and his wholehearted support for Eugene's demands for more troops and money. These demands had been conveyed to him in August while he was still in Barcelona, Eugene having complained that the main problem was that the funds assigned to the army never reached it.[24]

The unity and determination shown in Austrian ruling circles from the time of Charles's accession was, however, to prove useless when faced by the desertion of the English. The Tories had never liked Marl-borough's continental war and looked on the Dutch as commercial rivals rather than as allies, and on their assumption of power in 1710 peace became their main concern. By the summer of 1711 the secret and hesitant moves made by Harley towards the French over the past year were taken up more boldly by St John, the young secretary of state. He wanted peace even at the expense of the allies and he soon came to think of the latter as more of a danger to England than the French. Above all he was ready to see Philip king in Spain and could now point to the absurdity of continuing a war which the allies seemed unable to win for the sake of making one man ruler of Spain and Austria. He was in any case no friend of the Habsburgs and wrote in November 1711 that 'the house of Austria has been the evil genius of Britain. I never think of the conduct of that family without recollecting the image of a man braiding a rope of hay while his ass bites it off at the other end.'[25] A month before, as Charles was being elected at Frankfurt, Louis had reached a tacit understanding that Philip should have Spain in return for his conceding all the English demands and signing peace preliminaries in preparation for a congress in the new year at Utrecht.

When Charles met his new ministers at Innsbruck, they felt fairly certain that the English intended to sacrifice Spain. In the past this would have caused far less concern, especially to Wratislaw and Eugene, who had never wanted Spain and were more interested in Italy. But now the emperor's own personal commitment to Spain made its loss a very different matter. For as the English minister, Whitworth, reported: 'He is more a Spaniard than the greatest part of his councill could wish & that Monarchy will no longer be lookt on as a seperate interest.'[26]

Not surprisingly Charles's first discussions with his ministers at Innsbruck were heated ones. Eugene was incensed at what he saw as bad faith on the part of the English in negotiating separately with the French, and he suggested that the emperor should boycott the proposed Utrecht congress. Charles was impressed, noting that 'Prince Eugene gives good, brief and succinct advice', unlike Sinzendorff who 'prattles a lot'.[27] Finally, however, Wratislaw's more realistic arguments prevailed and Charles agreed that his ministers should attend the congress. The ministers were also beginning to recognize that they might have to agree to a partition of the Spanish empire. Over the following months it was to become even clearer to them that 'we cannot hope for all the monarchy', but it was never felt expedient to admit this and the ministers came to see that their main hope lay in delay until yet another change of government in England might transform the situation.[28]

Such a change would take time. There seemed a more direct way: to send Eugene to England to persuade the existing government to carry on the war. A mission of this kind had been suggested by Marlborough in early November and it was immediately taken up. Wratislaw considered it a useful card to play which would 'extremely embarrass the peace party' there.[29] As soon as Charles had been crowned, therefore, Eugene left Frankfurt for The Hague to make the crossing to England.

XV

Denain and Rastadt

The Tory leaders in England were 'terribly afraid of Prince Eugene's coming'.[1] The worst time for his arrival would have been December 1711, because that month saw the culmination of their struggle to dismiss Marlborough as commander-in-chief and to win parliamentary approval for their peace policy. In the event they managed to achieve both before Eugene sailed in January, as well as to mount a fierce propaganda campaign against the Dutch and Austrians, opening with the publication of Jonathan Swift's *The Conduct of the Allies*. All the same the Tories tried to stop, or at least delay, Eugene's visit.

Thus Strafford at The Hague was obstructive, telling Eugene that the visit would be a waste of time as the English ministers would only discuss the peace terms at the coming congress, and warning him that he would be attacked by the pro-peace London mob. Then in a final bid to stop the mission St John ordered Strafford to refuse the prince a yacht or a frigate convoy, adding: 'It is high time to put a stop to this foreign influence in British councils; and we must either emancipate ourselves now, or be for ever slaves.'[2]

Eugene was not the man to be put off by these threats and St John's orders came too late to stop him leaving Rotterdam with a small party which included his nephew Eugene. Their English yacht took a week to battle its way through winter storms to Harwich. As the boat sailed up the Thames on 16 January 1712 there were thick crowds waiting to welcome the prince at Greenwich and the Tower. To avoid them he insisted on going on to Whitehall, where he disembarked at nightfall and took an ordinary cab to Leicester House, which the Austrian resident, Hoffman, had ready for him.

Eugene's visit lasted two months and proved a political failure. Although he showed himself openly sympathetic towards Marlborough, nothing could be done to save his friend. The Tory leaders were studiously polite but resolutely refused to discuss their peace terms, and

Harley, now earl of Oxford, found a ready excuse in his own poor French. Repeated memorials by the prince were answered by complaints about the Austrian war effort, and Eugene's offers to increase the number of Imperial troops in Spain produced no effect. Audiences with the queen were no more successful: Anne would not be drawn and seemed 'somewhat embarrassed and aloof'.[3] However, on her birthday she presented Eugene with an expensive sword, 'very rich and genteele, and the diamonds very white'. On this occasion the usually unpretentious prince, who normally visited with 'but one footman', appeared 'in great splendor . . . in a fine equipage'.[4] Although the Tory ministers were worried he might interfere in domestic politics, he did not. The *Hof-kammer* had provided him with credit notes to exchange with Jewish bankers in London, but when the Hanoverian minister, Bothmer, suggested he bribe fifteen members of parliament in the name of the elector of Hanover, who was expected to succeed Anne, he refused because 'the proposed amount was so large'.[5] The credits went undrawn.

Why did Eugene stay in London so long, especially as he soon recognized that the ministry would not change its mind? Largely it seems because he was being pressed to stay by letters from Wratislaw[6] – the Imperial government continued to believe that their alliance with England still had some meaning and that they could influence queen Anne's ministers.

On another level Eugene had every reason to stay on: socially his visit was an enormous success. Jonathan Swift had accurately predicted it would 'all end in a journey of pleasure' because 'the great men resolve to entertain him in turns'.[7] At times he seemed 'in some danger of being kill'd with good cheer, having been allow'd but one day to dine at home'.[8] He accepted invitations from both Tories and Whigs and went out to Richmond more than once to shoot in the park with Ormonde, Marlborough's Tory successor as commander-in-chief. The two men got on well: on one visit the prince bagged 'a brace of pheasants and a hare'.[9] The prince also dined with Oxford, who toasted him as 'the greatest general of the age', to which Eugene is said to have replied, hinting broadly at Marlborough's dismissal, 'If that be true I owe it to your lordship.'[10] The most splendid reception, however, was an all-Whig occasion at the duke of Portland's where, after a dinner of 60 meat dishes and 41 desserts, the guests danced for an hour, although both Eugene and Marlborough pointedly refused to join in the French dances, the prince declaring he knew only the Hussar dance.

The ordinary Londoners were keen to see Eugene, who had been a popular figure throughout the war. Everywhere his coach drew a crowd;

so many people pressed their way into Leicester House that the floor cracked. Contemporary observers had a field day, particularly the malicious Tory lookers-on. Although the prince made a point of going to various great ladies' assemblies, Lady Strafford wrote to her ambassador husband at The Hague that 'The Ladys here dont admire Prince Eugene for he seems to take very little notis of them',[11] adding later: 'I have taken it into my head that Prince Eugene has been some time wounded in the —, for I never saw anybody sit down so stiff.'[12] While Swift had written on first seeing him that he was not, as rumoured, 'an ugly faced fellow, but well enough and a good shape', political feeling got the better of him a month later when he declared the prince to be 'very plain . . . plaguy yellow, and tolerable ugly besides'.[13]

The visit was marred by the death of the prince's twenty year old nephew Eugene from the ever-present smallpox, but we have no idea what effect, if any, this had on the prince; he was as reticent as ever about his own feelings. According to Lord Berkeley of Stratton it was

> drinking which threw him into it, for he fell in with the young debauchez here, who kept him continually drunk. They say his uncle was not well satisfied with him, nor did honour him with any great share of his kindness. Never having had the small pox, he was persuaded to remove out of Leicester house, and to lye at the D. of Grafton's in my neighbourhood. I saw a little more of him on Sunday . . . , but found him as reserv'd, tho' better bred than any English man.[14]

The young Eugene, who was buried in Ormonde's family vault in Westminster Abbey,[15] was typical of the children of Eugene's eldest brother Louis Thomas. All caused the prince a good deal of worry, and he tried to be strict with them. He had threatened to abandon one nephew, Maurice, unless 'he changes his conduct', although he nevertheless gave him 200 louis d'or just before his death in 1710.[16] The other two nephews, Emmanuel and Eugene, were both found Imperial commands, which the prince insisted they take seriously.[17] He wrote bluntly to Emmanuel to conduct his regiment properly and not to borrow from its funds because he would be unable to count on protection from his uncle if irregularities occurred.[18]

Eugene left London in March 1712 convinced that the ministry intended to make peace with France regardless of the allies. He feared that this was merely the first step to an English alliance with France and Bourbon Spain, the division of the world's commerce among them to the exclusion of the Dutch, and the succession of the Stuart pretender rather than the Protestant house of Hanover to the crown at Anne's death.

Both he and the Whigs felt this could only be prevented by the Austrians and Dutch continuing the war. This assessment of the Tory ministers' aims was surprisingly accurate, except over the question of the pretender, and was already being borne out by the progress of the peace congress at Utrecht from January 1712. Here the Imperialists and Dutch soon discovered that the important discussions were those held privately by the French and English.

To influence public opinion in England to persuade the government to continue the war and to force the French to make substantial concessions, Eugene wanted a vigorous campaign in Flanders in 1712: extra efforts were therefore made to increase Imperial numbers by moving troops from Hungary and the Rhine. Although Ormonde led the English national and auxiliary troops, the Dutch had put Eugene in command of their own forces. At the beginning of the campaign Eugene believed he would be able to force Villars to a battle and then march victoriously on Paris. Unfortunately things were to go badly wrong.

Although the prince was initially well-inclined towards Ormonde, who had no experience as a general, he soon found him hesitant to take the offensive. Ormonde's reluctance came not so much from caution or inexperience as from secret orders sent from England. On 6 May viscount Bolingbroke (as Henry St John had now become) warned him to 'be jealous of Prince Eugene's conduct' and to be 'more cautious for some time of engaging in an action, unless in the case of an apparent and considerable advantage'.[19] Then on 21 May, when the Tories felt they had squeezed all the concessions they wanted out of their private negotiations with the French and feared that an allied victory would entail a revision of the terms, Anne sent the famous 'restraining orders', forbidding Ormonde to take part in any siege or battle. Although these orders were kept secret from Eugene, they were communicated to Villars. This led G. M. Trevelyan to say that they amounted to 'little short of a plot' between the English and French governments to allow Villars to defeat Eugene. Although Trevelyan blamed Bolingbroke most, it now seems that Oxford was equally to blame. Bolingbroke was the more outspoken, however, telling the French agent in London, Gaultier, once the orders were sent, that he would not object if Villars fell on Eugene 'and cut him to pieces, him and his army'.[20] In October the Tory government even communicated what they knew of Eugene's war plans to the French.

Eugene had some idea of the 'restraining orders' because he was kept informed from within the English camp by Cadogan. As Ormonde became increasingly embarrassed at making excuses for his inaction,

Eugene grew contemptuous, calling him 'a blockhead'[21] in his correspondence with Sinzendorff at Utrecht. But he made the best of the
situation by beginning yet another siege, at Le Quesnoy, and by sending
2,000 hussars on a huge week-long terror sweep around Paris from
Rheims to Metz. This force pillaged and 'burned the country houses of
all those who could not produce money to ransom them'.[22]

Le Quesnoy fell in the first week of July but less than a fortnight
later, on 17 July, Ormonde announced an armistice with the French and
tried to separate all the troops under his command from the rest of the
allies. Only the 12,000 native English troops would follow him, as the
leaders of his German and Danish auxiliaries had been in close contact
with Eugene and took their men over to him. Now in control of the
bulk of the allied troops, Eugene could use them as he wanted. Yet he
did not attack Villars, but besieged Valenciennes and Landrecies. Once
these had fallen he felt he would then be in a position 'to thrust into the
heart of this kingdom'.[23] Although he hoped 'to fight the enemy
successfully if they came near',[24] he was really no freer of the siege
mentality to which he was wedded than he had been two years before.
Nevertheless the French court were frightened enough by Eugene's
reputation to contemplate leaving Versailles. While France's food stocks
and financial position were now much better than two years before,
Louis had feared that this year's campaign might finally destroy him. He
had told Villars privately in April that if the marshal were defeated he
would join the army himself for a last battle, as 'I do not intend to live
to see the enemy in my capital'.[25]

In besieging Landrecies, Eugene was handicapped because the Dutch,
who now had to shoulder most of the financial burden of the campaign,
had refused to pay for supply bases to be set up nearby; Eugene's own
main bases were some sixty miles in the rear. This meant that his long
line of communications was open to attack. Villars was quick to see that
the most exposed point was a Dutch garrison on the Scheldt at Denain.
On the night of 24 July he made a surprise attack on this position and
completely defeated the Dutch troops there under Albermarle. As the
Dutch fled panic-stricken over the Scheldt, Eugene arrived but could not
send reinforcements across the river as the only bridge had collapsed
under the weight of retreating baggage waggons. Although he was
furious at the cowardice of the Dutch troops – four battalions 'threw
down their arms upon the first discharge'[26] – he excused Albemarle and
assured Heinsius 'he did all that a brave, prudent and vigilant general
can do'.[27]

The battle was a minor one, which Eugene was inclined to dismiss at the time; nevertheless, in Napoleon's words, 'Denain saved France'. Villars followed up his victory by seizing the allies' main supply magazine at Marchiennes. These successive mishaps sapped the Dutch will to continue the war both at The Hague and in the army. By 8 August Eugene had been forced to retreat to a defensive position around Lille, from where he wrote to Sinzendorff in despair at the Dutch field deputies: 'No one would believe what I have to put up with from these people.'[28] Although the Dutch had largely taken the ground from under his feet, the auxiliary troops also became obstructive and restless as they began to worry about who would pay them. On the other hand Villars's forces were growing in strength and before the two armies went into winter quarters in October Douai, Le Quesnoy and Bouchain had all fallen to the French. It was a depressing end to the campaign but Eugene managed to keep his temper with the Dutch deputies, and the Hanoverian officers in the allied army were impressed that he could still laugh a lot and hearten those round him – he was 'very magnanimous and appeared more cheerful and witty than ever'.[29]

There were no doubts in Eugene's mind where the blame for the disasters lay: the extraordinary behaviour of the English, who he felt 'really deserve to be hanged'. But the conduct of the Dutch had been almost as bad, for, as he explained to Sinzendorff on 3 October, '. . . the poor success of this campaign should not be blamed on the Denain affair but to this mood of fear and irresolution which reigns in the Republic and which has spread among the deputies and generals.'[30] It was clear enough to him now that the emperor must decide whether he could afford to continue the war on his own. Both Eugene and Sinzendorff had believed during the summer that it would be impossible to fight without the Dutch.

The defeats in the Netherlands strengthened the hand of the English and French in the peace negotiations taking place throughout 1712 at Utrecht. For the most part the Imperialists were helpless spectators, unable to impose a military solution or to take the diplomatic initiative. Without their participation a settlement was gradually being decided on by which Philip of Anjou would renounce France – after a series of deaths in the French royal family Louis's direct heir was now his only remaining great-grandson, a child of two – and keep Spain and the Indies, while Charles would receive the Netherlands and the Italian lands except for Sardinia and Sicily.

Charles's German ministers had unanimously agreed during most of 1712 that the emperor would have to make peace. Trautsohn had been convinced from April that 'the war cannot be continued successfully against France and Spain without England',[31] but only Wratislaw dared point this out to Charles in July. Moreover, by the end of the year Wratislaw was also convinced that Austria would have to accept English mediation. He put it starkly to Sinzendorff, in charge of the negotiations at Utrecht: ' . . . we have to deal tactfully with England, as we are in her hands; we must no longer print, say or write anything which might offend her or her ministers, but we must cajole in order to obtain what we can.'[32] Under Wratislaw's guidance Austrian policy was also moving gradually towards renouncing Spain, a step which had been urged as early as February by Sinzendorff. Wratislaw worked hard to impress this on Charles and was consequently being criticized by the emperor's Spanish ministers, who accused him of being an 'enemy of Spain and of the Spaniards'.[33] His main aim, as before, was to create a compact Austrian state based on the hereditary lands and Italy. He would also have preferred to exchange the Southern Netherlands for Bavaria. His views about Italy had always been shared by Eugene and his experiences in 1712 made the prince also believe 'that it would be far better, if we could exchange a part [of the Netherlands] for Bavaria . . . I do not see how, if Holland and England do not want to do anything for the Emperor, we can accept this province which will be of no use to him but only a burden.'[34]

It was unfortunate that at the end of 1712 Wratislaw fell seriously ill from dropsy. When Eugene returned home on 9 December he found him too weak to get out of bed. Public prayers for his recovery were ordered by the emperor, but he died on the 21st. The death of such a close personal friend was a great blow to Eugene. In Wratislaw's will the only beneficiary outside the immediate family was Eugene, who was left a 'pair of companion Indian writing tables'.[35] Wratislaw, who had also been a bachelor and shared the prince's addiction to snuff, had not only provided friendship but had been Eugene's closest political ally for more than ten years. In every issue over this period they had stuck together. Wratislaw had furnished the firm political base which Eugene could count on while he was away on campaign. A confidant of the two young emperors, Wratislaw had also eased the transition from one brother to the other and had ensured Eugene's acceptance by Charles. No German minister was ever to have the same intimacy with Charles.

His friend's death left Eugene undisputed first minister, even though he never held any such formal title. When he was in Vienna he presided over the conference and during his absence prince Trautsohn acted for him. All the leading ministers were his close political allies. In the conference, besides the loyal and upright but ineffectual Trautsohn, was the deaf and punctilious Seilern, who was the most hardworking minister. Another member waiting to step into Seilern's shoes as first chancellor was the ambitious Sinzendorff, who was quite capable of changing his friends to suit the occasion. Of particular value to Eugene was the renewal of personal and political friendship in 1712–13 with another minister now admitted into the inner conference, Gundaker Starhemberg. The two men's friendship had been somewhat clouded by past enmity between Starhemberg and Wratislaw, but over the next twenty years the relationship with Starhemberg was to serve Eugene very much as that with Wratislaw had done, although there was not the same personal warmth and the prince was to be the leader rather than an equal in this partnership. For the moment both men seemed to have the complete confidence of the young emperor, even though they were ministers he had inherited rather than chosen himself. Judging from the great deference and affection as well as confidence he expressed in his letters to Eugene, Charles seems to have particularly valued him.[36] The prince fostered this regard by the friendship he established with one of the ministers Charles had brought back with him from Spain, count Stella, who, according to Charles's former tutor Liechtenstein, had the emperor under his spell.

Wratislaw's death did not affect Vienna's moves towards peace, but it did result in a shortage of diplomatic expertise in the difficult months ahead. The lead in pressing for peace was now taken over by Eugene, who accepted with the other members of the conference that further war in the Netherlands or Spain was out of the question without the help of the Maritime Powers. Neither the reluctance of the ministers who had returned with him from Spain nor that of Charles himself was strong enough to resist this pressure from the conference, and by the last day of 1712 the emperor had in effect agreed to the Anglo-French peace terms. Consequently at Utrecht Sinzendorff not only signed a convention in March 1713 for the evacuation of Catalonia and the neutrality of Italy but had also been empowered to sign peace terms which would have brought Charles the Southern Netherlands, Milan and Naples, but not Sardinia or Sicily. It had not been easy to overcome Charles's hostility to these terms and on 1 April Trautsohn wrote warning Sinzendorff: 'It seems that the Emperor inwardly harbours a bad impression of all us German ministers, as though we had no feelings for the Spaniards and had no great scruple in sacrificing them. This happens to be completely untrue.'[37]

In the event neither the emperor nor the majority of the Imperial princes signed the treaty of Utrecht with the other combatants on 11

April – it was actually signed on the 12th but was backdated at the request of the English as the old-style date in England would have been 1 April. Last-minute demands for the cession of Luxembourg to Max Emmanuel, as well as the restoration of Bavaria, the withdrawal of the Imperialists from Mantua and the immediate formal recognition of Philip V as king of Spain, were too much for Charles, but also for his German ministers, to stomach; they were as concerned over Italy as he was. Eugene, who had certainly not wanted the war to continue, was particularly angry at these new French demands. The Dutch minister in Vienna noticed when he wished Eugene well for yet another summer campaign that 'there were tears in the eyes of the good Prince'.[38]

Abandoned by the Maritime Powers, the Imperialists had to limit the 1713 campaign to the Rhineland, but their prospects were poor. Charles VI's early efforts to overhaul the monarchy's finances had had little effect, as he admitted in a letter to Eugene on 19 December 1713: 'The Chamber is as disordered as ever; the reorganization has still not begun.'[39] The hereditary lands were exhausted and the estates truculent about voting further contributions. To make matters worse, in 1713 the plague, which had been endemic in Hungary during the rebellion, spread westwards. Both Vienna and Prague were hit despite a military cordon to keep 'Jews, Swabians, beggars and Serbs' away.[40] Drastic measures were taken in Vienna: all Jews and pedlars found trying to get into the city were summarily hanged at the gates, the homeless population of the capital was transported on to the Danube islands, processions were forbidden and church services held in the open air. While the emperor created a good impression by staying in the city throughout the crisis, great care was taken when he went out to keep him away from any sick being carried in chairs and from death carts. Once autumn approached, the disease began to abate, but by then thousands were dead.

During 1713 all the hereditary lands, as well as Hungary, found real difficulties in filling their quotas and paying contributions. The estates of Upper Austria and the area of the Vorarlberg known as Further Austria proved the most obstinate in resisting Eugene and the *Hofkriegsrat*'s demands and drove Eugene, who never had much patience with estates, to write in exasperation: 'During all my life I have never seen a province like that of Further Austria, which complains about bagatelles and makes difficulties . . . over everything.'[41] The brunt had to be borne, as ever, by the Bohemian crown-lands and by Upper and Lower Austria: of the new recruits demanded at the end of 1712 Bohemia provided 60 per cent and Lower and Upper Austria 20 per cent. The contributions were assessed on much the same ratio.

1 Eugene Maurice, prince of Savoy-Carignan (1635–73), Eugene's father. An officer in the army of Louis XIV of France, he died on campaign during the Dutch war of 1672–78.

2 Olympia Mancini (1640–1708), a niece of cardinal Mazarin and Eugene's mother. She was forced to flee from France and her family in 1680.

3 Leopold I (1640–1705), the cultured but rather ineffective ruler of Austria from 1657 and Holy Roman Emperor from 1658. The first emperor Eugene served and the one who supported his military campaigns the least.

4 Maximilian Emmanuel (1662–1726), elector of Bavaria from 1679. An erratic a[n]d often brilliantly successful general, he was Eugene's patron and mentor during the 16[...] and his enemy during the War of Spanish Succession.

5 A page – much reduced in size – fr[om] Eugene's campaign diary for the Bosnian [...] of 1697, written in French, the prince's [...] language, in his own ha[nd.]

6 View of Sarajevo, the major trading centre of Turkish Bosnia, with its many mosques. The town was sacked by Eugene's expedition in autumn 1697.

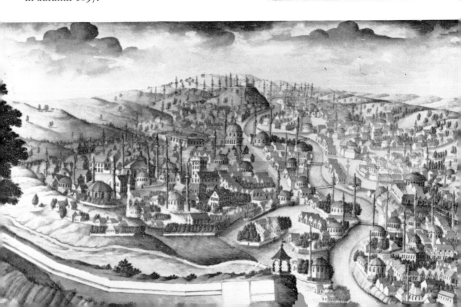

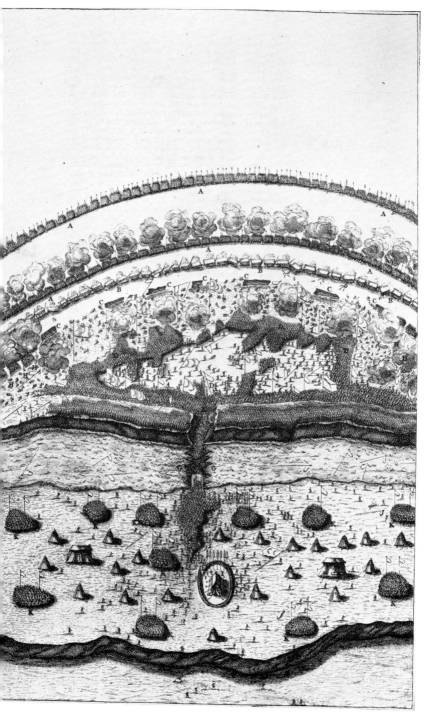

Eugene's first great victory, Zenta (11 September 1697), seen from the Turkish side of the Tisza. The Imperial troops are shown in two lines (A). The Turks retreated from their defences (B and C) and tried to flee over the pontoon bridge across the river. The sultan's tent, which Eugene claimed for himself, can be seen in the centre foreground.

8   The Judenplatz in Vienna during the first years of the eighteenth century. Leading off from the centre of the square is a typical narrow street (or *Gasse*) with tall buildings on either side.

9   Eugene's city or winter palace in the Himmelpfortgasse, as it appeared in the 1720s after Hildebrandt's extensions to the original by Fischer von Erlach. The engraver has greatly exaggerated the width of the street in order to show the building to its best advantage.

10 Infantry, drawn up in battle line, firing on the enemy.

11 Punishments used in the Imperial armies during Eugene's time, including running the gauntlet and riding a wooden horse.

12 Caricature depicting an Imperial
cavalryman billeted on a
long-suffering peasant.

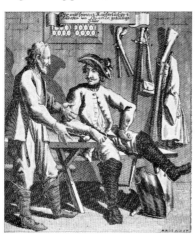

13 German camp surgeons at work.
Paid no more than N.C.O.s, they
provided the only medical services
available to the bulk of the troops.

16 (Oppo
Count He
von Mansf
prince of Fc
(1640–171;
time-serv
courtier
disast
president of
Imperial
council (1701–
who was repl
by Eug

14 Drawing of 'a market Tent in Camp' by Marcellus Laroon, who
accompanied the British troops in Flanders in 1707. It shows a side of army life
usually ignored by memoir writers of the time.

15 Eugene's army crossing the Alps at the beginning of the Italian campaign of 1701, a feat which astounded contemporaries and took the French completely by surprise. Engraving from the *Helden-Thaten*, a eulogizing history of the prince's life and deeds, published between 1736 and 1739.

17 The unsuccessful allied siege of Toulon (July 1707). The strongly defended base of the French Mediterranean fleet withstood the attack by Eugene and Victor Amadeus's army from the east, although the fleet itself was eventually destroyed by an Anglo-Dutch fleet.

20 Victor Amadeus II (1666–1732), duke of Savoy from 1675. As a ruler of a minor state, he successfully played on the rivalries of his stronger neighbours. Eugene's early gratitude towards him turned into intense distrust, but he always afforded him respect as head of his 'house'.

18 John Churchill, duke of Marlborough (1650–1722), commander of the allied forces in the Netherlands during the War of Spanish Succession and Eugene's 'especial good friend'. Portrait of *c.* 1706 by Godfrey Kneller.

19 Eugene of Savoy, painted by Godfrey Kneller, probably during the prince's visit to London early in 1712. An only slightly romanticized portrait which shows him, contrary to his usual practice, wearing a full wig as well as the order of the Golden Fleece. The date of death is incorrect.

21–22 (Left) Medal to commemorate the decisive allied victory of Blenheim
(13 August 1704), the first major defeat of Louis XIV of France during the War of
Spanish Succession. Prince Louis, margrave of Baden-Baden, is shown between
Eugene and Marlborough although he did not take part in the battle. (Right) Medal
to commemorate the taking of Mons by Eugene and Marlborough (October 1709),
shortly after the battle of Malplaquet.

23 The bloody allied victory of Malplaquet (11 September 1709). Eugene
appears on horseback in the left foreground, but his part of the army actually fought
its way through the woods on the right. The arms and uniforms are accurate.

25 Field-marshal Guido von Starhemberg (1657–1737), a distinguished Imperial infantry general. His close friendship with Eugene turned to bitter rivalry after 1703.

24 Joseph I (1678–1711), Austrian ruler and Holy Roman Emperor from 1705. An energetic and usually decisive man, he was the emperor Eugene enjoyed serving best.

26 Count John Wenzel Wratislaw von Mitrowitz (1669–1712), Eugene's closest friend and political collaborator during the War of Spanish Succession.

27 Charles Theodore Otto, prince Salm (1648–1710), tutor to the young Joseph and uncle of his wife Amelia. He was a constant critic of Eugene's generalship and of his conduct of the war council.

29 Count Michael John Althann (1679–1722), the closest friend of Charles VI in both Spain and Austria. He was used as a tool by the cabal which was formed unsuccessfully against Eugene in 1719.

8 Charles VI (1685–1740), the last male Habsburg, ruler of Austria and Holy Roman Emperor from 1711. While archduke he had been the allied candidate for the Spanish throne as 'Charles III' (1703–11). An excellent father but an indifferent ruler.

30 The moated palace at Laxenburg just outside Vienna, a favourite summer residence of the Imperial family because of the hunting available around the Danube.

32 Count Gundaker von Starhemberg (1[...] 1745), a financial expert and compe[...] president of the chamber (1703–15) and [...] of the *Finanzconferenz* (1716–45). Euge[...] firmest political ally during the first [...] decades of Charles VI's re[...]

31 Balthasar Permoser's white marble apotheosis of Eugene as conqueror of the Turks surrounded by cherubs and Fame. The statue, which was disliked by the prince, was executed in 1721 and set up in the 'Marble Room' of his Upper Belvedere palace.

33 Count Philip Louis von Sinzendorff (1671–1742), second and then first court chancellor (1705–15, 1715–42). A *bon-viveur* and an accommodating servant of Charles VI, he pursued an imaginative but futile foreign policy in the 1720s.

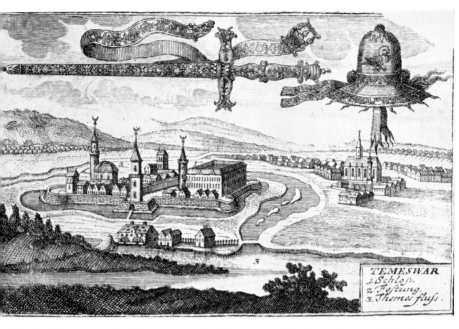

The Turkish stronghold of Temesvár on the Tisza, captured by Eugene's army in October
16. Note the sword and papal hat bestowed by Clement XI on the prince for this achievement.

Eugene's last and greatest victory over the Turks at Belgrade (16 August 1717). Surrounded
d apparently on the point of disaster, the Imperial army delivered a crushing and final defeat on
e Turks and then took Belgrade. Engraving by Huchtenburg.

36 South and front view of Eugene's double garden palace, the Belvedere. The Upper Belvedere seen here was built by Hildebrandt between 1720 and 1722. Shown in the engraving are the huge wrought-iron gates, the rows of chestnut trees and the pond which reflected the building beyond.

37 Eugene's picture gallery in the Upper Belvedere with 'the piece representing Adam and Eve as big as the life' in the centre. Note the heavily ornamented ceiling and the display furniture at the sides of the gallery.

38 The Schlosshof palace in the Marchfeld, the centre for the hunting parties which Eugene enjoyed in his last years. This painting by Bellotto dates from the 1750s when the palace had been bought by Maria Theresa from Eugene's niece Victoria.

39 Countess Eleonora Batthyány (1672–1741), generally thought to have been Eugene's mistress. A portrait of her as a young woman in Hungarian dress – the only one known.

40 Eugene in late middle age. Although this portrait by Kupetzky is conventional in style, it captures the prince's Latin features well.

41 Eugene in old age, wearing the ceremonial robes of the order of the Golden Fleece.

42 Count Frederick Charles von Schönborn (1674–1746), Imperial vice-chancellor (1705–34). Eugene's closest political friend during his last years and one who shared his interests in collecting and building. Note the hunting dog and gun in this portrait of 1715.

43 Jean-Baptiste Rousseau (1670–1741), French writer of odes and satirical verses. Eugene admired and patronized him for nearly a decade after 1716.

To spread the burden of the war strenuous efforts were made to persuade the German princes that France was still just as much a threat to them as to the emperor, and when Eugene reached Mühlberg on 23 May 1713 to take up command of the Imperial army, 8 million gulden and large numbers of troops had been promised by the Empire. But these promises were illusory. Only 10,000 gulden had been paid by August and Eugene reckoned that at this rate it would take thirty years for the rest to appear. The southern and western German states could not afford to pay, as the chief burden of supporting the Imperial army during the war had weighed on the Franconian and Swabian circles; the northern states were more interested in the renewal of fighting between Denmark, Russia and Sweden in northern Germany. There were, however, plenty of German troops for hire and the emperor had to turn to Dutch bankers for a loan of 1 million gulden to pay for them. Inevitably Eugene's freedom of movement was to be severely limited by lack of money and supplies: by the autumn the Hanoverian contingent in the Imperial army were eating acorns as no money was available to buy bread.

Villars deployed vastly greater numbers of French troops across the Rhine opposite Eugene and could continually keep him guessing about his intentions by sending columns in all directions from Speyer down to the Black Forest. The prince therefore concentrated on preventing any massive breakthrough and had to accept the loss of both Landau and Freiburg during the year.

Throughout these summer months Eugene was unhappy about carrying on the war and wrote to Charles in June that a bad peace would be better than being 'ruined equally by friend and foe'.[42] When his German colleagues in the conference agreed to Charles's suggestion that Austria should attack Savoy in order to force Victor Amadeus to surrender Sicily, which had been allotted to him at Utrecht, Eugene quickly quashed the plan by refusing to release any troops. On the French side, Louis, despite his success on the Rhine, also wanted peace – he had never expected that the Imperialists would reject his further demands at Utrecht and force him into another campaign. Eventually, using the elector palatine as intermediary, both sides agreed that Villars and Eugene should negotiate in November at Rastadt in the castle built by the late Louis of Baden in the style of Versailles.

On 26 November 1713 the two generals and their hundred or so entourage met in the courtyard to a fanfare of trumpets before moving off to separate wings of the castle. Having known each other from the Turkish campaigns of the 1680s, Eugene and Villars soon established an excellent relationship, dispensing completely with the formality which usually hindered diplomatic negotiations and treating each other as belonging to the same class of *honnêtes hommes*. The two men dined together, entertained by musicians Villars had brought with him, and then spent their evenings talking or playing cards. They began by playing *piquet* but as Eugene lost heavily, the tactful Villars gradually switched to the less expensive *brelan*.

In the actual negotiations Eugene came off best. While he could count on total support from home, Villars, who was permanently reduced to hobbling around on a stick and wanted to crown his military exploits by achieving a peace settlement, felt anxious about opposition groups at court, especially the foreign minister Torcy, eager to criticize him and urging a tough line in the negotiations. Villars was also an inept and confused negotiator, while Eugene, who persuaded him that he wanted to help confound his enemies at Versailles, continually acted fiercely, standing up, putting on his hat and threatening to break off the talks at the slightest provocation. After a week Eugene described the marshal brutally to Sinzendorff: 'Villars is timid, badly informed about previous negotiations, and wants peace; if it depended on him, he would sacrifice everything to achieve something which would increase his credit at court.'[43] Although the Imperialists would have given way on several points, Eugene convinced Villars they had every intention of fighting on even if the French reached Linz. Eventually in February 1714 the two generals drafted a final peace settlement and then withdrew from Rastadt, temporarily breaking off the talks until Louis accepted its terms. Villars threatened not to continue as negotiator unless he did. Louis gave way.[44]

By the treaty of Rastadt, the *Reich* frontier as fixed by the peace of Ryswick was accepted, which meant that the French kept Alsace, Strasbourg and the three Lorraine bishoprics. The French were also given Landau and Fort Louis, but the emperor was not asked to renounce his claims to Spain formally nor to recognize the Italian settlement reached at Utrecht. The French also agreed that Charles should have Sardinia, although it had been settled on Max Emmanuel of Bavaria at Utrecht.[45]

Eugene's achievement at Rastadt was all the greater because of the failure of the 1713 campaign and the desire in Vienna for peace. He was fêted as a hero on his return and even the normally reserved Charles kissed him. By fighting for a further year the Imperialists had beaten the French attempt to limit their influence in Italy and they now controlled Naples, Milan, Mantua, Mirandola, enclaves on the Tuscan coast and Sardinia. In possession of the Southern Netherlands and Hungary as well, 'the creation of Austria's position as a great power was completed'.[46]

Despite its long years of sacrifice the Empire itself had gained no territory and had even lost Landau. No minister in Vienna, including Eugene, was prepared to put the interests of the Empire before those of Austria and the dynasty. The Habsburgs' attempt to reverse the gains made by France in Germany since 1648 had failed, but at least the process seemed to have been halted. In Europe as a whole the universal predominance of France was no more and a balance of power appeared to have been created between the three great states of England, France and Austria. But Villars's cryptic comment on the settlement and the war itself provided a fitting afterthought:

> Thus after a war of fourteen years, during which the emperor and the King of France had nearly quitted their respective capitals; Spain had seen two rivals kings in Madrid, and almost all the petty states of Italy had changed their sovereigns; a war which had desolated the greater part of Europe, was concluded almost on the very terms which might have been procured at the commencement of hostilities.[47]

XVI

Charles VI and his Ministers

While the war lasted Charles VI had impressed both his ministers and outside observers as a ruler, but after his wife and his former Spanish court returned from Barcelona in 1713 and the urgency of the war years ended, he soon revealed a different self.[1] Notice was taken of his increasing slowness in transacting business and of his irritating habit of evading direct questions by gabbling so fast that 'the most skilful magician would not understand him'.[2] He was also, like Eugene, inclined to be extremely reticent and taciturn. His ministers soon learned to tread warily: the president of the aulic council, Windischgrätz, confided to the Hanoverian minister Huldenberg in 1716 that Charles was more difficult to deal with than his father or brother, because he was 'quite Spanish' and 'sensitive . . . about his authority', insisting that he should decide everything in person.[3] On the other hand he would not take the lead in directing government himself and spent a good deal of his time in listening to tittle-tattle, allowing his ministers to intrigue against each other. Consequently they not only found it hard to agree among themselves but also dared not act on their own initiative,[4] and, according to the same Huldenberg, 'In the 26 years that I have been here, they have never been so reserved and secretive.'[5] Many of Charles's problems with his ministers probably came from his inheriting men from his brother whom he gradually came to dislike but could never bring himself to get rid of. Like his father he was too much of a traditionalist to dismiss anyone, especially loyal servants.

As he grew older – he was only twenty-nine in 1714 – Charles increasingly isolated his real self from his public one, rejecting contact with those outside his immediate family and friends except on a very formal level. He stressed the ceremonial aspects of his rule, preferring communication with ambassadors and ministers to be in writing. He only rarely sat in on the conference. At the same time he was becoming more aware of and oppressed by his isolated and responsible position as the last male Habsburg. At the news of Joseph's death he had written in his diary, 'I am the only one of our house left; everything depends on me.'[6] Although he kept this diary regularly in his odd, monotonous angular writing till he died, the entries were limited to noting daily trivia and tell us little about his ideas. They do show, however, that he continually harked back to his days in Spain and also what a shattering effect the death of his first-born child and only son had on him in 1716. The loss of this baby, after eight years of waiting for an heir, and the subsequent births of three archduchesses, was plainly an enormous jolt to his sense of dynasty.

The succession issue had been with him since his accession. On 19 April 1713, while still without children of his own, he ordered his *Hofkanzler* Seilern to read to his councillors a document – the Pragmatic Sanction – which settled the succession of all his lands on his future male or female heirs, then on the daughters of Joseph. The aim was to keep the inheritance together – significantly described as 'indivisible and inseparable' – and to avoid another crisis like that which had been precipitated by the issue of the Spanish succession.

In his style of living Charles differed little from his father or brother. As they had done, he moved with the seasons from one residence to another. During the winter months the court lived in the medieval palace of the Hofburg in the heart of the inner city. Charles made few improvements to it and compared with Versailles or the smaller German palaces, it appeared cramped and dismal. When Pöllnitz saw the palace in 1729 he thought it 'so wretched a Mansion that few Monarchs are lodged worse than the Emperor. The Furniture too is old-fashioned and not very rich.'[7] In the Hofburg the court stuck rigidly to the Spanish ceremonial and dress of Leopold's time, and the wearing of black clothes made it difficult for observers to know whether the court was in mourning or not. The Hanoverian Keysler has left us this description of Charles in the Hofburg:

> [He] affects no great shew in dress, and has a professed aversion to all affectation of French modes; and particularly large open sleeves. On solemnities, he generally appears in a large black Spanish habit, with small cuffs of purple, embroidered with silver; his shoe ribbons are also embroidered, and he wears a red feather in his hat.[8]

He kept this hat on when sitting at table, only taking it off for grace or when the empress drank his health.

There were said to be 20,000 people in 'the greatest and most magnificent court in Europe'.[9] As there was not enough room in the Hofburg most of the courtiers were housed by custom on the second floor of citizens' houses, paying nominal rents. The corruption of the officials was notorious; half Vienna was said to live on the emperor's kitchen and cellar. The French minister du Luc in July 1715 complained of having to dispense 2,000 louis d'or to the households of the emperor and three empresses: 'They not only put their hands out but actually come to your house to claim their gratifications as a right.'[10]

The emperor's whole year, like his every day, was governed by a precise calendar of events and ceremonies that had to be performed, and pride of place was still taken by religious observances. The latter were the cause of much complaint from the envoys of Catholic powers who were expected to take part in them with the emperor. The French duke of Richelieu wrote in 1726 that 'Only a Capucin in excellent health could stand up to this life during Lent.' A sympathetic cardinal friend told him that it sounded very like the life of a cardinal in Rome but they at least were paid for it.[11]

Every April the court left the Hofburg for the summer palace at Laxenburg where it stayed till June. Originally a fishing village, two hours' ride from Vienna, most of the notables and ministers, though not Eugene, also built themselves houses there, so Charles was unable to escape from them. The palace was a tower-like building, which reminded Montesquieu of a dovecote when he saw it in 1728. Although the rooms were small Charles and his predecessors liked Laxenburg because it was ideal for hunting. The Imperial family spent every day from six to ten o'clock in the mornings and three till six in the afternoons in a shelter made out of leafy branches, releasing specially-trained falcons to catch herons, crows, ducks and hares. During quiet periods they played cards.

At the beginning of July the Imperial court moved to the Favorita palace – the modern Theresianum – in the Wieden suburb of Vienna, where it remained till the autumn. As at Laxenburg, the ceremonial was less formal and German clothes were worn – it was not till Joseph II's reign that military dress was allowed at court and even generals like Eugene had to wear court dress. The Favorita was hot, dark and cramped, so that a great deal of time was spent in the large billiards room and in the shady walks in the garden. Although Charles and his wife enjoyed billiards as well as cards, their favourite family occupation here was shooting at targets in the garden, the women being as expert as the men.

Yet the emperor had more cultured tastes. As a youth he already spoke Latin, Italian, French and Spanish as well as German.[12] He was a great collector of coins and books. He eventually bought the two famous private collections of Eugene and of the prince's adjutant, Hohendorff, which formed the basis of the modern Nationalbibliothek in Vienna. He spent some time every day in this library, which was also open for others to use; it was looked after by his physician Nicholas Garelli. When he travelled Charles took a *Handbibliothek* with him. But his greatest love was his music, which despite the economies at his accession eventually cost 200,000 gulden a year. In 1715 John Joseph Fux was appointed his *Kapellmeister* at a salary of 3,100 gulden. The Imperial orchestra was made up of 26 violins, 13 trumpets and 24 other instruments, and there was a twenty-eight-strong choir. Charles was himself a composer and under him Vienna took its first firm steps to becoming the eventual musical centre of Germany and Europe.

The highlight of the musical year at court was the operas performed on special occasions, like royal birthdays, either in the opera house in the Hofburg or in the gardens of the Favorita. After an opera in 1724, to celebrate the birth of his third daughter,

> His Imperial Majesty made a Lottery, where there were prizes drawn for all the performers, some of 2000, others of 1000 or 500 florins [gulden] value, viz. jewels, gold repetition watches, etuys etc. The Emperour himself play'd upon the harpsicord to accompany the voices during the whole opera, & the eldest of the young Archduchesses [Maria Theresa] sung upon the stage.[13]

Less costly pleasures, especially during the February carnival before the austerity of Lent, were the *Wirtschaft* parties in which we saw Eugene and Peter the Great taking part during Leopold's reign. During the winter months, when the snow was deep enough, several Vienna streets were often shut off from traffic to keep them clear of slush, and sledge processions were organized with small carved and gilded wooden sleighs, drawn by horses suitably decorated and carrying glockenspiels.

After the war years Charles's life became more and more bound up with these private and family interests. There is little doubt that he was devoted to his wife and daughters. It was specially commented on how he was 'very happy in his marriage'. When his youngest child died, aged four, in 1730 he was visibly upset and refused to allow his court painter, the Swede Meytens, to complete a portrait of the whole family.[14] His wife Elizabeth was a large voluptuous blonde with coarse rather than fine features. She had a dazzling white complexion, which caused Charles to call her his 'White Lizzy'. As she grew older, 'notwithstanding the pimples in her face and her present corpulency' she could 'still be reckon'd in the number of the beautiful Princesses'.[15] But what endeared her so much to Charles was that she entered into his own interests with equal enthusiasm. It was this concentration on his family, his indolence as far as government was concerned and his moderation even in his pleasures – he shot rather than chased animals on horseback – which made observers believe that Charles was someone who took life fairly easily. The Hanoverian Huldenberg was convinced that he would live to be an old man:[16] in fact he was fifty-five when he died in 1740.

The only people outside his immediate family who managed to get close to Charles were members of the coterie of Spaniards and Italians who had followed him from Spain. He felt a particular obligation to these men who had voluntarily exiled themselves for his sake. Count Michael John Althann was one of them, although he was a Bohemian noble: he had gone to Spain with Charles and became his inseparable friend until his death in 1722. His wife was often thought to be Charles's mistress but this seems unlikely: there are no references to her in his diary, and in any case the two men were particularly close themselves. Althann was one of the privileged few who played billiards with Charles, winning his respect because of his obvious indifference towards money or office for himself. Although he pursued no active political role of his own, he delighted in supplying Charles with gossip, much of which was often directed his way by others with a political motive.

In the early years of his reign Charles continued to believe himself to be, and to act, very much as king of Spain. Although he never seriously tried to regain the Spanish throne, it was not mere obstinacy which made him hold on to his Spanish titles. By doing so he strengthened his position in the former Spanish lands in Italy and emphasized the continuity of Habsburg rule. In these provinces, as in the Southern Netherlands and Hungary, Charles carefully preserved the existing historic constitutions: the only common link which these territories shared with the other Habsburg lands was rule by the emperor. Continuity with the Spanish past was particularly shown in the transformation of his royal council from Madrid and Barcelona into the *Consejo de España*, set up in Vienna in December 1713 with twice the original number of members at double the salary. This Spanish council was no makeshift or temporary institution but a properly organized body with its own secretariat. Its members were all Spaniards or Italians and only Spanish was used in the proceedings. Although, as we shall see, the Southern Netherlands were kept outside the council's jurisdiction, Charles's lands in Italy were controlled by it for the next twenty or so years. The emperor shared the council's view that the German ministers should be excluded from any influence in Italy, but the troops stationed in the Italian provinces and the resident governors were usually German. The administration ran on traditional lines, no attempt being made to reform the tax system. The revenues of Naples and Milan paid for the salaries and pensions of Charles's Spaniards, although most of these funds had to be diverted to the military establishment there and the lesser Spaniards in Vienna often found their pensions in arrears.

The most senior member of the council and an implacable enemy of Eugene till his death in 1724 was the archbishop of Valencia. More important, however, was count Stella, a Neapolitan soldier, who had gone to Spain with Charles and became his closest adviser there. An ugly man with a very dark complexion tinged with yellow – the effect of syphilis – he had at first amused the emperor with his farmyard imitations but Charles came to depend on him as the only man who would tell him the truth. His frequent visits to the emperor after dark earned him the nickname of 'the nighthawk'. Next in importance was Perlas-Rialp, a Catalan, who had been Charles's secretary of state since 1706 and was more hardworking and capable than Stella. After Stella's death he became Charles's closest confidant and dominated the council of Spain. All nomination to offices in Italy went through his hands and he had to be paid his cut. Although Charles knew of this, he did nothing to stop it. Unlike most of the Spaniards Rialp always tried hard to keep in with the German ministers. He and the other leading Spanish émigrés had their city palaces and lived very much the life of the greater nobility, but there were also scores of lesser Spanish officials.

Although the Spaniards, particularly Stella and Rialp, were friendly during their first years in Vienna towards Eugene and the other German ministers, the latter were edgy, wishing secretly that they could return to the old system and that 'Austrian mildness had not been mixed with Spanish maxims'. They feared that the Spaniards secretly influenced Charles but they were not sure in what way. Consequently they were very careful not to criticize them.[17]

There is no doubt that Charles held Eugene in a great deal of respect, particularly at the beginning of his reign, although his actual affection for the prince seems gradually to have worn off. The prince's opinion was the one which counted for most and all important questions were referred to him. In February 1714 Charles urged him to hurry back from Rastadt so that he would once more have 'a person in whom I can confide, which is not the case now . . . Although they work and I grumble and lecture, yet little happens.'[18] During the first six years of the reign, Eugene was treated by Charles and all his ministers as 'in effect premier minister'.[19] The prince himself came to accept this position. Envoys considered it unwise on their arrival to see anyone else before Eugene,[20] and the English minister Schaub warned his government in 1715 that the prince 'was jealous of anyone who knew the Emperor and who could reach him through any other hands than his own'.[21]

Eugene's position was built and continued to rest on his military reputation. He seems therefore to have hoped to remain above parties and factions, but his actual power was expressed through his role as president of the war council and *de facto* president of the conference. The permanent conference members were all ministers, who held the highest office in the hereditary lands – Trautsohn, Seilern, Gundaker Starhemberg and Sinzendorff – although both the Imperial and Spanish ministers joined in on occasions. The conference discussed foreign policy almost exclusively. Usually it was held in Eugene's town or garden palaces. At one of these conferences in 1726, when the Bavarian minister was called in, he found Eugene sitting in the centre with Sinzendorff on his right and Starhemberg on his left. Further to the left sat the secretary (*Referendar*), Buol. While Buol had a leather chair, the others had green damask ones. It was Buol who took the minutes in his scrawl of abbreviated Latin and German and then drew up the conference's proposals, under first Seilern's and then Sinzendorff's supervision, for Charles in writing. Only after the emperor's consent, which in some cases could take weeks and was liable to influence from his Spanish ministers, could the proposals be put into effect. The conference itself was a slow-moving institution and was often accused by foreign observers of laziness and lack of attention to business: the ministers were reluctant to act by themselves and during the summer when they moved off to their estates it was sometimes months before they could all be assembled to discuss a specific point, by which time they had often forgotten what had been put before them by foreign envoys.[22]

Of the ministers who made up the conference during the early years of Charles's reign, Seilern was dead by January 1715; his death left Sinzendorff as sole chancellor with control of foreign correspondence as well as the domestic chancery. While Sinzendorff had been an ally of Eugene's from almost the beginning of his career, he now worked hard to ingratiate himself with the emperor and his Spaniards and eventually formed a close relationship with Perlas-Rialp. He did not push himself very hard, often stayed in bed till the afternoon[23] and was determined to live up to his reputation of having the best table in Vienna, which was said to cost him 70,000 gulden a year. His favourite way of evading a direct question during a meal was to answer with 'Don't you think that this soup or this stew is excellent?'[24] He was also proud of his sexual prowess, which led to Charles's teasing him with 'very free and merry letters'.[25] Eugene was always suspicious of him and felt far less easy with him than with the nonentity Trautsohn or with Gundaker Starhemberg. Starhemberg was the prince's closest ally and impressed observers by his intelligence and critical ability, although he had a 'natural reservedness'.[26] He remained a member of the conference throughout Charles's reign, but his position as a minister was often ambivalent. In April 1715 he resigned as head of the *Hofkammer* in protest at Charles's plans for financial reorganization, objecting to the way in which Charles wished to rationalize the finances by the creation of a new receipt and credit institution, the *Bancalität*, to take over the functions of both the *Hofkammer* and Starhemberg's own Vienna City Bank. The *Bancalität* was the idea of his and Eugene's enemies among the German ministers, the Bohemian chancellor Schlick and his friends Mikosch and Walsegg. That the emperor carried it through against their advice[27] shows that even in these first years of Charles's reign Eugene's power was by no means absolute. The prince was to grow increasingly annoyed at the efforts of the *Bancalität* to challenge the financial independence of his war council, and both he and Starhemberg seem to have been determined to wreck it from the beginning.[28] In the event it collapsed under the pressures of the Turkish war of 1716 but there was chaos in the finances throughout 1715, for, in Schaub's words, 'of all those who are now responsible for them, there is no one who understands them'.[29] Eventually in August 1716 a new body, the *Finanzconferenz*, was set up to supervise all the financial institutions; Starhemberg was to be its most influential member, although the *Hofkammer* remained in the hands of Mikosch and Walsegg.[30]

While Eugene and his German colleagues were essentially concerned with Charles's role as ruler of the Austrian hereditary lands, there were also other ministers in Vienna who saw him chiefly as head of the German Empire – in particular the Imperial vice-chancellor, Frederick Charles Schönborn, who had been denied any real influence in the past by Seilern, the skilled Imperial lawyer, and by Wratislaw, the determined champion of Austrian state interests. Even after the latters' deaths any attempt to extend the powers of the Imperial chancery was strongly resisted by the court chancellor, Sinzendorff, so that Schönborn never regained the influence and control of foreign affairs which had been exercised by earlier vice-chancellors like Kaunitz. Charles himself had considered him a 'foreigner',[31] and until about 1720 he was firmly excluded from dealings with envoys, even those from the German states and northern powers, who were usually referred by the emperor to Eugene.[32] Gradually, however, his credit increased, particularly as difficulties developed over religious differences in Germany. He learnt how to work the myriad institutions of the Empire so as to get his own way. The German princes consequently tried to bribe him in order to obtain favourable decisions in Vienna, and there is clear evidence that in 1721 he accepted money from Hanover to complete their investiture of Hadeln.[33] Although Eugene did not share Schönborn's belief in the primacy of the emperor's Imperial interests, the two men were to become increasingly friendly because of their common pursuits of building, collecting and gardening.

And what of Eugene himself now that he was called on in his fifties to act in the unusual capacity of a desk-bound minister? To most foreign observers, he appeared a cold, formidable man, his own and his servants' simple clothes only emphasizing the severe impression. He was to change very little over the years, for in 1729 when he was sixty-six Pöllnitz described him in this way:

> [He is] of a middling stature, and well made. His air is extremely serious, and his deportment grave and reserv'd . . . He is perfectly genteel and civil, very polite to the Ladies, respectful and submissive to his Lord and Master, but without flattery or servility. He is generous and noble in everything except his apparel.[34]

His overriding concern seemed to be to preserve his own military reputation: an old friend, who was still an admirer of Eugene in 1718, the Swiss St Saphorin, now an English envoy in Vienna, remarked that 'The Prince's love of glory is superior to every other consideration.'[35] Feeling that his conduct and reputation were defence enough, he saw no need to demean himself by destroying his enemies or even by answering his critics. The Hanoverian Huldenberg summed him up in 1715 as 'incorruptible and disinterested in everything, very hardworking, just and upright'.[36]

But was he hardworking or a particularly good minister in these first years after the War of Spanish Succession, when his physical and mental powers were still strong? The comments which we have from foreign envoys – unfortunately there are none from within the court – indicate that he was not a gifted administrator and that he was afraid of responsibility or of failure. The French diplomat du Luc and St Saphorin both agreed that although he wanted to be consulted in everything and would stand no interference in his conduct of the war council, he was reluctant to advance any ideas of his own or make any decisions without close consultation with his colleagues.[37] The prince was also criticized for leaning too heavily on the advice of less experienced subordinates, to whom he left a great deal of administrative freedom: 'Even in the military department he suffers himself to be governed by his deputies, who follow their private interests.'[38] One of these secretaries, Brock-hausen, was believed to be easy to bribe.

Although Eugene seemed unaware of his own shortcomings, and no one would have dared point them out to him, St Saphorin believed they were surmountable if only the prince could have been persuaded to give a lead. He suggested that one way in which this might be achieved was if Charles chaired the conference and forced Eugene to put forward his own views, which were usually the soundest ones. One must conclude that although Eugene was the minister who undoubtedly had the most influence in the first years of peace, his natural reluctance to initiate and direct policies made him unable to compensate for a similar defect in Charles VI's own political character. St Saphorin expressed it thus in February 1718:

> He is not beloved by the Emperor. Yet he might be dictator in all affairs, if he would only give himself the trouble, and profit by the Emperor's idea that it is absolutely necessary to keep well with him . . . So intrepid before his enemies, he is one of the most timid of men in business, daring to take the least upon him of anyone.[39]

As to Eugene's private life in these years, it seems to have been pretty humdrum and much the same as that of the other great nobles, except for his love of reading. In August 1715 du Luc reported: 'He gets up late, gives short audiences and then joins the so-called Conference. He dines at home or elsewhere with large numbers of people. They then play [cards] till late at night, and in this way 24 hours are filled.'[40] All the ministers without exception, according to Huldenberg, spent most afternoons and evenings playing cards like the prince, but the Hanoverian felt Eugene worked harder than the rest.[41] It was, however, a sedentary existence differing completely from his active life on campaigns.

An essential part of Eugene's life after his return to Vienna in 1714 was his friendship with countess Batthyány, the widowed daughter of the former *Hofkanzler*, Stratmann. They played cards alone or with friends at their own houses or elsewhere, particularly at the home of Sinzendorff's widowed mother, countess Rabutin, till her death in 1725. Countess Batthyány was generally believed to be the prince's mistress. Du Luc said so, and Huldenberg had no doubts either, writing home that 'The day before yesterday, a Monday, Prince Eugene spent the whole day at my country house at Weidlingsein with his coterie of ladies, particularly with the widowed Countess Bathiani, his mistress.'[42] His close association with her meant that for the first time he began to enjoy at least a kind of domestic life.

XVII

A New Turkish War

The treaty of Rastadt brought the long struggle between Austria and France to a close but no peace was made between Charles and Philip V of Spain. Both men remained convinced of their right to the whole Spanish inheritance and neither would recognize the titles or possessions of the other. Although this division caused considerable instability in southern Europe, what eased the situation and contributed to a period of almost twenty years without a major European war was the reluctance of both England and France to engage in further conflict. In France after the death of Louis XIV in 1715 there was a long minority government for his great-grandson Louis XV, whose regents, first Orleans and then Bourbon, were more afraid of Philip V claiming the succession than of France's traditional enemies. At the same time in England, although George Louis of Hanover had succeeded Anne in 1714 as George I and brought the Whig party back to permanent power, the Whigs preferred to keep the peace and trade with Philip V's Spain and colonies rather than open up the old sores of the past war. Threatened also by Jacobite claims to the throne and by rebellion, the Whigs based their policies after 1716 on an alliance with France which was to be the main safeguard of European peace for more than a decade.

On the whole Eugene had no wish to upset the peace settlement of 1713–14.[1] He refused to contemplate a future conquest of Spain and in a conference of 12 April 1715, when Sinzendorff and Starhemberg both thought it wiser to agree, Eugene argued strongly against a proposal from Charles and his Spanish ministers to seize Sicily from Victor Amadeus. In the event the idea never got off the ground because the Imperialists had no navy of their own and the English refused to help.

For most of his life prince Eugene saw that the chief danger to Austrian security came from the great strength and ambitions of France, particularly under Louis XIV. It was because of this that he recognized the value of a close association with the Maritime Powers, especially

England. But he was not prepared to follow the latter dogmatically at the expense of specific Austrian interests and was ready to explore other ways of ensuring Austrian safety. In the year before Louis XIV died, Eugene proved responsive to overtures made by the old king for a *rapprochement* as a way of turning the peace settlement into a more permanent one. He also took a particularly tough line in the negotiations throughout 1715 with the Maritime Powers for the erection of Dutch Barrier fortresses in the Austrian Netherlands. Dutch desertion after Denain seems to have angered him far more than that of the English, who had the excuse of a change of ministry. He was contemptuous of Dutch military strength and realized the Republic wanted the fortresses not so much as a barrier against France but as a way of exploiting the Netherlands economically. It was the emperor who would be saddled with having to pay for the Dutch garrisons. Consequently a succession of English ministers had to listen to his complaints about the Dutch and he told one bluntly that the only way to deal with them was 'to show them your teeth'.[2] Finally in November 1715 a Barrier treaty was signed, largely to please the English who needed Dutch military help during the Jacobite revolt, and the Netherlands were handed over to Charles VI by the Anglo-Dutch condominium which had governed them since Ramillies. As we shall see, the prince was to be the first governor.

Eugene's chief reason for wanting peace in western Europe was the growing danger from the Turks and his own wish to be free to challenge them. Turkish military ambitions had revived after 1711 when the Turks humiliated a Russian army led by Peter the Great on the river Pruth: in December 1714 they struck at the Venetians in the Morea and clearly intended to attack Hungary in the near future and undo the whole Karlowitz settlement. In January 1715 Eugene warned Charles that the army and Hungarian forts must be put in a state of readiness and he immediately began to take the necessary steps himself. On 16 April the conference agreed that 'war is certain'[3] and that it would be best if Austria took the offensive the following year.

Ineffective opposition to the war came from two quarters: from Charles's Spanish ministers who wanted to concentrate on the Mediterranean and feared reasonably enough that their pensions would go unpaid during wartime, and from the group of German ministers who had supported the erection of the *Bancalität*. If anything this made Eugene more determined on war and, according to the English minister Schaub, he and Gundaker Starhemberg saw it as a chance to consolidate their own control: the financial strain would destroy the *Bancalität* and force the emperor 'to throw himself completely into the arms of him [Eugene] and those of Count Staremberg'.[4] Although Sinzendorff had supported the *Bancalität* and really opposed the Turkish war, he was too scared of offending Eugene to say so openly and he tried hard to keep a foot in both camps.[5]

Once committed to the war it became essential for the Imperialists to have security in their rear and here they were to be far more successful than during past struggles. The greatest danger threatened from an attack on their Italian lands by Philip V, which Louis XIV might be tempted to join. But in September 1715 Louis died and the danger of war in the Mediterranean receded. His death also brought the Imperialists, under Eugene's direction, to abandon the idea of a *rapprochement* with France: while Louis XIV might have had enough influence on his grandson Philip V to restrain him from attacking Italy during the Turkish war, the new regent, the duke of Orleans, and Philip were rivals for the succession to the French throne in the event of the death of the young Louis XV. Under a regency France was unlikely to indulge in foreign adventures of her own. By late November 1715, therefore, Eugene and Starhemberg were convinced that they should ally with England, who had the means in her fleet to restrain Philip V, although at the same time they saw the advantage of keeping the new French régime friendly by further talks of *rapprochement*. Those opposed to the Turkish war in Vienna were as eager for an English alliance, since they hoped for eventual English naval help against Savoy or Spain. On 5 June 1716 the treaty of Westminster was signed with George I. The main purpose of this alliance in Eugene's eyes was summed up by Starhemberg in a conference on 19 May, when he declared it would give 'security during the Turkish war'.[6]

Hostilities were judged to have broken out four days earlier, on 15 May 1716, when no reply was received from the Turks to a request asking them to maintain the Karlowitz settlement. Of all Eugene's wars this was the one in which he was to exercise most direct control over Austria's war effort and the difficulties he met came largely from the inbuilt weaknesses of the monarchy. It was also a war which Austria fought and won on her own. The Venetians, who were quickly expelled from the Greek peninsula by the Turks, could do no more than hold on to their outposts in the Ionian islands. The Imperial princes only contributed token sums and men, although the renegade Max Emmanuel of Bavaria sent more because he wanted an archduchess as a wife for his son. On the other hand the Papacy considered the war a crusade and gave direct subsidies as well as allowing the emperor to levy taxes on the clergy in the Habsburg hereditary lands.

However, the bulk of the cost of the war fell on Austria and, inevitably, this proved as much a problem as the enemy. Debts from the last war had not been paid off, especially those owed to the Dutch. Back pay and pensions owed by the war commissariat alone in 1714 amounted to 23 million gulden. Yet a further loan of 2 million gulden to finance the new war was floated in the United Provinces early in 1716. The new *Bancalität* soon failed miserably to cope with the heavy demands of the military and Eugene was not slow to point this out. By the summer of 1716 the financial system had to be reorganized under the *Finanzconferenz* as he and Starhemberg wanted.

Preparations for the war had been under way for over a year and already in September 1715 troops were moved into Hungary. The time available and the control exercised by Eugene produced a sound enough army, one which he himself declared to be 'in a very fine serviceable condition'.[7] Although the provisioning of the troops was largely left to the Oppenheimer family, the specialist services were taken care of directly. Three hundred bakers were collected from Nuremberg and Frankfurt and an artillery train assembled. A start was also made on a new Danube fleet: special agents were sent to the Dutch and Baltic ports at the end of 1715 to recruit sailors and shipwrights, and a yard was set up near the Prater. However, instead of the seven ships expected, only three armed galleys could be launched in July 1716.

It had originally been hoped to attack Belgrade in 1716, but this was never a viable aim during the first campaign. Drought and then floods delayed the assembly of the army and Eugene himself could not leave Vienna before 2 July because he wanted to ensure a continuing flow of cash and supplies for his army. By the time he reached his troops near Peterwardein in southern Hungary, the Turkish field army under the grand vizier Silahdar Ali Pasha, the sultan's son-in-law, was already at Belgrade. It therefore seemed best to let the Turks move towards him, which they did, crossing the Sava on 26/27 July. They probably numbered no more than 120,000, of which only 40,000 were janissaries and 30,000 spahis, the rest being Tartar, Wallachian, Egyptian and Asiatic irregulars.

The grand vizier intended to seize the fortress of Peterwardein and camped near the Imperial army to prepare for an attack. But Eugene gave him no chance to do so. Without bothering with a council of war, the prince decided to strike at once, as his forces were fresher and a quick victory would silence any critics at home. With the protective guns of the fortress behind him, Eugene unleashed his force of 70,000 men at seven o'clock on the morning of 5 August. Although the janissaries had

some unexpected success against the Imperial infantry, there was confusion and collapse after an Imperial cavalry attack on their flank. The
Turkish cavalry abandoned the field, fleeing towards Belgrade and
leaving the janissaries to be slaughtered. Possibly 30,000 of the enemy
were killed. One of Eugene's officers wrote: 'We took no more than 20
prisoners because our men wanted their blood and massacred them all.'[8]
One of the Turkish dead was the grand vizier, who had first watched the
battle impassively from his tent and then flung himself into the fray.

The victors found the usual vast pile of booty in the Turkish camp:
jewels, clothes and animals for the soldiers, and the grand vizier's tent
for the prince. There was so much that three hundred carts were kept
busy for three days carrying it away. Although the Turkish war chest
was also captured, it had already been pillaged by the Imperial troops,
the first man on the scene filling his knapsack with ducats and the next
pouring them into his shirt and hat. A less pleasant sight awaiting the
victors in the camp, however, was that of the decapitated bodies of Imperialists captured by the Turks in an earlier skirmish. Atrocities were
common on both sides in this as in earlier wars. Turkish spies found
among Eugene's own Serbian troops were impaled. No attempt was made
to bury the dead: Eugene quickly moved his army away from the battlefield to avoid infection from the rapidly decomposing bodies. The
following February the field was still 'strew'd with the Skulls and
Carcases of unbury'd Men, Horses and Camels'.[9]

Although it was only early August, Eugene was unwilling to attack
Belgrade. He had too few of the ships needed to invest the city which
was surrounded by rivers, and the defeated Turkish army was still
strong enough to defend it till the end of the year. Instead he decided to
use the oxen, buffaloes and camels taken in the battle as draught animals
and to march against Temesvár to the north. On 26 August his army
reached this stronghold which had remained in Turkish hands throughout
the last war. It was an exhausting march, largely undertaken at night to
escape the heat; many of the men were already ill from a campaign
which one of their officers described as 'far more tiring and arduous than
that on the Rhine or in the Netherlands'.[10]

As well as its natural defences of river arms, islands and swamps,
Temesvár had new fortifications built by 13,000 Wallachians impressed
into this work as punishment for not paying their taxes. Nevertheless the
fortress surrendered in mid-October after artillery fire had badly dam-
aged the wooden houses in the town and the citizens were beginning to
turn against the garrison.[11] Those Turks who wanted to leave with their
families were given waggons and an escort as far as Belgrade. The

administration of the town and the area around it, the Banat, was entrusted to the Lorrainer, Mercy, who was emerging as one of Eugene's favourite officers. He was ordered to restrict the fortress area of the town to German Catholics, and the prince also warned him to exclude any Jews from Temesvár. He claimed that they were dishonest traders who practised usury, but the real reason was that they travelled extensively throughout the Turkish empire and could act as agents for the Turks.

The success of the first year of the war was a personal triumph for Eugene. Throughout the campaign Charles had written to him, in his own hand, asking his opinion on everything and showing much personal warmth. When Clement XI honoured the prince with the gift of a papal hat for his victory, the emperor was highly amused at the thought of Eugene's embarrassment on being presented with it, and he wrote: '. . . I should have really liked to see you, my dear Prince, with your fine hat in this ceremony, so that I could laugh a little in secret, as I know what Your Highness feels about such ceremonies.'[12]

When Eugene returned to Vienna in November 1716 all parties recognized his ascendancy; and his determination to pursue the campaign the following year,[13] so that he could achieve what he saw as the main aim of the war, the capture of Belgrade, met with no opposition.[14] Belgrade controlled the Turkish invasion route: once in Habsburg hands it would finally secure central Europe from the threat of further Ottoman attacks. The capture of Belgrade was an objective which he felt confident Austria could achieve on her own. Offers made by Peter the Great for Russia to enter the war on the Austrian side were rejected because it was feared that the tsar would only try to cash in on Turkish weakness to expand into the Danubian provinces. However, princely volunteers from Germany and France were welcomed. Forty-five were to arrive for the 1717 campaign, so many that they proved almost an embarrassment. There were also said to be 8,000 volunteers among the ordinary soldiers.[15]

Valiant efforts were made to raise large sums of money in the hereditary lands through a special levy for the Turkish war, the churches continued to contribute funds and a gift of half a million gulden was extorted from the Jewish community. Nevertheless this was still not enough to pay the army on a regular basis during the coming year. On the other hand a determined and successful attempt was made to build more galleys. By the summer ten were ready, some with as many as 56 guns and carrying a total complement of 1,000 men. New sailors had been recruited and those from the previous year forced to stay on, although they had wanted to leave, complaining that they were not even paid enough to afford beer. Their commander declared he had never seen men drink as they did.

If Belgrade was to be taken, the Danube had to be crossed and the city invested long before another Turkish field army could be brought up to defend it under the new grand vizier Halil Pasha. Consequently Eugene left Vienna early, on 14 May 1717, the day after the birth of the future empress Maria Theresa. He had had geographical surveys and adequate preparations carried out previously by Mercy, so the army could move quickly over the Danube to the east of Belgrade on 15 June. Ahead of the Imperialists lay a formidable undertaking, as the city was protected by its position on a triangle of land formed by the Danube to the north and east and by the Sava, which flowed into the Danube at this point, to the west. The Imperial camp was set up on the remaining south side of the city where the army was intended to act both as a besieging force and as a defensive shield against the probable arrival of a Turkish relieving army. Pontoon bridges were built and ships and troops positioned on the river and banks in such a way that the Imperialists could maintain contact with Hungary while Belgrade was cut off from any outside contact by land and water.

The siege proceeded slowly. A great trading centre and the capital of Serbia, Belgrade was garrisoned by 30,000 men under the able Mustapha Pasha. A Bavarian contingent, again contributed by Max Emmanuel, arrived late after a gruelling march in the July heat across the arid and treeless Hungarian plain. The construction of the lines was held up by shortage of timber; Turks in small rowing boats, *caïques*, made repeated attacks on the Imperial ships; and raiding parties surprised groups of Imperialists, killing and decapitating many – 'a ducat is given for every Christian brought in by their soldiery, which profit tends to animate them in the fight'.[16] Then on 13 July a fierce storm struck: much of the pontoon bridging over the Sava and Danube was wrecked, some supply ships were sunk, and waggons with their oxen washed away. However by the end of July, when bands of cavalry heralded the approach of the Turkish field army, large parts of Belgrade had been destroyed by the Imperial artillery fire.

During the first days of August the whole of the grand vizier's army established itself on a high plateau to the east of the city and began a heavy bombardment of the Imperialists who were caught between two fires: it was like the siege of Vienna in reverse. In size and shape the Turkish force was much the same as the previous year. Regular troops only made up 'a small proportion of their whole body. The rest . . . are a mob collected from the population of the vast territories of the

Grand Seigneur . . . ignorant of all discipline, and are neither armed nor trained sufficiently well to make a stand against a regular force.' The Turkish camp with its multicoloured tents had 'quite the appearance of a gigantic flowerbed full of every kind of bloom'. The showpiece was the grand vizier's richly-embroidered tent, which had so many ante-chambers and courtyards that it was like a 'vast palace'.[17]

Eugene was in a dangerous position and alarming reports spread throughout Europe that he was trapped and that his army would be destroyed. But he kept his head and had no intention of raising the siege: he hoped the Turks would either attack him or be forced to return home through lack of food.[18] Instead for two weeks the grand vizier kept up a continuous deadly artillery fire on to the Imperialists below, who were increasingly suffering from dysentery, which had affected Eugene himself slightly the month before. When it became clear that his army was on the point of collapse, Eugene's hand was forced:[19] on 15 August he summoned his generals to a council of war and announced his intention to attack the Turks the next morning. No one dissented. While 10,000 men were left to watch the city, the remaining 60,000 moved quickly towards the Turkish camp under the cover of darkness. They had orders to keep closely together and to pour continuous volleys into the undisciplined Turks. Wine, brandy and beer were issued to keep their courage up, especially in the face of the terrifying noise which the Turks always made in battle.

Halil Pasha, who had been counting on starving and bombarding the Imperialists into submission, was caught unawares as the enemy came through the fog on the morning of 16 August. The Turkish army collapsed and fled towards Niš (Nish). Once more quarter was refused and stragglers were pursued and killed by hussars and Serbian infantry. The victorious soldiers were allowed to loot the camp, but a tight control was kept over them to ensure that the booty was divided equally and that Eugene had the grand vizier's tent for himself. In fact the amount seized was disappointing as the Turks had left most of their baggage on ships further down the Danube.

A week after the battle Belgrade surrendered, despite having supplies for a further six months. As the Imperialists moved into the city on 22 August, 60,000 Muslims, including 20,000 soldiers, who had wanted to leave were allowed to go with their belongings. The shrouded faces of the women were a source of amazement to Eugene's troops.

Immediate measures were taken to rebuild both the fortifications and the town, for as Eugene remarked to the war council on 3 November, 'there isn't a single house left undamaged in the upper or lower town'.[20]

Meanwhile the field army was moved northwards and then into winter quarters. There was no need for it to be deployed any further: the news of the victory was enough to frighten home Tartar raiders who had spent the summer terrorizing Hungary. These bands, which included Wallachians and Cossacks, as well as Tartars, usually armed only with bows and arrows, swords and spears, had seized whole communities as slaves, killing and destroying what they could not carry off.

On 19 October 1717 Eugene returned to Vienna where he was welcomed by the emperor and presented with a diamond-studded sword. The victory was the crowning point of his military career and it was also to be his last. A fitting and permanent memento of it was the famous German soldiers' song, *Das Prinz-Eugen Lied*, which was probably composed by one of the Bavarian troops who took part in the battle. Belgrade completely eradicated the humiliation of Denain and confirmed Eugene as the leading European general. Victories against the Turks were always spectacular and this battle showed the prince at his best: his ability to snatch victory at the moment of defeat. Eugene's latest triumph also demonstrated once more the continuing superiority of the Imperialists over the Turks and their capacity to mount effective campaigns, at least in the Balkans.

The principal objectives of the war had been achieved: the Karlowitz settlement had been safeguarded and the new conquests of Temesvár and Belgrade would now serve as outer bastions of Imperial power in the Balkans. It only remained to get the Turks to accept their losses. Eugene himself had no wish for a further push into the Danubian provinces or southwards towards Niš because the distances involved were too great. In any case the international situation had been changing in such a way that it was unwise to prolong the war. The Spanish king, Philip V, encouraged by his ambitious Italian wife and his chief minister Alberoni, had embarked on an expansionist Italian policy in the summer of 1717: the Spanish fleet was sent to take Austrian Sardinia. At first it was feared that it was heading for Naples and on 8 August the worried conference agreed to Stella's demand that the Turkish war be concluded.[21] But Eugene, trapped at Belgrade, had refused to listen to Vienna, and even when Sardinia was rapidly conquered by the Spaniards, he would not release any troops for Italy, suggesting that men be raised in Milan and Naples. He hoped a diplomatic solution might be possible through the intervention of England and France, who had formed an alliance during the past year, one of the objects of which was to reconcile Charles and Philip. On 17 September Eugene wrote to Sinzendorff from Semlin, that he had always thought Austria's accession to the Anglo-

French alliance was 'useful and necessary, and still believe it with this difference that at this time it will appear that fear makes us act. If the duke of Anjou has no allies I do not believe he will do much harm outside Sardinia.'[22]

Once the prince returned to Vienna with the Turks decisively beaten, he agreed to increase the number of troops in Italy to 36,000. Although the Imperial possessions there clearly had to be defended, and Eugene himself saw that no further gains could be made by continuing the war in Hungary, he had no intention of sacrificing what he had won by making a bad peace in order to concentrate on Italy. He was, however, to come under intense pressure to withdraw from the Balkans quickly. There were signs at the beginning of 1718 that Charles himself was prepared to abandon the Imperial advantage there,[23] and some of his ministers wanted to use the opportunity of the Spanish attack to revive their own aggressive designs on Savoy and Spain.

Unfortunately it was not easy to bring the Turks to admit their losses: they rejected the suggestion of direct talks and insisted on Anglo-Dutch mediation. As the Imperialists needed the protection of the British navy from Spain in the Mediterranean they had to agree to this. But the mediation delayed serious talks till June 1718, by which time Eugene was back in Hungary with enough troops to fight a further campaign if it proved necessary. He intended, however, to use the army as an ultimate threat and he did what he could to get the Imperial negotiators to finish quickly.

The peace talks were held at Passarowitz (Požarevac), where all the diplomats had to live under canvas as the whole area between Belgrade and Niš had 'not only been utterly destroy'd by the two Armys last campaign, but even the inhabitants are all fled, and have abandon'd their houses'.[24] The treaty of Passarowitz was signed after a month on 21 July 1718: the Turks surrendered the Banat of Temesvár and Belgrade with most of Serbia, although they regained the Morea from the Venetians. At the same time they agreed to grant Austrian merchants favourable terms to trade throughout the Ottoman empire: this was to form the basis for serious but unsuccessful efforts at commercial expansion through an Eastern Company established at Trieste and Fiume (Rijeka) after 1719.

The conquered territories, largely through Eugene's insistence on their military importance, were to be ruled directly from Vienna instead of through Hungarian institutions. On 3 August 1719 a meeting of ministers under the prince set up a *Subdelegation in Neoacquisitis* composed of members from the war council and the chamber. Directly responsible to this new body were two military governors, at Belgrade and Temesvár, who were instructed to embark on a full-scale immigration policy to fill these sparsely-populated lands. Although Alexander of Württemberg managed to turn Belgrade into an imposing defensive point for all southern Hungary in the early 1720s, he had less success in the resettlement of Serbia. Far more successful was the governor in the Banat, Mercy, whose task was made easier because most of the Turks had left and the people who remained were not Magyars but Serbs and Rumanians. He made great efforts to get the local nomadic people to settle down, and free land, transport, implements and tax concessions encouraged a steady stream of settlers, first of artisans and then of peasants after 1722. Ex-soldiers were particularly welcomed. Although he made sure that Temesvár was dominated by German Catholics, he allowed other Germans, Serbs, Slovaks, Italians and Lorrainers elsewhere in the Banat. These tended to settle in one-nationality villages, which remained isolated from one another and were to prove a headache to the advocates of national self-determination in the twentieth century. The economic advance of the Banat was certainly spectacular: a wasteland was turned into a flourishing agricultural area with mining and textile manufacturing. But for Eugene's nineteenth-century biographer, von Arneth, it had a deeper cultural significance: 'The lands which had lain under the dead hand of Turkish rule for centuries quickly blossomed through the reviving breath of Christian civilization.'[25]

An encouraging sign for the Imperial government during the war had been the passivity of the Hungarian population despite appeals from the exiled Rákóczi for further revolt. The war itself had spelt the end of the Turkish military threat to Hungary, but the same could not be said for the new acquisitions. Despite the defensive works built at Belgrade, both the fortress and Serbia, but not the Banat of Temesvár, were to fall to the Turks in the late 1730s shortly after Eugene's death.

XVIII

War over Sicily and the Cabal against Eugene

During Eugene's campaigns in Hungary, Austria under his direction was forced to be a largely passive observer of events in western Europe where a massive diplomatic venture was taking place.[1] Following their revolutionary alliance of 1716, the leading ministers of England and France, Stanhope and Dubois, began to work for a series of interlocking international guarantees for the Hanoverian dynasty in England and the succession of the regent Orleans in France. At the same time they hoped to prevent further warfare in the west by settling differences left over from the peace of Utrecht/Rastadt. They believed that if Philip V found security in Spain he would give up thoughts of challenging Orleans for the French throne in the event of the death of the young Louis XV. But to give him this security it was essential for Charles VI finally to renounce his claims to Spain. One way of persuading Charles to overcome his scruples would be to force Victor Amadeus of Savoy to cede Sicily to him.

In the last months of 1716 Stanhope was floating this idea in Vienna, where it was received with a good deal of interest. Although reluctant to say so openly, in case of offending him, few of Charles's ministers now took his claims on Spain seriously.[2] Even the Spaniard Rialp admitted to an English minister in October 1716 that they were no longer practicable,[3] while Sinzendorff echoed what had been Austrian policy for the past decade and a half when he said he was prepared to see Charles 'renounce this monarchy [Spain] so as to establish himself more securely in Italy'.[4] In a conference of 5 January 1717 Eugene gave his decisive support to the idea and Charles himself raised no serious objections,[5] although it was hoped that any recognition of Philip should be as a *de facto* king rather than as one by right (*de iure*).

Unfortunately Stanhope and Dubois had miscalculated in believing that Philip V would be satisfied with guarantees for the Spanish throne. Subject to bouts of incapacitating mental illness, both Philip and his foreign policy were controlled by his second wife, Elizabeth Farnese, who was a daughter of the duke of Parma and was determined on pursuing her own dynastic claims in Italy and on reviving Spain's empire there. Philip's chief minister Alberoni, who was an Italian, fell in with these ideas, and, as we have seen, the Spanish fleet took the first step in the summer of 1717 by invading and conquering Austrian Sardinia.

Spain's provocation not only deeply insulted the Imperial court but it also naturally revived ambitions among Charles's Spanish ministers for an expansive policy of their own: to seize 'the Duke of Parma's country'[6] and then to conquer Spain.[7] It was in this atmosphere that Eugene returned to Vienna after his victory at Belgrade. He came determined to prevent an escalation of the conflict, at least in the immediate future, and had written contemptuously during the recent siege to his secretary George Koch that 'two wars cannot be waged with one army'.[8] His stand on this question led for the first time to a split between himself and the Spanish coterie around Charles, a split which in the coming two years nearly destroyed the prince and considerably reduced his power.

Although Eugene agreed in November 1717 to release some troops from the Balkans for Italy, he did so reluctantly and not without blaming the emperor's Spanish council for the poor state of the defences there, assuring Charles that he had warned the council of this long ago. The prince was counting on Austrian military intervention in Italy being unnecessary. He preferred to depend on Anglo-French diplomatic pressure and hoped that, if the English could be persuaded to use their navy and act the part of Mediterranean policeman, Italy would be safe. Unfortunately for him, the English wanted to avoid a clash with Spain which could only harm their commercial interests. Consequently both Stanhope and Dubois tried hard to satisfy Philip V and to silence his supporters in the French court by extracting further concessions for him from Austria. For the English Whigs it was becoming more important to stay friends with France and Spain than risk offending Austria.

In November and December 1717 Charles was asked not only to renounce Spain formally and to recognize Philip as *de iure* king but also to give Sardinia to Savoy in exchange for Sicily and to agree to the eventual succession of Philip V and Elizabeth's son to Parma and Tuscany – sons by Philip's first marriage were his heirs to Spain. The conference ministers were stunned. Eugene was particularly incensed, warning the English minister St Saphorin that 'we will not suffer ourselves to be intimidated', being ready to 'run all risks, rather than suffer a son of the

Queen of Spain ever to possess' Tuscany. St Saphorin, who had known Eugene for twenty years, was suitably taken aback, having 'often seen the Prince in a passion but never did I hear him speak with such rage and violence'.[9] Enraged he might well be, because the Austrian supremacy in Italy, built up since his victory at Turin and confirmed at Rastadt, was seriously threatened.

Nevertheless the western allies called his bluff and stood firm: the Imperialists knew full well that only the British fleet could prevent further Spanish landings, added to which was the serious danger of pro-Spanish groups in France forcing the regent Orleans into war. Consequently in a series of conferences held by the German and Spanish ministers in March and April 1718, although all shared a sense of outrage, a realistic approach had to be adopted. Only the archbishop of Valencia pursued a consistently bellicose line. Eugene, backed up by Sinzendorff, gradually moved over to accepting the allies' demands: both were haunted by memories of 1711–13 and feared that the English would abandon them to a Franco-Spanish assault on Italy. The most they felt it possible to retain was Charles's right to keep the mere title of Catholic king and for some guarantees that Parma and Tuscany should not come under direct Spanish control. Both Stella and Rialp accepted the force of their arguments and in a conference held before Charles himself on 4 April Stella 'advised the acceptance of the treaty to avoid the present evil and the loss of all Italy'.[10] There was now a general acceptance of Eugene's policy, that it was best to leave it to England and France to restrain the Spaniards,[11] especially as no peace had yet been signed with the Turks.

Charles, however, was to put up a more determined resistance. He was annoyed not so much over Tuscany as at having to renounce Spain formally.[12] For two months he delayed the drawing up and signature of a definitive treaty. His ministers were reluctant to press him, bearing out what the Hanoverian Huldenberg had remarked earlier in the year: 'He is completely master over all his ministers . . . all of them fear him.'[13] But at the beginning of August England, France and Austria signed what came to be known as the Quadruple Alliance – quadruple because the Dutch were expected to sign, but did not. In it Charles recognized Philip and renounced Spain, Sardinia was given to Savoy in exchange for Sicily, the eventual succession of a Spanish prince to Parma and Tuscany was agreed, and the successions and territories of all the signatories were guaranteed.

Throughout, the English and French had hoped that Spain would join the treaty, although they were ready as a last resort to force it on

Philip. In the event it came to this because he rejected the treaty and unleashed a further naval assault in the summer of 1718, this time on
Savoyard Sicily. When this happened Eugene was in Hungary for the
conclusion of the Turkish peace. He was confident that the British fleet
would soon reach the Mediterranean and put an end to the Spanish
adventures,[14] but he was less sure about how the French would act. His
optimism was rewarded on 11 August when this fleet destroyed the
Spanish one off Cape Passaro. Unfortunately Philip's troops had already
landed in Sicily and although the Italian mainland was safe these troops
had to be ejected.

The Quadruple Alliance hung together remarkably well. By the turn
of 1718–19 both England and France declared war on Philip but were
determined to finish it quickly because of its unpopularity at home. In
April 1719 French troops under Eugene's old adversary, Berwick,
crossed into northern Spain to apply direct pressure, and they met with
early success. For their part the conference ministers, including Eugene,
stuck firmly to the new system, supporting the connection with France
as well as England: they knew well enough that their own operations
against Sicily and Sardinia 'depended on England' and her continuing
goodwill.[15]

Yet effective action to expel the Spaniards was slow to start. Eugene
himself could have gone south after Passarowitz, but he was content to
direct from Vienna: the small enemy forces involved hardly required his
personal intervention. An Imperial commander, Zumjungen, was only
appointed early in the new year and then superseded by Mercy. Excellent
subordinates – both men were Eugene's personal choice – neither shone
as a leader. The more obvious candidate, Guido Starhemberg, had been
vetoed not by the prince but by Rialp and Charles who had had enough
of him in Spain.[16]

Despite English naval support Austria's military effort proved derisory
and a forerunner of her performance in the 1730s rather than a repetition
of her success in the recent Turkish war. The Spanish troops, isolated in
Sicily, managed to hang on around Palermo till the end of 1719, while
no expedition could even be attempted against Sardinia. The Imperial
generals had quarrelled incessantly among themselves but they also
faced serious problems not of their own making. While Eugene seemed
to do his best to ease their difficulties, there was probably less urgency in
his actions than when he was personally involved in the field. We have
the evidence from one of Eugene's closest friends at this time, a renegade
Frenchman like himself, Bonneval, who had served well at Belgrade and
was appointed to command the proposed expedition against Sardinia.

He was critical in private to the English minister St Saphorin about the conduct of the council of war.

The basic problem as ever was the failure of the financial institutions to cope. There had been much wrangling among Charles's German and Spanish ministers over who should pay for the war. Eventually it was agreed that the German lands should provide the men and animals but that Naples and Milan should support the Imperial forces while they were in Italy. Although Eugene was very critical of the *Hofkammer* which he blamed for the difficulties experienced in sending the Imperial troops to Italy, more than enough men did reach there. Unfortunately the Spanish council's administrations in Naples and Milan failed to support them.[17] When the Imperial troops disembarked at Sicily from English ships, they were faced by a hostile pro-Spanish population and were desperately short of clothes and boots. Everything they needed had to be shipped over from Naples, where the administration was incapable even of feeding those troops still on the mainland.

It was not Austrian military action but the French invasion of northern Spain and English attacks on his shipping which decided Philip V to dismiss Alberoni as a scapegoat in December 1719 and join the Quadruple Alliance. Sicily then passed into Austrian hands and Sardinia was given as compensation to Victor Amadeus of Savoy. With the reunion of Sicily to Naples coming so soon after the gains at Passarowitz, Austria reached her greatest territorial extent, and on the face of it was at a pinnacle of power. Yet Sicily was just one more exposed province to defend and Charles's position in Italy had been maintained and extended only through English sea power and French goodwill. Once these were lost it would prove to be very precarious.

The Sicilian campaign proved an ignominious affair but it was made worse by the collapse of government in Vienna during 1719, when the ascendancy of Eugene and the conference ministers was challenged and shaken. Until 1718 the prince had enjoyed good personal relations with the emperor, his Spanish advisers and his favourite Althann. The letters which survive from Charles to the prince until this time show a constant, and probably genuine, concern for Eugene's health and safety as well as great deference to his advice. An extract from one letter will suffice: on 25 July 1717 Charles ordered Eugene not to run so many personal risks at Belgrade for 'Generals can always be found but not a Prince Eugene, whom I love and esteem so much.'[18]

What went wrong? The strains created by the Spanish attacks on Sardinia and Sicily broke up the fragile unity of the various interests which had co-operated since Charles's accession. Accusations flew about:

the Spanish council demanded the weakening of Eugene's army in Hungary, he complained about the council's administration in Italy and about the inefficiency of the Germans Mikosch and Walsegg at the *Hofkammer*, and there were countercharges about the failure of Eugene's generals in Sicily and the running of the *Hofkriegsrat*. Gradually all those under attack combined against Eugene and found a rallying point in Althann. It is not clear why Charles's friend threw off his previously passive role, but the men who turned against Eugene were those Althann had always been closest to and he was probably just following their lead.

Both Althann and what came to be called the cabal found a ready listener in Charles. Exceedingly suspicious of anyone and always eager for gossip, he had been deeply hurt by the way the Quadruple Alliance had been forced on him. It was also clear to him how Eugene had put the safeguarding of his conquests in Hungary before everything else and that the ultimate responsibility for failure in Sicily also had to rest on Eugene. Charles therefore had every reason to look on the prince less kindly. Moreover he was now reaching his mid-thirties and must have begun to have his doubts about ministers he had taken over wholesale from his brother nearly a decade before, and especially about their ultimate loyalty to himself and his immediate family, since the future of his own dynasty was still very much in doubt. Although he had two infant daughters by 1719, there was still no son and Charles was very concerned about anyone who showed too much attention towards his brother Joseph's daughters, now in their late teens and of marriageable age. It was to be Eugene's misfortune to advocate their marriage into the Bavarian and Saxon families[19] and thus to put himself in the position of appearing to support the succession of possible male heirs from these marriages if Charles died without a son.

In February 1719 Eugene and the other conference ministers came under fierce attack. Ranged behind Althann were the Spaniards, especially Valencia and Stella, the *Hofkammerpräsident* Walsegg and the *Hofkammerrath* Mikosch, and a crowd of lesser men. For most of the year the court was in uproar: foreign and domestic business went by the board as the ministers jostled for power. In September 1719 government came to a complete standstill when Eugene refused to hold the conference.

The cabal had plenty of cash: it was supplied from an outside source, Eugene's cousin Victor Amadeus of Savoy. The latter had felt humiliated when the great powers had taken Sicily from him without any consultation and was now looking for a way of acquiring claims for his family to the Austrian succession by marrying his son to one of Joseph I's daugh-

ters. Through his minister in Vienna, San Tommaso, he paid the cabal
to push a Savoyard match and to attack the conference ministers who
wanted the archduchesses married, following the recent pattern of Habsburg marriages with German families, to the electoral princes of Saxony
and Bavaria. But in attacking the conference ministers, trying to turn
them against each other and to destroy them one by one, the cabal was
not acting merely as a tool of Victor Amadeus. The Spanish ministers
hoped to force Eugene from the post of governor of the Netherlands,
which he had held since 1716, and to bring this province as well as
Italy under their control. Mikosch and Walsegg, already in charge of the
Hofkammer, had a serious reform programme: they felt the monarchy's
financial problems could only be solved by overcoming the obstruction
of the estates to voting adequate taxation. To do this, they had to be rid
of the unco-operative Sinzendorff at the *Hofkanzlei*. They also argued
the need to end the war council's independence from the *Hofkammer*, an
independence which Eugene was determined to uphold.

A systematic campaign of character assassination was begun against the
conference ministers both at court and privately before the emperor. It
was largely conducted by Althann and the Spaniards but Althann's
brother-in-law Nimptsch, who was being paid by San Tommaso
through the intermediary of a bogus Italian priest, Tedeschi, was also
involved. Faults with the conference ministers were easily found:
Sinzendorff was lazy and his extravagant entertaining smelt of the corruption which his father had practised unashamedly as president of the
chamber in Leopold's reign; Gundaker Starhemberg was widely believed to be under his wife's thumb; and Eugene was accused of being
influenced by his friend countess Batthyány and his secretaries, who were
said to be in Bavarian pay.

Sinzendorff quickly took fright and handed over his share of domestic
business to a second chancellor, Stügkh, while he was left in charge of
diplomatic correspondence. In doing so he had become in some measure
dependent on Althann and the Spaniards, who then turned on Eugene.
The prince characteristically refused to answer slanders against him, as he
felt it was beneath his dignity and that his reputation should be proof
enough against such attacks, nor would he discuss these with his close
colleagues. At one time he believed the latter had deserted him and he
began to speak to them 'drily and contemptuously'.[20] He was on the
point of resigning and told the English minister St Saphorin that it
would be no great loss as he could live on 10,000 gulden a year, adding,
'I have more than enough books not to be bored.'[21] That he stood his
ground seems largely to have been the work of St Saphorin, who be-

lieved English interests at Vienna were best served by the survival of the conference ministers. He acted as mediator between the prince, Starhemberg and Sinzendorff, persuading them to present a more united front.

In September 1719 a surprising piece of luck occurred: one of Nimptsch's valets arrived on the prince's doorstep with conclusive proof of his master's financial dealings with San Tommaso. Armed with this information, Eugene stormed into the Favorita and demanded satisfaction. Brushing aside Charles's attempts to soothe him with platitudes about his confidence in him, he refused to transact any business in the conference. He was backed up strongly by a known ally, the president of the aulic council, Windischgrätz, and surprisingly by Rialp, who was probably hoping to destroy Valencia and Stella. The reluctant Charles had to instigate an enquiry headed by Windischgrätz. By the end of the year this commission condemned both Nimptsch and Tedeschi, having discovered that the latter had received 80,000 gulden from San Tommaso.[22] Charles had no alternative but to banish Nimptsch to Graz in a sealed waggon to begin a sentence of two years' imprisonment. Tedeschi was expelled from Austria after being roped to a cross and publicly flogged in the Weidenmarkt – not surprisingly the thirty lashes made him squeal a lot. San Tommaso was also asked to leave Vienna and with him went Victor Amadeus's hopes of an Austrian marriage for his son.

Eugene had defeated the plot against him but his victory was a costly one. Charles was deeply embarrassed, as he had been an avid listener to the stories put about by Nimptsch and Althann. During the enquiry he had made a point of showing himself in Althann's house and garden, and the emperor's friendship with his favourite remained as close as ever till the latter died in 1722. St Saphorin feared that the affair would 'embitter his master more and more against him [Eugene]', and he believed it was the prince's great sense of 'duty' rather than love for Charles which made him continue to serve him.[23]

After being attacked in this way, Eugene might have been expected to try to rebuild his influence. But this is to misunderstand the prince. Unlike Wratislaw, he was not a politician and had stepped into his offices on the basis of his military success and from loyalty to the dynasty and his own troops. He had little interest in political power for its own sake and was now primarily concerned with defending his own reputation. In any case he did not have the application to make himself administratively indispensable. Despite all his posts, he worked no more than four or five hours a day, although even then he probably worked harder than most ministers: business piled up or was dealt with by his secretaries in the war council. Instead of protecting himself against charges of negligence by holding conferences regularly and reforming the war council, which according to St Saphorin 'had great need of it',[24] he was not prepared for the effort involved and seems to have been quite content to retain control of the war council and the Netherlands and to settle into a fairly undemanding domestic routine. He had no further interest in military adventures after the end of the Turkish war and by 1720 observers commented that his health and physical appearance were beginning to deteriorate. His position as effective first minister, and his own insistence on being treated as such, gradually slipped away.

As Eugene entered a period when his great influence and control of policy was coming to an end, there was a similar decline in the power of the conference. In foreign policy the lead was increasingly taken by Althann and the Spaniards and, to some extent, by the Imperial vice-chancellor Schönborn. Unfortunately the conference remained the main institution for the discussion and direction of foreign policy, and this was to produce confusion and, at times, paralysis in Austrian diplomacy in the coming years. There was no other member of the conference who could, or dared, provide the lead Eugene was failing to give. While Eugene had a measure of independence as he had no family, the other ministers had to think of their children's futures. Sinzendorff felt this more keenly than most; he had been careful during the troubles of 1719 not to identify himself too closely with Eugene.[25] His daily contact with Charles as *Hofkanzler* convinced him that he should keep in well with both Althann and the Spaniards. As for Gundaker Starhemberg, he was becoming more and more alienated from political life as he saw the *Hofkammer* firmly in the hands of Mikosch and Walsegg, men whom St Saphorin believed were mainly interested in financial reform to pay pensions on time rather than to support the army and reduce debts, as Starhemberg had tried to do in the past.[26]

The decline of the influence of Eugene and the conference and a lack of firm direction in Austrian policy can be seen in Charles's relations with the other European powers in the two years following the defeat of the cabal. Austria began to slide into a decade of isolation, which was reflected in her policy in both the Mediterranean and northern Europe.

In 1700, a year before the outbreak of the War of Spanish Succession, the Great Northern War had begun and it was to continue somewhat intermittently until 1721. Although the war was fought for much of the time on German soil, all three emperors and their ministers, because of their involvement against France, the Turks and Spain, had had to look on impotently as first Denmark, Saxony-Poland and Russia, and then

Prussia and Hanover, broke up the Swedish Baltic empire. While Eugene in the first years after Rastadt had been personally glad to see Sweden ejected from Germany because of her long association with France,[27] he felt keenly the insult to Charles as head of the Empire in the way the northern allies had ignored him. He also feared the growth of the territorial and military power of the Prussian state under the militarist Frederick William I (1713–40) and Prussia's increasingly close friendship with Peter the Great, whose Russian troops entered Germany in 1716 and occupied Mecklenburg. As the anti-Swedish powers fell to quarrelling over their spoils, Austria gave her moral support to Denmark, Saxony-Poland, and George I as elector of Hanover, against Prussia and Russia. And in the autumn of 1718, after making peace with the Turks, the Imperial government, and Eugene in particular,[28] eagerly took up suggestions from Hanover and Saxony-Poland to contain the two powers by an alliance concluded in Vienna in January 1719. Under the threat of this Vienna alliance the Russians quickly left Mecklenburg and Poland, and Frederick William quietly acquiesced. The Russian danger now appeared less to the Austrians, but that from Prussia with her large standing army lingered on. Eugene himself knew very well the value of Prussian troops from the War of Spanish Succession and he made no secret of his concern about 'Prussia's great army'.[29]

While Eugene had taken a determined enough stand on the problems of northern Europe until the first months of 1719, he subsequently began to play a much more secondary role. When George I, as English king and elector of Hanover, allied with Prussia during 1719 and then tried to persuade Austria to join in a broad coalition of the northern powers to push Russia out of Sweden's Baltic provinces, Eugene was sympathetic[30] but neither he nor anyone else in Vienna could contemplate joining in a conflict where Austria would have to bear the brunt of any fighting.[31] Austrian reluctance to co-operate infuriated George I's English ministers who felt they had saved Charles VI's neck from Spain in the Mediterranean. Relations between George I and Charles deteriorated rapidly in 1719 and 1720[32] as the English king aligned more closely with Protestant Prussia and supported the Protestant side in religious squabbles within Germany. Gradually the anti-Protestant Imperial vice-chancellor Schönborn stiffened Austrian policy towards these powers and went out of his way to be obstructive when the Prussians and Hanoverians tried to have their gains in northern Germany from Sweden confirmed by the emperor. Eugene did nothing to stop Schönborn moving into the centre of Imperial policy on this issue and reasserting the Imperial vice-chancery's traditional paramountcy in dealing

with the Imperial princes and the northern powers.[33] Although we know
from what he said himself in conferences and to foreign ministers at this
time, that Eugene would have been willing to compromise in these disputes, he did not push his views strongly nor did he try to direct policy.
Besides his own declining influence with Charles, there were other
reasons for standing on the sidelines. He had no wish to offend those in
Vienna who wanted to support the Catholics in the Empire, 'out of fear
that he might be accused of being prompted by irreligion',[34] but also he
was always as touchy as Schönborn about what he considered to be in-
sults to the Imperial dignity in the *Reich*.

The increasing coolness between George I and Charles VI in the
Empire and northern Europe after 1719 was matched by similar developments in the south. While the conference ministers and Eugene
were prepared to honour the terms of the Quadruple Alliance,[35] they
were unable to prevent the difficulties and obstructions which Charles
himself, encouraged by his Spaniards, was raising, particularly over
wanting to retain the mere title of king of Spain.[36] In exasperation the
English turned more towards the Bourbon powers and after the death of
Stanhope, the new directors of English policy, Townshend and Carteret,
made a Triple Alliance with France and Spain in June 1721.

The deterioration of Austrian policy into what appeared to be petty
obstruction was the result of the collapse of the direction of policy by
Eugene and the conference. Charles's policy was now managed from
behind the scenes by Althann and the Spaniards, with Sinzendorff as one
of their dependants.[37] Only in the Empire, where Schönborn controlled
policy as much as possible, was there any Austrian initiative or firmness
of purpose. As an experienced English under-secretary of state, Tilson,
put it, the Austrians seemed to be 'in a lethargy, who may start up a
little upon a great noise, but fall asleep again immediately'.[38]

XIX

Governor of the Netherlands

Except for his work in the war council, Eugene played little part in the day-to-day administration of the monarchy by its central institutions. He was not involved in the formulation of the Pragmatic Sanction (1713) nor in the attempts by Charles in the early 1720s to have this settlement accepted by the estates of his various lands. On the other hand for nearly a decade he was directly concerned in the administration of one particular area of the monarchy, the Southern Netherlands.

Before becoming governor of the Netherlands, he had been viceroy of Milan. But while recognizing the strategic importance of the duchy and making it contribute heavily to the war effort, he took little interest in it otherwise and seems to have looked on his appointment as a temporary wartime expedient: he never returned there after 1707. After Charles's accession his influence was in any case curtailed by interference from the Spanish council. No doubt it was the income from the post rather than anything else which made him hang on to Milan till he was made governor of the Netherlands in 1716.

Eugene was to take a much closer interest in his new charge, but he never seems to have intended to go there in person. The Southern Netherlands were only handed over to the emperor on the conclusion of the Barrier treaty at the end of 1715 and Eugene was not invested as governor till the following June. By then he was fully occupied with the first campaign against the Turks. Once the war was over and he was free to go to Brussels, he made no serious attempt to do so, although he occasionally spoke about going when he grew disgusted with Viennese politics. But it would have meant losing personal contact with the emperor and probably resignation from his chief interest, the war council.[1] He would also have had to abandon his palaces and his friends. The latter, particularly countess Batthyány, pressed him to stay, for in St Saphorin's words '. . . la Badiani fears he will find another mistress in the

Netherlands'.² Consequently during his eight years as governor, the province was administered by a permanent representative, the marquis de Prié.

While prince Eugene might be an absentee governor, he was determined to keep ultimate control in his own hands. He would brook no interference, particularly from members of Charles's Spanish council, and he insisted on the creation in Vienna of a separate council of Flanders, which was packed with trusted Flemings, Spaniards and Germans. He dealt with all important matters personally and this entailed a considerable administrative burden: he coped by delegating the routine work to his secretaries.

How did he view his position as governor? Undoubtedly, whether he realized it or not, he treated the post partly as a sinecure, which he could enjoy from Vienna and which brought him a substantial annual income of about 150,000 gulden; given his contribution to winning the Netherlands for Charles, he need have few qualms about doing so. Having little understanding of, or interest in, the complexities of the province's political life or economic needs, his approach was very simple: he saw the problem chiefly as one of security. The territory had to be kept politically quiet and should support as large a garrison as possible to defend it from France. The new government, which lacked the sanction of tradition rule from Madrid had enjoyed, inherited serious problems, which it never came to grips with. Both the towns and the nobility possessed extensive local privileges, which had survived the attacks of Philip V's administration under Bergeyck before 1706. The Netherlanders were jealous of their privileges and ever on the look out for a chance to extend them. They viewed their new ruler and his representatives with equal contempt, and it was said that all classes spoke of 'their august sovereign, the Emperor Charles VI, as though they were speaking only of a drummer boy'.³ They also had ample grounds for complaints. Their ruler had been changed without their leave, the continual campaigns and the exactions of the Anglo-Dutch condominium had weighed heavily on them, and after 1715 the Barrier treaty imposed the permanent financial burden of the Dutch garrisons, who were there to defend the province from France by manning a number of fortresses; even after some modification of the treaty in 1718, one third of the revenues went to support these Dutch troops. This and the favourable tariffs allowed to English and Dutch goods, which were a part of the treaty, meant that the Netherlands were never out of debt throughout Charles's reign. Any chance of increasing the wealth and revenues of the country by commercial expansion through overseas trade from Antwerp was denied by

Anglo-Dutch insistence on maintaining the century-old closure of the river Scheldt.

It was above all the conclusion of the Barrier treaty which meant that the new régime began on a sour note. Deputies from the estates came to Vienna to protest in 1716, but they found little sympathy from their new governor who was furious when they approached members of the Spanish council behind his back. However, his attitude was largely shaped by his determination not to alienate the Maritime Powers at the beginning of the Turkish war[4] and he was always to be chiefly concerned with the strategic position of the Netherlands: it was a link with England and the United Provinces in a system for containing France. French expansion into a traditional area would now be effectively blocked in a way which had been impossible under the previous weak Spanish administration and the three powers would be in a position to renew their attack directly on northern France if need be.

Given that the problems facing the new administration were large and were unlikely to decrease, the choice as resident in Brussels of the marquis de Prié was an unfortunate if not disastrous one. His appointment was Eugene's own. He was a Savoyard who spoke French and Italian; the two men had known each other well before 1705 when de Prié was one of Victor Amadeus's diplomats and afterwards when he entered Austrian service. His proven diplomatic skill, his French speech, non-Spanish or Austrian origins and personal loyalty made him seem the ideal man to act for Eugene in Brussels. But he proved unpopular with the local population and largely excluded them from the more important posts in the administration. Sensitive to any slights on himself and his family, de Prié remained isolated in Brussels. He was widely believed to be corrupt and to traffic in public and church offices, but the large personal debts left at his death suggest that this was not extensive. His natural laziness, age and increasing ill health made him an erratic administrator. Months would go by without his answering letters. Whitworth, an English diplomat who knew him well, sympathized with his subjects, 'who must perish under such slow jaws'.[5] His director of posts, Jaupain, complained that 'Prié now and again has attacks of dizziness; it is noticeable that they usually affect him on the days when the post arrives from Vienna, so that one could say he gets them by post.'[6]

Eugene was aware of de Prié's faults. He heard of them through his own correspondence with other officials in the Netherlands but he also knew about them when he appointed him, for as he told an English diplomat in 1721, 'when the Marquis de Prié was Ambassadour at Rome, they were sometimes here above a month without receiving any dispatches from him, & that then there would come a Bundle of papers of a foot high, & that he expected now a Packet of that size, which would take up fifteen days in the reading'.[7] Yet the prince showed remarkable patience and refused to accept that a wrong choice had been made, although he must have been aware that criticism of his deputy rebounded on him. He continually urged the man to be regular in his correspondence and above all to follow his own example by delegating the actual drafting of letters to his secretary after he had given the sense of it to him, for 'letter writing is not a minister's business'.[8]

De Prié has been accused by Belgian historians of trying to introduce absolutism but he was only defending what he saw as the status quo. Charles VI was always careful to maintain the existing constitutions of his territories, especially those forming part of the Spanish monarchy, having observed to Wratislaw in 1711 that 'every country will be governed best in accordance with its own privileges and customs'.[9] Eugene similarly had no intention of pushing through changes and advised de Prié to manage the estates like the English parliament rather than intimidating them.

What Eugene was determined to prevent was any attempt to extend local privileges at the expense of the crown, especially when accompanied by civil disturbances. In fact there was a good deal of unrest and mob violence in the main cities before 1719. It was provoked by the guilds, who were trying to resist the financial demands of the administration and also to re-establish the medieval idea of complete municipal independence. Although de Prié himself shied away from a direct confrontation, Eugene encouraged him to stand his ground and to take swift and sharp military action. After Passarowitz large numbers of troops were moved in to cow the province, and by 1719 Brussels was occupied by 10,000 men. De Prié could now seize troublemakers and with Eugene's backing he had the seventy year old guildmaster, Francis Anneessens, tortured to reveal his accomplices and then publicly beheaded with a great show of military force.

Eugene had insisted on using the mailed fist because of his horror at street rioting and looting, particularly as there had been some calls for the restoration of Philip V, and this might have encouraged French intervention. He told de Prié bluntly that when the troops encountered rioters they should 'kill any who try to escape or show the least signs of resistance, and in this way strike terror into this audacious and insolent populace, who deserve neither consideration nor leniency'.[10] The use of military force certainly worked and the disorders in the towns were effectively suppressed. Eugene was then the first to advocate easing the tense situation by withdrawing most of the troops. There was no thought of using them to overturn established municipal privileges, and the number of troops had to be reduced in any case because the burden of supporting them had led to an alarming deterioration in the financial position in the Netherlands.

If the régime successfully maintained internal order, the other success which Eugene was not slow to point out was that besides paying for the Dutch garrisons de Prié also managed to finance a permanent military establishment of 18,000–21,000 men. As far as Eugene was concerned, this was the most important side of his rule in the Netherlands. He had no personal interest in doing anything to increase the crown's revenues or its subjects' prosperity by direct intervention, although he did agree to some economies and even overcame his personal distaste at the sale of offices – both reflected in a moderately successful attempt by de Prié to reduce the debt after 1719. The real pressure for financial reform seems to have come from Charles VI, who from 1717 asked that proper accounts be kept in Brussels of income and expenditure and that the various financial institutions be reorganized. Whereas Eugene showed complete indifference to commercial enterprises, Charles had been convinced of their value since his days in Spain.[11] The possibilities in Austria were of course limited. Nevertheless after Passarowitz Charles had encouraged the setting up of a company to use Trieste as a port for trade with the Levant and had also initiated the building of an access road over the Semmering. He was to find sympathetic helpers in his Spaniards and Sinzendorff, and he took a keen interest in the development of Adriatic commerce in the 1720s, suffering bitter disappointment when he went to see the results of it at Trieste in 1728.[12]

The Netherlands should have provided a fine opportunity to break into the Atlantic and Asian trade, but the Maritime Powers were determined to prevent any interference with their own monopoly. They had not only refused to allow the opening of the Scheldt but were hostile to the development of trade elsewhere in the Netherlands. However, the success of John Law's Mississippi Company in France and of the South Sea Company in England in 1719 inevitably produced demands in the Netherlands and Vienna for a similar venture based at Ostend. While Charles was enthusiastic – 'the emperor has it intirely at heart as much as it is possible to imagine'[13] – Eugene was not: he was highly suspicious of commercial schemes and feared the political burden of having to defend them from the Maritime Powers. He effectively blocked all attempts by foreign speculators to interest the emperor in ambitious Law-type ventures and his caution was borne out by the collapse of both the Mississippi and South Sea Companies. He explained his attitude in this way: 'It is enough for someone to appear as a promoter for me to lose my good opinion of him. For, in most cases, I have found very little worth and sincerity in people who concern themselves with such things.'[14] But Charles insisted, and in 1720 Eugene reluctantly gave way, ordering de Prié to set about forming a company. The marquis dragged his feet, probably because he was being paid by the small group of merchants who were sending the occasional ship from Ostend to the Far East. Charles grew increasingly angry and Eugene had to demand a project in the summer of 1721. De Prié then produced a sound enough scheme and it was not his or Eugene's opposition but the interminable delays which plagued everything in Vienna which caused another two years to pass before the Ostend Company was floated in August 1723.

The company was to pay the emperor six per cent of its profits in return for protection and a charter to trade and colonize in the Far East. The first subscription was taken up immediately: the bulk came from Flemish nobles and capitalists and it was largely a Netherlands enterprise, but de Prié swallowed his opposition to become the largest subscriber with 150,000 gulden. Rialp and Sinzendorff shared another 100,000. Although de Prié reserved 500,000 for Eugene, the prince only took up 60,000. While wanting to support it publicly, he did not wish to appear to be profiteering and in any case had little interest in making money in this way. However, despite his previous doubts, his loyalty to Charles made him work hard for the success of the company and to work towards its acceptance by the Maritime Powers. But there was no chance of this because of the jealousy which the success of the venture aroused in the English and Dutch East India Companies. Profits on voyages often reached 80–100 per cent, and by 1730 6 million gulden had been paid in dividends.

A year after the formation of the Ostend Company Eugene resigned as governor of the Netherlands. He did so because de Prié's position there was becoming untenable and it was impossible for him to support him any longer. The marquis had fallen completely out of favour with Charles after his initial opposition to the Ostend scheme but he was also coming under intolerable pressure from the native nobility within his own council of state in Brussels. The most vocal of his opponents was the marquis de Mérode-Westerloo, who was a personal enemy of Eugene's from the War of Spanish Succession and bitterly attacked him in his memoirs, which were to be published a century later. When he overreached himself and slandered de Prié, Eugene was quick to have him arrested and imprisoned in 1724, wanting to make an example of him.

But the aristocratic opposition to de Prié was too strong and almost immediately another focus of dissent emerged around the Imperial general Alexander de Bonneval. An impetuous and argumentative Frenchman, who was to end his days as a Moslem and reformer of the Turkish army, he had left French and then Venetian service for that of the emperor. He rapidly became one of Eugene's favourites, going to Rastadt with him, and becoming a member of his circle in Vienna. But he was always a man of suspect views. In 1718 his close friend St Saphorin remarked that Bonneval 'very often spouts republican ideas' and was already in contact with opposition elements in the Netherlands.[15] Soon after the Sicilian war he and the prince fell out as he felt Eugene was not advancing him to the military posts he deserved. In 1723 he left Vienna for Brussels, although he had been told plainly by Eugene that he would find nothing there, '. . . my intention never having been to appoint him nor any other Frenchman in these lands next to France'.[16] Once in Brussels he immediately joined the nobles in opposition to de Prié, but, like Mérode-Westerloo, he went too far and was arrested for what amounted to treason in September 1724. Eugene felt particularly bitter about the episode and interpreted the attacks on de Prié as directed at himself, which they were probably meant to be, and he used all his power, as in the Nimptsch-Tedeschi affair, to insist, successfully, that Bonneval be imprisoned at Brno (Brünn).

Although both Mérode-Westerloo and Bonneval came unstuck, the furore accompanying their attacks and arrests in both Brussels and Vienna ruined de Prié and undermined Eugene's own position. The prince finally realized he could not keep on protecting de Prié and putting his own reputation at risk. The final straw was the growing opposition to the marquis from the previously docile council of Flanders in Vienna and open sympathy from both Charles and Sinzendorff for Bonneval. They may even have originally encouraged him to go to Brussels to gather information against de Prié. Whatever the truth of this, Eugene's final alienation from Sinzendorff stems from the time of the Bonneval affair. It also seems that the *Hofkanzler* threatened countess Batthyány that Eugene would be forced to go to the Netherlands in person if the prince did not resign. On 16 November 1724 he went to Charles and resigned.

As compensation Charles conferred on him the completely honorary post of vicar-general of Italy, worth 140,000 gulden a year, and gave him an estate for hunting at Siebenbrunn in Lower Austria, said to be worth double this amount. Eugene cynically remarked on this occasion that Charles's Spaniards obviously wanted to make him one of them, but the effect was spoilt by Rialp being given a larger estate. His resignation distressed him a great deal and he was already in very low spirits at Christmas 1724 when he had a bad bout of flu. This attack was the beginning of permanent bronchitis and regular acute infections every winter for the last dozen years of his life.

Once Eugene had resigned de Prié was finished and stood down in the spring of 1725 to avoid dismissal. He returned to Vienna in virtual disgrace and died a year later. The Netherlands reverted to the tradition of rule by a resident archduchess, in this case Charles's spinster sister Maria Elizabeth, an arrangement more suited to the semi-autonomous position of the province. Although an enthusiastic German writer of the 1930s claimed that de Prié and Eugene's régime 'laid the foundations of a new era',[17] it did nothing of the sort. The privileges of the province and the independence of the nobility had not been curbed and the economic weakness of the Netherlands remained: no solution to any of these problems was to be found before the end of Austrian rule at the close of the century. On the other hand under Eugene's administration open disaffection had been crushed and the position of the Netherlands as a barrier against France had been maintained. It was as much as could be expected from a governor whose authority was exercised from a thousand miles away.

XX

Eugene as a Patron

Palaces and religious buildings sprang up everywhere in the inner city and suburbs of Vienna in the half-century after the defeat of the Turks in 1683, and the same process was taking place in most of the smaller cities of the monarchy, particularly Prague and Pressburg (Bratislava), as well as on the estates of the nobility and clergy. These buildings represented the most impressive part of a great upsurge of activity in all the visual arts in south Germany and central Europe during what has been called the age of 'Imperial baroque' (1684–1740). The lead in bringing baroque art and artists from Italy in the seventeenth century was taken by the religious orders, especially the Jesuits, but the equally wealthy lay aristocracy soon followed suit on a similarly grand scale. For two hundred years the main artistic influences in Austria had been Italian and there was no dramatic change of direction in this period. Although native artists and architects were increasingly employed after the turn of the century, they were usually men who had learnt their craft in Italy, and the majority of artists continued to be Italians.

Imperial baroque tried and succeeded in creating a spectacle of grandeur, colour and opulence both in buildings and in their furnishings and decorations. Architecture reigned supreme, and all the other arts, including music, were used to embellish it. The great aristocratic builders became collectors of works of art of the past and patrons of living artists. Charles VI, like his father before him, joined in far less than many of his leading subjects and was unable to match them in their building enterprises: this is some indication of where the real wealth in his realm lay. He had to abandon Joseph's grandiose plans for a palace at Schönbrunn to rival Versailles and to be satisfied with a fine building for his library (Hofbibliothek) and with the Karlskirche in the Wieden suburb. Yet all around Charles his ministers and courtiers seemed to have little difficulty in building. Whether they were from established families like Liechtenstein, Sinzendorff and Trautsohn, or comparatively new arrivals like

Caprara, Rialp or Schönborn, one or more palaces appeared bearing their name. The most spectacular of them all as builder, collector and patron was prince Eugene.

Most of the great nobles found the enormous sums demanded by their extravagances from the income of their inherited estates rather than from the rewards of Imperial office. In the case of the richest of them, Adam Liechtenstein, we have seen that he enjoyed 400,000 gulden a year.[1] On the other hand neither Eugene nor Schönborn came to Vienna with inherited lands, yet both ended up very rich men. Schönborn's income from Imperial offices in 1720 amounted to about 50,000 gulden a year, but his family helped him purchase an estate in 1710 and he also received lands in Hungary from Charles VI in 1728. Gifts of land from the crown were important factors in the wealth of many of the ministers, but Schönborn benefited as well from presents tendered him by interested parties in disputes within the Empire where his influence was decisive: in 1720 George I's minister Cadogan paid him 20,000 gulden to settle the investiture of Hadeln on him as elector of Hanover.[2] Eugene similarly benefited from gifts of crown land, but it is highly unlikely that he accepted bribes. Du Luc, the French diplomat, believed in 1715 that he was the only minister who could not be bought. The magnificent presents he received on occasions from foreign rulers were to serve as ornaments for his palaces rather than as negotiable assets.

As we have seen the bulk of Eugene's personal correspondence and all his personal accounts, which would also have told us much about his palaces and treasures, have been lost. This means that it is not possible to identify exactly where his vast wealth came from, but we have a fairly good idea about his income and how he financed the building of his homes and his collections. He managed to purchase and build the first stages of the winter palace as well as the site for the later Belvedere and the Danubian island of Czepel largely out of the revenues from his abbeys in Savoy. But from 1703, when he became president of the war council, he could count on a steadily mounting income from Imperial office. The presidency was probably worth 100,000 gulden a year, while the governorships of Milan and the Netherlands are both likely to have brought in 150,000 gulden. When he lost the Netherlands in 1724, the post of vicar-general of Italy more or less made up for it with a salary of 140,000 gulden. In addition there were gifts from Leopold of largely worthless land in Hungary between 1698 and 1702. More substantial was the gift of 400,000 gulden between 1710 and 1717 in lieu of further Hungarian land, and of the Siebenbrunn estate in 1724–25. In 1729 Pöllnitz believed – and Keysler reached the same conclusion a year later

– that the prince's income from his offices was 300,000 gulden with another 100,000 from his various estates.[3] His share of the booty from such battles as Zenta and Peterwardein would be additional bonuses. He therefore enjoyed sums which put him well into the Liechtenstein class, and it should consequently be of no surprise that he could build on as lavish a scale as any of the leading magnates within the monarchy. In fact he could afford to spend more because he had no immediate family, few servants and was indifferent to his own appearance. Moreover, as he grew older he went back on his earlier decision not to build up an estate for himself and became one of the largest landowners in the fertile plain of the Marchfeld which lies between the rivers Danube and March, buying land there in 1726 to add to the Siebenbrunn estate. One reason for this, besides his increasing interest in hunting, was that there was a limit to what he could spend on his Vienna palaces from his large income. When he died in 1736 his total wealth, which did not include the estates in southern Hungary, was put at 2 million gulden and this was probably an underestimate: the Belvedere and Himmelpfortgasse palaces were only valued at 100,000 gulden each, yet individual items in them cost 10,000 or more gulden.

As with so much of Eugene's personal life, we know little about how he administered his estates. It is clear that he only visited those in Savoy and Hungary once or twice. Although he could not administer the estates directly, judging from a letter of his to the administrator of the Savoyard abbeys in 1711, he probably kept a tight enough personal control: he asked for an accurate account 'so I can make a correct balance for myself'.[4] The man responsible for the overall administration of the various estates, as well as for all Eugene's financial affairs and his purchases, was George Koch, 'Old Koch', the father of his secretary Ignatius Koch. He entered the prince's service after Zenta and stayed with him for the rest of Eugene's life. A man such as Koch was essential to him because, although his great collections and palaces at Belvedere and in the Marchfeld at Schlosshof were assembled in the long period of peace after the War of Spanish Succession, he had built nearly as lavishly during the previous twenty years of almost continual warfare and absence from Vienna. While the campaigns made direct supervision impossible, Eugene scrutinized all the building plans and in many cases chose the materials and furnishings himself.

There is no need to enquire too deeply into why Eugene built and collected. As he rose through Imperial service there was every reason why he should try to emulate his contemporaries. Military men such as Caprara and Daun built, commissioned and collected in Vienna; outside

Austria Marlborough created his own palace of Blenheim at Woodstock and in Venice marshal Schulenburg collected paintings on a truly regal scale. Moreover Eugene came from a princely family, had grown up in the Hôtel de Soissons in Louis XIV's Paris and had for his great-uncle Mazarin, one of the greatest collectors and patrons of the seventeenth century.

Eugene's winter palace in the Himmelpfortgasse had been constructed in its main essentials before the end of the seventeenth century by the Austrian architect Fischer von Erlach. The choice of this man and his lofty and idealistic architecture, which fitted so well into the narrow confines of the inner city, was a natural one. The leading architect of the day, he had built a city palace for Eugene's early powerful friend chancellor Stratmann, and he was also later to build one for the latter's daughter and son-in-law, count and countess Batthyány. The prince's association with Fischer ended in 1701. There is no indication of a quarrel: it is more likely that the prince found something more to his taste in the less heroic and more elegant architecture of John Lukas Hildebrandt. This man was in fact a protégé of the prince, having accompanied him in Italy as a siege engineer in 1695–96. It was probably through Eugene's influence that he was made Imperial court engineer in 1701. Hildebrandt extended and improved the Himmelpfortgasse palace throughout the war years, although essentially he was completing Fischer's conception. Because of the confined site these extensions had to wait till the court hatter, Fauconet, agreed to sell a house he had been using as a theatre and until another neighbour, a court usher, died. The work was also continued during the plague year of 1713 when everyone else was laying off workmen. According to the *Helden-Thaten*, a eulogizing history of his life and deeds which appeared soon after the prince's death, Eugene had felt obliged to keep them employed and even 'engaged more men, ending up with 1,300, saying "it would be unchristian to force people to fight hunger as well when they are already having to wrestle with death" '.[5]

Contemporaries regarded Eugene's winter palace as the most beautiful of all those in the inner city. It was here that he spent most of his life, presided over conferences and eventually died. Yet it was difficult then, as now, to view it properly except from an angle because of the narrowness of the Himmelpfortgasse. Today all that is left, in what has become the Finanzministerium, is the façade, without the original figures on the roof, a cave-like entrance vestibule, the magnificent curved staircase and two ceiling frescoes.

As one would expect, the motifs on the outside and the internal decoration stressed martial themes and we find the same in the palaces built for two other soldiers, Daun and Batthyány. At Blenheim Marlborough had his great victories depicted on tapestries; Eugene had his painted on massive canvases. Classical themes were also strongly represented in the Himmelpfortgasse: the myth of Hercules in particular – just as in the Batthyány palace – and that of Apollo, the god of arts and sciences.

The great houses of the early eighteenth century were sparsely furnished: frescoes, hangings, mirrors and display furniture were used to create the main effects. Differences between rooms were emphasized by stressing one particular colour – gold or blue and so on. Eugene's palaces were no exception and we are lucky in having contemporary accounts of them. The winter palace was visited in 1729 and 1730 by Pöllnitz and Keysler, whose descriptions are not only interesting in themselves but also in showing how easy it was for foreign visitors to be shown round the palaces much the same as tourists today:

> The Palace of Prince Eugene of Savoy is stately, but situated in a narrow street with a very little court before it. . . . [It] consists of four stories; the third is the most magnificent, but the apartments and staircase are somewhat darkened by the houses on the other side of the street. In the front are three doors opening into so many balconies; and in every story are seventeen windows. The roof is flat, in the Italian taste, and adorned with eighteen large statues. . . . The stair-case is very well contriv'd were it not too much confin'd. The apartments of the first story are as well laid out as the ground wou'd admit of. We enter first into a spacious salon adorn'd with great pictures [by Huchtenburg] representing the chief victories of Prince Eugene over the French and the Turks. . . . In the two rooms next to this are very rich hangings wherein the maker Devos [de Vos][6] at Brussels has very correctly delineated the whole military science. . . . that representing a ship-wreck is particularly admired. Some of the apartments are finely hung with crimson velvet, especially that in which the prince, some years ago, gave audience to the Turkish ambassador under a canopy and in a chair of state. The stove in this room is made of brass and represents Hercules vanquishing the Hydra. In another apartment is a book-case and desk made entirely of tortoise-shell. . . . every part of this superb palace is embellished with exquisite pictures, glasses of all kinds, and fine chimney-pieces; one of which of grey marble, cost twenty thousand guldens. . . . The bed-chamber . . . has a set of furniture of green velvet richly embroider'd with gold and silk. In the same room there is a lustre of rock crystal which is said to have cost 40,000 florins. All the other furniture is extraordinary magnificent, and wou'd be cry'd up at Paris itself.[7]

The Himmelpfortgasse palace was only one of Eugene's palaces; from almost the beginning of his life in Austria he seems to have intended to have several. Hildebrandt was employed to draft plans for a palace on his Danubian island at Ráckeve, and the building was nearly finished by the time of the Hungarian rebellion, probably eventually costing 100,000 gulden. It was built at the edge of the river and had a large octagonal dome and curved wings. As the prince only seems to have gone there once, after the siege of Belgrade in 1717, we must conclude that he lost interest in the place both as a palace and a country retreat, probably because of the Rákóczi revolt.

Throughout the War of Spanish Succession Hildebrandt was laying out gardens on the land Eugene had bought a few years earlier to the south east of Vienna, but no buildings were erected there until the war was over. The site gave a superb view of the city and was large enough for a more flamboyant structure than in the Himmelpfortgasse. Eventually Hildebrandt was to fulfil an architectural dream in the double Belvedere palace which surpassed all the palaces being built in the suburbs.

Between 1714 and 1716 a modest single-storey building, the Lower Belvedere, was constructed at the bottom of the sloping gardens. Almost immediately afterwards Eugene decided to build the much larger and impressive Upper Belvedere at the top of the slope. The actual building was probably completed between 1720 and 1722, although the interiors must have taken longer. A great deal of work was done on the gardens in 1717 and 1719 by the French landscape gardener Girard, a pupil of the famous Le Nôtre, lent to Eugene by Max Emmanuel of Bavaria. He reversed the layout of the gardens so that they could be viewed sloping downwards rather than upwards. They were planned in the manner of Versailles to show nature tamed by man: straight lines and geometric patterns in complete contrast to the curves and twirls of baroque buildings and art.

The Upper Belvedere was Hildebrandt's as well as Eugene's showpiece and both had the money to create what they wanted. A fairy-tale palace with sparkling white stucco walls and a copper roof, it soon became the wonder of Europe: between 1731 and 1740 Salomon Kleiner of Augsburg produced a hundred engravings of it.* Then, as today, visitors entered the enclosed grounds from the south through huge wrought-iron gates and immediately came upon 'a very large piece of water, with a row of chestnut-trees on each side, that leads to the House'.[8] The pond was large enough for small gondolas to sail on it and reflected the building behind it. This palace with its three-storeyed central section and

---

* One contemporary critic was Montesquieu who thought the façade 'is in bad taste: a mass of fancy bits and pieces', *Voyages* I (1894), p. 5.

lower pavilions on both sides with squat cupolas at all four corners gave the impression of a vast tent. The interiors have changed over the palace's two hundred years as an Imperial and state residence, but we have two contemporary accounts of its original appearance, one published by J. B. Küchelbecker in Hanover in 1730[9] and the other printed at a later date by the Hanoverian Keysler after a visit in 1730.

The main rooms were, and still are, on the first floor – the ground floor housed the servants and kitchens. Going round the palace from the front towards the east, the visitor entered the prince's bedroom through a 'blue' room hung with fine pictures. The bedroom contained a costly bed, mirrors and other furniture, and led to a room with walls covered from floor to ceiling with miniatures in gilt frames with floral mouldings. Here the prince also kept a collection of optical and scientific instruments. At the far corner of the palace, under one of the cupolas, was a small chapel decorated in brown marble, with a painting of the Resurrection on the altar. In the next corner room, which had a floor made of multi-coloured wood, were several heavily-gilded mirrors and 'four small tables of black marble, with brown veins, brought hither from Rome'. As the visitor moved west he reached the 'Audience Room' which had walls draped with tapestries in Indian floral patterns and a ceiling fresco of Apollo. He next came to the 'Conference Room' with crimson-damask walls and a crystal chandelier, said to have cost 18,000 gulden, before entering the two-storey high 'Open Room' which provided views of the gardens and the city beyond. Shaped like 'an oblong octagon', the room had a ceiling 'finely painted in fresco' and a floor of red marble. Next to the 'Open Room' was another double-storeyed room, the 'Marble Room', which had an apotheosis of Eugene as a warrior on the ceiling. After passing through three more rooms the visitor reached the prince's narrow picture gallery, where his best paintings were hung, many in the semi-erotic style so popular in Germany at this time:

> Among the excellent paintings . . . are a piece representing Adam and Eve as big as the life, which is said to have cost fifty thousand gulden; a woman embracing a youth in a bath, valued at thirty thousand, with Endymion and Diana worth twelve thousand gulden. Here is also a copy of Rubens's three graces, which is very much esteemed.

At the extreme west corners of the palace were a 'white' room made out of marble-like gypsum and another decorated in what was known as the Indian style with much lacquer work and gold-inlaid porcelain. Scattered throughout most rooms were gold-brocade couches and chairs.

The intention of the whole was for the rooms to be walked around in and admired rather than lived in. The prince used the large palace mainly for receptions, staying himself in the summer in the Lower Belvedere.

The strictly symmetrical gardens contained several fountains, an elaborate cascade and a mass of topiary work. No large trees were planted which might obscure the views. The long walks running the length of the gardens were edged with box trees, and busts were set at intervals along the sides. One drawback, however, was 'that the Salesian nunnery, founded by the empress Amelia, commands this garden, so that a person cannot walk in it, without being overlooked'. As at Versailles, there was an orangery for tropical plants, many needing to be sheltered with glass in the winter. There were said to be two thousand different kinds drawn from the Mediterranean, the Far East and South America, 'among which are dragon's blood, coffee, date, and musk trees'. In the grounds there was also 'a spacious aviary made of curious wire-work' and a zoo, arranged in 'eight small courts embellished with fountains and rows of chestnut-trees'.[10] The prince had an extensive collection of tropical birds, including large ostriches and multi-coloured sparrows and swallows. Besides a lion and some apes, there was a porcupine, a bearded Transylvanian ox, a Russian fox, an Indian wolf and many others.

Even while the internal decorations of the Belvedere were being completed, Eugene was building elsewhere. In the late 1720s he asked Hildebrandt to convert an existing structure on his Marchfeld estates into a country seat, the Schlosshof. Finished by 1729, this was a much less elaborate building than his other palaces and was strong enough to serve as a fortress in case of need. Its main purpose was to accommodate the large hunting parties Eugene wanted to take there in the autumn. As it was only a day from Vienna by land or water, the prince spent a good deal of time there in his last years. The inside was richly decorated and furnished, and it housed yet another great collection of pictures, many of them specially commissioned to illustrate his plants and animals at the Belvedere.

In decorating and furnishing his palaces Eugene became one of the greatest patrons of his age and he has been called 'the most grandiose and influential private patron in Europe'.[11] If the architects he employed were Germans, the men who came to Vienna to paint the frescoes and who took commissions for most of his paintings were Italians. In choosing them, he was not asserting his own Italian associations but following the pattern of other great nobles like the Liechtensteins and ruling princes such as Max Emmanuel of Bavaria or Augustus the Strong of Saxony. He particularly liked classical themes and his taste was for 'the sumptuous and heavy'.[12] On the other hand when he wanted paintings of his great victories, these were executed by John van Huchtenburg of Haarlem. Although Eugene sent him details for these ten battle scenes, which, as we have seen, were hung in the winter palace, they were inevitably romanticized ones. In 1720 Huchtenburg published them as prints.[13] Eugene's sculptures were mostly commissioned in Italy, especially with Lorenzo Mattielli and Domenico Antonio Parodi; but probably the most famous, and expensive, was executed by the Salzburg artist at the Saxon court, Balthasar Permoser: a huge white-marble statue of Eugene. This apotheosis, which shows the prince trampling a Turk underfoot, was finished in 1721 and set up in the marble room of the Upper Belvedere. According to George Koch Eugene did not like 'the posture'[14] of the figure, and it does present him in a rather awkward position with cherubs and Fame pressing closely round.

Besides special commissions Eugene was systematically collecting furniture, statues and paintings for his palaces, and plants and animals for his gardens. Like other leading men of his time he called on diplomats throughout Europe to help: one example of this was in 1709 when he asked the Imperial minister in London, Gallas, to buy porcelain and paintings.[15] Every ship coming into Ostend from the East was met to see if any fine work or exotic animals were on board.

All his palaces had picture galleries. He had begun to collect paintings during the War of Spanish Succession: there is a print in Nicholas Henderson's biography of the prince, which shows him kneeling down to choose a picture at an Amsterdam dealer's. What he eventually amassed cannot be known exactly because no catalogue of the whole collection was drawn up and it was dispersed after his death, but the more important paintings were bought by the duke of Savoy and many are still in Turin. Sixteenth- and seventeenth-century Italian and seventeenth-century Dutch and Flemish works seem to have predominated, although it is likely that 'the pictures ascribed to the great names of Titian, Raphael, Correggio, Guercino and Holbein were in fact school works, or copies, or the work of lesser painters'.[16]

The prince found collecting plants for his gardens just as absorbing as filling his galleries, and this brought him into particularly close contact with the Imperial vice-chancellor Schönborn, who was 'a great Florist'.[17] The two men took a keen interest in each other's gardens and when Schönborn began to spend much of his time at Bamberg, where he had become bishop, they continued to exchange plants.

While collecting works of art and furnishings was not exceptional for a man in Eugene's position, if not on such a grand scale, what is more surprising is the prince's famous collection of books and engravings. At his death he left a library of 15,000 printed books and 237 manuscripts as well as 500 or so volumes and cartons of prints, which today are in the Nationalbibliothek and the Albertina.[18] It is usually said that he began to collect his first books during his visit to London in 1712, but we have the evidence from the Tory agent and businessman in The Hague, Drummond, of June 1711 that he and Eugene had a common interest in books and paintings and that the prince 'makes me a sort of favourite in his own little affairs'.[19] The decisive influence may have been his adjutant, the Prussian Hohendorff, a great bibliophile and a formidable modern and classical scholar. When Eugene went to London in 1712 Hohendorff accompanied him and the two men spent a good deal of their time buying books, many of them from Christopher Bateman in Paternoster Row.[20] It was Hohendorff who acquired for him the Parisian bookbinder Stephen Boyet at a salary of 1,500 livres. Boyet stayed in the prince's service from 1713 till his death and was responsible not only for the binding but also for buying and transporting his books. The prince only wanted the finest copies and obtained them either through catalogues or through Imperial agents, friends and collectors throughout Europe. From 1718 the young P. J. Mariette, son of a Paris engraver and bookdealer, had what amounted to a roving European commission to buy for Eugene. It is clear that his collection was built up systematically. He particularly liked illustrated books on natural history and geography, but collected little on military matters. As one would expect, the mass of works were in French, Italian and Latin rather than in German.[21] All were bound in impressive morocco leather with the title embossed in gilt and with his own arms on the front and back. The books, mainly folios, were divided into three broad classes, indicated by the colour of the binding: blue for theology and jurisprudence, red for history and fiction, and yellow for natural science. They were kept in three rooms of the Himmelpfortgasse palace and arranged on 'bookshelves made of boxwood, each row being on green cloth on account of the dust'.[22]

A question which naturally occurs, is whether he actually read all his books. At the end of his life there were so many that this is rather doubtful, and we never hear of him taking books on campaigns like Frederick the Great. But we have noted him telling St Saphorin that he had enough books to make retirement pleasant and in 1716 Jean-Baptiste Rousseau wrote to a friend:

> . . . the astounding fact is that there is hardly a book which the Prince has not read, or, at least looked through, before sending it to be bound. It is hardly

believable that a man who carries on his shoulders the burden of almost all the affairs of Europe ... should find as much time to read as though he had nothing else to do. He understands a little of everything, but shows no pre-dilection for anything special. Since he reads entirely for recreation, he under-stands how to gain advantage from his reading just as he does from his official duties. His judgment is extraordinarily accurate ... [23]

As Eugene was Rousseau's protector and patron at this time one would expect flattery but there was no need for it to be directed towards his reading habits. On the other hand we have a different view from Lady Mary Wortley Montagu who was not fond of the prince and associated more with the Spanish group in Vienna. She visited his library in 1717, being shown round by Rousseau and Bonneval as well as Eugene, and wrote:

> ... the library, though not very ample, is well chosen; but as the Prince will admit into it no editions but what are beautiful and pleasing to the eye ... this finikin and foppish taste makes many disagreeable chasms in this collection. The books are pompously bound in Turkey leather ... Bonneval pleasantly told me that there were several quartos on the art of war, that were bound with the skins of spahis and janissaries; and this jest, which was indeed elegant, raised a smile of pleasure on the grave countenance of the famous warrior.[24]

XXI

Eugene and his Friends

In the twenty or so years after the peace of Rastadt Eugene's collecting brought him into contact with a large number of literary men. He was ready to accept their advice, particularly on buying books, and they were eager to give it. Two of his closest military friends in the 1710s, Hohendorff and Bonneval, were men with broad cultural interests. On the other hand one should be careful not to accept too uncritically the epithet of 'philosophe guerrier',[1] which the poet Rousseau gave him. He was no Frederick the Great and had no literary pretensions of his own: his letters were plain and factual without literary or classical allusions or attempts at imagery. Like Marlborough he was not tempted to join those soldiers – Montecuccoli, marshal de Saxe or even Villars – who wrote memoirs or books on the art of war.[2] His written contacts with authors were limited to courtesy letters, where it is certainly not possible to see a mutual exchange of ideas. It is difficult for us to assess what he understood of the books he collected, although Rousseau and Leibniz believed, or said they did, that his understanding on many subjects was very good. This might have been flattery, but there is no reason why it should not have been true. His knowledge of religion was certainly too much for Villars at Rastadt. Here Eugene explained to the French general the differences between the various kinds 'and spoke about them so knowledgeably, that Marshal Villars, who was no theologian, was taken aback &, being unable to give a reply, said to him on rising to leave: "Take care, monsieur, for your vast knowledge will damn you, but my ignorance will be my salvation".'[3]

Literary men had every reason to flatter Eugene. Given his position and his receptiveness, they were keen to meet him: few in this period could exist without patronage and this was probably the chief motive in Leibniz's association with him. The leading contemporary German philosopher got to know the prince during 1714, when he was in Vienna trying to persuade Charles VI to found an Academy of Science. While

Eugene sympathized – Leibniz wrote 'I am convinced that no man will advance the cause of science to a greater extent than Prince Eugene'[4] – as did Charles VI and Sinzendorff, the project failed from lack of money. Nevertheless, Leibniz presented Eugene with a manuscript of an abbreviated version of his difficult philosophical tract, the *Monadologie*, which delighted him so much that, according to the cynical Bonneval who may have brought him and Leibniz together, he kept it locked away, treasuring it like 'the priests keep the blood of St Januarius at Naples; that is to say he lets me kiss it and then closes it up again in its casket'.[5]

The contact with Leibniz, who left Vienna after a few months, was short-lived and there were to be no others with German writers. The cultural world in which Eugene felt most at home was that of Latin Europe, although he certainly could speak and dictate in German, and he received the Turkish ambassador with a speech in it in 1719. We have the evidence from one of his contemporaries that 'His speech is deliberate but not slow, and he also speaks German fluently enough, although he is careful never to say more than he has to.'[6] Yet he was clearly never at ease with German because not a single sentence written by him in it has been found: in 1705 he confessed to Joseph that he 'was not used to writing' in German.[7] When he wrote letters in his large bold hand, they were in French or Italian. Those written in German were dictated, sometimes with a sentence or two of his own in French, and always signed with the curious *Eugenio von Savoy*: this was not an attempt to sum up his life in a mixture of Italian, German and French but the result of his mistaken belief that this was the correct German form. When he signed French letters it was always as Eugene de Savoye. It is also clear that despite his early training for the church he was no classical scholar, at least in his old age, for in January 1731 the English diplomat Robinson showed him a draft treaty in French rather than in Latin 'knowing that the Latin Tongue is not familiar to His Highness'.[8]

The only author to whom Eugene acted in any real sense as a patron was in fact a Frenchman, the popular writer of odes and satirical verse, Jean-Baptiste Rousseau. He came to Vienna with the French minister du Luc, was quickly invited to dine with Eugene and by 1716 was being supported financially by the prince. He wrote rather mechanical, sickly odes to the appreciative Eugene and countess Batthyány, and he stayed on attached to Eugene's household, probably helping in the library, till he left for the Netherlands in 1722. Throughout this time he had his sights on a permanent post in Vienna or Brussels, but none materialized, and when he reached the Netherlands he soon became involved with his friend Bonneval in the faction opposed to the marquis de Prié. Although

Eugene was hurt at this, writing to a correspondent in the Netherlands, 'I had not believed Rousseau capable of getting mixed up with these kind of cabals',[9] he continued to write to him and their connection only gradually died out.

Eugene was always enthusiastic about Rousseau's poems and looked forward to receiving them from Brussels. When Rousseau informed him in 1723 that he was thinking of trying his hand at history, he advised against it:

> ... it is far more hazardous to write history than poetry because it is very tiring to search through the sources to carry out one's work on the past properly; and if one turns to the present, it is not easy to satisfy everyone or to say too much or too little about matters which are particularly delicate because they concern people who are still alive.[10]

Eugene probably enjoyed Rousseau's poems because they were in the style of Boileau and similar to those he had read in his youth, and the poet certainly had a vogue at the time. One person who disliked him, however, was Lady Mary Wortley Montagu, who condemned him not so much for being 'a free-thinker' but as 'a man whose heart does not feel the encomiums he gives to virtue and honour in his poems'.[11]

The prince's taste in literature was conservative and he had his doubts about modern trends. Rousseau, despite being a last champion of the 'Ancients' against the 'Moderns', introduced him to Voltaire's *Oedipus* in 1719, and could write to the author that Eugene enjoyed reading it and 'spoke to me about it in awe'.[12] But when Rousseau later sent him the *Henriade* from Brussels the prince admitted, 'I have tried to read Voltaire's poem which was enclosed with one of your last letters, but I have to confess, that I didn't find the satisfaction I expected by the way you praised the author to me.'[13] He was, however, interested enough to ask Rousseau to mark and comment on those passages he felt were the best and worst.

While Eugene neither met nor wrote to Voltaire, he did meet the other early eighteenth-century political writer, Montesquieu, who was already famous for his *Persian Letters*, when he arrived in Vienna in 1728. Eugene quickly welcomed him at his table and Montesquieu some twenty years later recollected the 'delicious moments'[14] he had spent on these occasions. A less fortunate contact was the utopian abbé St Pierre, whose *Project for Perpetual Peace* Eugene had read with some interest and scepticism by 1727. When the abbé sent him and several European statesmen further observations and projects, they produced no response and it is doubtful whether the prince bothered to read them.

It would be wrong on the evidence of occasional meetings and exchange of complimentary letters to make too much of Eugene's contacts with European intellectuals and to suggest that he was a forerunner of Frederick or Catherine the Great: they had far closer and more substantial relations with contemporary writers. On the other hand the prince did have a circle of less well-known educated friends in Vienna, whom he met through his love of books. In the early years Bonneval and Rousseau belonged to it and then in the 1720s and 1730s an equally frequent visitor was the emperor's physician and chief librarian, Garelli, reputedly 'a person of extraordinary erudition and judgement', who had charge of the best library of printed books in Europe.[15] It was through Garelli that the anti-clerical Italian historian Giannone became a friend of Eugene throughout the eleven years he lived in Vienna from 1723.

Eugene took his friends indiscriminately from orthodox and unorthodox Catholics, Protestants like St Saphorin and Hohendorff and free-thinkers such as Rousseau and Bonneval. He had no qualms about corresponding in the 1710s with the English deist John Toland, whom Hohendorff already knew well and who bought books for both men. There were works by Toland in Eugene's library, but with these as with the *Scienza Nuova* of the Italian philosopher of history, Vico, which was also there, we have no way of knowing whether they had been read or understood.

Two of Eugene's friends, Garelli and the papal nuncio Passionei, were leading figures in the spread of the controversial Catholic reform movement, known as Jansenism, in Austria, but the prince refused determinedly to take sides. He saw well enough, as he told Montesquieu, the appalling way in which the controversy was tearing France apart. While he had been governor of the Netherlands he had tried to prevent the struggle between the orthodox Jesuits and the Jansenists spreading from France to the province. With Charles's backing he refused to allow the publication of what he saw as the provocative papal bull, *Unigenitus*, and roundly condemned the archbishop of Malines for doing so. He was determined that the crown should not be dragged into the quarrel as in France, although, like Schönborn, he was a firm protagonist of the supremacy of the state over the church. Yet he never showed any real hostility towards the Jesuits, who for their part had exploited the propaganda value of his victories over the Turks and represented him as a militant Christian. At his death the Jesuit preacher Peickhardt could not praise his achievements or his piety highly enough.

While Eugene was interested in and clearly liked listening to the men who were eventually to be important in the encouragement of the growth of Jansenism and of the Enlightenment in Austria, his own role in the advancement of both was an indirect one, and he himself was unaware of the direction in which these men were leading. A much better case could be made for Charles VI having opened the way for these developments: Garelli and Giannone had both been closer to the emperor than to Eugene. Moreover the prince evidently felt out of sympathy at the end of his life with what he saw as the modern world. He told the English diplomat Robinson in disgust in 1733, when Austria was attacked by France, that it was only to be expected, as 'everywhere, as arts and sciences, for example, were visibly decayed in the world'.[16]

The group of intellectuals who were invited into his home were probably of less importance to him personally than the aristocrats and diplomats with whom he dined and played cards almost every evening. In his middle and old age these friends made up for the family he still lacked. Long before the end of the War of Spanish Succession only his youngest sister, Louise, was still alive, in a convent near Turin. He kept in touch with her and seems to have been genuinely upset at her death. With no direct heirs of his own, his expectations came to rest on the children of his eldest brother, Louis Thomas, although, as we have seen, he had few illusions about their characters. The only nephew to survive after 1712, Emmanuel, evidently benefited from his uncle's no-nonsense attitude towards him: he became a competent soldier, serving on the Rhine and in the Netherlands and then in the Turkish war, rising to the rank of lieutenant general. Eugene arranged a good marriage for him with one of the daughters of prince Liechtenstein, 'Adam the Rich', and by 1714 they had a son, who was christened Eugene. Prince Eugene was clearly fond of the couple and hunted on their estates in Bohemia. The question of the succession to his wealth now seemed settled, but unfortunately in 1729 smallpox claimed yet another victim in Emmanuel. However, the young Eugene showed every promise and he joined his great-uncle's campaign along the Rhine in 1734. But in the November of this year he died and with his death there were no close male relatives left to succeed the prince. Now in his early seventies, Eugene seems to have lacked the energy or interest to sort out what should happen after his own death and he did not draw up a will.[17] His closest relative was his brother Louis Thomas's unmarried daughter Victoria. He had never met her and made no effort to, as he had heard nothing but bad of her as she flitted from one Savoyard or French convent to another.

Despite Eugene's close interest in Emmanuel and his family, they were not part of his household and he continued to live alone. Yet during the last twenty or so years of his life he had a relationship with one woman,

Eleonora Batthyány, which amounted to a marriage, although they lived apart. After his early thirties he never seems to have contemplated marrying and although he was always very charming and gallant towards women, he certainly had no time for romance. His early biographer, Mauvillon, explained his attitude to love in a way which rings true: 'Love always appeared to Prince Eugene one of those frivolous emotions which reasonable men should never give way to. He used to say that in civil society those who were in love were like religious fanatics, people who were out of their mind.'[18] On the other hand he could quite well have had affairs, particularly during wartime. That there are no specific references to them does not mean that there were none. If one reads the reports and memoirs on the War of Spanish Succession, there are few signs that women accompanied the armies. Yet they were there, as is shown by the French officers' women being captured at Blenheim.[19] The only pointer we have in this direction for Eugene is the disparaging comment made by Schulenburg in 1709 that the prince enjoyed 'la petite débauche et la p . . . au delà de tout'. Max Braubach, Eugene's foremost twentieth-century biographer, believed Schulenburg's discrete 'la p . . .' meant either 'paillardise' (lewdness) or 'prostitution'.[20] It might also have indicated 'puterie' (whoring).

There is one reference to a mistress before countess Batthyány and this was made by the Swedish minister in Vienna, Stiernhöök, who wrote in 1713 that countess Maria Thürheim, the wife of one of Eugene's military dependants and the daughter of the former president of the chamber, Salaburg, had been his mistress for several years. Although we have no other evidence for or against this suggestion, it could well be true.

When we come to the prince's friendship with Eleonora Batthyány, there is no doubt about their long association: most foreign diplomats were convinced she was his mistress. As to their actual feelings for each other and whether the relations between the middle-aged couple were physical or not, we are in the realm of speculation. Eugene never mentioned her in any of his surviving letters, and the Austrian historian Srbik spent a long and fruitless search for their correspondence.[21] Whatever the relationship between them, it kept them constantly together at dinner, receptions and card games almost every day till his death. Eugene's evenings at her house became the subject of popular Viennese legend: his cream-coloured horses were said to be able to find their own way from the Himmelpfortgasse palace to her house. When they reached it, so the story goes, the old prince, his coachman, guard and footman, whose total ages came to 310, would all be asleep and no one would stir till the countess's servants fetched them.

Eleonora was nine years younger than the prince. The only portrait we have of her, painted when she was in her twenties, shows a woman with raven hair and fine, rather sharp features. She had known the prince most of her life as he had been a constant visitor to her father's house when he was court chancellor. In 1692 she had married Adam Batthyány, the Ban of Croatia, who died in 1703 leaving her a great fortune and two sons born in 1696 and 1697. These were rumoured to be Eugene's children and Maria Theresa called them 'Eugene's codicil'[22] but this is doubtful, not only because her husband was still alive but also because there are no references to Eleonora's being the prince's mistress before 1715. Countess Batthyány's closest friend was another Eleonora, who had married her brother Henry and was also widowed early. Eugene's friendship with Eleonora Batthyány entailed that with her sister-in-law as well, and the two women were usually mentioned together as accompanying him at receptions. A French report of 1725 even suggested that, as the more intelligent woman, Eleonora Stratmann had the greater influence on the prince.

What influence did countess Batthyány have over Eugene? There was no doubt in the minds of his enemies, particularly during the Nimptsch-Tedeschi crisis, that she had a good deal, and this was also the view of foreign diplomats, who believed she worked with his secretaries behind his back. She was also generally thought to be corrupt and the French minister du Luc felt it worth his while to give her presents to the tune of 1,200 livres, including eighteen pairs of shoes and slippers, a scarf and a gold vanity set. More than a decade later the Englishman Waldegrave, who was a frequent guest at Eugene's and her dinner and card parties, wrote that

> ... their smiles or frowns go seldom asunder tho their views are very different, the one is not to be corrupted, the other tho immensely rich will stoop to the lowest prey ... P. Eugene never lets her meddle in foreign affairs. Her power consists chiefly in military preferments and of these she makes her market. It is the general opinion that this trade is carryed on without the Prince so much as suspecting it ...[23]

As to her political influence, Waldegrave felt that she only managed this indirectly in that 'nobody is admitted to his dinners and private parties but by her direction'. Eugene himself was not unaware of what was said about her and he was very sensitive to any comments about 'his foible for this Lady',[24] but it is unlikely that she or countess Stratmann ever had any direct influence on him. In fact he had nothing but contempt for women's political capacities, saying on one occasion that politics should not be discussed with women: 'they do not have the necessary stability as men, easily become careless, allow their feelings to dictate what they say and therefore you cannot depend on their discretion.'[25]

Eugene's greatest pleasure after the War of Spanish Succession consisted in the evenings he spent playing cards with his close friends. In this he was typical of most of the Viennese nobility. However, he did not share the contemporary enthusiasm for music, the theatre or the spectacles put on at court. He told Villars, in a letter written in 1728, that he did not go to plays, although he intended to go to the opera when he had the time. He added, 'I have to spend a lot of my time working and the job of being a minister for someone who hasn't been used to this kind of work since he was young is hard enough. In the evenings, I usually go to a gathering where I play a game of piquet.'[26]

Who were the regular members of his little coterie besides his two ladies? Non-noble intellectuals and various visiting foreign nobility took part frequently, but more permanent members, especially in his last ten years, were certain foreign diplomats. Both the French Richelieu and Waldegrave were admitted for the relatively short periods they spent in Vienna. More long-standing friends were the Dane Berkentin, the Portuguese Tarouca and the papal nuncio, Passionei. Berkentin came to Vienna in 1722 when he was thirty and he stayed there for eighteen years. He was quickly accepted by countess Batthyány and Eugene, began to play cards with them and was invited to stay at Schlosshof. An even older friend than Berkentin was Tarouca, whom the prince had met at The Hague in 1710 and corresponded with till he came to Vienna as Portuguese ambassador in 1726. Tarouca was a good conversationalist with interests in building, and Montesquieu found both him and Berkentin good company when he was in Vienna.[27] Just as close in the prince's last years was Passionei, whom he had also come across in The Hague, and who was eventually appointed nuncio in Vienna in 1731 after a long period when their only contact was by letter. He shared many of Eugene's interests including book collecting. Probably none of these men had any political influence on the prince. He assured the Imperial minister in Prussia, Seckendorff, that 'I have never had the least confidentiality'[28] with Berkentin; and Waldegrave noted his ability to establish close social relationships while managing to avoid discussing politics: '. . . it is hardly to be imagined how close the Prince is . . . I see him every day and play at cards with him which creates a kind of freedom but for all this he avoids as much as he can talking upon any of the matters under consideration . . . He barely answers yes, or no, and changes the discourse as soon as he can.'[29]

As to Imperial ministers, although Eugene co-operated longest with Gundaker Starhemberg and Sinzendorff, there seems to have been little warmth between them and the prince. They did not share his collecting interests and their association was largely on a business level. A far more satisfying political and personal friendship of his later years was with the Imperial vice-chancellor Schönborn. Their letters show mutual respect and affection. Yet they were very different men. The urbane Schönborn, who according to the English diplomat Robinson 'talks like an angel and appears to act like one',[30] was not only corrupt but was universally distrusted. The Hanoverian minister Huldenberg compared him to a ball which was continually bouncing out of your hand.[31] But Eugene clearly enjoyed his company a great deal; they spent long periods on each other's estates and were particularly fond of their *Hasenkrieg* (hunting hares). One of the portraits painted of Schönborn shows him characteristically with a gun tucked under his arm. Although no portrait exists of Eugene in the same pose, the prince's delight in hunting, especially shooting, has often been ignored. Professor Max Braubach drew up an extensive itinerary of his activities on the estates of various nobles as well as at Schlosshof in the 1720s, which shows that he spent a good deal of time in summer and autumn hunting deer and boars and shooting ducks and hares. In October 1729 we also find Waldegrave writing that he had been a week 'fishing daily in the country with Prince Eugene'.[32]

With the rigours of campaigning behind him, Eugene for most of his middle and old age settled into a pleasant routine of official business in the mornings and relaxation after noon either with his books or his friends in splendid surroundings which he had created himself. It was a greatly satisfying way to spend his last years.

XXII

Cold War in Europe

The defeat of the cabal late in 1719 did nothing to stem the decline in Eugene's political influence: it would take Charles some years to forgive the humiliation of these months. The deaths of Eugene's chief antagonists hardly changed the position. In October 1720 count Stella died, Charles describing him in his diary as 'the one I depended on most, also trusted in foreign affairs'.[1] A year later it was Mikosch's turn, and in March 1722 Althann followed them, a victim of 'a polypus grown at his heart'. Charles was 'so much concerned and disordered . . . that the Physicians thought it proper to bleed him'.[2] Devastated, he wrote in his diary of 'My comforter, my most loyal servant, who loved me dearly, as I him, for 19 years in true friendship.'[3] He was never to forget him and no one was to replace him.

Eugene drew little benefit from these deaths not only because of Charles's hostility but also because what could be called the German party had long since split up through mutual quarrels. Eugene refused to try to hold it together: he was not the man to create or maintain a political connection. Both Trautsohn and Windischgrätz had joined Sinzendorff in dissociating themselves from Eugene and Gundaker Starhemberg by the time of Althann's death and in looking to the Spaniard Rialp, who welcomed their approaches. This desertion was partly compensated for by Eugene's closer relationship with the Imperial vice-chancellor Schönborn, and their increasing friendship was to be one of the most solid of the next decade. In the early 1720s, however, it counted for little, as Eugene, Starhemberg and Schönborn only had 'a very little part of the Emperor's confidence'.[4]

If the emperor listened to anyone in the early 1720s it was to Rialp, Sinzendorff and Savalla, president of the council of Spain and a particular friend of Charles, men who made up a kind of triumvirate and shared his enthusiasm for commercial ventures. Only one of them, Sinzendorff, was a regular member of the conference, and as court chancellor was closely involved in negotiating with the estates to have the succession of Charles's daughters guaranteed. Although he hoped to become a prime minister in the manner of Salm, Sinzendorff lacked the dead man's ruthlessness and consistency and he was very loath to upset people.

The five years after the Nimptsch-Tedeschi affair of 1719 saw continual quarrels and backbiting among the ministers and an apparent aimlessness in Austrian foreign policy, which was not lost on outside observers. For the Hanoverian Huldenberg who had been there since the 1690s, it was like living in 'another world'.[5] Charles refused to assume control himself or to stop the bickering. Instead he would usually drag out his replies or even sign resolutions from his various councils which were flatly contradictory. Individual ministers found it easy to sabotage what they did not want, as Eugene once told St Saphorin. What he said is as revealing of his own loyalty to the emperor as of the situation:

> If I had wanted to carry on like the other ministers, this major reform which has been made over the troops,* against my advice, would never have been effected, for I could have raised so many incidental points that I could have put it off till the next war when it would have been impossible to carry out; but as it is my duty to execute the Emperor's orders, even when I do not agree with them, I began to put it into effect from the moment the Emperor directed me to. If the others acted in the same way, at least something would get done, whether good or bad. But because they know how to avoid doing anything, nothing gets done.[6]

Charles's European policy in the early 1720s was moulded largely by what he saw as the needs of his Spanish lands in Italy and the Southern Netherlands. This led him to hold on to the Spanish titles, which infuriated France and England as much as Philip V, and to refuse to remove the remaining legal obstacles to Don Carlos's eventual succession to Parma and Tuscany, which were regarded as Imperial fiefs. It was also to lead to the foundation of the Ostend Company, and his attempt to use Trieste both as a trading post and as a naval base, since Charles was 'bent upon making a figure at sea'.[7]

To outsiders Charles's determination to go his own way seemed a sinister attempt to become the 'arbiter of Europe',[8] an ambition which they believed Rialp and Sinzendorff encouraged. But in fact Austria's international position was rapidly growing weaker and more isolated as England and France moved closer to Spain after 1721 and backed Philip V against Charles. Relations with England deteriorated further with the opening of the Ostend Company and because George, as elector, was working with Prussia to present a resolutely Protestant and anti-

* This was a reduction in their number demanded by the *Hofkammer*.

Habsburg front in the Empire. While Sinzendorff would have compromised in Germany, Schönborn insisted on a hard line and was increasingly backed by both Eugene and Gundaker Starhemberg,[9] partly from loyalty to their new friend but also because they were equally determined not to allow the emperor's dignity to be threatened by bullying from the north-German Protestant states. The increasing power and hostility of Hanover and Prussia undermined the emperor's position in Germany and made it weaker than at any time since the death of Leopold; and this was probably the main reason for Eugene's growing interest in the Empire and his comparative neglect of Italian issues. In any case the Habsburg position in Italy seemed fairly secure, despite the potential threat from Elizabeth Farnese's son in the central duchies, while the dominance of Charles's Spanish ministers in Italy may have made the prince, at least subconsciously, less concerned about Austria's interests there.

Although Eugene had little direct influence over the policies being pursued by Charles in the early and mid-1720s, he always supported them loyally when they were adopted, and he appeared at this time to be the most intransigent of the emperor's ministers, causing the French diplomat du Bourg to comment in February 1725 that 'Whatever engagements the Emperor makes, Prince Eugene will support them arrogantly.'[10]

By the close of 1724 Austria's isolation in Europe seemed complete: France and England were supporting the pretensions of the Spanish prince Don Carlos to succeed to Parma and Tuscany, and both the English and the Dutch were determined to have the Ostend Company suppressed. But then, out of the blue, a Dutch adventurer, Ripperda, arrived in Vienna early in 1725: he had been sent secretly by queen Elizabeth Farnese of Spain to tempt Charles with an offer of a guarantee of the Austrian succession (the Pragmatic Sanction) and commercial concessions for the Ostend Company in return for guarantees for her own son Don Carlos's succession to the Italian duchies and marriages between him and his younger brother Philip with the emperor's daughters. Although it was a reversal of much of what Charles had worked for since his accession, he jumped at the bait, as did Sinzendorff and Rialp. Commercial expansion and the future of his dynasty seemed now more important to him than his long quarrel with Philip of Anjou.

Sinzendorff was put in charge of the negotiations, which proceeded well. Eugene and Starhemberg were kept fully informed but were opposed to the talks from the beginning: they believed they were a ploy by Elizabeth to gain land for her children and feared that they would lead to the total alienation of England and France. Ripperda eased the way by substantial gifts to Sinzendorff and Rialp, which Charles knew about but merely insisted that half should be handed over for his own privy purse.

Eventually on 30 April/1 May 1725 Charles signed the first treaty of Vienna with Philip V. It provided for mutual recognition and guarantees of each ruler's possessions and successions, gave trading concessions to the Ostend Company and confirmed Don Carlos's rights in Italy. Charles also promised his diplomatic support for Spain's demands for the return of Gibraltar and Minorca from England. The treaty was a clear triumph for the emperor. He had managed to avoid committing himself to marriages for his daughters and had gained two important advantages: commercial concessions for the Ostend Company and the first international guarantee of the Pragmatic Sanction.

Unfortunately these gains were soon shown to be largely worthless because of the fury which the treaty aroused among the western powers. In September 1725 France, the Maritime Powers and Prussia joined together in the Alliance of Hanover to intimidate the new allies. This forced Spain and Austria closer together and a further alliance was signed two months later. Charles was promised subsidies and in return agreed that two of his three daughters should marry Elizabeth and Philip's sons. He also agreed that if he should die himself his eldest daughter, Maria Theresa, should immediately marry Don Carlos. But as his children were aged only eight, seven and one, the marriages seemed a long way off and, in Oswald Redlich's words, were 'as good as illusory',[11] especially as Charles and his wife really wanted Francis Stephen of Lorraine to marry Maria Theresa. The young duke had been brought to Vienna in 1723 to be raised as part of the Imperial family. Charles hoped in this way to avoid a marriage into one of the major European families who would absorb his own house. Because of his bitter experience over the Bavarian marriage negotiations in 1719, Eugene had kept well clear of any discussion of marriages for Charles's daughters and in a conference of 20 July 1725 he refused to advise the emperor on such a personal matter, coming out with the remarkable statement that it was 'difficult for a foreigner' to do so.[12]

The second treaty with Spain inflamed the international situation even further and for the next three years there was continual danger of war between the western powers and the Austro-Spanish bloc. The most belligerent powers were England and Spain; in France, however, cardinal Fleury, the seventy year old ex-tutor of Louis XV, became chief minister in 1726 and was determined to avoid war as well as to hold fast to the connection with England. Although the English feared a clash with Spain in case their commerce should suffer, they were particularly exasperated by the threat of the Austrian Ostend Company. The northern secretary Townshend, who had been resolutely anti-Habsburg since coming to power in 1721, adopted a very threatening tone which culminated in George I's aggressive speech to parliament in January 1727 and the expulsion of the Austrian minister from London and St Saphorin from Vienna. However, it was to be the Spaniards who made the first direct move towards war when they besieged Gibraltar in February. Reluctantly the English responded by a blockade and a short naval war against Spain but more enthusiastically by raising a mercenary army in the Empire to frighten Charles. At the same time French troops were moved towards the German and Spanish frontiers.

War was the last thing Charles and Sinzendorff wanted. Backed and possibly led by Charles, Sinzendorff had hoped to use the Spanish alliance as the basis for a new European system which would ensure wide international acceptance for both the Ostend Company and the Pragmatic Sanction. The court chancellor was soon to become convinced that this could best be achieved by reaching an agreement with Fleury to separate France from the Maritime Powers, although he always seems to have hoped for an agreement with the latter as well.[13]

Eugene's approach to the crisis did little to solve it and may in fact have prolonged it. He had no interest in the commercial gains which the Spanish treaty was expected to bring and was pessimistic enough about the Ostend Company's prospects to sell his own shares, making a profit of 41,145 gulden. But in public he always supported the new orientation towards Spain and in fact he was genuinely annoyed at English threats. He railed against both Townshend and his former friend St Saphorin, complaining about the latter's 'poisonous correspondence, filled with barefaced lies'.[14] He was particularly vexed at the way the Anglo-Prussian association in the Alliance of Hanover had totally undermined the emperor's position in the Empire. Although St Saphorin's reports of the 1720s point to Eugene having lost interest in further military adventures of his own, being far more caught up with his palaces and gardens as increasing ill-health and age affected him, most of the bellicose remarks made to foreign envoys in Vienna during the next few years came from him. There was probably more than a grain of truth in St Saphorin's accusation that Eugene and Schönborn's animosity towards Sinzendorff was such that they were willing to contemplate war, or at least a war crisis, which would undermine his diplomacy and make themselves indispensable to Charles.

From January 1726 strenuous efforts were made to increase the size of the standing army. It seemed a formidable task: the condition of the Imperial fortresses along the Rhine had deteriorated, and in the Netherlands, where the hostile Dutch had their garrisons, the Imperial troops' pay was in arrears. Financial problems would be inevitable: it had already proved impossible to find the 8 million gulden needed annually to support a peace-time force of 90,000 men. There had been an overall deficit in 1725 and the chamber had been driven to complain about Charles's expenditure on his music. Nevertheless during 1726 it was to be asked to find an extra 5 million gulden for more recruits for the army. Although a powerful inducement to stick by the Spanish alliance was provided by promises of annual subsidies of 3 million gulden, a total of only 2 million was ever paid. By the end of 1726, however, the army had been raised to 125,000 men, although most of these troops were tied down by garrison duty in Italy and Hungary, while a quarter of the cavalry had no horses. Because of this and the almost open secret that Austria could only afford one campaign, St Saphorin was unimpressed by the threats of officers in Eugene's circle that they would winter in Hanover. St Saphorin himself put the blame for Austrian military weakness on the eclipse of Eugene in recent years and on the prince's inability to persuade the emperor and *Hofkammer* to spend money on the army.

It was clear that the emperor on his own could not support a war against the western powers, and no one was more aware of this than Eugene. While recognizing the need to maintain the Spanish alliance now that it had been made, he had no confidence in Spain's military and financial strength or in the loyalty of her rulers. But instead of following Sinzendorff's lead in working towards an accommodation with France and the Maritime Powers, he looked round for other allies. From 1726 we see the beginnings of what developed into a full-blown personal secret diplomacy, one which was completely separate from that of the court chancery and was directed by Eugene in consultation with Charles. It is remarkable that it should have begun at a time when Sinzendorff and Rialp still had the greater influence at court. Yet the emperor was prepared not only to co-operate with Eugene but to hide its existence from the other two ministers. Given Charles's liking for secrecy and keeping several strings in his own hands, this is not so surprising.

Gradually from 1726 Eugene, closely supported by Starhemberg and Schönborn, recovered his political importance. His skill in managing a vast secret diplomatic network over the next seven or eight years was the main reason why Charles came to depend on him so heavily once more.

Eugene was to show far more finesse in this field than in direct diplomatic talks, where 'his excessive positiveness joined to his natural pride,
render him . . . very intractable'. The English diplomat Waldegrave was
to complain that 'once he has taken a thing into his head, there is no
reasoning of him out of it and you must be convinced because he says he
is, that he knows it to be so, and thus he answers most arguments'.[15]

Eugene was in an ideal position to undertake this diplomatic venture
because he had dozens of contacts throughout Europe who had always
been ready to send him information, some of which he paid for. But
from the late 1720s the regular Imperial ministers abroad, several of
whom had been his military subordinates, also wrote him secret letters,
often with special codes, separate from the 'ostensible' ones sent to
Sinzendorff as *Hofkanzler*. Letters reached Eugene through special
couriers or by means of cover addresses – in Berlin, for instance, a mer-
chant was employed – and they were only seen by Charles, Eugene, his
secretary Ignatius Koch, and sometimes by the secretary (*Referendar*) of
the conference, Bartenstein. The bulk of the paperwork was undertaken
by Koch. Because of Eugene's belief in delegating business to his subordinates and giving the drift of a letter rather than dictating directly, a
man of Koch's industry and intelligence was essential, and he was even
allowed to discuss the correspondence with the emperor when Eugene
was away.

The secret diplomacy involved wholesale buying of men and information. A great deal of money was used, sent mostly through the Viennese
banking house of Palm, but some by special messengers. The exact
amounts are unknown as no accounts were kept, but they were paid out
of the emperor's secret fund. Although the money was spent throughout
Europe, the most fruitful area was Prussia: from 1726 one of Frederick
William's leading ministers, Grumbkow, received an annual pension of
1,000 ducats in return for supporting Austrian policy and providing
copies of his own letters to the king and those from Prussian ministers
abroad.

The first effects of Eugene's diplomacy were alliances with Russia and
Prussia. The death of Peter the Great in 1725, and the accession first of
his wife Catherine till 1727 and then of the child Peter II till 1730, made
Russia appear a far less menacing power and brought the possibility of
using her strength in Austria's interest. Schönborn had long pressed for
agreement, but it was Eugene who took the lead at the end of 1725,
declaring in a conference of 2 October that 'there is no doubt that we
cannot survive without an alliance':[16] it would serve as an immediate
reply to the Alliance of Hanover. One of Eugene's military subordinates,

Rabutin, was dispatched to Russia to negotiate, and Eugene kept in close contact with him throughout, advising on how to act towards members of the Russian court and warning against being too free with offers of presents. By April 1726 a preliminary treaty had been signed and in August Russia acceded to the Austro-Spanish alliance in a ceremony presided over by Eugene. The Russians guaranteed the Pragmatic Sanction and both powers promised to help the other in case of attack. It was the beginning of a long-standing relationship between Austria and Russia. The Russians immediately proved loyal allies, and had troops ready for dispatch by 1727 should they be needed.

Sinzendorff could be kept out of these negotiations because relations with Russia, as with the German states, were still conducted through Schönborn's Imperial chancery rather than the *Hofkanzlei*. Eugene had been able to count on total support from Schönborn, but the latter was far less enthusiastic about the next power Eugene wished to approach, Prussia. The Imperial vice-chancellor found it difficult to swallow his hatred of Frederick William, whose intransigent support for George of England/Hanover and the Protestant side in the Empire had culminated in the Alliance of Hanover. The contempt of these two rulers for Imperial authority had led to a complete collapse of any idea of common *Reich* interests – Charles VI was far less of a 'German emperor' than his brother or even his father had been – so that it was only possible to appeal to the German princes in cash terms, an area where England and France had a decided advantage.

Eugene had run Schönborn a close second in the previous ten years in his hostility towards Prussia, but this did not blind him to the fact, especially after the Alliance of Hanover, that Frederick William had to be won over. With his large standing army and full treasury, his defection from the allied camp would effectively destroy the emperor's position in Germany. Consequently during 1726 prince Eugene asked the Saxon general Seckendorff, whom both he and Frederick William had known from the campaigns in Flanders, to accept a standing invitation to the Prussian king's precious military manoeuvres and to try to wean him from the western powers. Seckendorff was tailor-made for the job; he fell in easily with the barrack-room atmosphere of the Berlin court and joined the king's 'tobacco-college', evenings of smoking, hard drinking and crude jokes. Despite his bombast, Frederick William was a rather sensitive soul who appreciated having a fuss made of him, especially by Eugene and the emperor. He had tried his best to please Eugene the previous year in May 1725 when he had offered him a team of Prussian horses for his stables and a couple of elks and a bison for his zoo at the Belvedere. Embarrassed at what seemed an obvious bribe, Eugene had replied that he never accepted presents and that his zoo was full.

Peter the Great once described the Prussian king as someone who liked fishing but hated getting his feet wet,[17] and this was certainly true in 1726. The conclusion of the Austro-Russian alliance brought home to Frederick William that he would be the member of the Alliance of Hanover to bear the brunt of any fighting. Consequently in October 1726 he made a mutual defensive treaty (of Wusterhausen) with Charles, following this with another in 1728. These treaties guaranteed the Pragmatic Sanction and promised Imperial support for Prussia's claims on the duchy of Berg. The first was sealed by the dispatch to Berlin of the almost classical tribute of twenty giant recruits for the Prussian army; then in 1727 Eugene willingly accepted the king's animals for his zoo and in return sent some Spanish stallions for the royal stud. Frederick William was delighted and asked for a portrait of Eugene to hang in his own cabinet. A very good relationship now developed between them, and although Eugene was still wary of what he described to Seckendorff as the king's 'fickle temperament',[18] he came increasingly to value Frederick William.

Largely through prince Eugene's personal efforts the almost total isolation of Austria in Europe had been ended and her most exposed flank in Silesia and Bohemia covered. Nevertheless it would still have been a risky venture for her to have gone to war with France and the Maritime Powers when her Spanish ally began the unsuccessful siege of Gibraltar at the beginning of 1727. That no general conflict broke out was largely due to the restraining hand of the French minister, Fleury. Making it clear that France would join the Dutch in suppressing the Ostend Company by force, he proposed a temporary suspension of the company for seven years and the discussion of this and other European issues at a congress to meet at Soissons.

Charles accepted these Paris preliminaries in May 1727. Eugene and Gundaker Starhemberg, who had no interest in preserving the Ostend Company, had urged him to accept the terms of the preliminaries, warning him that he would have to face an immediate war if he did not. Both the emperor and Sinzendorff hoped that by agreeing to them it would be possible to win France away from the Maritime Powers and eventually save the company or transfer its activities to Trieste. All parties in Vienna, and Eugene was no exception, saw England as the main antagonist both over Ostend and within the *Reich*. Consequently when the first Hanoverian king George died in June 1727, it was hailed by the pro-Austrian Prussian general Anhalt-Dessau as yet another 'Austrian miracle'.[19] But hopes that the new king, George II, would dismiss his Whig ministers, Walpole and Townshend, or that there would be a Jacobite rising were soon dashed, and by December 1727 Eugene was declaring that George 'demonstrated as bad if not worse principles than his father'. He also insisted to Seckendorff that the blame for Europe's problems lay at England's door: under the guise of defending the Protestant religion she had reduced the German Empire 'to turmoil' and her vaunted policy of creating 'a balance' was nothing more than a way of achieving her 'predominance over all other powers'.[20]

Despite the Paris preliminaries and the conclusion of the brief Anglo-Spanish conflict, armed confrontation between the European powers persisted throughout 1727 and 1728 during the delays in opening the proposed congress. In Austria the army was supposed to be on a war footing but this was not taken very seriously by her enemies. When the English minister Waldegrave came to Vienna in 1728, he doubted whether Austria could field more than 30,000 men and he believed her ruler's financial problems were increasing because every year the army was kept on the alert, it 'adds four or five millions of florins [gulden] to their Debt, and yet they will not begin a reform'.[21] By the end of 1728 he was convinced that no one really wanted war:

> He [Charles] . . . desires nothing but to enjoy what he already has, and to see his succession secured as he would have it. . . . His ministers are equally agt. war, and Prince Eugene is more averse to it than any of the others tho' upon occasion talks big. He has got to be pretty well with his Master, and he sees from the example of others that his absence might alter the case without having their suppleness and address to recover his credit. He would dislike to see any but himself at the head of the army. He is satisfied with the reputation he has acquired and cannot but be sensible that the loss of a battle or any other misfortune might blast the glory of twenty years. Perhaps he knows his own constitution and feels that he could not be able to go thro' the fatigues of a campaign.[22]

Waldegrave also summed up Eugene's position and character as he saw them at this time. His assessment is interesting in showing how the prince was adopting the approach he had condemned so roundly in others to St Saphorin seven years before:

> . . . in my mind P. Eugene's parts may be decayed. I did not know him formerly but by what appears now I should not have taken him to be the great man he has been thought upon occasion. This gives him the weight he bears here which consists more in obstructing what he does not like than promoting any scheme of his own.[23]

Whether Eugene was as negative as Waldegrave complained or not, he had regained his own political influence. In the last months of 1728 his enemy Sinzendorff went to the congress of Soissons, hoping to pull off a diplomatic coup and to do a deal with Fleury. At the same time Charles undertook an extensive journey to see how his commercial and naval schemes were progressing at Trieste. He came back disappointed, and probably annoyed with Sinzendorff who had been largely responsible for the enterprise there.[24] The court chancellor's own mission to Soissons gave the prince and Starhemberg a splendid opportunity to work against him. Rialp, who had in recent years been rather overshadowed by Sinzendorff, was hedging his bets by moving over to them. Eugene was now back in enough favour for Charles to allow him to open his correspondence while he was away in Trieste,[25] but their relationship seems to have been largely a business one. Waldegrave reported that 'Pr Eugene's dryness and old Starhenberg's pedantry hinder, I am told, the Emperor from talking to them in private any more than is absolutely necessary.'[26]

Eugene and Starhemberg's warning about Sinzendorff's diplomacy, voiced since the first treaty with Spain, was confirmed at the end of 1728 when Sinzendorff returned from the congress at Soissons with his mission a complete failure. The hunting and the meals had been excellent but Fleury had given nothing away. From his accession to power in 1726 the French cardinal had aimed at winning back Spain from Austria and keeping his more bellicose English ally in check. This necessitated isolating Austria, and he had no intention whatsoever of guaranteeing the Pragmatic Sanction or supporting the Ostend Company without massive concessions, since it would have entailed confirming Austria's existing vast territorial size as well as the addition of Lorraine through the eventual marriage of Maria Theresa and Francis Stephen.

Eugene had never expected anything useful to emerge from Sinzendorff's mission. He felt Habsburg policy ought to be based firmly on the principle that 'Austria, Brandenburg and Moscow should keep together and in all occurrences stand as one man.'[27] If any of the western powers should be won over it should be England rather than France: since the Austrian alliance with Prussia, England was less of a problem in the Empire and could be satisfied cheaply, as he saw it, by the surrender of the Ostend Company. He had told Waldegrave in May 1728 of 'his sincere desire to see a perfect reconciliation with England . . . and he took notice of the figure we made in the world whilst we were friends', adding an interesting self-characterization on this occasion: 'You may depend upon it says he I will not mislead you; I know how to hold my tongue when it is necessary; but I do not know how to lie.'[28]

Eugene was now openly contemptuous of Sinzendorff. At a dinner party shortly after the court chancellor returned from Soissons a guest remarked on the fine things he had brought back with him from France, but 'the Prince replyed with a snear that he had brought a great many bad things with him also'.[29] Charles was also beginning to realize that it was impossible to come to an agreement with the French. The total deadlock over Ostend, which had emerged at Soissons, and his sense of let-down over Trieste were inevitably to turn the emperor away from his commercial plans and to concentrate more and more on getting international guarantees for the Pragmatic Sanction.

The final blow to Sinzendorff's diplomatic system came when the Austro-Spanish alliance collapsed in 1729: its advantages for Austria were minimal once the Ostend Company had been suspended and Spanish subsidies dried up. It was Elizabeth Farnese who ended it, however. As Charles could not be drawn into the marriage pact she wanted, she concluded that the best security for her son's succession to Parma and Tuscany lay with England and France. Consequently in November 1729 Spain signed the treaty of Seville with these two powers: Spanish garrisons were to be allowed into the Italian duchies to safeguard Don Carlos's rights, and the final suppression of the Ostend Company was demanded.

The Imperial ministers were thunderstruck by the news and in a conference of 20 December Eugene declared that the treaty of Seville was 'an event which is seldom to be found in history'.[30] It had been presented to them in the form of an ultimatum which was both insulting to the emperor's dignity and seemed to foreshadow Spanish control of Italy. Eugene therefore insisted that Austria stand up to the western powers. Brushing aside Sinzendorff's pleas for accommodation, Charles put himself in Eugene's hands and sent troops to Italy to prevent the entry of Spanish garrisons into Parma or Tuscany. By the beginning of 1730, therefore, Eugene was once more back in control of Austrian policy.

During the long crisis which the Spanish treaty precipitated, Eugene's militancy had made a diplomatic settlement with the western powers more difficult. Whether his attitude was guided by a genuine belief that the Imperial dignity demanded that Austria resist what he saw as intimidation, or by a more dubious attempt to reassert his own influence and ruin that of others by creating a war situation,[31] the results were the same: a period of prolonged crisis which necessitated keeping the army on an almost permanent war footing throughout these years and which progressively undermined Austrian finances.

XXIII

The Second Treaty of Vienna
and Fleury's Revenge

In the winter of 1729/30, following the treaty of Seville, Eugene and his friends continued to rattle their sabres and to rub salt in Sinzendorff's wounds by blaming Austria's troubles on his original treaty with Spain. There was no thought of compromise with the western powers and in February Eugene 'spoke in a most heroick strain to the Emperor & says he was very glad Almighty God had spared his life in his last illness since he could once more draw his sword in his Imperial Majesty's service'. Behind these brave words lay real fear at the Viennese court: the Seville treaty appeared a prelude to an assault on Italy by the Bourbon powers and an attempt to snatch Milan and Naples from Charles. It was a struggle which no one could look forward to, especially as it was clear that England would stand aside or even help France and Spain. The English minister Waldegrave was convinced that in Eugene's case, it was all a massive game of bluff, since he doubted 'whether he would be able to bear the fatigue of a campaign'.[1] There had been a marked decline in the prince's health and physical appearance. Now in his sixty-seventh year, it was noticed that 'of late he droops very much'.[2] During the winter he had such a bad attack of influenza that Waldegrave feared 'should his cough hang much longer upon him, it may cost him his life'. He had refused to see a doctor and had 'grown as lean as is possible'.[3]

Eugene was not to be called on to fight his last campaign yet, because the western powers had no intention of enforcing the treaty of Seville unless Charles tried to revive the suspended Ostend Company. Fleury in France was quite content for the cold war to continue, knowing full well that the continual preparations for war were as ruinous to Austria as any conflict. But then in 1730 there was a significant shift in English policy. The pacific Robert Walpole had grown increasingly concerned about Townshend's policies which had threatened war with Austria, a war which he feared would only benefit the two Bourbon states. He therefore sacked him and tried to come to terms with Charles VI, although he intended to maintain the connection with Spain. In doing so he was taking a definite step away from the close association with France which had been the cornerstone of English policy for more than a decade. In France itself the increasing influence of the secretary of state Chauvelin, and the growing friendship with Spain, was leading to a similar coolness towards England. The birth of a dauphin to the young Louis XV and his wife Maria Leszczyńska in 1729 secured the succession, making France less dependent on England and keener on agreement with Spain, as Philip's claims to the French throne were now less dangerous.

Walpole knew from diplomatic reports that the price for an Austrian alliance would be recognition of the Pragmatic Sanction. Eugene had made it clear in 1729 that this was a *sine qua non*,[4] but Townshend had always refused to consider it, not only because of France but also in case it strengthened Charles's position in the Empire. Walpole was prepared to offer an Anglo-Hanoverian guarantee of the Pragmatic Sanction in return for the final surrender of the Ostend Company and the entry of Spanish garrisons into the Italian duchies. In June 1730 Thomas Robinson was sent to Vienna to put these proposals to Charles.

Long wrangles ensued over the Spanish garrisons and George II's demands in the Empire as elector. Robinson realized, however, that all Charles VI's ministers, including Eugene, wanted a reconciliation. The most accommodating was Sinzendorff, who continually stressed 'the advantages his majesty [George II] would reap in returning to the antient system'.[5] Eugene was at first far more reticent, complaining about England's past behaviour and about George's actions in the Empire,[6] but as it became clear that the English were serious and wanted to resume their former close relationship, Eugene grew openly enthusiastic, assuring Robinson in November that he wanted agreement 'more earnestly than any person whatever in the Emperor's service'.[7] By the following January the English minister was writing home that all the progress made so far 'was entirely owing to his [Eugene's] encouragement',[8] and although Sinzendorff was proving just as eager for a treaty, he was kept out of the negotiations which Charles entrusted to Eugene and the conference secretary Bartenstein. The prince was now convinced in his own mind that a treaty was needed because of Austria's isolation in western Europe,[9] but he also seems to have become worried that the house of Habsburg would die out (Charles's youngest daughter had died in April 1730), and in mentioning this to Robinson 'he shed a tear upon this occasion'.[10] The eldest archduchess Maria Theresa was now thirteen and with the onset of puberty it was possible to think seriously of an early marriage; in fact one seemed advisable for in August 1730 she had been unwell, and '. . . looks ill, pale & consumptive. Her sickness is attributed to the ceasing of those Evacuations which nature has apropriated to that sex, & it is said that the Physicians advise marriage as the only remedy.'[11] Unfortunately her marriage to Francis Stephen of Lorraine could not but offend the French.

In March 1731 Austria and England signed the second treaty of Vienna, which the Dutch soon joined. Charles sacrificed the Ostend Company and agreed to Spanish garrisons in Parma and Tuscany, as well as investing George as elector with the duchies of Bremen and Verden. In return George guaranteed the Pragmatic Sanction as king and elector. The long period of isolation from the major powers was now at an end as was the conflict with the Maritime Powers.

One sceptic, John Joseph Harrach, remarked that the agreement could have been made years before without the waste of so many million gulden,[12] while Robinson himself was convinced that much of the hostility and the danger of war in the past had come from Eugene's 'own former obstinacy'. The prince had been visibly shaken when Robinson told him, on the conclusion of the alliance, that the western powers had intended to impose the treaty of Seville on Austria by force.[13] To be fair to Eugene, however, an agreement with England similar to the one just concluded would have been impossible previously because of Charles's personal commitment to the Ostend Company and the English association with France. The prince now became firmly committed to upholding the new system which he had done so much to create, and he looked upon it as complementary to rather than as separate from the alliances with Prussia and Russia. The English alliance seemed to give Austria real security from any possible danger from France or Spain, and when Fleury made a personal approach to Eugene in July 1731 for a Franco-Austrian agreement, he turned him down flat on the grounds that it was irreconcilable with the English alliance. His personal view of Fleury was that he was 'a knavish old Priest'.[14] But agreement with France was impossible because she was pressing, as she had done over the past two years, for the cession of Luxembourg in return for a guarantee of the Pragmatic Sanction. She was also proposing that Charles's eldest daughter should marry a Spanish prince.

It was largely through Eugene's secret diplomacy that the Imperial position was further strengthened in January 1732 when the Imperial diet guaranteed the Pragmatic Sanction. Ominously, both Saxony and Bavaria protested at this: the electoral prince of Saxony and the elector

Charles Albert of Bavaria had both married daughters of emperor Joseph. But at the time their protests seemed of little importance.

The treaty with England and the acceptance of the Pragmatic Sanction by the Empire following on the earlier treaties and guarantees by Russia and Prussia mark the culmination of Eugene's diplomacy and seemed to offer Charles VI and his succession as much safety as could be achieved through paper agreements. Although he was said to be sceptical of the value of such paper guarantees,[15] Eugene had worked as hard as anyone to secure them. The Venetian ambassador to the Imperial court was suitably impressed and wrote in 1732, 'Not since Charles V has a prince of the House of Habsburg enjoyed such an imposing position of power as the current emperor. The imperial house seems at its fullest bloom and the fame and glory of the emperor at its height.'[16] He seemed to have grounds enough for this observation because the vast gains from the reigns of Leopold and Joseph as well as Charles were still intact and Austria was undoubtedly a territorial giant. But it was an over-optimistic and superficial view: the distant and exposed territories in Italy and the Netherlands depended ultimately for their defence on the goodwill of the Maritime Powers, the financial position of the monarchy had not improved, all hopes of commercial expansion through Ostend and Trieste had had to be abandoned or were collapsing and the army would soon prove inadequate. The reckoning was not far off.

In France the situation was very different: under Fleury the finances had been repaired, economic prosperity restored and the army rebuilt. Although the old cardinal preferred diplomacy to war, he and all Louis XV's court had been infuriated by the second treaty of Vienna. They had been ignored and the Pragmatic Sanction guaranteed: now Charles VI clearly intended his heiress to marry Francis Stephen of Lorraine, which would present an unacceptable threat on France's border. Fleury had warned Sinzendorff in 1728 that he would occupy Lorraine if a marriage took place, and behind all French moves from 1731 was a determination to seize the duchy even before the marriage.[17] A direct attack on Austria was considered in 1732 and all the while efforts were being made successfully to reach agreement with Spain and Savoy and to build a pro-French bloc in the Empire around Bavaria. By the beginning of 1733 the French army was ready for war: all that was needed was a pretext and one which would avoid the intervention of the Maritime Powers. This was to be found over Poland.

In February 1733 the Polish king and elector of Saxony, Augustus the Strong, died. He had been an unpopular figure in Vienna. Both he and his court had proved impervious to Eugene's secret diplomacy and he had always refused to guarantee the Pragmatic Sanction. Unfortunately worse was in store when the Polish diet showed every sign of electing in his stead Stanislas Leszczyński, the father-in-law of Louis XV. This opened up the possibility of a French satellite in eastern Europe. In a bid to prevent the election of Leszczyński Russia, Austria and Prussia reluctantly threw their weight behind the candidature of Augustus's son and the new ruler of Saxony, Augustus, although Austria used the opportunity to extract a guarantee of the Pragmatic Sanction from him. In supporting the Saxon elector the lead had been taken by Russia, but when she moved her troops towards the Polish frontier in the first months of 1733, Austrian forces were sent into Silesia as well. It seemed safe enough to do so because the English government was also backing the Saxon candidate.

There is little doubt that Eugene supported this policy but by the first months of 1733 he was playing little active part in business because of a steady decline in his physical and mental faculties. Now approaching seventy, his memory was deteriorating noticeably. He had suffered increasingly during recent winters from his chest and catarrh. One of the inevitable results was a permanent hacking cough which led the other ministers as early as 1731 to keep their conversations with him as brief as possible.[18] Charles's letters to him from this period often contain a sentence or two in French about the prince's health. In November 1729 he wrote, '. . . let Garelli [Charles's physician] pay you a short visit and confide in him, take all possible care of your health'; and in January 1733, 'I beg you to take care of your health, keep out of the bad weather and stay in bed a bit later.'[19]

Eugene's increasing senility and incapacity were accompanied by a gradual slipping away of his political control. He could no longer fall back on the support of Schönborn, since the Imperial vice-chancellor was spending ever longer periods in his new bishoprics of Bamberg and Würzburg. This made him very unpopular with Charles VI, who wrote furiously to Eugene in March 1733 that his friend ought to resign because '. . . the Imperial Chancery is run badly and is totally confused under his direction . . . the work doubles and becomes more difficult, and my governing is already difficult enough without this'.[20] Although the prince tried to support him and urged him to stay on, Schönborn eventually resigned in the summer of 1734.

Charles now had to turn to others for advice: to Sinzendorff once more[21] and to Gundaker Starhemberg, but above all to Bartenstein who had been secretary of the conference since 1727. One of the many lawyers from the Empire who made his way up through the Imperial bureaucracy by his own efforts, he was and had to be hardworking, clever and ambitious. He used to the full his position as the link between the conference and the emperor and gradually came to guide the decisions of the conference at a time when Eugene found increasing difficulty in presiding over it. The only minister who had tried to stem his influence had been Schönborn, who told him to his face in one conference that 'his business was not to speak but to write'.[22] As Charles became aware of what he described to the secretary in January 1733 as Eugene's 'loss of memory and *vigor naturalis*',[23] he came to depend on Bartenstein. If any minister directed Austrian affairs from this period until Charles's death, it was Bartenstein, although it has been suggested[24] that the emperor himself was really in control and that the secretary merely agreed with and executed his policies.

Unfortunately neither Charles nor Bartenstein had the diplomatic expertise to see where the Polish crisis was leading during 1733, and they fell largely unawares into the trap France was setting for them. From the beginning Fleury was determined to seize the opportunity afforded by the Polish succession issue to attack Austria. The clear intention was to use the war to take Lorraine from Francis Stephen and to force Charles VI to hand over Naples and Sicily to Don Carlos – the latter would ensure Spanish support for France.

The Austrians had plenty of notice of what was going on but they failed to react as they should have done. As early as January 1733 Eugene warned Charles that the French were arming and preparing their magazines along the Rhine, and that their Bavarian allies in Germany were taking similar steps. He suggested that they should follow suit. At the same time the reports which were coming in from Eugene's secret diplomatic network, now largely directed by Gundaker Starhemberg and Bartenstein, should have made it clear enough that France and Spain were about to strike, that Savoy was likely to take their side and that the Maritime Powers were determined not to become involved. But it was not till conferences held on 14 and 16 July that the Imperial ministers finally faced up to the fact that the Polish crisis could lead to a direct clash with France, and even then they failed to see the immediacy of it and were lulled by Sinzendorff's assurances that he knew Fleury well enough to know he would never involve France in war. If there was to be war, they agreed that it would not come till the following year and that it would be fought along the Rhine and not in Italy. Eugene was more convinced of Austrian security in Italy than anyone: he counted on the loyalty of the new duke of Savoy, Charles Emmanuel, and in August, in his capacity as president of the war council, he began to withdraw troops from Lombardy, leaving only 16,000 men there. At that moment Charles Emmanuel finally decided to move into the Bourbon camp in the hope of seizing part of Lombardy for himself.

In September 1733 Stanislas Leszczyński was elected king of Poland by the diet. Russian troops immediately moved in to expel him and to form a new diet which would be more amenable to the election of Augustus III. Although no Austrian troops had entered Poland, France declared war on the emperor as the ally of the Russians and Augustus. Fleury was convinced that he could count on the passivity of the Maritime Powers because the war had the appearance of being confined to the question of Poland. Although it was already October, French troops rapidly seized Lorraine and took Kehl on the Rhine, while Charles Emmanuel of Savoy co-operated with another French force under the octogenarian Villars which simply occupied Lombardy: the vastly outnumbered Austrian garrison fled. The onset of winter brought this dramatic campaign to a close without an Imperial army having taken the field, and it was only at the end of the year that the various estates of the Habsburg hereditary lands agreed to raise extra troops.

The Imperial court was numbed and in total disarray. Eugene, who had been particularly hurt by the behaviour of his young Savoyard cousin, declared publicly that he thought 'the world was near its end' and claimed to see 'a decay in the common sense and wisdom of mankind'.[25] What had really gone wrong? Bartenstein and Charles were later to put the blame squarely on Eugene on two counts – his diplomacy had led to the war and his mismanagement of the army ensured the Austrian defeat.

The diplomatic system created by Eugene in the early 1730s did in fact prove a fiasco when put to the test. The Maritime Powers refused to come to Austria's defence, while her association with Ruisia and Prussia appeared to have led her into the War of Polish Successson. But was Eugene responsible for the war? During the most crucial period of 1733 he had little influence over policy, and the main fault lay with the indecision at the centre which led Charles VI to follow the Russians blindly over Poland. But more important than the Polish issue was France's determination to seize Lorraine; and the reason for this was Charles VI's own pet project of a marriage between Francis Stephen and his eldest daughter. Eugene had kept strictly out of discussions of whom she should marry. While his diplomatic system was to prove no match for Fleury once France had decided on war, the prince was less to blame for the actual conflict than most. Where Bartenstein and Charles had far more justification was in blaming him for the defeats the Austrian army suffered once the war began.

XXIV

Eugene and the Austrian Army

The outbreak of the War of Polish Succession came fifty years after prince Eugene began his military career in Imperial service and thirty years after he became president of the war council. For most people, therefore, his name was synonymous with the Austrian army.

In battle and during wartime Eugene's talents as a military leader were self-evident. No other Imperial general managed to win a major victory against the French and it is unlikely that Austria would have made such vast territorial gains by 1718 without his military genius. In battle he led his men from the front, showed great personal bravery and had a direct effect on the outcome of the fighting; during the wars as a whole he squeezed the most out of an inadequate and creaking system, one which often produced armies more reminiscent of the Thirty Years War than those of Marlborough. It was this ability to make the best out of inferior material, combined with his belief in attack and in swift movement as well as his faculty for quick decisions, which made him a great general. He was no tactical innovator but deployed his troops in a conventional manner which differed little from that of his French opponents. However, for most of his career he had the great advantage over the latter of not having to follow the orders of a minister of war or of a Louis XIV. As president of the war council he was largely his own master and suffered little interference from the emperor.

The Austrian army was not Eugene's creation but Montecuccoli's: Eugene only made minor changes in the organization of regiments, standardization of weapons and the famous order of 1707 for all infantrymen to wear the same light-grey uniforms. Nevertheless he moulded the army to his own requirements through close personal control. On becoming president of the war council he worked systematically to have the officers he wished appointed and to resist any meddling from outside, even from the crown.[1] His criteria for promotions were not so much social position as obedience to orders and bravery under fire, since he believed only officers of this stamp could win the respect of their men. He was also convinced that this respect depended on the officers being well dressed and mounted. On the whole we find that he had few complaints about the quality of his officers and he never felt the need to set up a cadet school to train them, believing that the best training for an officer was war itself. However, the poor showing of the allied army at the sieges of Lille and Tournai made him appreciate the value of an engineering school and one was set up in 1717. Even during the long period of peace before the War of Polish Succession the calibre of the junior officers does not seem to have deteriorated and Eugene's standards were applied to their appointment. In 1727 St Saphorin wrote: 'The army's best officers come from the lower nobility and the better-educated bourgeoisie who know they can only depend on their own merit to advance and consequently apply themselves with tremendous zeal.'[2]

In an age when warfare increasingly required troops to form into precise lines and to fire or charge at controlled intervals, one of the keys to success was a force which could respond instantly to orders. Throughought his military career the prince was to insist on obedience at all levels. One reason he complained so bitterly about Heister's conduct in Hungary was that he continually ignored instructions from the war council. When ordinary soldiers disobeyed during battle, he was prepared to shoot them himself, and he approved if others did the same. However, he rejected the blind brutality often shown towards troops in contemporary armies. In May 1728 he wrote to general Traun: 'the common soldiers should not be exhausted except with good reason, and you should only be harsh when, as often happens, kindness proves useless'.[3] Although there were continual complaints during the War of Spanish Succession about the disorder of the German troops, these usually referred to auxiliaries acting under their own generals. Eugene always tried to maintain tight control over the troops immediately under him, issuing annual edicts on matters of discipline: he wanted to prevent desertions and to keep his troops together as a fighting unit but also to avoid alienating local populations. In 1710 he ordered that all soldiers found 100 paces away from the rest of the army on the march or 1,000 paces from camp should be 'hanged without favour or clemency', and the same was to happen to those who plundered religious buildings or private houses.[4] He expected similar self-control among his generals and in 1705 threatened to courtmartial two field-marshals, Gronsfeld and Herbeville, when they were suspected of exacting money for themselves in Bavaria. No accusations were ever levelled at him of looting or raising contributions for his own pocket.

It was not easy to insist on discipline and to forbid looting in the Imperial armies. As Eugene did not have the financial resources or sound supply systems of other western forces, his men were usually inadequately paid and fed. Their physical condition was always poor, but he never let this stand in the way of rapid movement. He expected the troops to march and fight where and when he wanted. On the whole they responded, if only because it was clear that he drove himself as hard as them. He lost little sleep over casualties, provided men had died bravely. Only in the case of his friend Commercy did he ever show any open signs of anguish or regret. In his indifference he reflected the contemporary disregard for life. The younger unmarried sons of the European nobility, who made up the mass of junior officers in all armies, had a notorious contempt for their own personal safety. If they survived, they would do well, as Eugene himself had proved.

There were few rewards for the ordinary soldiers, brave or otherwise. Promotion from the ranks was almost unknown, pay amounted to less than a gulden a week, and the opportunities for material gain largely disappeared except in the Balkans as looting was brought under control. The ex-soldier had little to look forward to besides begging, and to Eugene's credit he did believe that the injured and those too old for active service had a right to expect to be provided for. He gave away himself '15,000 florins per annum in settled pensions',[5] and insisted that every garrison include a company of invalids, as in France, arguing that this would keep them off the roads and provide a fund of experience in time of crisis.

Most men in the Austrian army were produced by the levies of the estates on the peasantry in the hereditary lands. The prince saw nothing wrong with this system and made no attempt to reorganize it himself in a more systematic way as was done during his own lifetime in Prussia or Russia. He wrote to Guido Starhemberg in 1703: 'As to the peasant levies you speak of, all the old soldiers were peasants and the army can only expand and be put in a proper state in this way.'[6] Recruiting officers, sent out to find men to supplement those provided by the estates, were ordered not to recruit artisans, students or nobles and to look for volunteers who were 'large, strong, and between twenty-five and thirty years of age'. Eugene also ordered them, in a regulation of 1722, to avoid 'forbidden nationalities', namely Frenchmen, Italians, Swiss, Poles, Hungarians and Croats, since 'they do not adjust easily to our comradeship and are the greatest cowards and braggarts, who go from one army to another and even lead astray and debauch good men'.[7] Separate Croat and Hungarian regiments did exist and Eugene encouraged the raising of Italian regiments in the peninsula, but he wanted the bulk of the army, especially that which would be called on in wartime to provide the field army, to be German so as to keep it homogeneous and to instil into it a sense of pride in serving the emperor.[8]

On the battlefield Eugene's approach was personal and dictatorial. He had little time for councils of war: he made his own decisions and subordinates were expected to execute his orders and to act bravely. However, he was willing enough to co-operate with someone he regarded as his equal, as with Louis of Baden and Marlborough.

St Saphorin claimed in 1727 that Eugene's successes were not built on strategy and planning, but on decisive action in battle.[9] He cited both Peterwardein and Belgrade as victories where the prince had allowed his position to become critical. Certainly he needed to be present physically in the thick of the fight, but neither Zenta nor Turin can be explained in St Saphorin's way. In fact Eugene always tried to find out as much as possible about his areas of operations and the state of the enemy. Desperate strategic situations did, however, bring out the best in him. Except for Zenta, all his major victories were ones which he conjured up from a position of almost inevitable defeat. Paradoxically, he was to prove far less successful and far more cautious when fighting from a position of strength, as after Oudenarde.

Despite his great tactical and strategic skill and his ability to galvanize domestic support in wartime, Eugene was hardly a successful peacetime president of the war council. He worked best in situations where the pressures and tensions would have broken other men, and he coped well with the problems posed by the practice of European states of disbanding the bulk of their field armies between wars and building them up piecemeal as new conflicts began and progressed. The length of the wars and the high wastage rates meant that most armies in any case had to be largely rebuilt during a war. The Austrians moreover could not afford to keep more than garrison troops between wars. Much of Louis XIV's success had been based on his ability to keep large forces in a state of readiness during peacetime, and in the eighteenth century the European powers became increasingly aware that the outcome of wars depended on who could strike first and hard. This meant that armies had to be at their maximum strength and training the moment war broke out. This was ruinously expensive and called for more concentrated effort in peacetime than most rulers and generals could summon up. The model for these ever-ready armies was the Prussian forces developed under Frederick William I with large cash and manpower resources, rigid training and regular manoeuvres. Such an army contrasted markedly with existing standing armies, where the troops were largely left idle in garrisons during peacetime.

In the War of Polish Succession the Austrian army was outclassed by a much larger and more adequately prepared French force. It was not just a matter of the Austrians being caught by surprise and their forces being in the wrong place as hostilities began. Their performance hardly improved during the war and they performed even more disastrously after Eugene's death in a war against the Turks in 1737–39. Although Eugene remained war president and commander-in-chief during the war with France, he was unable to repeat the marvels of improvization of the past because of his own physical and mental collapse. There was no one else able or willing to usurp his position. It was therefore particularly unfortunate that during the long years of peace after the Turkish war of 1716–18 no proper efforts were made to create a fighting force, however small, which would have formed the core of a larger wartime army and which to some extent might have carried the monarchy through a crisis of failure in military leadership. For this Eugene himself was largely to blame.

If prince Eugene had been determined to build up such a force in the period before the War of Polish Succession, he was in a better position than anyone else to have done so. His control over the army had been more complete than ever because he could direct it in person from the centre in Vienna. All his subordinates in the war council were hand-picked soldiers and the supremacy of the council in the military sphere was complete: the separate provincial war councils at Graz and Innsbruck had been abolished in 1705 and 1709, while the war commissariat lost much of its independence after 1713.

How did Eugene use this absolute position? He certainly had little time or interest in the minutiae of administration and he left this very much to his secretaries within the war council. His subordinates, Öttel, Brockhausen and Ignatius Koch, were evidently hardworking and capable, but there was a good deal of adverse contemporary comment about their influence over the military machine. If they were not actually corrupt, it does seem that they allowed their own or countess Batthyány's friends into posts which they did not deserve. It may well have been their fault that such capable generals as Bonneval and Schulenburg were lost to the Imperialists – the former driven to treason in the Netherlands and the latter compelled to enter Venetian service. Yet they probably had little to do with the advancement of those generals whom Eugene clearly intended to be his successors, Mercy, Seckendorff and Königsegg, as these were men he had known and trusted over a long period. All, unfortunately, proved disastrous as independent commanders, Mercy in Italy during the War of Polish Succession and Seckendorff and König-segg in the Balkans during the Turkish war after Eugene's death, when a series of Austrian mistakes and defeats led to the loss of Belgrade. In advancing these men the prince's judgment may have been at fault.[10] His nineteenth-century biographer Arneth has suggested, in his life of Guido Starhemberg, that the Imperial generals would have benefited from being consulted and instructed in the kind of councils of war held by Guido but which Eugene refused to hold.[11] The prince also failed to set up a permanent general staff, separate from the war council. Instead he insisted rigidly on obedience and hierarchy which probably stifled the development of any military initiative.

When we look at the state and size of the army during the period before the War of Polish Succession, there is no doubt that Eugene saw the need to have as large a peacetime force as possible and for it to be provided with adequate funds. The garrisoning demands of the monarchy were vast and on the whole they were met, although the prince never had the number of troops at his disposal that he would have liked. Yet nothing was done with the available troops except allowing them to deteriorate at their garrison posts.[12] The idea of having a separate field army or of providing the garrison troops with enough training for them to be turned into such an army quickly was never considered by Eugene. In his view the time to create actual fighting men was when war came, and this would also be the time for him to leave his own palaces. There was war and there was peace: by his standards the two were completely separate. Despite his almost exclusively military life till his late fifties, Eugene was no militarist. As we have seen, he adjusted well into civilian life and showed no inclination whatever to face the rigours of the camp again until forced to do so. His non-militarist approach is evident also in his refusal to consider training troops in peacetime, although he was the first to insist on it during campaigns. The drilling and manoeuvres carried out in Prussia after the accession of Frederick William seemed to him irrelevant to real warfare. He was contemptuous of Prussian generals who, in many cases, had no experience of war, and he was sure that the well-fed giant soldiers and their huge mounts would crack under the rigours of an actual campaign and that if the chance occurred, undoubtedly more than a third of the troops would desert. Yet when his own army had to face war in 1733–35 their lack of previous drill and training was apparent to all, especially to Charles VI. When the emperor complained in June 1734 that the infantry in Italy were shooting at each other instead of the enemy, the prince defended himself: '. . . while I am against unnecessary musket practice in peacetime, I am equally aware that men must be drilled in how to shoot during wartime. Consequently I am having the regiments here exercised every day.'[13] After further bitter complaints from Charles, he admitted 'the difference . . . between what our troops once were and what they are now', and explained it as '. . . the natural consequence of a long unbroken peace, during which much disorder and abuse has crept into the regiments, while many officers have also forgotten part of their duties'.[14]

The condition of the army at the outbreak of the War of Polish Succession was only part of a much wider problem. As essential as the training of the men was the ability of the monarchy's central institutions to provide cash and supplies. During the Turkish wars and the War of Spanish Succession Eugene had been ready to interfere in and invigorate other areas of the administration besides the military. He had usually supplied the dynamism at the centre lacking in successive emperors. Presumably if he had been twenty years younger, he could have done the same in 1733 and shored up the system for at least a while. But it would clearly have been preferable for him to have initiated long-term reforms during the years of peace. What we find, however, is that during these years he had not considered it his duty to interfere outside his own immediate areas of the military, the Netherlands and Austrian foreign policy. He had consciously kept clear of interfering in the domestic administration handled by the court chancery and in the financial administration of the *Hofkammer*.

In the early years of the reign of Charles VI's daughter Maria Theresa, the main weaknesses of the monarchy were diagnosed as the lack of centralization among government departments and the various lands and the totally inadequate revenues of the state. Fairly effective measures were taken to cope with these problems and the monarchy gradually recovered from the low ebb of the 1730s and 1740s, but throughout his career Eugene had to live with a system which was incapable of financing an adequate army for war or peace. Despite the commercial ventures of Charles VI, it is doubtful whether the state's revenues had increased significantly from the time of Leopold's reign when they were assessed at a fifth of those of France. The revenues were divided into two main groups. The money which came directly to the crown from its own land and mines and from indirect taxes was used to finance the court and civil administration, while that raised from the contributions of the estates was used to support the military. The latter was a far less dependable source than the former and entailed a lengthy process of bargaining by the *Hofkammer* with the various estates. The contributions were also liable to direct deductions by the estates for existing crown debts and were not paid wholly in cash, but partly 'in cloathing and other furniture necessary to the troops'.[15]

As the contributions from the estates were irregular and could never be calculated accurately, the monarchy had to borrow during wartime, and even in peacetime money destined for the court and civil administration had to be used to subsidise the needs of the military. In wartime the annual financial demands of the military could reach 20 to 35 million gulden. After 1721, under pressure from the *Hofkammer*, a fixed sum of 8 million gulden was allocated from the contributions of the Austrian, Bohemian and Hungarian lands to support a permanent peacetime force of 90,000 men. With the addition of the contributions from the remaining territories, it was hoped to finance a total force of 140,000 men. The attempts to raise twice this number during the diplomatic crises of the late 1720s led to considerable strain on the *Hofkammer*, which in 1721 had fought to reduce the number of troops and was to do the same in 1731–32 against Eugene's advice. In 1733 when the War of Polish Succession broke out, the army, on paper, was made up of 117,000 infantry and 36,000 cavalry, but it is doubtful whether the combined numbers ever amounted to half this. The next year, 1734, the contributions which the monarchy managed to extract out of its estates were nearly 2 million less than the peacetime target of 8 million gulden.

While the monarchy was so dependent on the estates for finance and recruiting, it could never maintain an adequate peacetime army, let alone meet the extra demands of war, without outside help. The financial measures of Charles VI's *Hofkammer* officials after 1716, however well-intentioned in their desire to balance the budget and save money, were always directed to cutting down the number of troops. This naturally led to conflict with Eugene who saw his main task as maintaining as large a military establishment as possible and fighting off attempts by the *Hofkammer* to interfere within his military sphere. Neither Eugene nor the *Hofkammer* was prepared to tackle the underlying problem posed by the estates' control over the size of the army. Although Eugene grumbled continually about the reluctance of the estates to vote contributions and during wartime browbeat both estates and officials, he did not act in this way during peacetime. He had little interest in the sources of the government's revenue and was particularly indifferent and impatient on questions of taxation. He told Montesquieu in 1728, 'I have never listened to these financial experts and their schemes, because if you put a tax on slippers or on wigs it comes to the same thing.'[16] Professor Braubach has rightly concluded that Eugene 'was far from wanting to be a reformer or revolutionary'.[17] The suggestions made in the conferences of 30 December 1720 and 27 January 1726 for the emperor to make a 'totum'* out of all his territories did not come from Eugene himself, but from the conference as a whole. The aim in any case was not to centralize the multitude of various councils and administrations in the several territories (as was to take place in the next reign), but to ensure that the emperor's territories, particularly the former Spanish ones, should bear an equal burden of supporting the army. If Eugene ever advised the emperor[18] that the best way of safeguarding his daughter's succession was not through paper guarantees but by having a strong army and a full exchequer, he contributed very little to effecting this himself.

* A 'whole'.

XXV

The War of Polish Succession and Eugene's Death

It was a cruel fate which spared Eugene beyond his seventieth birthday and forced him to spend his last years in the field. He entered the War of Polish Succession (1733–35) under far more serious handicaps than any war in the past: what troops he had were raw recruits or men rapidly scraped together from the garrisons throughout the monarchy; further men and funds would have to depend on the estates and a *Hofkammer* already embarrassed by the extra demands of the armed confrontations of the late 1720s. Above all the prince was handicapped by the collapse of his own political, physical and mental powers. Nevertheless the main burden of the war was to fall on him as president of the war council and commander-in-chief. The enormity of the task was not lost on Eugene: after the shock defeats of the autumn of 1733 he warned Charles on 25 October that the monarchy was in graver danger than it had ever been and that the war had to be as short as possible.

Austria had to fight the French along the Rhine, as well as Louis XV's allies Savoy and Spain in Italy, largely on her own. The Russians were too occupied in Poland to send any help and it proved impossible to accept more troops from Frederick William of Prussia than the 10,000 he immediately contributed under his existing treaties with the emperor. They would have had to be paid for by the Austrians and it was feared in Vienna that he might be seen to be taking control of the war. As elector of Hanover George II also contributed troops, but the Empire as a whole let Charles down badly. The electors of Bavaria, Cologne and the Palatinate pointedly declared their neutrality and clearly intended to support France if the chance came. Several Imperial princes were willing to hire men to the emperor but he would have to pay for them. Here, of course, was the Habsburgs' perennial problem. The Imperial diet voted 2.5 million gulden in May 1734 for that year's campaign but by the following January less than an eighth had been paid. In this war there were no direct subsidies nor indirect ones through the hiring of auxiliary troops by the Maritime Powers. Both England and the Dutch were determined to stay neutral, having no desire to be involved in a war with France and being even less willing to jeopardize their trade by a war with Spain. Robert Walpole had made the second treaty of Vienna in order to avoid a war, not to get himself involved in one; and Fleury encouraged this attitude by resisting the temptation to attack the Austrian Netherlands, which would have posed a direct threat to England and the Republic. The decision of the Maritime Powers to stay out of the war spelt certain defeat for Austria: in Benedikt's words, 'Without English money victory for Imperial arms was impossible.'[1]

No one was more shocked and upset at the English refusal to help than Eugene. He had been the minister most responsible for the English alliance of 1731, and had agreed to allow the Spaniards to garrison Parma and Tuscany in 1732 to please them. Secretly, he tried to contact factions opposed to Walpole in parliament, at the same time making an impassioned appeal to the ministry, warning that the Bourbons would turn on the Maritime Powers and their trade once they were masters of Italy. He saw the spectre of Louis XIV's universal monarchy once more. On 30 December 1733 he wrote to the Austrian ambassador in London, Kinsky: 'The efforts we are making exceed our powers. We cannot continue them without bringing the Austrian lands to their knees . . . It is indispensable that the other Powers who have the same interest in saving freedom should make the necessary contribution towards its defence.'[2]

It was to be a depressing winter for the prince. His bronchitis prevented his interfering directly in the preparations for the coming year. Yet there was no doubt in his or anyone's mind that he would command the army in the spring whatever his physical state. His name alone was expected to work wonders and, as his card-playing friend the Danish minister put it, even if Eugene died beforehand, they need only send his 'stuffed body along with the army for his spirit alone to produce good luck and respect'.[3]

When spring came he travelled slowly to take command on the Rhine, where the greatest threat to the hereditary lands as well as to Germany existed. During the summer months he had to content himself with a careful defence of the river from a base at Bruchsal. He may have lacked the energy to risk a battle but he was in any case vastly outnumbered by the French and his own troops were ill-trained and his generals inexperienced.

Charles saw the need for an initial defensive stance and had written reassuringly in May 1734 of his confidence in Eugene's 'loyalty, love, intelligence, bravery and experience, which had been proved over many years'.[4] Yet he grew impatient when Philippsburg fell to the French, and he urged on Eugene that 'a successful decisive blow either in the Empire or Italy is the only human way left of saving me, my archducal house and the whole of Europe from the supremacy of the house of Bourbon'.[5] Eugene, however, was convinced that any hasty move, especially while Bavaria had still not declared her hand, would risk the army, and he replied to Charles on 19 July, '. . . as long as this army is kept intact the hereditary lands are protected and Bavaria held in check'.[6] He saw this as his main task for the rest of the year. Meanwhile in Italy his protégé Mercy, although almost blind and deaf after a stroke, had taken the offensive and been killed. His replacement, Königsegg, failed to shake the allies' control of Milan. Further south Naples and Sicily welcomed a successful Spanish invasion and conquest.

The campaign in Germany had begun with considerable brutality on the part of the French as they occupied areas of the Upper Rhine in April and May. Their supposed atrocities may have been magnified for general German consumption, but whatever the truth of specific allegations, Eugene made a successful appeal to the French commander Berwick to bring his men under control, declaring that he would punish any of his own men who dared to act in this way: 'The afflictions of war have their bounds and it seems to me that the laws of humanity should never be disregarded.'[7] A few months after this appeal from Eugene the duke of Berwick was dead, decapitated by a cannon ball at the siege of Philippsburg. Another of the prince's opponents from the last war, Villars, also died that summer at Turin. The two men had continued to correspond throughout the twenty years after Rastadt. Their generation now was clearly coming to an end. Yet Eugene still clung on and had summoned up the strength to conduct an intelligent campaign reminiscent of that of 1713. He had to depend on others for scouting and intelligence work and for the first time he was quick to ask for advice. At one point during the summer he suffered the indignity of a special agent, the emperor's favourite general Hamilton, coming to his camp to report on his physical condition. His reports have not been found, but we have the comments of Frederick the Great, when, as Prussian crown prince, he had been sent by his father to Eugene's camp in 1734 to learn the art of war. Although Frederick William had insisted that Eugene treat his son as an ordinary volunteer officer, he had him dine with him every day: it seemed wise to cultivate him as Frederick William was so ill during the summer that he was expected to die. Eugene found the twenty-two year old Frederick 'wholly French-minded' and wrote to Charles that 'Much is at stake in gaining this young prince, who one day will be able to make more friends in the world than his father has and be able to do as much harm as good.'⁸ For his part Frederick and the other Prussian generals were shocked at the chaos in the Imperial camp, at the static way the campaign was being conducted, and especially at the fact that Philippsburg was seized by the French 'under the eyes of Prince Eugene without anyone taking a step to stop it'.⁹ Frederick was aghast at the physical condition of the most famous general of the age, writing later 'his body was still there but his soul had gone'.¹⁰ However some of the conversations he had with Eugene left an enduring impression, especially the old man's advice to plan in detail and to seize an opportunity when it was presented.

Frederick's youthful assessment of the prince was certainly too harsh, given the fact that he had held the army together during the campaign. When Eugene returned to Vienna at the end of 1734, however, he was obviously a very sick and dispirited man. His close friend Schönborn had resigned a few months before and in the November his last male heir, Eugene, died. A French agent in the Imperial capital reported that he could not see how the prince could possibly undertake another campaign: his memory was so poor that Ignatius Koch and his military aide Philippi 'direct all the business of Prince Eugene, who only gives the orders, and the rest of the time he is seen to play at trictrac, smiling from time to time, saying very little, afraid that it will be noticed that his memory is gone and that his spirit is depressed'.¹¹ Eugene's political influence which had been declining rapidly over the previous two years now disappeared completely. The conference was clearly dominated by Gundaker Starhemberg and Bartenstein, but there seemed to have been no thought of superseding the prince.

The advice which Eugene was giving at this time, in his depressed state, was the most sensible one: end the war. Too ill to attend the conference for most of the winter, he had Koch point out that Austria's lack of allies, the uncertainty over Bavaria and also over the Turks, and the monarchy's financial exhaustion meant that Austria must consider 'any peace better than the present war'. He was willing to see Naples and Sicily handed over to Don Carlos and part of Milan to Charles Emmanuel of Savoy so as to preserve 'these hereditary lands which in fact make up the strength of the monarchy'.¹² Yet Charles thought he knew better and believed that the Maritime Powers would soon have to come to his help. Although the Imperial troops had to survive by looting during the winter of 1734–35, a loan was being negotiated in England. The emperor could not bring himself to contemplate the loss of his former Spanish crown lands in Italy and he rejected Eugene's advice to withdraw completely from the peninsula to concentrate on the Rhine.

The prince conducted a further campaign in Germany in the spring and summer of 1735. Once again he managed to pursue a sensible defensive strategy with the resources available, even though he now found it difficult to remember what had been told him from one hour to the next. The Bavarians still held back from declaring for the French and Eugene's name alone seemed to make the French army wary of testing the Rhine barrier. Fleury in any case did not want to pursue too active a war there since it might provoke intervention by the Maritime Powers, and he was eager for a speedy diplomatic settlement and the confirmation of French gains. Charles, however, still deluded himself into hoping that a victory would be conjured up from somewhere; in May Bartenstein spoke of the possibility of a new Blenheim. But the Maritime Powers had no intention of sending a new Marlborough.

Charles began to adopt a more realistic approach during the summer and responded to direct peace feelers put out by Fleury. Eugene was consulted, but it was for form's sake: in sarcastic marginalia on his dispatches Charles and Bartenstein blamed him first for getting Austria into the war and then for losing it.

Even if Charles and Bartenstein had been prepared to listen, they would hardly have been ready to accept Eugene's advice, which was the counsel of despair. In August he wrote to Charles: 'In former times, as your majesty will recollect, no one was more opposed to an alliance with the house of Bourbon than I and no one more than I in favour of one with the Maritime Powers.'[13] He then went on not only to suggest an alliance with France but also to propose that the only way of propping up the hereditary lands was by marrying the eighteen year old Maria Theresa to the eight year old Bavarian crown prince. This infuriated Charles, who had never wavered in his intention of marrying her to Francis Stephen of Lorraine. The archduchess herself was equally determined on this and was already showing how tenacious she could be.[14]

The peace preliminaries granted by Fleury to Charles in October 1735 were far better than he deserved: Naples and Sicily were to be handed over to Don Carlos and a slice of Milan to Savoy, but in return Charles received Parma. At the same time Fleury achieved France's original aim in the war: Francis Stephen was to surrender his duchy of Lorraine to Louis XV's father-in-law Stanislas Leszczyński and accept the succession to Tuscany instead. In both cases it was envisaged that the duchies would eventually be absorbed by the French and Austrian crowns. Francis Stephen had at first baulked at accepting this settlement but did so after the blunt warning from Bartenstein, 'Highness, no cession, no archduchess.'[15] Fleury was also prepared to guarantee the Pragmatic Sanction, as he felt Austria in her present humiliated and truncated state was no great threat to France.*

Although the territorial settlement of 1735 had some advantages for Austria, particularly in the gain of Parma and the expectation of Tuscany which brought the chance of consolidation in northern Italy around Milan, it spelt the final destruction of Charles's mirage of regaining the Spanish monarchy. The loss of Naples and Sicily had been the inevitable consequence of an over-extended empire, indefensible without a navy. As serious, however, were the implications of Francis Stephen's surrender of Lorraine: it was a recognition of the collapse of Austria's position in the German Empire and to a great extent of her traditional role as guardian of the Rhine barrier. That the Southern Netherlands survived was the result of a tacit understanding between France and the Maritime Powers that this area be neutralized. When Charles became involved in 1737 in the disastrous war with the Turks – which was to lead to the loss of Eugene's prize of Belgrade – what remained of Austria's territories were left intact largely through the reluctance of Fleury to deliver the final blow. In fact Austria passed into an almost satellite relationship with France. In her unreformed state and without outside financial support, the position of Austria as a great power had proved a myth. Except against the Turks, even Eugene's victories, great as they had been, were built largely on the belief of the Maritime and German powers that a strong Austria was vital to contain France. Only in the 1740s did this belief take hold once more, and by that time the Austrian monarchy under Maria Theresa was taking the first halting steps towards becoming a great power in its own right.

Eugene was not to live to see the disasters of the late 1730s and early 1740s nor the rejuvenation of the monarchy. He returned to Vienna in October 1735 in a wretched condition but was able to stay for a while on his estates at Schlosshof. One of the empress Elizabeth's friends, countess Fuchs, described him in a letter to Schulenburg of 29 October: 'He came, as he had left, feeble in mind and body. He had plenty of company and everyone tried to keep him happy with masques and children's games,

---

* Yet at Charles VI's death, this French guarantee of Maria Theresa's succession was no more honoured than most of the others which the emperor had extracted from the European powers since 1725. The French war party insisted that Fleury should break his promise.

which were more appropriate to the feebleness of his age than to his character.'[16] It was at this time that his old enemy Guido Starhemberg, now paralysed in his legs, commented maliciously: 'I am growing old from the feet upwards, but I know someone it is happening to just as fast from the head downwards.'[17]

When the prince returned to the Himmelpfortgasse, the cold weather and his weak chest kept him indoors for most of the winter. He had become so politically unimportant that the English diplomat Robinson never mentioned him in his correspondence. Eugene's contact with Charles was now only in writing; and he had excused himself from an audience in a letter of 28 November 'because of this persistent catarrh which makes talking difficult . . . but as soon as my chest gets any better I will wait on Your Imperial Majesty most humbly'.[18]

When Maria Theresa and Francis Stephen were finally married in February 1736, Eugene was too ill to attend. With the return of the warm weather in April, however, he seemed to rally and began to go out once more. To the undoubted dismay of Charles and the other ministers, it looked as though he might try to work again. On 20 April he ate with friends at midday in his own palace, insisted on sitting, military style, on a stool, and then went to countess Batthyány's in the evening to play cards. He was quieter than usual and breathed heavily through his mouth. The Portuguese Tarouca took him home at nine o'clock and his servants put him to bed after he had refused to take anything 'to loosen the phlegm'. The next morning when they went to wake him, surprised at not hearing him coughing, they found him dead, 'extinguished in his bed like a taper'. When the surgeons opened him up later, they discovered he had choked from phlegm in his throat; presumably he had had pneumonia. Robinson added a suitable epitaph in his letter home: 'In a word, My Lord, his life was glorious and his death was easy.'[19]

For three days Eugene lay in state in the winter palace, dressed in a wig and in his uniform of a colonel of dragoons: red tunic with gold braid and black velvet facings, and spurred boots. Laid out next to him were 'on one side his cap as Prince, his sword, his gloves and *baton de marechal*, on the other the bonnet and great sword sent him by the Pope after one of his victories against the Turks', a victory which seemed such an age ago that the observer who wrote this description did not know which one.[20] Throughout the day and night six huge candles in silver candlesticks burnt round the body. The more curious of those who came to stare were kept away by the lieutenant colonel of the prince's own dragoon regiment, standing guard with a drawn sword.

Eugene's heart was cut out and sent to be buried with those of others of his family in Turin. The remains were carried in a long procession of soldiers, clerics and state officials through Vienna. In front of the cortège went his decorations and behind it came his riderless charger. The cortège took two hours to reach St Stephen's Cathedral, where the body was interred in the *Kreuzkappel*. Charles and his court accompanied the procession, but etiquette prescribed that they go incognito as the prince had not been a member of the Habsburg family.

All Eugene's possessions, except those in Hungary which the crown reclaimed, went to his unmarried niece Victoria in Savoy, now fifty-two years old. Robinson was aghast at what would happen to the prince's inheritance, especially as there was no will:

> Would you have believed that P. Eugene should dye without a will, that a sister as old as himself [there was none], and a niece fifty years old should inherit, the finest library, the finest pictures and the finest furniture of all kinds that any one less than a crowned head had in Europe. His estates in Hungary return to the Emperor for want of a will, and God knows how the rest will be dissipated. He thought indeed the day before he died of making a disposition, mostly in favour of decayed officers' widows, but there were only found minutes to that purpose. Not one of his old domestics, coevals or rather friends than servants are provided for. This is unpardonable.[21]

Victoria was quick to come to Vienna to claim her inheritance, and a husband soon appeared to share it, the prince of Sachsen-Hildburghausen. Over the next sixteen years, before she finally left both the city and her husband, she systematically broke up and sold the collections and palaces. The prince's fortune had been reckoned to be worth 100,000 gulden for each of the Vienna palaces, 600,000 gulden for the Marchfeld estates, 150,000 for estates in Savoy and France (we have no indication what these were), 150,000 for the library, 100,000 for the paintings, 170,000 in silver, 100,000 in jewels, 200,000 in cash and another 200,000 in the bank. The library with its books and prints was bought by Charles VI in 1737. Most of the pictures were bought by the house of Savoy but many were dispersed during the Revolutionary wars. The Belvedere, Himmelpfortgasse palace and Schlosshof were eventually acquired by Maria Theresa as Imperial residences.

Although the prince's political influence had long been dead and his actual death was expected to make 'no change here',[22] Charles was relieved. He shared the general feeling that the prince had outlived his usefulness, and had also persuaded himself that many of his problems were Eugene's fault. He noted clinically in his diary that Eugene had died and added 'now, see, everything will be put in a better order'.[23] However, as Austria's problems increased after Eugene's death, there was

a natural tendency in Vienna to see him in a better light, especially once
his subordinates and the remaining ministers plunged the monarchy
from one defeat to another in the Turkish war of 1737–39. Even before
these occurred Robinson wrote to Robert Walpole about the divisions
among Charles's ministers, which Eugene's death had done nothing to
settle, and he passed this judgment on the prince.

> ... the very remains, during the last two years, of what he had been, kept
> things in some order, as his very yes, or no, during his sounder age, had kept
> them in the best; & the notable difference, that there will be in the loss of this
> great man from other disasters, is, that time the great remedy of common mis-
> fortunes, will only serve to increase this.[24]

While Robinson was to be proved only too right in his prediction of
what was in store for the monarchy, he overestimated what Eugene
could have done or indeed had done. He had shown himself no more
capable of solving the problems of Charles's empire than any other
minister and he had played his part, as they had, in ensuring that they
would not be solved.

Conclusion

Eugene's career spanned the same years that saw the establishment of Austria as a great power, one based on the destruction of the Turkish empire in central Europe and of French hegemony in the west. At the same time Austrian expansion into Hungary and Italy was determining the future course of the monarchy over the next two centuries. The prince won important, in fact decisive, victories against both the Turks and the French, and to the extent that it is possible or desirable to give credit to individuals for these things, he was the creator of the modern multi-national Austrian state, linked with the rest of Germany but possessing a distinct identity of its own.

As the greatest of the victors over the Moslem Turks, Eugene has quite naturally captured the Austrian and German imagination as the last of the defenders of Christendom, the 'noble knight' of the *Prinz-Eugen Lied*. Many German historians of this and the last century praised him, despite his French speech and Italian background, as a German nationalist hero, determined to defend and extend German civilization in the west and the east.[1] There is no doubt that Eugene's victories were won with German-speaking troops from Austria and the Holy Roman Empire and that they led, at least in Hungary, to extensive German immigration and influence. The prince also preferred German troops to all others and tried to keep control of the conquered areas in German hands. If successful generals have to be turned into national heroes, Eugene certainly belongs to Austria and Germany rather than to anyone else. But this is a far cry from saying that he was a conscious protagonist of pan-Germanism or of German culture. His own cultural world was always that of Latin Europe, and if he was the servant of any state it was not the Greater Germany of nineteenth- and twentieth-century nationalists but the Austrian monarchy of the early eighteenth century. In fact, in common with most ministers of his day, Austrian or otherwise, he saw himself not so much as a servant of a state as of a dynasty, the house of Habsburg.

Eugene's commitment to three emperors and their family was essentially a commitment to the Habsburgs as rulers of the Austrian hereditary lands. He rejected the notion of accumulating provinces merely because the Habsburgs had dynastic claims to them; they had to be territories with some strategic or political importance to the Austrian heartland which made up 'the strength of the monarchy'. Italy and Hungary were needed for strategic reasons and the Southern Netherlands served as a political link with the Maritime Powers. The prince was therefore the servant of a dynasty but of a distinctly Austrian one. Yet the Habsburgs were also the heads of the Holy Roman Empire and derived much of their prestige and, on occasion, their strength from Germany. It was a fact which Eugene increasingly appreciated and became determined to maintain, not so much through territorial expansion – although he saw the value of Bavaria to the monarchy – or by the direct subjection of the German princes, but through diplomacy and an appeal to common political and military interests, particularly in relation to France.

The danger posed to Austria and to European stability by the territorial and dynastic ambitions of the French royal house largely determined Eugene's approach to European politics. His own resentment towards Louis XIV reinforced his appreciation of the Bourbon threat, a threat which preoccupied him more than that from the Ottoman empire. In dealing with France, Eugene showed a good deal of flexibility, being ready to explore several diplomatic combinations ranging from alliances with the Maritime Powers to ones with Prussia and Russia. At the same time, however, he was not blind to the fact that all these powers themselves could present threats almost as great, if not as permanent, as those from France or Spain. Although he began his diplomatic career very much in the shadow of Wratislaw, he proved almost as skilled as his mentor over the next twenty years. Where he showed less imagination, however, and this is why Charles VI turned against him in the 1720s, was in developing Austria as a commercial and Mediterranean power.

Napoleon counted Eugene among the seven great generals of history, but on the whole later military critics have not agreed with him. The prince was no military innovator; others also won victories against the Turks, if not so decisively, and against the French, except at Turin, his victories were shared with the equally compelling figure of Marlborough. Yet Eugene was undoubtedly the greatest Austrian general: he had the knack of making an inadequate system work and managed to give Austria the appearance, and for a time the reality, of being a great power on a par with England and France. Prepared to shoulder the burdens of policy-making and campaigning, he was equally adept as organizer, strategist and tactician. He took full advantage of the hussar regiments in the Austrian army to gather information, and one of his greatest strengths was having detailed knowledge of the movements of his enemies. He shared with Marlborough a belief in the primacy of battle and his ability to seize the right moment to launch a successful attack. Although he displayed a tendency after 1708 to play safe and to accept the rules set by the French, less than a decade later his two victories against the Turks had all the marks of his earlier triumphs. The main criticism that can be levelled against him as a general is in his legacy – he left no school of officers nor even an army able to function without him. There was a comparable lack of concern for what would happen after his death in his failure to draw up a will for the disposal of his magnificent collections and palaces.

While in wartime Eugene could make the best of the existing Austrian system, what he could not do was to transform the monarchy into a power capable of competing equally with France or England on a permanent basis and without continually resorting to outside financial help. He had no answer to the problems of poor revenues, particularism and economic backwardness. He was, moreover, uninterested in these problems and probably never even appreciated them. At the same time he was hardly in a position to grapple with them because of his reluctance to usurp the role of the emperor or to become a Wallenstein. He kept largely within the bounds of his military and diplomatic duties, and the Nimptsch-Tedeschi episode of 1719 must have underlined for him the jealousy which these offices brought him. Only very briefly, between 1714 and 1718, can he be said to have acted as a premier minister.

Although the guiding political and military principle of Eugene's life was loyalty to three successive emperors, just as important was loyalty to his own ideals. He considered himself, to the end of his life, not as a mere subject of a French or Austrian ruler but as a prince in his own right, a member of one of the ruling families of Europe, the house of Savoy. Evidently he never felt himself to be a Frenchman: this is shown in his refusal to allow Bonneval to fill a military post in the Southern Netherlands, Eugene's own province, because he was French. Nor do we find his claiming to be Austrian: he excused himself from advising Charles VI on Habsburg family matters because he was a 'foreigner'. When it came to a marriage within his own immediate family, of his nephew Emmanuel in 1713, he thought it necessary to ask Victor Amadeus's permission as head of his house. Yet membership of the house of Savoy brought with it no feeling of political loyalty to its dukes but only a sense of independence which allowed him to pledge himself by his own choice to the Habsburgs. What is also apparent throughout Eugene's career is the importance he attached to being true to his own personal values[2] – physical bravery, loyalty to his sovereign, the preservation of an untarnished reputation, a word that could be trusted implicitly, self-control in all things. The result was an austere cold figure with a 'reservedness which makes him almost inaccessible'.[3] Yet it was often a strain: the anger and the sarcasm would break through and he was said to show 'dissatisfaction by his countenance more than any body'.[4] He could also be vindictive, particularly as he grew older – he pursued both Mérode-Westerloo and Bonneval unmercifully – and he was always impatient of men he considered fools, especially those who stood in his way, whether they were Mansfeld, Salm or Sinzendorff. Although he could show good humour on campaign or over cards with his friends, he inspired respect and admiration rather than affection or sympathy. If the 'posture' of Balthasar Permoser's white marble statue of the prince was wrong, the material was right.

Notes to the Text

List of abbreviations

BA Bernstorff Archives, Gartow, West Germany
BL British Library, London
FE *Feldzüge des Prinzen Eugen von Savoyen*, published by K. K. Kriegsarchiv, Abteilung für Kriegsgeschichte (20 vols, Vienna 1876–92)
HHSA Haus-, Hof-, und Staatsarchiv, Vienna
HMC *Historical Manuscripts Commission*
MIÖG *Mitteilungen des Instituts für österreichische Geschichtsforschung*
MM *Mémoires militaires relatifs à la succession d'Espagne sous Louis XIV*, edited by F. E. de Vault and J. J. G. Pelet (11 vols, Paris 1835–42)
MÖS *Mitteilungen des österreichischen Staatsarchivs*
NSA Niedersächsisches Staatsarchiv, Hanover
PRO Public Record Office, London
WG *Weensche Gezantschapsberichten, 1670–1720*, edited by G. Antal and J. C. H. De Pater (2 vols, The Hague 1929, 1934)

Chapter I

1 H. Oehler, *Prinz Eugen im Urteil Europas* (Munich 1944) 109. All Elizabeth Charlotte's remarks were made some twenty-five years later, most of them after Eugene had defeated her son at the battle of Turin (1706). In 1682 there was a homosexual scandal among the young aristocrats at the French court, but there is no direct evidence that Eugene was involved.
2 H. L. Mikoletzky, *Österreich: Das Grosse 18. Jahrhundert* (Vienna 1967) 32.
3 According to the Dutch envoy Hop: *The Lexington Papers*, ed. H. Manners Sutton (London 1851) 339.
4 S. Riezler, *Geschichte Bayerns* (Gotha 1913) VII, 595.

Chapter II

1 *The New Cambridge Modern History*, vol. V: *The Ascendancy of France*, ed. F. L. Carsten (Cambridge 1961) 475.
2 *HMC, Bath MSS.*, III (London 1908) 9–10.
3 J. Bérenger, 'La Hongrie des Habsbourgs au XVIIe siècle. République nobiliaire ou monarchie limitée', *Revue historique* (1967) 31.
4 P. Rycaut, *The History of the Turks Beginning with the Year 1679 . . . until the End of the Year 1698 and 1699* (London 1700) 24.

Chapter III

1 *HMC, Downshire MSS.*, I (London 1924) 190–91.

2 Ibid., 191.

3 Rycaut, 217.

4 *The Letter Book of Sir George Etherege*, ed. S. Rosenfeld (London 1928) 430.

5 Rycaut, 247.

6 For the adventures of one of these Turkish captives see Osman Aga, *Der Gefangene der Giauren*, tr. R. F. Kreutel and O. Spies (Graz 1962).

7 Riezler, 298.

8 Oehler, 156.

Chapter IV

1 *Letter Book of Etherege*, 432, Etherege to Preston, 3 Jan. 1689.

2 D. Carutti, *Storia della diplomazia della corte di Savoia* (Turin 1879) III, 148.

3 13 July 1690, W. Paget to Colt, BL, Add. MS. 34095.

4 M. Braubach, *Prinz Eugen von Savoyen* (Munich 1963–65) I, 164.

5 *Mémoires et correspondance du maréchal de Catinat* (hereinafter Catinat, *Mémoires*), ed. B. le Bouyer de Saint-Gervais (Paris 1819) I, 130.

6 Braubach, *Eugen*, I, 164.

7 27 June 1693, Vienna, G. Stepney to W. Blathwayt, PRO, London, S.P. 105/59.

8 *HMC, Bath MSS.*, III, 13, Stepney to J. Trenchard, 20 Oct. 1693.

9 P. Frischauer, *Prince Eugene* (London 1934) 182.

10 Riezler, VII, 361.

11 A. Arneth, *Prinz Eugen von Savoyen* (Vienna 1864) I, 455.

12 See 29, 31 Jan., 14 Feb. 1692, Paget to Nottingham, S.P. 80/17.

13 Catinat, *Mémoires*, II, 89.

14 E. Mauvillon, *Histoire du Prince François Eugène de Savoye* (Vienna 1790) I, 164.

15 J. B. Wolf, *Louis XIV* (London, Panther ed. 1970) 587.

16 S. B. Baxter, *William III* (London 1966) 341.

17 William III thought it 'the only place' they could attack France 'with some hope of success', Carutti, 206, William III to Heinsius, 11 March 1693.

18 The devastation can be followed in Catinat, *Mémoires*; Eugene had described the whole area between the Po

and Pinerolo as having been 'ruined for a long time', *Militärische Korrespondenz des Prinzen Eugen von Savoyen* ed. F. Heller (hereinafter Heller) (Vienna 1848) I, 78–79, Eugene to Leopold, 18 June 1696.

19 However, in Hungary indiscriminate looting still took place, and both Caprara and Caraffa were inclined to resort to it on occasions in Italy.

Chapter V

1 *Lexington Papers*, 101.

2 A. Arneth, *Das Leben des kaiserlichen Feldmarschalls Grafen Guido Starhemberg* (Vienna 1853) 168, 182–83.

3 13 July 1692, Harbord to Blathwayt, PRO, S.P. 80/17.

4 Arneth, *Eugen*, I, 96.

5 V. Bibl, *Prinz Eugen: Ein Heldenleben* (Vienna 1941) 72.

6 Arneth, *Starhemberg*, 187.

7 *Lexington Papers*, 278.

8 *FE*, II, Supplement, 42.

9 *Eugenius Nummis Illustratus. Leben und Thaten des Grosen Printzen Eugenii* (Nuremberg 1736) 122.

10 Mauvillon, I, 230.

11 Heller, I, 171.

12 Rycaut, 553.

13 Frischauer, 197.

14 Rycaut, 557.

15 *FE*, II, Supplement, 93, Eugene's 'Journal de la marche en Bosnie'.

16 This aspect is discussed in the unpublished dissertation by M. Baratta-Dragono, 'Prinz Eugen von Savoyen in der Publizistik seiner Zeit' (Univ. of Vienna 1960).

Chapter VI

1 F. Hennings, *Das barocke Wien* (Vienna 1965) II, 18.

2 17 Sept. 1701, Vienna, R. Sutton to Blathwayt, PRO, S.P. 105/63.

3 J. G. Keysler, *Travels through Germany, Bohemia, Hungary . . .* (London 1760) IV 165–6.

4 Quoted in I. Barea, *Vienna, Legend and Reality* (London 1966) 60.

5 C. L. de Pöllnitz, *The Memoirs of Charles Lewis Baron de Pöllnitz* (2nd ed., London 1739) I, 253.

6 1 May 1715, Vienna, D. Huldenberg

to A. G. Bernstorff (George I's chief Hanoverian minister in England), BA, A.G. 63.

7 Lady Mary Wortley Montagu, *The Complete Letters*, ed. R. Halsband (Oxford 1965) I, 273.

8 Eugene told the French general Villars in 1713 that he had not wanted to buy a country estate like him: 'You have a family and so it is no surprise to me that you should think in this way: but I have none, and I can assure you that if I retire a million in revenues or 12,000 livres in income would be the same to me.' Oehler, 161.

9 Arneth, *Starhemberg*, 215.

10 Braubach, *Eugen*, I, 155.

11 The fullest, but still rather coy, discussion is in M. Braubach, *Geschichte und Abenteuer: Gestalten um den Prinzen Eugen* (Munich 1950) 108 ff.

12 On the other hand, as Oehler, 10, points out, very few men said much about their feelings in writing at this time.

13 For St Saphorin see S. Stelling-Michaud, *Les Aventures de M. de Saint-Saphorin sur le Danube* (Paris 1934) 154 ff.

14 *Lexington Papers*, 307–8.

15 Ibid., 290, A. Prior to Lexington, 6 Aug. 1697, The Hague.

16 Ibid., 252, Stepney to Lexington, 26 March 1697.

17 4 Aug. 1700, Vienna, Sutton to Blathwayt, and see further letter of 10 July, BL, Add. MS. 9736.

18 A. Gaedeke, *Die Politik Oesterreichs in der Spanischen Erbfolgefrage* (Leipzig 1877) II, 171* [*sic*].

19 4 Aug. 1700, Sutton to Blathwayt, Add. MS. 9736.

20 Gaedeke, II, 203*–4* [*sic*].

Chapter VII

1 4 May 1701, Vienna, Stepney to Hedges, PRO, S.P. 105/62.

2 *FE*, III, Supplement, 18, Eugene to Leopold, 26 May 1701.

3 As Eugene recorded in his campaign diary, ibid., 160.

4 W. Erben, 'Prinz Eugens italienischer Feldzug im Jahre 1701', *MIÖG* XXXVIII (1920) 615–16.

5 See especially Heller, I, 195–201, 272.

6 *MM*, I, 290, Catinat to Louis XIV, 4 Aug. 1701.

7 Ibid., I, 600.

8 Mauvillon, I, 310.

9 10 Sept., Stepney to Blathwayt, S.P. 105/63.

10 4 Oct., Stepney to Blathwayt, S.P. 105/64.

11 *FE*, III, Supplement, 59.

12 19 Nov., Stepney to Blathwayt, S.P. 105/64.

13 *MM*, I, 375.

14 Ibid., 586.

15 Although the English only wanted him to have Milan in Italy, Leopold stood out for Naples and Sicily as well. 4 May 1701, Stepney to Blathwayt, S.P. 105/62, 20 May 1702, Stepney to Vernon, S.P. 105/65.

16 See correspondence between Stepney and C. Hedges for July 1702 in S.P. 105/65.

17 26 April 1702, Vienna, Stepney to Vernon, ibid.

18 *FE*, IV, Supplement, 56.

19 *MM*, II, 671.

20 N. Henderson, *Prince Eugen of Savoy* (London 1964) 68.

21 Frischauer, 229.

22 Henderson, 70.

23 31 May, Stepney to Vernon, S.P. 105/65.

24 16 Aug., Stepney to Hedges, S.P. 80/19.

25 Bibl, 107.

26 Heller, I, 493.

27 Henderson, 75.

28 12 July, Stepney to Hedges, S.P. 105/65.

29 19 Aug., Stepney to A. Stanhope, ibid.

30 18 Oct., Stepney to Hedges, S.P. 105/66.

31 23 Sept., Stepney to Hedges, S.P. 80/19.

32 23 Dec., Stepney to Hedges, S.P. 105/66.

33 25 Nov., Stepney to Hedges, S.P. 80/19.

34 *MM*, II, 280.

Chapter VIII

1 10 Jan. 1703, Stepney to Nottingham, PRO, S.P. 105/67.

2 28 Feb., Stepney to Aglionby, ibid.

3 H. Wendt, *Der Italienische Kriegs-schauplatz in Europäischer Konflikten* (Berlin 1936), Eugene to Starhemberg, 30 May.

4 *FE*, IV, Supplement, 17, Eugene to Starhemberg, 21 Feb.

5 Ibid., 20, Eugene to Starhemberg, 7 March.

6 4 April, Stepney to Hedges, S.P. 105/68.

7 *FE*, V [*sic*], Supplement, 61, Eugene to Starhemberg, 7 March.

8 23 June, Stepney to Hedges, S.P. 105/68.

9 Braubach, *Eugen*, I, 364.

10 Ibid.

11 24 March, Stepney to Hedges, private, S.P. 105/67.

12 Ibid.

13 Ibid. and 23 June, Stepney to Buckingham, S.P. 105/68.

14 28 Feb., Stepney to Hedges, S.P. 105/67.

15 2 May, Stepney to Hedges, S.P. 105/68.

16 23 June, Stepney to Buckingham, ibid.

17 2 June, Stepney to Hedges, ibid.

18 Bibl, 111.

19 7 July, Stepney to Hedges, S.P. 105/69.

20 Braubach, *Eugen*, II, 28.

21 Heller, II, 56–7, 103.

22 10 Jan., Stepney to Nottingham, S.P. 105/67.

23 Wendt, 30.

24 3 Oct., Stepney to Hedges, S.P. 105/70.

25 4 April, Stepney to Hedges, S.P. 105/70.

26 13 Oct., Stepney to Hedges, S.P. 105/70.

27 Arneth, *Starhemberg*, 304.

28 4 Aug., Stepney to Cardonnel, S.P. 105/69.

29 E. Frauenholz, *Prinz Eugen und die Kaiserliche Armee* (Munich 1932) 9–10.

30 8, 12 Dec., Vienna, C. Whitworth to Hedges, S.P. 105/70.

31 Braubach, *Eugen*, II, 22.

32 29 Dec., Whitworth to Hedges, S.P. 105/70.

33 Henderson, 89.

34 Ibid., 90.

35 15 March 1704, Stepney to Marlborough, S.P. 105/71.

36 9, 16 Jan., Whitworth to Hedges, ibid.

37 C. F. J. Noorden, *Europäische Geschichte im 18. Jahrhundert* (Düsseldorf 1870) I, 458.

38 See Stepney's reports in S.P. 105/72.

39 30 Dec. 1702 [*sic*], old style, Whitehall, Hedges to Stepney, private, 3 Feb. 1703, Vienna, Stepney to Hedges, private, S.P. 105/67.

40 25 April 1703, Stepney to Hedges, S.P. 105/68.

41 4 Aug. 1703, Stepney to Hedges, S.P. 105/69.

42 Stepney did not know of the family compact but was certain, none the less, that these would be ceded to Joseph; see correspondence in ibid. and his letter to R. Harley of 3 Oct. 1704, S.P. 105/74.

Chapter IX

1 17 May 1704, Stepney to Hedges, private, PRO, S.P. 105/72.

2 The correspondence would have been particularly useful because Wratislaw was largely Eugene's political mentor. Although it has been argued by E. Mezgolich, 'Graf Johann Wenzel Wratislaw von Mitrowitz: Sein Wirken während des spanischen Erbfolgekrieges' (Univ. of Vienna dissertation 1967) 97 ff., that Eugene was the driving force behind the Danube expedition, a more convincing argument for Wratislaw's being the initiator has been made by E. Jarnut-Derbolav, *Österreichische Gesandtschaft in London, 1701-1711* (Bonn 1972) 158 ff.

3 D. Chandler, *Marlborough as Military Commander* (London 1973) 121.

4 W. S. Churchill, *Marlborough: His Life and Times* (London, Sphere ed. 1967), II, 250–1.

5 Ibid., 253.

6 Heller, II, 192.

7 *WG*, II, 295–6; *FE*, VII, 545.

8 Frischauer, 251.

9 Churchill, II, 288.

10 25 Sept. 1704, Cron Weissembourg, Stepney to Whitworth, S.P. 105/73.

11 Henderson, 101.

12 H. L. Snyder, *The Marlborough-Godolphin Correspondence* (Oxford 1976) I, 316.

13 Twenty-one years later Max Emmanuel blamed this decision of Villeroy for the subsequent disasters, Riezler, VII, 614.

14 *Military Memoirs: The Marlborough Wars, Robert Parker and Comte de Mérode-Westerloo*, ed. D. Chandler (London 1968) 160–1.

15 J.-M. de la Colonie, *The Chronicles of an Old Campaigner*, tr. and ed. W. C. Horsley (London 1904) 173.

16 Churchill, II, 325.

17 Noorden, I, 546.

18 A. Schwenke, *Geschichte der Hannoverschen Truppen im Spanischen Erbfolgekriege, 1701–1714* (Göttingen 1862) 75.

19 *The Life and Adventures of Mrs Christian Davies, commonly called Mother Ross* (Oxford 1840) 294 (no editor is given for this edition). The original was printed in 1740, having been compiled by Daniel Defoe from Mother Ross's recollections. It might be fictitious, although it has more than a ring of truth.

20 Henderson, 104.

21 Heller, II, 183–84.

22 Mezgolich, 134.

23 Frischauer, 253.

24 Chandler, *Marlborough*, 140.

25 Bibl, 135.

26 Arneth, *Eugen*, I, 266.

27 R. Kane, *Campaigns of King William and Queen Anne* (London 1745) 56.

28 W. Coxe, *Memoirs of John Duke of Marlborough* (2nd ed., London 1820) II, 7–8.

29 Heller, II, 200.

30 Snyder, I, 354, Marlborough to Godolphin, 21 Aug. 1704.

31 Braubach, *Eugen*, II, 78.

32 Heller, II, 197.

Chapter X

1 Braubach, *Eugen*, II, 97–98.

2 24 Jan. 1705, Stepney to Cardonnel, and see Stepney's reports till April, PRO, S.P. 105/75.

3 4 March, Stepney to Cardonnel, ibid.

4 Braubach, *Eugen*, II, 128.

5 18, 21 March, Stepney to Harley, S.P. 105/75.

6 22 April, Stepney to Halifax, ibid.

7 21 March, Stepney to Marlborough, ibid.

8 18 April, Stepney to Harley, ibid.

9 *WG*, II, 314.

10 25, 29 April, 9 May, Stepney to Harley, S.P. 105/75.

11 23 May, Stepney to R. Hill, ibid.

12 1 Aug., Stepney to Harley, S.P. 105/76.

13 Arneth, *Starhemberg*, 366.

14 *MM*, V, 246–7.

15 Eugene sympathized with Victor Amadeus, writing to Joseph on 25 August, 'I know better than anyone the Fieldmarshal's bad temper.' *Prinz Eugen von Savoyen*, Catalogue to the Exhibition marking the 300th anniversary of his birth published by the Heeresgeschichtliches Museum (Vienna 1963) 92.

16 Heller, II, 541–42, Eugene to Guido Starhemberg, 29 June.

17 24 Dec., Stepney to Vernon, S.P. 105/76.

18 Heller, II, 595.

19 Braubach, *Eugen*, II, 114.

20 7 Aug., Stepney to Hill, S.P. 105/76.

21 Coxe, *Marlborough*, II, 251.

22 Henderson, 119.

23 15 Feb., Frankfurt, H. Newton to Blackwell, S.P. 98/22.

24 Churchill, III, 37–38.

25 22 April, Stepney to Harley, S.P. 105/75.

26 9 Nov. 1707, Vienna, P. Meadows to Harley, S.P. 80/29.

27 Braubach, *Eugen*, II, 447.

28 Braubach, ibid., 130 ff., is less sympathetic to Joseph than Mikoletzky, 75–76, 96, or K. O. Aretin, 'Kaiser Joseph I zwischen Kaisertradition und österreichischer Grossmachtpolitik', *Historische Zeitschrift* CCXV (1972) 533 and W. Bauer, 'Joseph I', *Mitteilungen des Oberösterreichischen Landesarchivs* IV (1955).

29 18 Jan., 28 July 1708, Meadows to H. Boyle, S.P. 80/29.

30 22 April 1705, Stepney to Halifax, S.P. 105/75.

31 Wratislaw felt that Gundaker Starhemberg was as bad as Salm: see A.

Arneth, 'Eigenhändige Correspondenz des Königs Karl III von Spanien mit dem Obersten Kanzler des Königreiches Böhmen Grafen Johann Wenzel Wratislaw', *Archiv für Kunde österreichischer Geschichtsquellen* XVI (1856) 60 (hereinafter Arneth, *Eigenhändige*).

32 7 Jan. 1706, Stepney to Cardonnel, 12 March, Stepney to Marlborough, S.P. 105/77.

33 *FE*, IX, Supplement, 27–28, Eugene to Salm, 16 Feb. 1707, Milan. There is no mention of this incident in the actual conference minutes, which show that rather non-controversial subjects were discussed – relations with the Swiss Cantons and the need for English ships in the Adriatic. Present, besides Eugene and Salm, were Moles, the marquis de Prié and Seilern, and it is likely that Seilern lectured Eugene. 22 March 1706, conference minutes, HHSA, Vorträge 12.

Chapter XI

1 Henderson, 125.

2 Although Victor Amadeus had 'little expectation of any help ... from Prince Eugene', he seemed determined to stick by the allies. 23 July 1706, Vibran, P. Methuen to Hedges, PRO, S.P. 89/19.

3 *MM*, VI, 200.

4 Ibid, 277; and see Churchill, III, 164.

5 Henderson, 132.

6 G. M. Trevelyan, *England under Queen Anne* (London, Fontana ed. 1965) II, 163.

7 *FE*, IX, Supplement, 54, Eugene to Joseph, 9 March 1707.

8 Ibid., IX, Supplement, 27–8, Eugene to Salm, 16 Feb.

9 Wolf, *Louis XIV*, 660.

10 Braubach, *Eugen*, II, 176.

11 For the Italian aspects of Imperial policy see Aretin, 544 ff. The imposition of contributions on the Italian states was part of this assertion of feudal rights. Particularly heavy contributions were imposed on Tuscany in 1707, because, according to the elector palatine, its duke was believed to be 'one of the chief instruments in procuring the will in favour of the Duke of

Anjou'. 10 April 1707, Frankfurt, Manchester to Harley, S.P. 80/29.

12 N. Tindal, *The Continuation of Mr Rapin's History of England* (London 1762) XVI, 449, Manchester to Sunderland, 19 Aug. 1707, Venice.

13 Churchill, III, 231.

14 *FE*, IX, 77.

15 Tindal, XVI, 443, 447, Manchester to Harley, 30 April, Manchester to Godolphin, 18 May.

16 18 May, Turin, W. Chetwynd to Sunderland, BL, Add. MS. 9099.

17 Tindal, XVI, 450.

18 Coxe, *Marlborough*, III, 284.

19 11 May, Milan, Eugene to Marlborough, Add. MS. 9099.

20 Wolf, *Louis XIV*, 665–66.

21 29 July, La Valette, near Turin, Chetwynd to Sunderland, Add. MS. 9100. And see D. de Visé, *The History of the Siege of Toulon* (London 1708) for the plundering and devastation by the army and navy and for the details of the expedition.

22 Ibid., 89 ff.

23 9 Aug., Chetwynd to Sunderland, Add. MS. 9100.

24 8 Aug., Toulon, Rehbinder to Marlborough, ibid.

25 15 Aug., Chetwynd to Sunderland, ibid.

26 Churchill, III, 238.

27 Henderson, 146.

28 25 Aug., Fréjus, Chetwynd to Sunderland, Add. MS. 9100.

29 Coxe, *Marlborough*, III, 318, Eugene to Marlborough, 19 Aug. 1707, Turin. If this letter was written from Turin, the date must be a month later than Coxe gives.

Chapter XII

1 Wratislaw warned Charles in Spain that Eugene had to be kept close by in case Joseph died, as 'the Emperor has not had the smallpox' and led a dangerous hunting life. Arneth, *Eigenhändige*, 57, Wratislaw to Charles III, 15 Jan. 1708.

2 15 Oct. 1707, Vienna, Meadows to Marlborough, BL, Add. MS. 9100.

3 Braubach, *Eugen*, II, 217.

4 Henderson, 120.

5 Braubach, *Eugen*, II, 222.

6 7/18 Jan. 1708, Vienna, Meadows to Boyle, PRO, S.P. 80/29.

7 2 March 1709 [*sic*], Meadows to Boyle, ibid.

8 Coxe, *Marlborough*, IV, 111.

9 J. Banks, *The History of Francis-Eugene, Prince of Savoy* (London 1741) 263.

10 *MM* VIII, 18.

11 Schwenke, 141.

12 *FE*, X, 332.

13 K. W. Schöning, *Des General-Feldmarschalls Dubislaw Gnemar von Natzmer auf Gennewitz Leben und Kriegsthaten* (Berlin 1838) 286.

14 Chandler, *Marlborough*, 215.

15 Ibid., 222.

16 Churchill, III, 360.

17 Henderson, 162.

18 J. M. Schulenburg, *Leben und Denkwürdigkeiten* (Leipzig 1834) I, 337.

19 Henderson, 162.

20 G. Murray (ed.), *Letters and Dispatches of John Churchill, duke of Marlborough* (London 1845) IV, 129.

21 Wolf, *Louis XIV*, 670.

22 Churchill, III, 398.

23 *MM*, VIII, 426.

24 M. Sautai, *Une Opération militaire d'Eugène et de Marlborough, le forcement du passage de l'Escaut en 1708* (Paris 1905) 9.

25 O. Klopp, *Der Fall des Hauses Stuart und die Succession des Hauses Hannover* (Vienna 1875 etc.) XIII, 154.

26 Coxe, *Marlborough*, IV, 238, 243.

27 Schwenke, 171.

28 24 Sept. 1708, Lanoy, A. Cardonnel to G. Tilson, S.P. 87/4.

29 Murray, IV, 271–72, 294–99.

30 Coxe, *Marlborough*, IV, 269.

31 *The Life and Diary of Lieutenant Colonel John Blackader*, ed. A. Crichton (Edinburgh 1824) 336.

32 Henderson, 167.

33 G. Otruba, *Prinz Eugen und Marlborough: Weltgeschichte im Spiegel eines Briefwechsels* (Vienna 1961) 63.

34 *FE*, X, Supplement, 318, Eugene to Thiel, 7 Nov. 1708.

35 Braubach, *Eugen*, II, 259.

Chapter XIII

1 Braubach, *Eugen*, II, 277.

2 W. Reese, *Das Ringen um Frieden und Sicherheit in den Entscheidungsjahren des spanischen Erbfolgekrieges, 1708–1709* (Munich 1933) 145.

3 On the other hand Eugene certainly did not go as far as Schönborn and some of the Imperial princes who wanted 'to sacrifice Naples and Sicily so as to keep a better barrier on the Rhine', Arneth, *Eigenhändige*, 167, Wratislaw to Charles III, 27 May 1711. For a reasoned criticism of the view of H. Srbik, *Aus Österreichs Vergangenheit* (Salzburg 1949) 7 ff., that Eugene pursued a strong *Reich* policy, see P. R. Sweet, 'Prince Eugene of Savoy and Central Europe', *American Historical Review* LVII (1951).

4 27 Feb. 1709, Meadows to Boyle, PRO, S.P. 80/29.

5 Churchill, IV, 58.

6 The main advantage for the emperor in this, as Eugene pointed out, was that it would ensure the rapid surrender of Strasbourg. See V. L. Tapié, 'Louis XIV's methods in foreign policy', in Ragnhild Hatton (ed.), *Louis XIV and Europe* (London 1976) 12.

7 Braubach, *Eugen*, II, 293.

8 See esp. Murray, IV, 505, Marlborough to Townshend, 13 June 1709.

9 Sweet, 55. For a lucid discussion of the above and of Marlborough and Eugene's attempt to shift the blame see M. A. Thomson, 'Louis XIV and the Grand Alliance, 1705–10', in Ragnhild Hatton and J. S. Bromley (eds), *William III and Louis XIV* (Liverpool 1967) 208.

10 Arneth, *Eugen*, II, 68, Eugene to Sinzendorff, 11 June.

11 Braubach, *Eugen*, II, 468.

12 Reese, 272.

13 Churchill, IV, 84.

14 Coxe, *Marlborough*, V, 4–5.

15 Chandler, *Marlborough*, 248.

16 I. F. Burton, *The Captain-General* (London 1968) 149.

17 Wolf, *Louis XIV*, 686–88.

18 *FE*, XI, 98, and Supplement, 252.

19 For this explanation see Schwenke, 196, and Schulenburg, I, 407–9.

20 Banks, 291.

21 26 Sept., Marlborough to Godolphin, BL, Add. MS. 9107.

22 Matthew Bishop, *The Life and Adventures of Matthew Bishop* (London 1744) 214–15.
23 Schulenburg, I, 432.
24 Schwenke, 210.
25 Kane, 85.
26 Wolf, *Louis XIV*, 690.
27 Arneth, *Eugen*, II, 93.
28 Schulenburg, I, 469–70, Schulenburg to Werthern (Saxon minister at Ratisbon), 6 Oct.
29 Vehse, II, 127.
30 Schöning, 297.
31 Braubach, *Eugen*, II, 475–76.
32 The inner conference, 'the secret or so-called small' conference, consisted of Wratislaw, Trautsohn, Seilern and the referendary Buol, but not Gundaker Starhemberg. Eugene and Sinzendorff joined this inner conference when they were in Vienna. The 'so-called large' conference included these men together with Starhemberg, Waldstein, Mansfeld, Windischgrätz, who had just become president of the aulic council, and Schönborn. In the *Deputation*, where the contributions of the estates were discussed, were Starhemberg, Seilern and Trautsohn. Arneth, *Eigenhändige*, 145, Wratislaw to Charles III, 22 April 1711.

Chapter XIV

1 For their need of money see 2 June 1710, Marlborough to Godolphin, BL, Add. MS. 9109.
2 *FE*, X, 77, and *FE*, XI, 43.
3 Arneth, *Eugen*, II, 475.
4 Schwenke, 215.
5 24 April, Marlborough to Godolphin, Add. MS. 9108.
6 5 May, Douai, Cadogan to Sunderland, PRO, S.P. 77/159.
7 *FE*, XII, 296; and see ibid., 315.
8 See Marlborough's correspondence during spring 1710 in Add. MS. 9109.
9 29 June, 7 July, Marlborough to Godolphin, ibid.
10 Schulenburg, I, 473.
11 18, 21, 30 Aug., 23 Sept., 3 Nov., Marlborough to Godolphin, Add. MS. 9110.
12 Klopp, XIII, 533.
13 Churchill, IV, 212.

14 6/17 July 1711, Vienna, Whitworth to H. St John, Add. MS. 9112.
15 6 Nov. 1710, Vienna, F. Palmes to Marlborough, Add. MS. 9110.
16 W. Coxe, *History of the House of Austria* (George Bell edition, London 1901) III, 79.
17 12 April 1711, Palmes to St John, S.P. 80/31.
18 Arneth, *Eugen*, II, 481.
19 Arneth, *Eigenhändige*, 158, Charles III to Wratislaw, 18 May 1711, Barcelona.
20 Wolf, *Louis XIV*, 704.
21 Arneth, *Eigenhändige*, 197.
22 5/16 Sept., Whitworth to Marlborough, Add. MS. 9113.
23 9/20 Oct., Whitworth to Marlborough, ibid.
24 *FE*, XIII, Supplement, 81.
25 *The New Cambridge Modern History*, vol. VI: *The Rise of Great Britain and Russia*, ed. J. S. Bromley (Cambridge 1970) 458.
26 20 Oct., Dresden, Whitworth to Marlborough, Add. MS. 9113.
27 Braubach, *Eugen*, III, 74.
28 25 Feb. 1712, Wratislaw to Sinzendorff, HHSA, Grosse Korrespondenz 71.
29 2 Jan. 1712, Wratislaw to Sinzendorff, ibid.

Chapter XV

1 *Correspondence of Jonathan Swift*, ed. H. Williams (Oxford 1963) I, 285.
2 Henderson, 188–9.
3 Churchill, IV, 430.
4 *The Wentworth Papers, 1705–39*, ed. J. J. Cartwright (London 1883) 259, 265.
5 Churchill, IV, 417. The heir was in fact still George's elderly mother, Sophia.
6 17, 25 Feb. 1712, Wratislaw to Sinzendorff, HHSA, Grosse Korrespondenz 71.
7 *Correspondence of Jonathan Swift*, I, 285.
8 *Wentworth Papers*, 258.
9 Abel Boyer, *The Political State of Great Britain* (London 1712) III, 58, 99.
10 Churchill, IV, 433.
11 *Wentworth Papers*, 244.
12 Henderson 198.

13 Braubach, *Eugen*, III, 397.

14 *Wentworth Papers*, 271.

15 Boyer, III, 101.

16 FE, XII, Supplement, 8, 25, Eugene to Tarini, 4 Jan., 8 March 1710.

17 Ibid., 81–2, Eugene to G. Koch, 18 May.

18 Ibid., 204–5, Eugene to Emmanuel, 9 July.

19 Churchill, IV, 451.

20 Trevelyan, III, 236 ff.

21 Braubach, *Eugen*, III, 109.

22 De la Colonie, 367.

23 M. de Vogüé, *Malplaquet et Denain* (Paris 1893) 73.

24 Arneth, *Eugen*, II, 240.

25 C. Sturgill, *Marshal Villars and the War of the Spanish Succession* (Lexington 1965) 113.

26 28 July 1712, Brussels, J. Laws to Bolingbroke, PRO, S.P. 77/61.

27 FE, XIV, 190.

28 Arneth, *Eugen*, II, 258–59.

29 Schwenke, 260.

30 Arneth, *Eugen*, II, 266, 500–1.

31 24 April, Vienna, Trautsohn to Sinzendorff, HHSA, Grosse Korrespondenz 70.

32 3 Nov., Wratislaw to Sinzendorff, ibid., 71.

33 25 July, Pressburg, Wratislaw to Sinzendorff, ibid.

34 *FE*, XIV, Supplement, 204–5, Eugene to Sinzendorff, 18 Aug.

35 Mezgolich, 275–76.

36 Already in Spain he had written of 'the love and affection . . . , which I have had for the Prince's person since my youth, and which I will always have till I die'. Arneth, *Eigenhändige*, 116, Charles III to Wratislaw, 28 April 1710.

37 Arneth, *Starhemberg*, 740.

38 O. Redlich, *Das Werden einer Grossmacht: Österreich von 1700 bis 1740* (Baden bei Wien 1938) 121.

39 FE, XV, 42.

40 Ibid., 45–46.

41 Ibid., 52.

42 Ibid., 222.

43 Arneth, *Eugen*, II, 511.

44 During the negotiations Louis had written cryptically to Villars: 'For long now I have grown accustomed to regard Prince Eugène as the Emperor's

subject and as such he has done his duty. I am pleased with what you tell me of him, and you may inform him of this from me.' Tapié in *Louis XIV and Europe*, 14.

45 The peace at Rastadt was between Louis and Charles as archduke. One between Louis and Charles as emperor was concluded by Eugene and Villars at Baden in September 1714 with no changes. No peace was made between Charles and Philip of Spain.

46 Redlich, *Grossmacht*, 128–29.

47 Coxe, *Austria*, III, 96.

Chapter XVI

1 In fact these traits were already there in Barcelona for those who wanted to see them: D. Francis, *The First Peninsular War, 1702–13* (London 1975) 285 ff.

2 H. Mercier, *Une Vie d'Ambassadeur du Roi-Soleil, . . . Comte du Luc* (Paris 1939) 191.

3 12 Feb. 1716, Vienna, Huldenberg to George I, NSA, Cal. Br. 24 Ö. II 99i.

4 5 June 1721, St Saphorin to Townshend, PRO, S.P. 80/43.

5 29 Feb. 1716, Huldenberg to Bernstorff, BA, A.G. 63.

6 Mikoletzky, 99.

7 C. L. Pöllnitz (2nd ed.) I, 234.

8 Keysler, IV, 186.

9 Pöllnitz (2nd ed.) I, 224.

10 Mercier, 193.

11 *Mémoires du Maréchal Duc de Richelieu* (Paris 1793) IV, 107–8.

12 13 Oct. 1703, Stepney to Hedges, S.P. 105/70.

13 24 May 1724, Colman to Townshend, S.P. 80/51.

14 Keysler, IV, 186.

15 Pöllnitz (2nd ed.) I, 232.

16 5 Oct. 1715, Huldenberg to Bernstorff, BA, A.G. 63.

17 29 Feb. 1716, Huldenberg to Bernstorff, ibid.

18 Braubach, *Eugen*, III, 235.

19 5 Oct. 1715, Huldenberg to Bernstorff, BA, A.G. 63.

20 2 Dec. 1716, Stanyan to Townshend, S.P. 80/34.

21 28 Sept. 1715, Schaub to Townshend, S.P. 80/32.

22 16 Nov. 1715, Schaub to Townshend, S.P. 80/32.
23 19 Feb. 1716, Huldenberg to George I, NSA, Cal. Br. 24. Ö. II. 99i.
24 Mercier, 189.
25 4 Dec. 1728, Waldegrave to Townshend, S.P. 80/63.
26 29 Oct. 1728, Waldegrave to Tilson, ibid.
27 19 Dec. 1714, Stanhope to Townshend, S.P. 80/32.
28 See especially 13 May 1716, Schaub to Townshend, S.P. 80/33; and J. W. Stoye, 'Emperor Charles VI: the early years of the reign', *Transactions of the Royal Historical Society* XII (1962).
29 9 Nov. 1715, Schaub to Townshend, S.P. 80/32.
30 26 Aug. 1716, Schaub to Townshend, S.P. 80/33.
31 Arneth, *Eigenhändige*, 197, Charles III to Wratislaw, 31 July 1711, Barcelona.
32 For this see D. McKay, 'Diplomatic Relations between George I and the Emperor Charles VI, 1714–19' (Univ. of London Ph.D. thesis 1971) 67 ff.
33 19 Nov. 1721, St Saphorin to Townshend, S.P. 80/44; 5, 18, 29 May 1720, Huldenberg to Bernstorff, BA, A.G. 63.
34 Pöllnitz (2nd ed.) I, 237.
35 21 Feb. 1718, St Saphorin to J. Robethon, BL, Add. MS. 35837.
36 5 Oct. 1715, Huldenberg to Bernstorff, A.G. 63.
37 Ibid.; 8 Feb. 1719, St Saphorin to Stanhope, S.P. 80/38.
38 21 Feb. 1718, St Saphorin to Robethon, Add. MS. 35837.
39 Ibid.
40 Braubach, *Eugen*, III, 246.
41 5 Oct. 1715, Huldenberg to Bernstorff, A.G. 63.
42 31 July 1715, Huldenberg to Bernstorff, ibid.

Chapter XVII

1 For the options open to Austria and Eugene's policies in 1714–16 see McKay, *Diplomatic Relations*, 16 ff., M. Braubach, *Versailles und Wien von Ludwig XIV bis Kaunitz* (Bonn 1952) 56 ff.
2 2 Feb. 1715, Cobham to Townshend, PRO, S.P. 80/32.

3 H. Hantsch, *Reichsvizekanzler Friedrich Karl Graf von Schönborn* (Augsburg 1929) 407.
4 18 Sept. 1715, Schaub to Townshend, S.P. 80/32, and see 13 May 1716, Schaub to Townshend, ibid.
5 11 Dec. 1715, 29 Jan. 1716, Schaub to Townshend, ibid. and S.P. 80/33.
6 Undated *Referat* over conference of 19 May 1716, HHSA, Vorträge 20.
7 Braubach, *Eugen*, III, 313.
8 *FE*, XVI, 204.
9 Lady Mary Wortley Montagu, *Letters*, I, 305.
10 W. Hacker, 'Das Regiment Hoch- und Deutschmeister, Prinz Eugen und der Türkenkrieg, 1716', *Südostdeutsche Archiv* XIV (1971) 117.
11 17 Oct., Schaub to Townshend, S.P. 80/33.
12 Redlich, *Grossmacht*, 354.
13 6 Oct., conference minutes, HHSA, Vorträge 21.
14 *FE*, XVII, Supplement, 10, Eugene to Mercy, 27 Jan. 1717: 'My sights are always fixed on Belgrade.'
15 23 June 1717, Stanyan to Sunderland, S.P. 80/34.
16 De la Colonie, 403.
17 Ibid., 415–17.
18 7 Aug., Vienna, Stanyan to Sunderland, S.P. 80/35.
19 This is suggested in a newsletter of 28 Aug., ibid.
20 Braubach, *Eugen*, III, 460.
21 8 Aug., conference minutes, HHSA, Vorträge 22.
22 17 Sept., Eugene to Sinzendorff, HHSA, Kriegsakten 287.
23 5 Feb. 1718, Huldenberg to Bernstorff, BA, A.G. 63.
24 4 April, Belgrade, Sutton to J. Addison, S.P. 97/24.
25 Arneth, *Eugen*, II, 446.

Chapter XVIII

1 For a detailed account of this see McKay, *Diplomatic Relations*, 133 ff.
2 10 April 1717, Huldenberg to Bernstorff, BA, A.G. 63: They felt 'in their hearts that hopes for the Spanish monarchy were chimerical'.
3 31 Oct. 1716, Schaub to Townshend, PRO, S.P. 80/33.

4 26 Sept., Schaub to Townshend, ibid.
5 16 Jan. 1717, *Referat* over conference of 5th, HHSA, Englische Korrespondenz 58 [*sic*].
6 28 Aug., Stanyan to Sunderland, S.P. 80/35.
7 13, 24 Nov., Huldenberg to Bernstorff, A.G. 63.
8 Braubach, *Eugen*, IV, 25.
9 5 Jan. 1718, St Saphorin to Schaub, BL, Add. MS. 35837.
10 See 3 March, 4 April, conference minutes, 23 March, *Referat* over conference of same date, HHSA, Vorträge 22.
11 13 April, Huldenberg to Bernstorff, A.G. 63.
12 23 March, St Saphorin to Sunderland, S.P. 80/36.
13 23 Feb., Huldenberg to Bernstorff, A.G. 63.
14 4, 27 July, Belgrade, Eugene to Perlas-Rialp, HHSA, Verzeichnis 7c (Belgien) 33.
15 7 Aug. 1719, conference minutes, 17 Sept., *Referat* over conference of 16th, Vorträge 23.
16 29 Sept. 1718, 9 Aug. 1719, St Saphorin to Stanhope, S.P. 80/36, S.P. 80/39. Starhemberg had spoken too bluntly to Charles for his taste and had wanted 'to be master in everything'. He had also not hidden in Spain that he wanted to be president of the war council. Arneth, *Eigenhändige*, 187, Charles III to Wratislaw, 25 June 1711, Barcelona.
17 29 Sept., 29 Nov. 1718, St Saphorin to Stanhope, S.P. 80/36, 9 Aug., 2, 3, Sept. 1719, St Saphorin to Stanhope, S.P. 80/39.
18 Arneth, *Eugen*, III, 33.
19 Maria Josepha married the electoral prince of Saxony in October 1719 and Maria Amelia the electoral prince of Bavaria in December 1722, both having to renounce their claims to the succession in favour of Charles's daughters.
20 12 Sept. 1719, relation of St Saphorin, S.P. 80/39.
21 Braubach, *Eugen*, IV, 74.
22 3 Dec. 1719, Huldenberg to Bernstorff, A.G. 63.
23 11 Oct., St Saphorin to Schaub, S.P. 80/39.

24 10 Feb. 1720, relation of St Saphorin, S.P. 80/40.
25 J. M. Graham, *Annals of Viscount and First and Second Earls of Stair* (Edinburgh 1875) II, 391–2, St Saphorin to Stanhope, 14 June 1719.
26 10 Feb. 1720, relation of St Saphorin, S.P. 80/40.
27 17 May 1715, conference minutes, Vorträge 20. For Austrian northern policy in these years see P. K. Sörensson, 'Keysaren, Sverige och de Nordiska Allierade från Karl XII's Hemkonst från Turkiet till Alliansen i Wien, 1719', *Karolinska Förbundets Årsbok* (1926–29) and D. McKay, 'The Struggle for control of George I's Northern policy, 1718–19', *Journal of Modern History* XLV (1973).
28 See especially 1 Sept. 1718, conference minutes, Vorträge 22.
29 J. G. Droysen, *Geschichte der Preussischen Politik* (Leipzig 1869) IV, 241.
30 See St Saphorin's dispatches to Stanhope of October 1719 in Add. MS. 35837 and of December in S.P. 80/39.
31 7 Jan. 1720, conference minutes, Vorträge 23.
32 16, 19 Sept., 10 Oct., 3 Nov. 1720, Hanover, C. Starhemberg to Charles VI, HHSA, Englische Korrespondenz 60.
33 28 Feb. 1722 [*sic*], Huldenberg to Bernstorff, A.G. 63.
34 Graham, II, 391–92, St Saphorin to Stanhope, 14 June 1719.
35 23 Aug., 6, 11 Oct. 1720, conference minutes, Vorträge 23.
36 7 Nov., Charles VI to Windischgrätz and Pendterriedter going to congress of Cambrai, HHSA, Friedensakten 24.
37 See St Saphorin's dispatches of June to Oct. 1721, S.P. 80/33 and 80/44.
38 2 May, old style, Whitehall, Tilson to Whitworth, Add. MS. 37385.

Chapter XIX

1 19 Jan. 1715, Huldenberg to Bernstorff, BA, A.G. 63.
2 25 Jan. 1719, St Saphorin to Stanhope, PRO, S.P. 80/38.
3 A. De Meeüs, *History of the Belgians* (London 1962) 225.

4 18 March 1716, Schaub to Townshend, S.P. 80/38.
5 19 Sept. 1721, Aix-la-Chapelle, Whitworth to Tilson, BL, Add. MS. 37386.
6 M. Huisman, *La Belgique commerciale sous l'Empereur Charles VI: La Compagnie d'Ostende* (Brussels 1902) 189.
7 9 July 1721, Colman to Townshend, S.P. 80/45.
8 Arneth, *Eugen*, III, 157–8.
9 Stoye, *Charles VI*, 74.
10 Arneth, *Eugen*, III, 532.
11 Arneth, *Eigenhändige*, 98, Charles III to Wratislaw, 14 Sept. 1709, Barcelona. He was prepared to 'introduce the Jews into Spain' to further commerce.
12 See Waldegrave's reports of July to Sept. 1728, S.P. 80/63.
13 A. F. Pribram, *Österreichische Staatsverträge, England* (Innsbruck 1907) I, 446, Colman to Townshend, 5 May 1723.
14 Frischauer, 329.
15 24 Oct. 1718, St Saphorin to Stanhope, S.P. 80/36.
16 Arneth, *Eugen*, III, 542.
17 J. Niessen, 'Prinz Eugen von Savoyen als Statthalter in der Südlichen Niederlanden, 1716–24', *Rheinische Vierteljahrsblätter* VI (1936) 165.

Chapter XX

1 17 Sept. 1701, Stepney to Blathwayt, PRO, S.P. 105/63.
2 See chapter XVI, note 33.
3 Pöllnitz (2nd ed.) I, 327; Keysler, IV, 178.
4 Braubach, *Eugen*, V, 23.
5 Baratta-Dragono, 34.
6 De Vos also made the Blenheim tapestries.
7 Pöllnitz (2nd ed.) I, 236; Keysler, IV, 177.
8 Pöllnitz (1st ed., London 1738) IV, 48.
9 The relevant part of Küchelbecker, *Allerneueste Nachricht von Römisch-Kayserl. Hofe . . .* is printed in H. Aurenhammer, *Das Belvedere in Wien, Zehn Stiche und eine Beschreibung von Zeitgenossen des Prinzen Eugen* (Vienna 1963).
10 Quotations are from Keysler, IV, 175–6.

11 F. Haskell, *Patrons and Painters* (London 1963) 201.
12 Ibid.
13 In the work *Batailles Gagnées par le Sérénissime Prince Fr. Eugène de Savoye*, ed. J. Dumont (3 vols, The Hague 1725).
14 Braubach, *Eugen*, V, 84.
15 *FE*, XI, Supplement, 36.
16 Henderson, 258.
17 23 Feb. 1729, Vienna, Waldegrave to Townshend, S.P. 80/64.
18 However, in England at this time there were other equally impressive collections. The Sloane collection amounted to 40,000 books and 4,100 manuscripts and the Harleys' *c.* 50,000 books and 7,639 manuscripts. I am grateful to Peter Barber for drawing this to my attention.
19 Ragnhild Hatton, 'John Drummond in the War of the Spanish Succession', in Ragnhild Hatton and M. S. Anderson (eds), *Studies in Diplomatic History* (London 1970) 83.
20 Pöllnitz (1st ed.) IV, 239, translator's note.
21 Oehler, 21–2, 312. They included seventeenth-century French poetry as well as classical authors, but there were also Latin and French translations of Milton, and English, French and Dutch philosophers of the seventeenth century, including a first English edition of Hobbes's *Leviathan*.
22 W. Suchier, *Prinz Eugen als Bibliophile* (Weimar 1928) 21.
23 Frischauer, 290.
24 Henderson, 261–62.

Chapter XXI

1 Oehler, 9.
2 Guido Starhemberg also did not write any memoirs. He was bracketed with Eugene by Montesquieu as 'the two greatest men of letters that there are in Vienna', Oehler, 97. Montesquieu also called Starhemberg 'a philosophe', *Voyages* (Paris 1894) I, 6.
3 Oehler, 150, using the *Mémoires* of de Quincy.
4 Frischauer, 287.
5 Braubach, *Geschichte und Abenteuer*, 303.

6 Baratta-Dragono, 30 – no indication of the source is given.
7 Heller, II, 563, Eugene to Joseph, 9 July 1705.
8 13 Jan. 1731, Robinson to Harrington, PRO, S.P. 80/70.
9 Arneth, *Eugen*, III, 522.
10 Oehler, 61. Oehler is the fullest on Eugene's literary contacts.
11 Henderson, 245.
12 Oehler, 73.
13 Braubach, *Eugen*, V, 182.
14 Oehler, 104.
15 Keysler, IV, 195–97.
16 24 Oct. 1733, Robinson to Harrington, secret, S.P. 80/100.
17 That there was no will is confirmed in the diary of Maria Theresa's lord marshal, prince Khevenhüller-Metsch, *Aus der Zeit Maria Theresias*, ed. R. Khevenhüller-Metsch and H. Schlitter (Vienna 1907) II, 178.
18 Braubach, V, 412. E. G. Rinck in his German life of Leopold I, published in 1708, described Eugene thus: 'He lets no pleasures disturb his noble ambition and he is a Mars without Venus, at least at the present time.' Oehler, 26.
19 Also see D. Francis, *The First Peninsular War*, 301, who shows that 128 women went with three English regiments to Portugal in 1703 and that there were 3 women per company of marines.
20 Braubach, *Eugen*, V, 412.
21 Srbik, *Aus Österreichs Vergangenheit*, 13.
22 E. Vehse, *Memoirs of the Court, Aristocracy and Diplomacy of Vienna* (London 1856) II, 140.
23 26 Feb. 1729, Waldegrave to Townshend, S.P. 80/64.
24 13 May 1728, Waldegrave to Townshend, very private, S.P. 80/62.
25 Mikoletzky, 140.
26 Braubach, *Eugen*, V, 404.
27 Both had 'l'esprit', *Voyages*, I, 8.
28 Braubach, *Eugen*, V, 164.
29 29 Oct. 1728, Waldegrave to Tilson, S.P. 80/63.
30 2 Sept. 1730, Robinson to Tilson, S.P. 80/68.
31 8 March 1724, Huldenberg to Bernstorff, BA, A.G. 63.

32 22 Oct. 1729, Waldegrave to Townshend, S.P. 80/65.

Chapter XXII

1 Braubach, *Eugen*, IV, 89.
2 18 March 1722, Colman to Townshend, PRO, S.P. 80/45.
3 Braubach, *Eugen*, IV, 92.
4 1 May 1722, St Saphorin to Townshend, S.P. 80/46.
5 18 Feb. 1724, Huldenberg to Bernstorff, BA, A.G. 63.
6 1 May 1722, St Saphorin to Townshend. S.P. 80/46.
7 14 Aug. 1728, Waldegrave to Townshend, S.P. 80/63.
8 7 Jan. 1722, Huldenberg to Bernstorff, BA, A.G. 63.
9 18 Feb. 1722, Huldenberg to Bernstorff, ibid.
10 M. Braubach, *Die Geheimediplomatie des Prinzen Eugen von Savoyen* (Cologne 1962) 56.
11 Redlich, *Grossmacht*, 239.
12 G. Mecenseffy, *Karls VI Spanische Bündnispolitik* (Innsbruck 1934) 34.
13 The British diplomatic documents point to this conclusion.
14 Braubach, *Eugen*, IV, 231.
15 26 Feb. 1729, Waldegrave to Townshend, S.P. 80/64.
16 W. Leitsch, 'Der Wandel der österreichischen Russlandspolitik, 1724–26', *Jahrbücher für Geschichte Osteuropas* (1958) 77.
17 Huisman, 333.
18 Braubach, *Eugen*, IV, 299.
19 Arneth, *Eugen*, III, 566.
20 Braubach, *Eugen*, IV, 290–91.
21 13 May 1728, Waldegrave to Townshend, private, S.P. 80/63, and see 8 Jan. 1729, Waldegrave to Townshend, S.P. 80/64.
22 29 Oct. 1728, Waldegrave to Tilson, S.P. 80/63.
23 26 Feb. 1729, Waldegrave to Townshend, S.P. 80/64.
24 See Waldegrave's reports of summer and autumn 1728 for Charles's disappointment and Sinzendorff's involvement, S.P. 80/63.
25 See especially 21 July, Graz, Waldegrave to Townshend, 29 Oct. 1728, Vienna, Waldegrave to Tilson,

ibid., and 18 March 1729, Waldegrave to Townshend, S.P. 80/64.

26 4 Dec. 1728, Waldegrave to Townshend, S.P. 80/63.

27 Braubach, *Eugen*, IV, 300.

28 7 May 1728, Waldegrave to Townshend, S.P. 80/62.

29 25 Dec., Waldegrave to Townshend, S.P. 80/63.

30 Pribram, I, 470.

31 21 June 1730, Robinson to Newcastle, S.P. 80/68: 'It is ... universally agreed, that the obstinacy and ill humour of this Court hitherto is mostly owing to Prince Eugene, partly out of a false glory with which he flatters and animates the Emperor, and partly at the risk of any consequences, the worse they are the more to his purpose, to throw the blame of them upon Count Sinzendorff's projects as the source of all.'

Chapter XXIII

1 15 Feb. 1730, Waldegrave to Townshend, PRO, S.P. 80/66. Eugene himself admitted to Waldegrave that there was not enough in the whole dispute 'to kill a chicken over it', 18 March, Waldegrave to Townshend, S.P. 80/67.

2 27 May, Waldegrave to Townshend, ibid.

3 30 Nov. 1729, Waldegrave to Townshend, S.P. 80/65.

4 11 Oct. 1729, Waldegrave to Townshend, ibid.

5 15 July 1730, Robinson to Harrington, S.P. 80/68.

6 See Robinson's reports from July to Oct. 1730, S.P. 80/68 and S.P. 80/69.

7 18 Nov., Robinson to Harrington, most private, ibid.

8 W. Coxe, *Memoirs of the Life and Administration of Sir Robert Walpole* (London 1798) III, 49–50, Robinson to Harrington, 16 Jan. 1731.

9 14 Feb., Robinson to Harrington, S.P. 80/71.

10 9 March, Robinson to Harrington, secret, S.P. 80/72.

11 26 Aug. 1730, Robinson to Harrington S.P. 80/68.

12 H. Benedikt, *Das Königreich Neapel*

unter Kaiser Karl VI (Vienna 1927) 404.

13 9 March 1731, Robinson to Harrington, S.P. 80/72.

14 29 Sept., Robinson to Harrington, S.P. 80/80.

15 The Venetian ambassador Capello in his relation of 1744 said that Eugene was always opposed to the idea of paper guarantees for the Pragmatic Sanction and stressed the need for a strong army and full treasury. Oehler, 262.

16 K. A. Roider, *The Reluctant Ally: Austria's Policy in the Austro-Turkish War, 1737–39* (Baton Rouge 1972) 3.

17 Although Schönborn told Robinson that Charles intended Francis Stephen to renounce the duchy to his younger brother, 20 Sept. 1730, Robinson to Harrington, S.P. 80/68, the French do not seem to have been told this.

18 9 March 1731, Robinson to Harrington, secret, S.P. 80/72.

19 Braubach, *Geheimediplomatie*, 43.

20 Hantsch, *Schönborn*, 342.

21 21 Oct. 1733, Robinson to Harrington, most secret, S.P. 80/100.

22 Coxe, *Austria*, III, 195.

23 Braubach, *Eugen*, V, 204.

24 By Hrazky. See bibliography.

25 24 Oct. 1733, Robinson to Harrington, S.P. 80/100.

Chapter XXIV

1 Heller, II, 553, Eugene to Joseph, 7 July 1705. The prince's attempts to eradicate the purchasing of commissions failed, however. The practice was still rife at his death. J. Zimmermann, 136. For Zimmermann see bibliography.

2 Arneth, *Eugen*, III, 525.

3 Ibid., 527.

4 Braubach, *Eugen*, V, 221, and see Frauenholz, *Eugen*, 13–14, for similar ones for 1707–08.

5 25 April 1736, Robinson to Tilson, PRO, S.P. 80/121.

6 *FE*, V, 102.

7 Roider, 20.

8 Similar efforts were made to keep them all German in German armies during the Thirty Years War. F.

Redlich, *The German Military Enter-priser and His Work Force* (Wiesbaden 1964) I, 456.

9 T. Gehling, *Ein Europäischer Diplomat am Kaiserhof zu Wien* (Bonn 1964) 69–70.

10 In 1729 Waldegrave remarked that except for Eugene and Guido Starhemberg 'the Emperor has not a general with whom he could prudently trust an army', although there were plenty of good second-rank officers. 1 Jan. 1729, Waldegrave to Townshend, S.P. 80/64.

11 Arneth, *Starhemberg*, 774.

12 The Venetian ambassador Foscarini was one of the few contemporaries to criticize Eugene for not attending to troops in peacetime: Oehler, 264.

13 Arneth, *Eugen*, III, 420–21.

14 Braubach, *Eugen*, V, 217.

15 20 Nov. 1717, Stanyan to Sunderland, S.P. 80/35.

16 Oehler, 98.

17 Braubach, *Eugen*, V, 211.

18 See chapter XXIII, note 15.

Chapter XXV

1 Benedikt, *Königreich Neapel*, 466.

2 Henderson, 277.

3 Mikoletzky, 137.

4 *FE*, XIX, 190–1.

5 Arneth, *Eugen*, III, 424.

6 Ibid., 428.

7 Ibid., 414.

8 Ibid., 431–32.

9 Braubach, *Eugen*, V, 280.

10 Redlich, *Grossmacht*, 257.

11 Braubach, *Geheimediplomatie*, 59.

12 Arneth, *Eugen*, III, 454.

13 Ibid., 477.

14 In 1730 she was said to be lovesick when Francis Stephen was away. 25 Feb. 1730, Waldegrave to Tilson, PRO, S.P. 80/66.

15 Coxe, *Austria*, III, 195.

16 Henderson, 286.

17 Arneth, *Starhemberg*, 781.

18 Bibl, 287.

19 21 April 1736, Robinson to Harrington, S.P. 80/121, and same source for quotations about Eugene's last night. This was the first Robinson had mentioned of the prince all that year.

20 25 April, Robinson to Tilson, ibid.

21 Ibid.

22 21 April, Robinson to Weston, ibid.

23 Braubach, *Eugen*, V, 323.

24 27 June 1736, Robinson to R. Walpole, private, S.P. 80/121, and see Coxe, *Austria*, III, 193, for abbreviated form.

Conclusion

1 The best brief guide in English to Eugene as a *völkisch* hero is in the article by Sweet.

2 Max Braubach points out that to live the life of the *honnête homme* was a fairly common ideal among the European aristocracy. Braubach, *Eugen*, V, 119.

3 15 July 1730, Robinson to Harrington, PRO, S.P. 80/68.

4 29 Oct. 1728, Waldegrave to Tilson, S.P. 80/62.

Select Bibliography

Sources

Most of Eugene's correspondence with rulers, statesmen and soldiers has been printed in F. Heller, *Militärische Korrespondenz des Prinzen Eugen von Savoyen* (2 vols, Vienna 1848) and in the *Feldzüge des Prinzen Eugen von Savoyen*, published by the K. K. Kriegsarchiv (20 vols, Vienna 1876–92) or has been quoted extensively in existing biographies. The original letters or copies are largely in the Austrian State Archives, Vienna, either in the Kriegsarchiv or the Haus-, Hof-, und

Staatsarchiv. Little of importance seems to have been missed, but I found useful material in the Haus-, Hof-, und Staatsarchiv, particularly among the *Conferenz* minutes and reports (Vorträge), the collection of letters, largely to Eugene, known as the Grosse Korrespondenz, and the correspondence over the Southern Netherlands (Belgien Verzeichnis 7c) and with England (Englische Korrespondenz). Previous biographers have drawn heavily on the reports of foreign envoys in Vienna. Many of the reports from Dutch ministers are printed in *Weensche Gezantschapsberichten, 1670–1720*, ed. G. Antal and J. C. H. De Pater (2 vols, The Hague 1929, 1934) and some of the Venetian relations in A. Arneth, 'Die Relationen der Botschafter Venedigs über Österreich im 18. Jahrhundert', *Fontes rerum Austriacarum* XXII (1863). I have worked systematically through the reports from the 1680s to 1730s of the English ministers in Vienna and, when appropriate, Savoy and Flanders in the collections in the Public Record Office, London, and in the British Library. Much of the present text is based on these collections. The best guide to the latter is D. B. Horn, *British Diplomatic Representatives, 1689–1789* (London 1932). The Coxe transcripts, particularly Add. MS. 9099 to 9113, and Add. MS. 35837 of the Hardwicke collection in the British Library, also proved very valuable. An observer in Vienna for most of Eugene's career was the Hanoverian minister Huldenberg. His official reports in the Niedersächsisches Staatsarchiv, Hanover, were of less interest than his private letters to George I's chief Hanoverian minister, A. G. Bernstorff. The latter are in the possession of the present Count Bernstorff at Gartow, West Germany.

For Eugene's campaigns the *Feldzüge* is an indispensable source, but for the War of Spanish Succession there is the equally full French collection *Mémoires militaires relatifs à la succession d'Espagne sous Louis XIV*, ed. F. E. de Vault and J. J. G. Pelet (11 vols, Paris 1835–42). Useful for both the Nine Years War and the War of Spanish Succession are the *Mémoires et correspondance de Tessé*, ed. M. J. B. R. de Froullay (2 vols, Paris 1806) and the *Mémoires et correspondance du maréchal de Catinat*, ed. B. le Bouyer de Saint-Gervais (3 vols, Paris 1819). Relevant to most of the years covered by the present book are the *Mémoires du maréchal de Villars*, ed. de Vogüé (5 vols, Paris 1884–92) and *The Chronicles of an Old Campaigner, 1692–1717* (a Frenchman, de la Colonie, in Bavarian service), ed. W. C. Horsley (London 1904). Both W. Coxe, *Memoirs of John Duke of Marlborough* (6 vols, London, 2nd ed. 1820) and G. Murray (ed.), *The Letters and Dispatches of John Churchill, First Duke of Marlborough from 1702 to 1715* (5 vols, London 1845) are major printed sources and contain many of Eugene's letters. There are also B. van 'T Hoff (ed.), *The Correspondence, 1701–11, of John Churchill and Anthonie Heinsius* (The Hague 1951) and H. L. Snyder (ed.), *The Marlborough-Godolphin Correspondence* (2 vols, Oxford 1976). Among the Military Expeditions collection of the Public Record Office, London, there are letters from Marlborough's secretary Cardonnel with graphic descriptions of the 1708 campaign (S.P. 87/4). Of the many military memoirs those most accessible to the general reader are *Military Memoirs: the Marlborough Wars, R. Parker and Comte de Westerloo*, ed. D. Chandler (London 1968). Particularly useful because of his close association with Eugene in Flanders are the *Leben und Denkwürdigkeiten* of

J. M. Schulenburg (2 vols, Leipzig 1834). However, there is a great lack of material on Eugene's personal life: his private papers have not survived and we have very few letters from him to close friends. The Austrian court also lacked a St Simon during the period covered by Eugene's career so that we are continually thrown back on the observations of foreign ministers and visitors. But there is a mass of information on Viennese politics during Joseph's reign in the 'Eigenhändige Correspondenz des Königs Karl III von Spanien mit . . . Grafen Johann Wenzel Wratislaw', *Archiv für Kunde Österreichischer Geschichtsquellen* XVI (1856). Other printed sources are referred to below and in the footnotes.

Biographies and works on Eugene's life

There are still no better accounts of the prince's military career than in the introductory sections of the *Feldzüge* and in A. von Arneth, *Prinz Eugen von Savoyen* (3 vols, Vienna 1858, reissued 1864). Arneth based his work firmly on primary material; he saw his hero as essentially a servant of the house of Habsburg but one conscious of the monarchy's German character and a champion of the civilizing effects of German culture. This is substantially the view taken by Max Braubach. Although in his pre-Second World War writings Braubach praised the prince as a German hero, in his *Prinz Eugen von Savoyen* (5 vols, Munich/ Vienna 1963–65) he emphasizes his involvement with Italian and French culture and his personal loyalty to successive emperors. His massive biography, the culmination of a lifetime's archival work and a succession of studies on the prince, considerably extends the scope of our knowledge of Eugene as a statesman and patron. It must serve as the main authority for all aspects of the prince's life and it has proved invaluable throughout the present study. Of several short modern biographies, that by V. Bibl, *Prinz Eugen: Ein Heldenleben* (Leipzig 1941) is probably the best despite its Nazi overtones. The changing view of Eugene as a German hero is discussed by P. R. Sweet, 'Prince Eugene of Savoy and Central Europe', *American Historical Review* LVII (1951). In English the only work which has referred to modern German scholarship is N. Henderson, *Prince Eugen of Savoy* (London 1964). This is adequate on Eugene's military career, good on his artistic tastes but very poor on his political role. A near contemporary biography, which has withstood time and modern research well, is E. Mauvillon, *Histoire du Prince François Eugène de Savoye* (5 vols, Amsterdam 1740, ed. used here of 1790). The short *History of Francis-Eugene, Prince of Savoy* (London 1741) is largely a translation of Mauvillon. A complete bibliography of all known works on the prince was compiled by B. Böhm, *Bibliographie zur Geschichte des Prinzen Eugen und seiner Zeit* (Vienna 1943); this can be supplemented by that in vol. I of Braubach, *Eugen*.

M. Braubach, *Geschichte und Abenteuer: Gestalten um den Prinzen Eugen* (Munich 1950) has chapters on Eugene's early life and final years, on his family, Hohendorff, Bonneval and Batthyány. *Diplomatie und Geistiges Leben im 17. und 18. Jahrhundert* (Bonn 1969) is a collection of the same author's published articles and includes ones on Eugene's relations with Schönborn, Salm and Bartenstein, as well as a discussion of his attitude to Jansenism. The best guide to the contemporary memoir literature on the prince and to his connections with writers and artists is H. Oehler, *Prinz Eugen im Urteil Europas: ein Mythus und sein Niederschlag in Dichtung und Geschichtsschreibung* (Munich 1944), but there is additional material on German writers in M. Baratta-Dragono, 'Prinz Eugen von Savoyen in der Publizistik seiner Zeit' (Univ. of Vienna dissertation 1960).

On particular aspects of his career there is W. Erben, 'Prinz Eugens italienischer Feldzug im Jahre 1701', *M.I.Ö.G.* XXVIII (1920) and E. Ritter, *Politik und Kriegsführung, ihre Beherrschung durch Prinz Eugen 1704* (Berlin 1934). Eugene's partnership with Marlborough is examined briefly by G. Otruba, *Prinz Eugen und Marlborough: Weltgeschichte im Spiegel eines Briefwechsels* (Vienna 1961). There are several discussions of Eugene's government of the Netherlands but all look at it too much from the Vienna end. The latest is A. Sprunck, 'Prinz Eugen als Generalstatthalter der österreichischen Niederlande', *M.Ö.S.* XV (1962). This problem can be partly solved by using L. P. Gachard, *Histoire de la Belgique au commencement du XVIIIe siècle* (Brussels 1880), M. Huisman, *La Belgique commerciale sous l'Empereur Charles VI: La Companie d'Ostende* (Brussels 1902) and H. Hasquin, 'Les difficultés financières du gouvernement des Pays-Bas autrichiens au début du xviiie siècle, 1717–40', *Revue internationale d'histoire de la banque* VI (1973). Essential for Eugene's role as a European statesman in the late 1720s is M. Braubach, *Die Geheimediplomatie des Prinzen Eugen von Savoyen* (Cologne 1962). On his building and cultural activities there are several insubstantial studies, which add little to Oehler and Braubach, *Eugen.* These include A. Ilg, *Prinz Eugen als Kunstfreund* (Vienna 1889) and H. R. Bludau, 'Kunst und Wissenschaft im Leben des Prinzen Eugen' (Friedrich-Wilhelms Univ., Berlin, dissertation 1941). Informative and profusely illustrated are B. Grimschitz, *Das Belvedere in Wien* (Vienna 1949) and H. Aurenhammer, *J. B. Fischer von Erlach* (London 1973). Relevant to Eugene's part in the Austrian Enlightenment is G. Ricuperati, 'Libertinismo e deismo a Vienna. Spinoza, Toland e il Triregno', *Rivista storica italiana* LXXIX (1967).

The Habsburg Monarchy

The chapters in *The New Cambridge Modern History*, vol. V, ed. F. L. Carsten and vol. VI, ed. J. S. Bromley (Cambridge 1961, 1970) are excellent on internal history, and V. L. Tapié, *The Rise and Fall of the Habsburg Monarchy* (London 1971) is particularly good on the non-German lands. Of the standard Austrian histories that by E. Zöllner, *Geschichte Österreichs* (Vienna 1961 and subsequent eds) is the best. Especially welcome is J. Spielman, *Leopold I* (London 1976): it has comprehensive accounts of the emperor's domestic and foreign policy with a full bibliography, which should be consulted. Two recent analytical articles are J. Bérenger, 'La monarchie autrichienne au xviie siècle (1650–1700)', *Information historique* XXX (1971) and T. M. Barker, 'Military entrepreneurship and absolutism', *Journal of European Studies* IV (1974). For the reigns of Joseph and Charles there is H. L. Mikoletzky, *Österreich: das grosse 18. Jahrhundert* (Vienna

1966). E. Wangermann, *The Austrian Achievement, 1700–1800* (London 1973) is an effective antidote to the outward splendour of the baroque period, and this is also true of E. Winter, *Barock, Absolutismus und Aufklärung in der Donaumonarchie* (Vienna 1971). A fine study of an aristocratic and ministerial family is G. Klingenstein, *Der Aufstiege des Hauses Kaunitz* (Göttingen 1975). Dated, prejudiced and full of errors, but of occasional value, are E. Vehse, *Memoirs of the Court, Aristocracy and Diplomacy of Austria* (2 vols, London 1856) and F. Förster, *Die Höfe und Cabinette Europa's von 18. Jahrhundert* (2 vols, Potsdam 1836). A revealing account of Charles VI's court based on the reports of Italian envoys is A. Lhotsky, 'Kaiser Karls VI und sein Hof im Jahre 1712/13', *M.I.Ö.G.* LXVI (1958); extracts from the emperor's diary are given by O. Redlich, 'Die Tagebücher Kaiser Karls VI', in *Gesamtdeutsche Vergangenheit. Festgabe für H. von Srbik* (Munich 1938). Attempts at administrative and financial reform are discussed by J. W. Stoye, 'Emperor Charles VI: the early years of the reign', *Transactions of the Royal Historical Society* XII (1962). F. Mensi, *Die Finanzen Österreichs von 1701 bis 1740* (Vienna 1890) is still an indispensable source for the central financial institutions. See also B. Holl, *Hofkammerpräsident Gundaker T. Starhemberg und die Österreichische Finanzpolitik der Barockzeit (1703–1715)* (Vienna 1976) which appeared too late for the present study. The best discussions of Charles's Spanish ministers and possessions are P. Gasser, 'Das spanische Königtum Karls VI in Wien', *M.Ö.S.* VI (1953) and H. Benedikt, *Das Königreich Neapel unter Kaiser Karl VI* (Vienna 1927). On leading figures there is M. Grunwald, *Samuel Oppenheimer und sein Kreis* (Vienna 1913); H. Hantsch, *Reichsvizekanzler Friedrich Karl Graf von Schönborn* (Augsburg 1929); H. Benedikt, *Der Pascha-Graf Alexander von Bonneval* (Graz 1959); J. Hrazky 'Johann Christoph Bartenstein, der Staatsmann und Erzieher', *M.Ö.S.* XI (1958); and see Braubach, *Diplomatie und Geistiges Leben (supra)* for articles on Salm and Bartenstein.

On baroque art and architecture perhaps the best introductions are Aurenhammer, *J. B. Fischer von Erlach (supra)* and V. L. Tapié, *The Age of Grandeur* (London 1960). Slight but well illustrated is F. Hennings, *Das barocke Wien* (2 vols, Vienna 1965). More substantial is A. M. Leitich, *Vienna Gloriosa* (Vienna 1947). A delightful introduction to the Vienna of this period is I. Barea, *Vienna. Legend and Reality* (London 1966).

Warfare

Fine surveys, particularly for western Europe, are D. Chandler, *The Art of Warfare in the Age of Marlborough* (London 1976) and the chapter in *The New Cambridge Modern History*, vol. VI *(supra)*. For warfare against the Turks there is W. H. McNeill, *Europe's Steppe Frontier, 1500–1800* (Chicago 1964) and T. M. Barker, *Double Eagle and Crescent: Vienna's Second Turkish Siege and its Historical Setting* (Albany 1967). On the Austrian army the *Feldzüge*, vol. I, is very comprehensive but a short modern account is J. Zimmermann, 'Militärverwaltung und Heeresaufbringung in Österreich bis 1806', part 3 of the *Handbuch der deutschen Militärgeschichte* (Frankfurt 1965). For a discussion of the army after

Eugene's death see J. C. Allmayer-Beck, 'Wandlungen im Heerwesen zur Zeit Maria Theresias', *Schriften des Heeresgeschichtlichen Museums in Wien* III (1967). Studies of warfare in a wider social context are F. Redlich, *De Praeda Militari: Looting and Booty, 1500–1800* (Wiesbaden 1956), F. Redlich, *The German Military Enterpriser and His Work Force* (2 vols, Wiesbaden 1964), G. Perjés, 'Army provisioning, logistics and strategy in the second half of the 17th century', *Acta Historica* XVI (Budapest 1970) and A. Corvisier, *Armées et sociétés en Europe de 1494 à 1789* (Paris 1976).

International relations and war 1680–1700

The best and most complete survey, which puts Austria in the centre of the picture, is O. Redlich, *Weltmacht des Barock. Österreich in der Zeit Kaiser Leopolds I* (Vienna, 4th ed. 1961). In English there is now Spielman, *Leopold I* (*supra*). Another excellent introduction is J. B. Wolf, *The Emergence of the Great Powers, 1685–1715* (New York 1951). J. W. Stoye has written an enthralling account of *The Siege of Vienna* (London 1964) and there is an equally impressive one by T. M. Barker, *Double Eagle and Crescent* (*supra*). E. Eickhoff, *Venedig, Wien und die Osmanen. Umbruch in Südosteuropa, 1645–1700* (Munich 1970) puts the Turks in a wider European context and has excellent bibliographies. An interesting contemporary history is by P. Rycaut, *The History of the Turks Beginning with the Year 1679 . . . until the End of the Year 1698 and 1699* (London 1700). Excellent on the campaigns in Hungary is A. Arneth, *Das Leben des kaiserlichen Feldmarschalls Grafen Guido Starhemberg* (Vienna 1853) and for the last stages S. Stelling-Michaud, *Les Aventures de M. de S. Saphorin sur le Danube* (Paris 1933). For the Nine Years War J. B. Wolf, *Louis XIV* (London, Panther ed. 1970) is valuable but heavy going. R. M. Hatton (ed.), *Louis XIV and Europe* (London 1976) contains several relevant articles. For the peace-making there is H. Srbik, *Wien und Versailles, 1692–97* (Munich 1944) and M. A. Thomson, 'Louis XIV and William III, 1689–97' in R. M. Hatton and J. S. Bromley (eds), *William III and Louis XIV* (Liverpool 1968). For the Spanish Succession crisis see M. A. Thomson, 'Louis XIV and the origins of the War of the Spanish Succession' in *William III and Louis XIV* (*supra*) and the Austrian documents printed in A. Gaedeke, *Die Politik Österreichs in der spanischen Erbfolgefrage* (2 vols, Leipzig 1877).

International Relations and War 1700–14

Once again the best survey is O. Redlich, *Das Werden einer Grossmacht: Österreich von 1700 bis 1740* (Baden bei Wien 1938). Essential for most aspects are W. S. Churchill, *Marlborough, His Life and Times* (4 vols, London, Sphere ed. 1967) and G. M. Trevelyan, *England under Queen Anne* (3 vols, London, Fontana ed. 1965). Relevant for the early campaigns in Italy is A. Arneth, *Starhemberg* (*supra*) and for all of them is H. Wendt, *Der italienische Kriegsschauplatz in europäischen Konflikten: Seine Bedeutung für die Kriegsführung an Frankreichs Nordostgrenzen* (Berlin 1936). Of recent biographies of Marlborough the best is D. Chandler,

Marlborough as Military Commander (London 1973). For the French side of the war see J. B. Wolf, *Louis XIV* (*supra*) and C. Sturgill, *Marshal Villars and the War of the Spanish Succession* (Lexington 1965). A recent study of Max Emmanuel is by L. Hüttl, *Max Emanuel. Der blaue Kurfürst* (Munich 1976). The successive peace negotiations should be approached initially by way of R. M. Hatton, 'Louis XIV and his fellow monarchs' in her *Louis XIV and Europe* (*supra*) where she gives a full bibliography. A résumé of J. G. Stork-Penning's work on the Dutch side of the negotiations is given by the latter in 'The Ordeal of the States', *Acta Historiae Neerlandica* II (1967). For Austrian policy important works are W. Reese, *Das Ringen um Frieden und Sicherheit in den Entscheidungsjahren des spanischen Erb-folgekriege 1708-9* (Munich 1933), K. O. Aretin, 'Kaiser Joseph I zwischen Kaisertradition und österreichischer Grossmachtpolitik', *Historische Zeitschrift* CCXV (1972), and O. Weber, *Der Friede von Utrecht* (Gotha 1891). Excellent introductions to the financial side of the war are in *The New Cambridge Modern History*, vol. VI (*supra*) and H. L. Mikoletzky, *Österreich* (*supra*).

International relations and war 1714-36

O. Redlich, *Das Werden* (*supra*) still covers this period. For the Turkish war there is the brief study by E. Odenthal, *Österreichs Türkenkrieg, 1716-18* (Düsseldorf 1938) and E. Pruckner, 'Der Türkenkrieg von 1716-18. Seine Finanzierung und militärische Vorbereitung' (Univ. of Vienna dissertation 1946). T. Gehling, *Eine Europäischer Diplomat am Kaiserhof zu Wien* (Bonn 1964) contains a great deal of information on the Imperial court and its policies from 1718 to 1727 gleaned from the reports of St Saphorin to London. Some of the latter are examined by H. Hantsch, 'Die drei grossen Relationen St Saphorins über die inneren Ver-hältnisse am Wiener Hof zur Zeit Karls VI', *M.I.Ö.G.* LVIII (1950). Splendid short diplomatic studies are O. Weber, *Die Quadrupelallianz vom Jahre 1718* (Gotha 1887) and G. Mecenseffy, *Karls VI spanische Bündnispolitik 1725-29* (Innsbruck 1934). Fundamental for an understanding of French policy is A. M. Wilson, *French Foreign Policy during the Administration of Fleury, 1726-1743* (Cambridge, Mass. 1936). M. Braubach, *Versailles und Wien von Ludwig XIV bis Kaunitz* (Bonn 1952) is better on the 1720s and 1730s than the 1710s. The con-frontation in the Empire is examined in M. Naumann, *Österreich, England und das Reich, 1719-1732* (Berlin 1936). More material can be found in W. Strobl, 'Österreich und der polnischer Thron, 1733' (Univ. of Vienna dissertation 1950), but C. Schar, 'Politik und Kriegsführung Kaiser Karls VI, 1719-40' (Univ. of Innsbruck dissertation 1966) is merely a sound summary of secondary sources. For the disasters Austria suffered after Eugene's death see K. A. Roider, *The Reluctant Ally: Austria's Policy in the Austro-Turkish War, 1737-9* (Baton Rouge 1972).

Chronology

1648 Peace of Westphalia ends Thirty Years War.
1657 Death of Ferdinand III. Accession of Leopold I, crowned emperor in 1658.
1661 Death of cardinal Mazarin, Eugene's great-uncle, and start of Louis XIV's personal rule.
1663–64 Austro-Turkish war. Turkish defeat at St Gotthard in 1664 followed by peace of Vasvár the same year.
1663 Birth of Eugene of Savoy.
1671–81 Revolt in Hungary and unsuccessful attempt by Leopold to impose his absolute rule there.
1672 Outbreak of war between France and the Dutch Republic, which Austria enters in 1674 on the Dutch side. Peace of Nymegen concluded in 1678/79.
1681 Louis XIV annexes Strasbourg.
1682 Outbreak of Austro-Turkish war.
1683 Vienna besieged by the Turks. Eugene arrives in Austria.
1684 Truce of Ratisbon (Regensburg). Holy League against the Turks formed between Austria, Poland, Venice and the Papacy, joined by Russia in 1686.
1686 Imperial troops take Buda.
1687 Imperial victory at Berg Harsan (Nagyharsány). Hungarian throne made hereditary in the Habsburg family.
1688 Max Emmanuel takes Belgrade. William III invades England. Outbreak of Nine Years War.
1690 Victor Amadeus of Savoy joins the anti-French coalition. Eugene sent to Savoy.
1696 Savoy withdraws from the war and treaty of Vigevano signed between France, Savoy, Austria and Spain.
1697 Nine Years War concluded by peace of Ryswick. Eugene defeats the Turks at Zenta.
1698 First partition treaty over the Spanish succession.
1699 Peace of Karlowitz between the Turks, Austria, Poland, Venice and Russia.
1700 Second partition treaty and death of Charles II of Spain. Outbreak of Great Northern War between Charles XII of Sweden, and Denmark, Russia and Saxony-Poland.
1701 Imperial troops under Eugene invade northern Italy.
1702 Death of William III. General outbreak of War of Spanish Succession.
1703 Savoy and Portugal join the anti-Bourbon coalition. The archduke Charles is sent to the Iberian peninsula, and Eugene becomes president of the Imperial war council. Hungarian revolt under Rákóczi begins.
1704 Eugene and Marlborough's victory at Blenheim.
1705 Eugene returns to Italy. Death of Leopold and accession of Joseph I.
1706 Marlborough's victory at Ramillies and that of Eugene at Turin. Eugene is made viceroy of Milan.
1707 Successful Imperial expedition against Naples but allied failure against Toulon.
1708 Eugene goes to Flanders. Allied victory at Oudenarde and fall of Lille.
1709 Defeat of Charles XII of Sweden at Poltava. Abortive peace

negotiations at The Hague are followed by battle of Malplaquet.

1710 Further unsuccessful peace negotiations at Geertruidenberg. The Whig ministry in England is replaced by a Tory one. Prince Salm finally retires.

1711 Death of Joseph I and accession of Charles VI. Marlborough is dismissed.

1712 Eugene goes to England and returns to Flanders where he is defeated by Villars at Denain. Death of Wratislaw.

1713 Peace of Utrecht brings peace between the Bourbons and all the allies except Charles VI and some German princes. Charles VI issues his Pragmatic Sanction.

1714 Peace of Rastadt/Baden ends War of Spanish Succession but no formal peace is made between Charles VI and Philip V of Spain. Death of queen Anne and accession of the elector of Hanover as George I. Outbreak of war between the Turks and Venice.

1715 Death of Louis XIV and accession of Louis XV. Philip of Orleans acts as regent till his death in 1723. Barrier treaty concluded between Austria, England and the Dutch Republic over the Southern Netherlands.

1716 Outbreak of Austro-Turkish war and Eugene's victory at Peterwardein. Eugene is made governor of the Southern Netherlands. Beginning of Anglo-French co-operation.

1717 Eugene's victory at Belgrade. Spanish assault on Sardinia.

1718 Peace of Passarowitz with the Turks. The Spaniards attack Sicily but their fleet is destroyed off Cape Passaro. Charles VI agrees to the Quadruple Alliance.

1719 Conclusion of alliance of Vienna between Austria, Saxony and Hanover against Russia and Prussia. The cabal is formed against Eugene, and French troops invade Spain.

1720 Spain makes peace and joins the Quadruple Alliance. Charles VI receives Sicily from Savoy in return for Sardinia.

1721 Peace of Nystadt between Russia and Sweden finally ends Great Northern War.

1722 Death of Charles VI's favourite Althann.

1723 Foundation of the Ostend Company.

1724 Eugene resigns as governor of the Southern Netherlands.

1725 First treaty of Vienna signed between Austria and Spain, followed by Alliance of Hanover between England, France, Prussia and the Dutch.

1726 Fleury becomes chief minister in France. Signature of Austro-Russian alliance is followed by Austro-Prussian treaty of Wusterhausen.

1727 Spaniards besiege Gibraltar. Charles VI accepts the Paris preliminaries. Death of George I of England and accession of George II.

1728 Unsuccessful mission of Sinzendorff to congress of Soissons.

1729 Spain abandons Austria and joins England and France in treaty of Seville.

1730 Fall of Townshend in England and mission of Robinson to Vienna.

1731 Anglo-Austrian accommodation through second treaty of Vienna.

1733 Death of Augustus II of Saxony-Poland is followed by outbreak of War of Polish Succession between Austria, Russia and Prussia, and France, Spain and Savoy. Milan and Naples are lost to Austria in the first year of war.

1734 Eugene commands the Imperial forces on the Rhine. His friend Schönborn resigns as Imperial vice-chancellor.

1735 War of Polish Succession ends with preliminary peace terms, final peace signed in 1738.

1736 Marriage of Maria Theresa to Francis Stephen of Lorraine. Death of Eugene.

1737–39 Outbreak of further Austro-Turkish war, during which Belgrade is lost.

1740 Death of Charles VI.

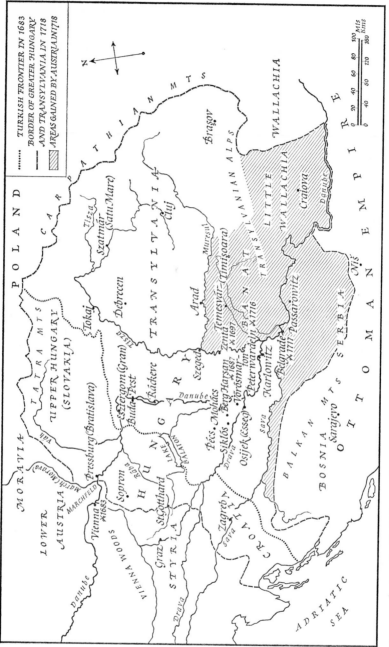

Hungary during the Turkish wars (1682–99, 1716–18)

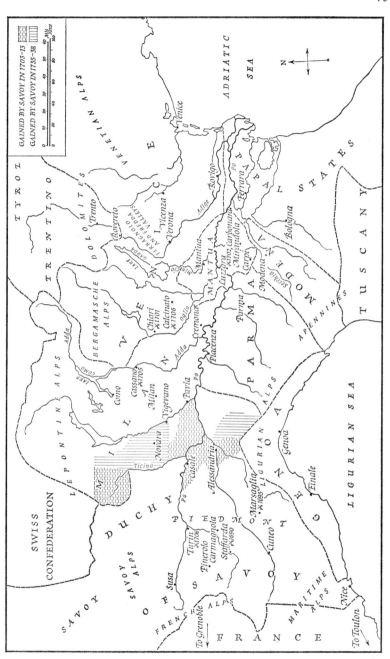

Northern Italy during the Nine Years War and War of Spanish Succession (1688–97, 1701–14)

274

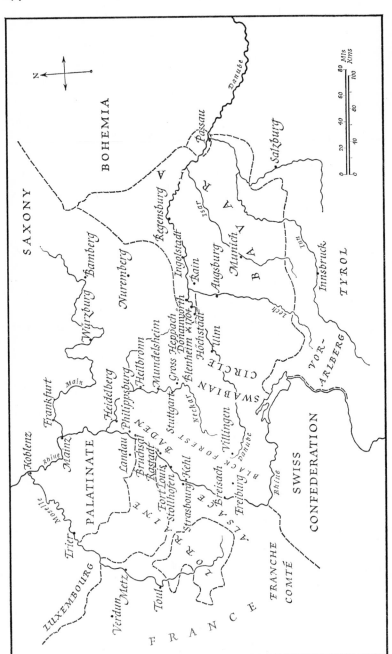

Southern and western Germany during the Wars of Spanish and Polish Succession (1702–14, 1733–35)

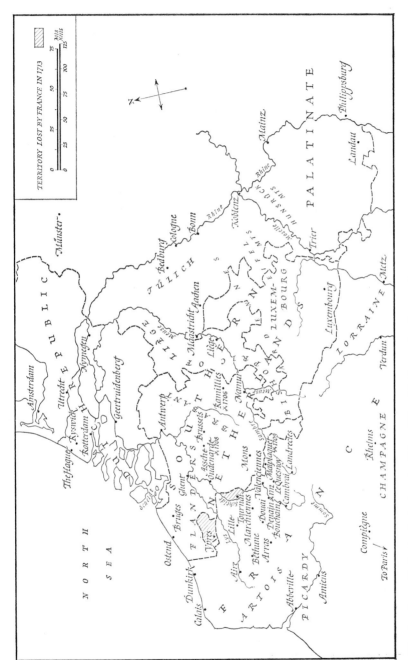

The Southern Netherlands during the War of Spanish Succession (1702–14)

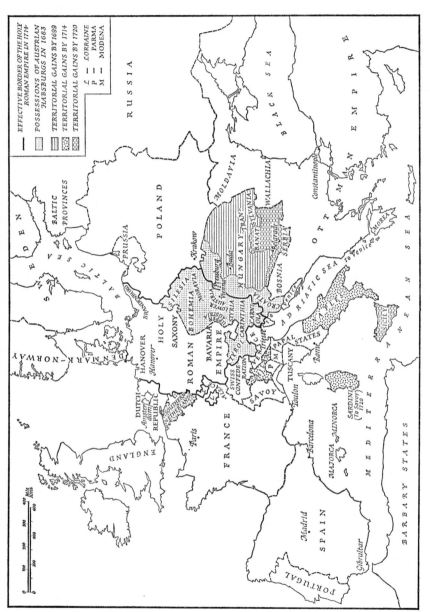

Europe in 1714

List of Illustrations

Index

Numbers in italics refer to illustrations